AQA Certificate in Biology (iGCSE) Level 1/2

SCIENCE

Ann Fullick

Margaret Cross

Faye Meek

Editor
Lawrie Ryan

Nelson Thornes

Published in 2012 by:
Nelson Thornes Ltd
Delta Place
27 Bath Road
CHELTENHAM
GL53 7TH
United Kingdom

12 13 14 15 16 / 10 9 8 7 6 5 4 3

A catalogue record for this book is available from the British Library.

AQA examination questions are reproduced by permission of the Assessment and Qualifications Alliance.

ISBN 978 1 4085 1710 9

Cover photograph: Science Photo Library / Getty

Page make-up by Wearset Ltd, Boldon, Tyne and Wear

Printed and bound in Spain by GraphyCems

Biology   Contents

Welcome to AQA Level 1/2 Certificate in Biology

This book has been written for you by the people who will be marking your exams, very experienced teachers and subject experts. It covers everything you need to know for your exams and is packed full of features to help you achieve the very best that you can.

Figure 1 Many diagrams are as important for you to learn as the text, so make sure you revise them carefully.

Key words are highlighted in the text. You can look them up in the glossary at the back of the book if you are not sure what they mean.

Learning objectives

Each topic begins with key statements that you should know by the end of the lesson.

Examiner's tip

Hints from the examiners who will mark your exams, giving you important advice on things to remember and what to watch out for.

Did you know ... ?

There are lots of interesting and often strange facts about science. This feature tells you about many of them.

links

Links will tell you where you can find more information about what you are learning and how different topics link up.

Activity

An activity is linked to a main lesson and could be a discussion or task in pairs, groups or by yourself.

Maths skills

This feature highlights the maths skills that you will need for your Science exams with short, visual explanations.

Practical

This feature helps you become familiar with key practicals. It may be a simple introduction, a reminder or the basis for a practical in the classroom.

Summary questions

These questions give you the chance to test whether you have learned and understood everything in the topic. If you get any wrong, go back and have another look. They are designed to be increasingly challenging.

And at the end of each chapter you will find …

Summary questions

These will test you on what you have learned throughout the whole chapter, helping you to work out what you have understood and where you need to go back and revise.

AQA Examination-style questions

These questions are examples of the types of questions you will answer in your actual exam, so you can get lots of practice during your course.

Key points

At the end of the topic are the important points that you must remember. They can be used to help with revision and summarising your knowledge.

B1.1 | Animal and plant cells

Learning objectives

After this topic, you should know:

- the main parts of animal and human cells
- the similarities and differences between plant and animal cells.

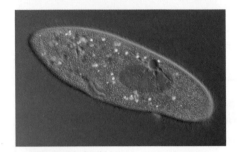

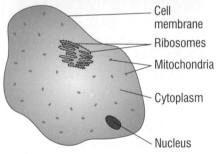

Cell membrane
Ribosomes
Mitochondria
Cytoplasm
Nucleus

Figure 1 Diagrams of cells are much easier to understand than the real thing seen under a microscope. This picture shows an animal cell magnified ×2000 times under an electron microscope. Below it is the way we draw a model animal cell to show the main features common to most living cells, including those in humans.

Earth is covered with a great variety of living things. However, they all have one thing in common – they are all made up of cells. Most cells are very small and you can only see them using a microscope.

Eggs are the biggest animal cells. Unfertilised ostrich eggs are the biggest of all – they have a mass of around 1.3 kg and you certainly don't need a microscope to see them!

The **light microscopes** in schools may magnify things several hundred times. Scientists have found out even more about cells using **electron microscopes**. These can magnify objects more than a hundred thousand times.

Animal cells – structure and function

All cells have some features in common. You can see these clearly in animal cells. Human cells have the same features as other animal cells, and so do the cells of most other living things.

- The **nucleus** – controls all the activities of the cell. It contains the **genes** on the **chromosomes** that carry the instructions for making the proteins needed to build new cells or new organisms.
- The **cytoplasm** – a liquid gel in which most of the chemical reactions needed for life take place, for example the first stages of cellular respiration.
- The **cell membrane** – controls the passage of substances such as glucose and mineral **ions** into the cell. It also controls the movement of substances such as urea or hormones out of the cell.
- The **mitochondria** – structures in the cytoplasm where oxygen is used and most of the energy is released during respiration.
- **Ribosomes** – where **protein synthesis** takes place, making all the proteins needed in the cell.

Plant cells – structure and function

Plants are very different organisms from animals. They make their own food by photosynthesis. They stay in one place, and do not move their whole bodies about from one place to another.

Plant cells have all the features of a typical animal cell, but they also contain features that are needed for their very different way of life. **Algae** are simple aquatic organisms. They also make their own food and have many similar features to plant cells. For centuries they were classified as plants, but now they are part of a different kingdom.

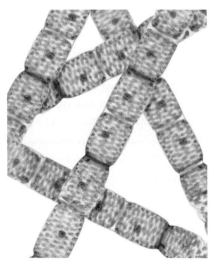

Figure 2 Algal cells contain a nucleus and chloroplasts so they can photosynthesise

All plant and **algal cells** have:

● a **cell wall** made of **cellulose** that strengthens the cell and gives it support.

Many (but not all) plant cells also have these other features:

● **Chloroplasts** are found in all the green parts of the plant. They are green because they contain the green substance **chlorophyll**. Chlorophyll absorbs light energy to make food by photosynthesis. Root cells do not have chloroplasts because they are underground and do not photosynthesise.

● A **permanent vacuole** is a space in the cytoplasm filled with cell sap. This is important for keeping the cells rigid to support the plant.

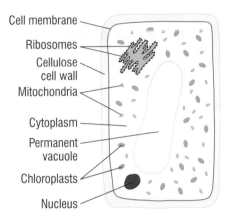

Cell membrane
Ribosomes
Cellulose cell wall
Mitochondria
Cytoplasm
Permanent vacuole
Chloroplasts
Nucleus

Figure 3 A plant cell has many features in common with an animal cell, as well as other features that are unique to plants

For more information on photosynthesis, look at 9.1 'Photosynthesis'.

Practical

Looking at cells

Set up a microscope to look at plant cells, for example from onions, *Elodea* and/or algal cells. You should see the cell wall, the cytoplasm and sometimes a vacuole. You will see chloroplasts in the *Elodea* and the algae, but not in the onion cells because they do not photosynthesise.

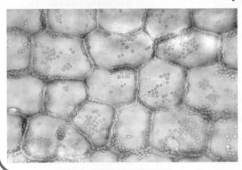

Figure 4 Some of the common features of plant cells show up well under the light microscope. Here, the features are magnified ×40.

Summary questions

1 a List the main structures you would expect to find in an animal cell.
  b You would find all the things we have in animal cells also in a plant or algal cell. There are three extra features that may be found in plant cells but not animal cells. What are they?
  c What are the main functions of these three extra structures?

2 Why are the nucleus and the mitochondria so important in all cells?

3 Chloroplasts are found in many plant cells but not all of them. Give an example of plant cells without chloroplasts and explain why they have none.

Examiner's tip

Remember that not all plant cells have chloroplasts. Don't confuse chloroplasts and chlorophyll.

links

For more information on photosynthesis, look at 9.1 'Photosynthesis'.

Did you know ... ?

The best light microscopes magnify cells ×2000. To give an idea of scale, this would make an average person about 3.5 km tall. An electron microscope magnifies cells ×2 000 000, making an average person around 3500 km tall!

Examiner's tip

Learn all the parts of cells and their functions. This will help you answer many different questions on the biology papers, not just the ones on cell structure.

Key points

● Most human cells are similar to most other animal cells and contain features common to all cells: a nucleus, cytoplasm, cell membrane, mitochondria and ribosomes.

● Plant and algal cells contain all the structures seen in animal cells as well as a cell wall. Many plant cells also contain chloroplasts and a permanent vacuole filled with sap.

B1.2

Bacteria and yeast

Learning objectives

After this topic, you should know:

● the similarities and differences between bacteria and yeast cells

● how they compare to animal and plant cells.

Maths skills

Using units

1 km = 1000 m

1 m = 100 cm

1 cm = 10 mm

1 mm = 1000 μm (micrometres)

Bacteria are single-celled living organisms that are much smaller than animal and plant cells. Most bacteria are less than 1 μm in length. You could fit hundreds of thousands of bacteria on to the full stop at the end of this sentence, so you can't see individual bacteria without a powerful microscope.

When you culture bacteria on an agar plate, you grow many millions of bacteria. This enables you to see the **bacterial colony** with your naked eye.

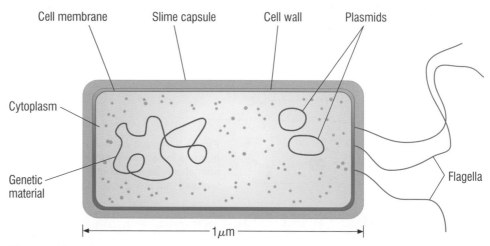

Cell membrane   Slime capsule   Cell wall   Plasmids

Cytoplasm

Genetic material

Flagella

⊢————1 μm————⊣

Figure 1 Bacteria come in a variety of shapes, but they all have the same basic structure

Bacterial cells

Each bacterium is a single cell. It is made up of cytoplasm surrounded by a membrane and a cell wall. Inside the bacterial cell is the **genetic material**. Unlike animal, plant and algal cells, the genes are not contained in a nucleus. The long strand of **DNA** (the bacterial chromosome) is usually circular and found free in the cytoplasm.

Many bacterial cells also contain **plasmids**, which are small circular bits of DNA. These carry extra genetic information. Plasmids are widely used by scientists in the process of genetic engineering.

Bacteria may have a slime capsule around the outside of the cell wall. Some types of bacterium have at least one flagellum (plural: flagella), a long protein strand that lashes about. These bacteria use their flagella to move themselves around.

Although some bacteria cause disease, many are harmless. Some are actually really useful to us. We use them to make food like yoghurt and cheese. Others are used in sewage treatment and to make medicines. They are vital as decomposers in food chains and webs, and in natural cycles such as the carbon and nitrogen cycles. They are also an important part of a healthy gut.

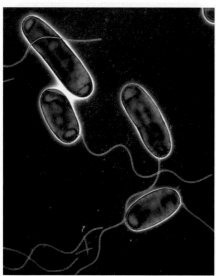

Magn
6500× ⊢————⊣ 5 μm

Figure 2 Bacteria come in several different shapes and sizes. This helps us to identify them under the microscope.

Yeast

Another type of microorganism that is very useful to people is **yeast**. Yeasts are single-celled fungi. Each yeast cell has a nucleus containing the genetic material, cytoplasm and a membrane surrounded by a cell wall.

The cells vary in size, but most are about 3–4 μm. This makes them bigger than bacteria but still very small.

The main way in which yeasts reproduce is by **asexual budding**. This involves a new yeast cell growing out from the original cell to form a separate yeast organism.

Yeast cells are specialised to be able to survive for a long time, even when there is very little oxygen available. When yeast cells have plenty of oxygen, they use **aerobic respiration**. They use oxygen to break down sugar to provide energy for the cell. During this process, they produce water and carbon dioxide as waste products.

However, when there isn't much oxygen, yeast can use **anaerobic respiration**. When yeast cells break down sugar in the absence of oxygen, they produce ethanol and carbon dioxide.

Ethanol is commonly referred to as alcohol. The anaerobic respiration of yeast is sometimes called **fermentation**.

Humans have used yeast for making bread and alcoholic drinks almost as far back as written records go. We know that yeast was used to make bread in Egypt 6000 years ago, and some ancient wine found in Iran is over 7000 years old.

Yeast is also important in the production of **antibiotics** such as penicillin, as decomposers in food chains and webs, and in the carbon cycle. However, yeast can cause problems too, particularly breaking down and decomposing food stuff that people are storing.

?? Did you know …?

When making sourdough bread, a mixture of yeast and bacteria is used to provide a natural raising agent. This gives the bread its typical sharp taste.

Examiner's tip

Be clear about the similarities and differences between animal, plant, algal, bacterial and yeast cells.

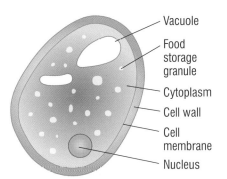
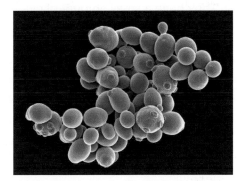

- Vacuole
- Food storage granule
- Cytoplasm
- Cell wall
- Cell membrane
- Nucleus

Figure 3 Yeast cells. These microscopic organisms have been useful to us for centuries

Summary questions

1 **a** What is unusual about the genetic material in bacterial cells?
  b Which are bigger, bacterial cells or yeast cells?
  c What are flagella and what are they used for?

2 Compare the ways bacteria and fungi are useful and/or damaging to people.

3 Make a table to compare the structures in animal, plant and algal, bacterial and yeast cells.

Key points

- A bacterial cell consists of cytoplasm and a membrane surrounded by a cell wall. The genes are not in a distinct nucleus. Some of the genes are in circular structures called plasmids.

- Yeast is a single-celled organism. Each yeast cell has a nucleus, cytoplasm and a membrane surrounded by a cell wall.

B1.3

Specialised cells

Learning objectives

After this topic, you should know:

- cells may be specialised to carry out a particular function.

∞ links

You can find out much more about the organisation of specialised cells into tissues, organs and organ systems in 2.4 'Cell growth and cancer' and 2.5 'Tissues and organs'.

The smallest living organisms are single cells. They can carry out all of the functions of life. These range from feeding and respiration to excretion and reproduction.

Most organisms are bigger and are made up of lots of cells. Some of these cells become **specialised** in order to carry out particular jobs.

When a cell becomes specialised, its structure is adapted to suit the particular job it does. As a result, specialised cells often look very different to the 'typical' plant or animal cell. Sometimes cells become so specialised that they only have one function within the body. Examples of this include sperm, eggs, red blood cells and nerve cells. Some specialised cells, such as egg and sperm cells, work individually. Others are adapted to work as part of a tissue, an organ or a whole organism.

Fat cells

If you eat more food than you need, your body makes fat and stores it in fat cells. The fat can be broken down and used for energy when it is needed. Fat cells help animals, including humans, to survive when food is in short supply. Fat cells together form adipose tissue.

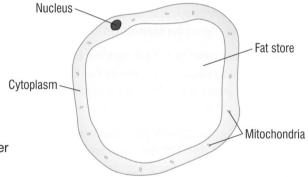

Fat cells have three main adaptations:

- They have a small amount of cytoplasm and large amounts of fat.
- They have few mitochondria as the cell needs very little energy.
- They can expand – a fat cell can end up 1000 times its original size as it fills up with fat.

Cone cells from human eye

There are cone cells in the light-sensitive layer of your eye (the retina). They make it possible for you to see in colour.

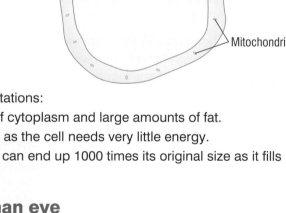

Cone cells have three main adaptations:

- The outer segment contains a special chemical, a visual pigment, that changes chemically in coloured light. It needs energy to change back to its original form. The visual pigments are based on the vitamin A in your diet.
- The middle segment is packed full of mitochondria. The mitochondria release the energy needed to reform the visual pigment. This lets you see continually in colour.
- The final part of the cone cell is a specialised synapse that connects to the **optic nerve**. When coloured light makes your visual pigment change, a nerve impulse is triggered. This makes its way along the optic nerve to your brain.

Root hair cells

You find **root hair cells** close to the tips of growing roots. Plants need to take in lots of water (and dissolved mineral ions). The root hair cells help them to take up water and mineral ions more efficiently. Root hair cells are always close to the **xylem tissue**. The xylem tissue carries water and **mineral ions** up into the rest of the plant. Mineral ions are moved into the cell by active transport.

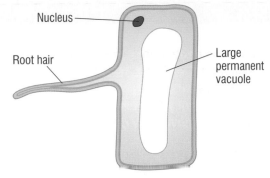

Root hair cells have two main adaptations:

● The root hairs increase the surface area for water to move into the cell.
● The root hair cells have a large permanent vacuole that speeds up the movement of water by osmosis from the soil across the root hair cell.

Sperm cells

Sperm cells are usually released a long way from the egg they are going to fertilise. They contain the genetic information from the male parent. Depending on the type of animal, sperm cells need to move through water or the female reproductive system to reach an egg. Then they have to break into the egg.

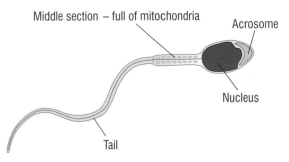

Sperm cells have several adaptations to make all this possible:

● A long tail whips from side to side and helps move the sperm towards the egg.
● The middle section is full of mitochondria, which provide the energy for the tail to work.
● The acrosome stores digestive enzymes for breaking down the outer layers of the egg.
● A large nucleus contains the genetic information to be passed on.

links

You can find out more about osmosis in 1.5 'Osmosis' and active transport in 1.6 'Active transport'.

Practical

Observing specialised cells

Try looking at different specialised cells under a microscope.

When you look at a specialised cell, there are two useful questions you can ask yourself:

● How is this cell different in structure from a generalised cell?
● How does the difference in structure help the cell to carry out its function?

Summary questions

1 Make a table to explain how the structure of each cell on this spread is adapted to its function.

2 a Muscle cells can contract (shorten) and are used to move the body around and also to move substances around your body. Muscle cells usually contain many mitochondria. Explain why this is an important adaptation.
   b The palisade cells are found near the top surface of a leaf. They contain many chloroplasts. Why is this an important adaptation?

3 Explain the types of features you would look for to decide on the function of an unknown specialised cell.

Key points

● Cells may be specialised to carry out a particular function.

● Examples of specialised cells are fat cells, cone cells, root hair cells and sperm cells.

● Cells may be specialised to work as tissues, organs or whole organisms.

B1.4

Diffusion

Your cells need to take in substances such as glucose and oxygen for respiration. Cells also need to get rid of waste products and chemicals that are needed elsewhere in your body. Dissolved substances and gases can move into and out of your cells across the cell membrane. One of the main ways in which they move is by **diffusion**.

Diffusion

Diffusion is the spreading out of the particles of a gas, or of any substance in solution (a **solute**). This results in the **net movement** (overall movement) of particles. The net movement is from an area of high concentration to an area of lower concentration. It takes place because of the random movement of the particles. The motion of the particles causes them to bump into each other, and this moves them all around.

Imagine a room containing a group of boys and a group of girls. If everyone closes their eyes and moves around briskly but randomly, children will bump into each other. They will scatter until the room contains a mixture of boys and girls. This gives you a good model of diffusion (see Figure 1).

Figure 1 The random movement of particles results in substances spreading out, or diffusing, from an area of higher concentration to an area of lower concentration

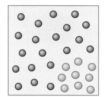

At the moment when the blue particles are added to the red particles they are not mixed at all

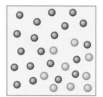

As the particles move randomly, the blue ones begin to mix with the red ones

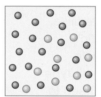

As the particles move and spread out, they bump into each other. This helps them to keep spreading randomly

Eventually, the particles are completely mixed and diffusion is complete

Rates of diffusion

If there is a big difference in concentration between two areas, diffusion will take place quickly. Many particles will move randomly towards the area of low concentration. Only a few will move randomly in the other direction.

However, if there is only a small difference in concentration between two areas, the net movement by diffusion will be quite slow. The number of particles moving into the area of lower concentration by random movement will only be slightly more than the number of particles that are leaving the area.

net movement = particles moving in − particles moving out

In general, the greater the difference in concentration, the faster the rate of diffusion. This difference between two areas of concentration is called the **concentration gradient**. The bigger the difference, the steeper the concentration gradient and the faster the rate of diffusion. In other words, diffusion occurs *down* a concentration gradient (see Figure 2).

Temperature also affects the rate of diffusion. An increase in temperature means the particles in a gas or a solution move around more quickly. When this happens, diffusion takes place more rapidly as the random movement of the particles speeds up.

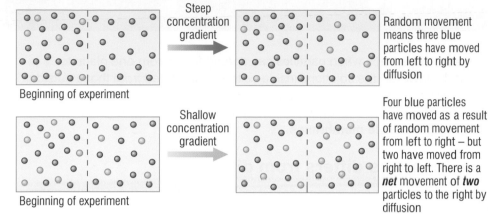

Both types of particles can pass through this membrane – it is freely permeable

Steep concentration gradient

Beginning of experiment

Random movement means three blue particles have moved from left to right by diffusion

Shallow concentration gradient

Beginning of experiment

Four blue particles have moved as a result of random movement from left to right – but two have moved from right to left. There is a *net* movement of *two* particles to the right by diffusion

Figure 2 This diagram shows the effect of concentration on the rate of diffusion. This is why so many body systems are adapted to maintain steep concentration gradients.

Diffusion in living organisms

Dissolved substances move into and out of your cells by diffusion across the cell membrane. These include **simple sugars**, such as glucose, gases such as oxygen and waste products such as urea from the breakdown of amino acids in your liver.

The oxygen you need for **respiration** passes from the air into your lungs. From the lungs it enters your red blood cells through the cell membranes by diffusion. The oxygen moves down a concentration gradient from a region of high to low oxygen concentration. Oxygen then also moves from the blood cells into the cells of the body where it is needed by diffusion down a concentration gradient.

Carbon dioxide moves out from the body cells into the red blood cells and then into the air in the lungs by diffusion down a concentration gradient in a similar way.

Individual cells may be adapted to make diffusion easier and more rapid. The most common adaptation is to increase the surface area of the cell membrane. Increasing the surface area means there is more room for diffusion to take place. By folding up the membrane of a cell, or the tissue lining an organ, the area over which diffusion can take place is greatly increased. Therefore the rate of diffusion is also greatly increased, so that much more of a substance moves in a given time.

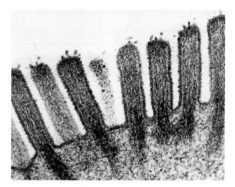

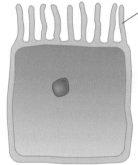

Infoldings of the cell membrane form microvilli, which increase the surface area of the cell

Figure 3 An increase in the surface area of a cell membrane means diffusion can take place more quickly. This is an intestinal cell.

Summary questions

1 Explain the process of diffusion in terms of the particles involved.

2 a Explain why diffusion takes place faster when there is an increase in temperature.
  b Explain in terms of diffusion why so many cells have folded membranes along at least one surface.

3 Explain the following statements in terms of diffusion:
  a Digested food products move from the inside of your gut into the bloodstream.
  b Carbon dioxide moves from the blood in the capillaries in your lungs to the air in the lungs.
  c Male moths can track down a mate from up to 3 miles away because of the special chemicals produced by the female.

Key points

- Diffusion is the net movement of particles from an area where they are at a high concentration to an area where they are at a lower concentration, down a concentration gradient.

- The greater the difference in concentration, the faster the rate of diffusion.

- Dissolved substances such as glucose and gases such as oxygen move in and out of cells by diffusion.

B1.5 Osmosis

Learning objectives

After this topic, you should know:

- how osmosis differs from diffusion

- why osmosis is so important in cells.

Examiner's tip

Remember, all particles can diffuse from an area of high concentration to an area of low concentration, provided they are **soluble** and **small** enough to pass through the membrane. Osmosis refers only to the diffusion of WATER through a partially permeable membrane.

Diffusion takes place when particles can spread freely from one place to another. However, the solutions inside cells are separated from those outside by the cell membrane. This membrane does not let all types of particles through. Membranes that only let some types of particles through are called **partially permeable membranes**.

How osmosis differs from diffusion

Partially permeable cell membranes let water move across them. Remember:

- A **dilute** solution of sugar contains a *high* concentration of water (the solvent). It has a *low* concentration of sugar (the solute).

- A **concentrated** sugar solution contains a relatively *low* concentration of water and a *high* concentration of sugar.

The cytoplasm of a cell is made up of chemicals dissolved in water inside a partially permeable bag of cell membrane. The cytoplasm contains a fairly concentrated solution of salts and sugars. Water moves from a dilute solution (with a high concentration of water molecules) to a concentrated solution (with fewer water molecules) across the membrane of the cell.

This special type of diffusion, where only water moves across a partially permeable membrane, is called **osmosis**.

Practical

Investigating osmosis

You can make model cells using bags made of partially permeable membrane (see Figure 1). You can see what happens to them if the concentrations of the solutions inside or outside the 'cell' change.

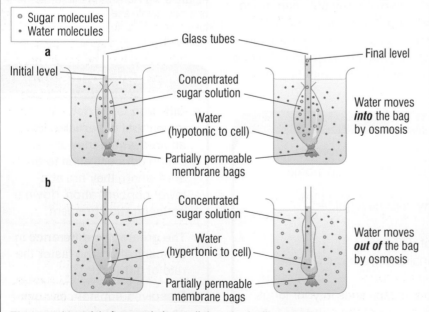

Figure 1 A model of osmosis in a cell. In **a** the 'cell' contents are more concentrated than the surrounding solution. In **b** the 'cell' contents are less concentrated than the surrounding solution.

The concentration inside your body cells needs to stay the same for them to work properly. However, the concentration of the solutions outside your cells may be very different to the concentration inside them. This concentration gradient can cause water to move into or out of the cells by osmosis.

- If the concentration of solutes in the solution outside the cell is **the same** as the concentration inside the cell, the solution is **isotonic** to the cell.

- If the concentration of solutes in the solution outside the cell is **higher** than the concentration inside the cell, the solution is **hypertonic** to the cell.

- If the concentration of solutes in the solution outside the cell is **lower** than the concentration inside the cell, the solution is **hypotonic** to the cell.

Osmosis in animals

If a cell uses up water in its chemical reactions, the cytoplasm becomes more concentrated. The surrounding fluid becomes hypotonic and more water immediately moves in by osmosis.

If the cytoplasm becomes too dilute because more water is made in chemical reactions, the surrounding fluid becomes hypertonic and water leaves the cell by osmosis. So osmosis restores the balance in both cases.

However, osmosis can also cause big problems in animal cells. If the solution outside the cell becomes much more dilute than the cell contents (hypotonic), water will move into the cell by osmosis. The cell will swell and may burst.

If the solution outside the cell becomes more concentrated than the cell contents (hypertonic), water will move out of the cell by osmosis. The cytoplasm will become too concentrated and the cell will shrivel up. Then it can no longer survive.

Once you understand the effect osmosis can have on cells, the importance of maintaining constant internal conditions becomes clear.

Osmosis in plants

Plants rely on osmosis to support their stems and leaves. Water moves into plant cells by osmosis. This causes the vacuole to swell and press the cytoplasm against the plant cell walls. The pressure builds up until no more water can physically enter the cell – this pressure is known as **turgor**. Turgor pressure makes the cells hard and rigid, which in turn keeps the leaves and stems of the plant rigid and firm.

Plants need the fluid surrounding the cells to always be hypotonic to the cytoplasm, with a lower concentration of solutes and a higher concentration of water than the plant cells themselves. This keeps water moving by osmosis in the right direction and the cells are turgid. If the solution surrounding the plant cells is hypertonic to (more concentrated than) the cell contents, water will leave the cells by osmosis. The cells will no longer be firm and swollen – they become flaccid (soft) as there is no pressure on the cell walls. At this point, the plant wilts as turgor no longer supports the plant tissues.

If more water is lost by osmosis, the vacuole and cytoplasm shrink, and eventually the cell membrane pulls away from the cell wall. This is **plasmolysis**. Plasmolysis is usually only seen in laboratory experiments. Plasmolysed cells die quickly unless the osmotic balance is restored.

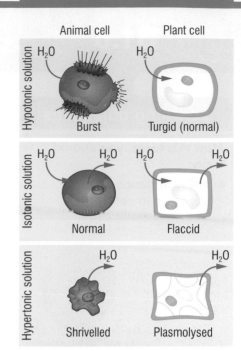

Figure 2 Osmosis is important in all living organisms

Examiner's tip

When writing about osmosis, be careful to specify whether it is concentration of water or solutes you are referring to. Simply saying 'higher concentration outside cell' will gain no marks!

Key points

- Osmosis is a special case of diffusion. It is the movement of water from a dilute to a more concentrated solution through a partially permeable membrane that allows water to pass through.

- Differences in the concentrations of solutions inside and outside a cell cause water to move into or out of the cell by osmosis.

- Osmosis is important to maintain turgor in plant cells. Animal cells can be damaged if the concentrations inside and outside the cells are not kept the same.

Summary questions

1 a What is the difference between osmosis and diffusion?
 b How does osmosis help to maintain the cytoplasm of plant and body cells at a specific concentration?

2 a Define the following terms: isotonic solution, hypotonic solution, hypertonic solution.
 b Why is it so important for the cells of the human body that the solute concentration of the fluid surrounding the cells is kept as constant as possible?

3 Explain why osmosis is so important in the support systems of plants.

4 Animals that live in fresh water have a constant problem with their water balance. The single-celled organism called *Amoeba* has a special vacuole in its cell. It fills with water and then moves to the outside of the cell and bursts. A new vacuole starts forming straight away.
 Explain in terms of osmosis why the *Amoeba* needs one of these vacuoles.

B1.6 Active transport

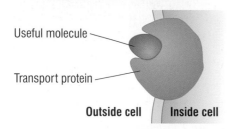

Useful molecule

Transport protein

Outside cell **Inside cell**

Transport protein rotates and releases molecule inside cell (using energy)

Transport protein rotates back again (often using energy)

Figure 1 Active transport uses energy to move substances against a concentration gradient

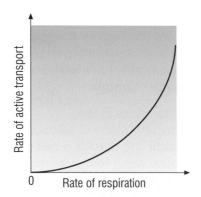

Rate of active transport

0   Rate of respiration

Figure 2 The rate of active transport depends on the rate of respiration

Cells need to move substances in and out. Water often moves across the cell boundaries by osmosis. Dissolved substances also need to move in and out of cells. There are two main ways in which this happens:

- Substances move by diffusion, down a concentration gradient. This must be in the right direction to be useful to the cells.
- Sometimes the substances needed by a cell have to be moved against a concentration gradient, or across a partially permeable membrane. This needs a special process called **active transport**.

Moving substances by active transport

Active transport allows cells to move substances from an area of low concentration to an area of high concentration. This movement is *against* the concentration gradient. As a result, cells can absorb ions from very dilute solutions. It also enables them to move substances, such as sugars and ions, from one place to another through the cell membranes.

It takes energy for the active transport system to carry a molecule across the membrane and then return to its original position (see Figure 1). The energy for active transport comes from cellular respiration. Scientists have shown in a number of different cells that the rate of respiration and the rate of active transport are closely linked (see Figure 2).

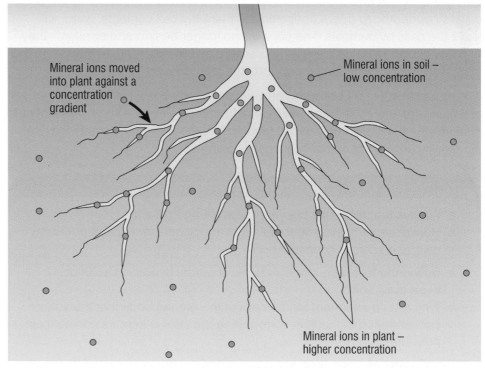

Mineral ions moved into plant against a concentration gradient

Mineral ions in soil – low concentration

Mineral ions in plant – higher concentration

Figure 3 Plants use energy from respiration in active transport to move mineral ions from the soil into the roots against a concentration gradient

In other words, if a cell is making plenty of energy, it can carry out lots of active transport. Examples include root hair cells and the cells lining your gut. Cells involved in a lot of active transport usually have many mitochondria to provide the energy they need.

The importance of active transport

Active transport is widely used in cells. There are some situations where it is particularly important. For example, mineral ions in the soil, such as nitrate ions, are usually found in very dilute solutions. These solutions are more dilute than the solution within the plant cells. By using active transport, plants can absorb these mineral ions, even though it is against a concentration gradient (see Figure 3).

Sugar, such as glucose, is always actively absorbed out of your gut and **kidney tubules** into your blood. This is often done against a large concentration gradient.

CO links

You can find out more about the absorption of glucose in the gut in 5.6 'The digestive system', and about the absorption of solutes in the kidney in 7.3 'The human kidney'.

Examiner's tip

Do not refer to movement *along* a concentration gradient. Always refer to movement as *down* a concentration gradient (from high to low) for diffusion or osmosis and *against* a concentration gradient (from low to high) for active transport.

Figure 4 Some crocodiles have special salt glands in their tongues. These remove excess salt from the body against the concentration gradient by active transport. That's why members of the crocodile species *Crocodylus porosus* can live in estuaries and even the sea.

?? Did you know ... ?

People with cystic fibrosis (see 10.6 'Inherited conditions in humans') have thick, sticky mucus in their lungs, gut and reproductive systems. This is the result of a mutation affecting a protein involved in the active transport system of the mucus-producing cells.

Summary questions

1 Explain how active transport works in a cell.

2 a How does active transport differ from diffusion and osmosis?
  b Why do cells that carry out a lot of active transport also usually have many mitochondria?

3 Explain fully why active transport is so important to:
  a marine birds such as albatrosses, which have special salt glands producing very salty liquid
  b plants.

Key points

- Substances are sometimes absorbed against (up) a concentration gradient by active transport.

- Active transport uses energy from respiration.

- Cells can absorb ions from very dilute solutions, and actively absorb substances such as sugar and salt against a concentration gradient, using active transport.

B1.7

Exchanging materials

Learning objectives

After this topic, you should know:

- how the surface area to volume ratio varies depending on the size of an organism

- why large multicellular organisms need special systems for exchanging materials with the environment.

 Maths skills

Surface area to volume ratio

The ratio of surface area to volume falls as objects get bigger. You can see this clearly in the diagram. In a small object, the surface area to volume (SA : V) ratio is relatively large. This means that the diffusion distances are short and that simple diffusion is sufficient for the exchange of materials.

As organisms get bigger, the surface area to volume ratio falls. As the distances between the centre of the organism and the surface get bigger, simple diffusion is no longer enough to exchange materials between the cells and the environment.

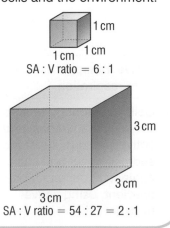

1 cm 1 cm 1 cm
SA : V ratio = 6 : 1

3 cm 3 cm 3 cm
SA : V ratio = 54 : 27 = 2 : 1

For many single-celled organisms, diffusion, osmosis and active transport are all that is needed to exchange materials with their environment. A single-celled organism such as *Amoeba* has a relatively large surface area compared to the volume of the cell. This is known as the surface area to volume ratio. So, for example, the diffusion distances are small enough for all the oxygen needed to be moved into the cells from the surrounding water by simple diffusion. The carbon dioxide produced during metabolism can be removed in the same way.

Surface area to volume ratio

The surface area to volume ratio is very important in biology. It makes a big difference to the way animals can exchange substances with the environment. Surface area to volume ratio is also important when you consider how energy is lost and gained by living organisms, and how water evaporates from the surfaces of plants and animals.

⚭ links

You will use the idea of surface area to volume ratio when you study the adaptations of animals and plants for living in a variety of different habitats in 12.1 'Adapt and survive' to 12.4 'Competition in animals'.

Getting bigger

As living organisms get bigger and more complex, their surface area to volume ratio gets smaller. This makes it increasingly difficult to exchange materials quickly enough with the outside world:

- Gases and food molecules can no longer reach every cell inside the organism by simple diffusion

- Metabolic waste cannot be removed fast enough to avoid poisoning the cells.

So in many larger organisms, there are special surfaces where the exchange of materials takes place. These surfaces are adapted to be as effective as possible. You can find them in humans, in other animals and in plants.

Adaptations for exchanging materials

There are various adaptations to make the process of exchange more efficient. The effectiveness of an **exchange surface** can be increased by:

- having a large surface area that provides a big area over which exchange can take place

- being thin, which provides a short diffusion path

- having an efficient blood supply (in animals); this moves the diffusing substances away and maintains a concentration (diffusion) gradient

- being **ventilated** (in animals) to make gaseous exchange more efficient by maintaining steep concentration gradients.

Different organisms have very different adaptations for the exchange of materials, such as the leaves of a plant, the gills of a fish and the kidneys of a desert rat. For example, scientists have recently discovered that the common musk turtle has a specially adapted tongue.

Its tongue is covered in tiny buds that greatly increase the surface area. It also has a good blood supply. These turtles don't just use their tongue for eating – they use it for **gaseous exchange** too. The buds on the tongue absorb oxygen dissolved in the water that passes over them. Most turtles have to surface regularly for air. However, the musk turtle's tongue is so effective at gaseous exchange that it can stay underwater for months at a time.

Examples of adaptations

Many of your own organ systems are specialised for exchanging materials. This is because the human surface area to volume ratio is so low that the cells inside your body cannot possibly get the food and oxygen they need, or get rid of the waste they produce.

One of these exchange systems is your breathing system, particularly your lungs. Air is moved into and out of your lungs when you breathe, ventilating the millions of tiny air sacs called **alveoli**. The alveoli have an enormous surface area and a very rich blood supply, both of which make your lungs very effective for gas exchange.

Animals are not the only organisms that need effective gas and solute exchange systems. Even the smallest plants need specialised exchange systems to get the water, mineral ions and carbon dioxide they need. Plants need to be able to take in plenty of water and dissolved mineral ions through their root systems. The roots have a very large surface area that is increased still more by the root hair cells. Water is constantly moved away from the roots in the transpiration stream, which maintain a steep concentration gradient into the cells.

Plant leaves are also modified to make gaseous and solute exchange as effective as possible. Flat, thin leaves, the presence of air spaces in the mesophyll tissue and the **stomata** all help to provide a big surface area. They also maintain a steep concentration gradient for the diffusion of substances such as water, mineral ions and carbon dioxide needed by plants.

Examiner's tip

Active transport requires energy. You will remember this if you think about mineral ions having to *push* into the root hair cells *against* a concentration gradient.

Summary questions

1 Explain clearly how the surface area to volume ratio of an organism affects the way it exchanges materials with the environment.

2 a How does the tongue of a musk turtle differ from the tongues of most reptiles?
   b How does this adaptation help musk turtles survive?

3 a Summarise the adaptations you would expect to see in effective exchange surfaces and explain the importance of each adaptation.
   b Explain how three different exchange surfaces show some or all of these adaptations to help them operate efficiently.

Figure 1 The common musk turtle has a very unusual tongue, which is adapted for gaseous exchange

∞ links

You will find out much more about the detail of the alveoli of the lungs as a site of gas exchange in 4.1 'Breathing and gas exchange in the lungs'.

∞ links

You can see how active transport and osmosis are important in plant roots in 1.6 'Active transport' and 9.4 'Exchange in plants'.
You can find out more about the transpiration stream in 9.5 'Evaporation and transpiration'.

∞ links

You can find out more about the adaptations of plant leaves for diffusion and the exchange of materials in 9.4 'Exchange in plants'.

Key points

- Single-celled organisms have a relatively large surface area to volume ratio so all necessary exchanges with the environment take place over this surface.

- In multicellular organisms, many organs are specialised with effective exchange surfaces.

- Exchange surfaces usually have a large surface area and thin walls, which give short diffusion distances. In animals, exchange surfaces will have an efficient blood supply or, for gaseous exchange, be ventilated.

B1.8

Exchange in the gut

After this topic, you should know:

- how the small intestine is adapted to enable you to absorb food efficiently
- why villi are so important.

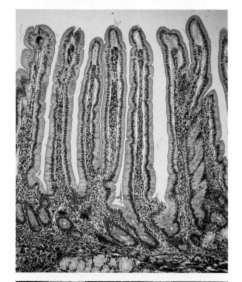

Figure 1 The villi of the small intestine increase the surface area available for diffusion many times. This means we can absorb enough digested food to survive.

The food you eat is made up of large insoluble molecules which your body cannot use. This food is broken down as it passes along your **digestive system** or gut. This is a tube which is many metres long and as your food passes along it, the large food molecules are broken down into simple sugars, such as glucose, as well as amino acids.

The food you eat is broken down in your gut. Food molecules get turned into simple sugars, such as glucose, as well as amino acids, fatty acids and glycerol. Your body cells need these products of digestion to provide fuel for respiration and the building blocks for growth and repair. A successful exchange surface is therefore very important. Your digestive system is adapted for the effective exchange of solutes, particularly the **small intestine**.

⚭ links

You will find out more about chemistry of carbohydrates, proteins and lipids as well as the breakdown of food in the digestive system in 3.1 'Carbohydrates, lipids and proteins' and 3.3 'Factors affecting enzyme action'.
You will find out more about the structure of the whole digestive system in 2.5 'Tissues and organs'.

Absorption in the small intestine

For the digested food molecules to reach your cells, they must move from inside your small intestine into your bloodstream. They do this by a combination of diffusion and active transport.

The digested food molecules are small enough to pass freely through the walls of the small intestine into the blood vessels. They move in this direction because there is a very high concentration of food molecules in the gut and a much lower concentration in the blood. They move into the blood down a steep concentration gradient.

The lining of the small intestine is folded into thousands of tiny finger-like projections known as **villi** (singular: villus). These greatly increase the uptake of digested food by diffusion (see Figure 1). Only a certain number of digested food molecules can diffuse over a given surface area of gut lining at any one time. Increasing the surface area means there is more room for diffusion to take place (see Figure 2).

Each individual villus is itself covered in many microscopic microvilli. This increases the surface area available for diffusion even more.

The lining of the small intestine has an excellent blood supply. This carries away the digested food molecules as soon as they have diffused from one side to the other. So, a steep concentration gradient is maintained all the time, from the inside of the intestine to the blood (see Figure 3). This in turn makes sure that diffusion is as rapid and efficient as possible down the concentration gradient.

Gut with villi ← Length 5 cm →

Gut without villi ← Length 5 cm →

Total stretched length = 5 cm

Total stretched length = 45 cm

Figure 2 The effect of folding on the available surface for exchange

links

You will find information on glucose, amino acids, fatty acids and glycerol in 5.6 'The digestive system'.

Active transport in the small intestine

Diffusion isn't the only way in which dissolved products of digestion move from the gut into the blood. As the time since your last meal increases, you will have more dissolved food molecules in your blood than in your digestive system. Glucose and other dissolved food molecules are then moved from the small intestine into the blood by active transport. The digested food molecules have to move against the concentration gradient. This makes sure that none of the digested food is wasted and lost in your faeces.

??? Did you know …?

Although your gut is only around 7 metres long and a few centimetres wide, the way it is folded into your body along with the villi and microvilli give you a surface area for the absorption of digested products of between 200 and 300 m²!

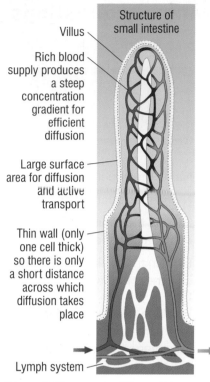

Structure of small intestine

Villus

Rich blood supply produces a steep concentration gradient for efficient diffusion

Large surface area for diffusion and active transport

Thin wall (only one cell thick) so there is only a short distance across which diffusion takes place

Lymph system

Figure 3 Thousands of finger-like projections in the wall of the small intestine – the villi – make it possible for all the digested food molecules to be transferred from your small intestine into your blood by diffusion and active transport

Summary questions

1 In the following sentences, match each beginning (A, B, C or D) to its correct ending (1 to 4).

A	Food needs to be broken down into small soluble molecules …	1	… by diffusion and active transport.
B	The villi are …	2	… carry away the digested food to the cells and maintain a steep concentration gradient.
C	Food molecules move from the small intestine into the bloodstream …	3	… so diffusion across the gut lining can take place.
D	The small intestine has a rich blood supply to …	4	… finger-like projections in the lining of the small intestine that increase the surface area for diffusion.

2 Explain why a folded gut wall can absorb more nutrients than a flat one.

3 Coeliac disease is caused by gluten, a protein found in wheat, oats and rye. Affected people react to gluten – the villi become flattened and the lining of the small intestine becomes damaged.
   a Why do you think people with untreated coeliac disease are often quite thin?
   b If someone with coeliac disease stops eating any food containing gluten, they will gradually gain weight and no longer suffer malnutrition. Suggest why this might be.

Key points

- The villi in the small intestine provide a large surface area with an extensive network of blood capillaries.

- The villi mean the small intestine is well adapted as an exchange surface to absorb the products of digestion, both by diffusion and by active transport.

Summary questions

1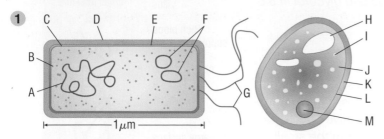

a Name the structures labelled A–G in this bacterial cell.

b Name the structures labelled H–M in the yeast cell.

c Explain the similarities and differences between a bacteria cell and a plant cell.

d Explain the similarities and differences between a yeast cell and a non-specialised animal cell.

2 a Produce a table to compare diffusion, osmosis and active transport. Write a brief explanation of the advantages and disadvantages of all three processes in cells.

b In an experiment to investigate osmosis two visking tubing bags were set up with sugar solution inside the bags and water outside the bags. Bag A was kept at 20 °C and bag B was kept at 30 °C (see Figure 1).

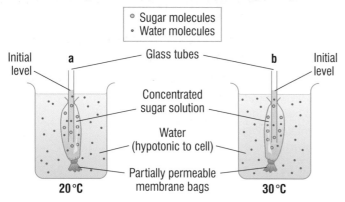

Figure 1

Describe what you would expect to happen and explain it in terms of osmosis and particle movements.

3 An amoeba is a single-celled animal that lives in ponds. It obtains oxygen for cell respiration from the water by diffusion across the cell membrane. Sticklebacks are small fish that live in the same habitat. They have a complicated structure of feathery gills to obtain oxygen. Water is pushed over the gills by muscular action.

a Explain why the amoeba can obtain sufficient oxygen for respiration by simple diffusion across its outer surface but the stickleback requires a special structure.

b Explain how the gills and the circulating blood will increase the diffusion of oxygen into the cells of the stickleback.

4 Exchanging materials with the outside world by diffusion is vital for most living organisms. Give four different adaptations which are found in living organisms to make this more efficient. For each adaptation, explain how it makes the exchange process more efficient and give at least one example of where this adaptation is seen.

5 An amoeba is a single-celled animal that lives in ponds. It obtains oxygen for cell respiration from the water by diffusion across the cell membrane. Sticklebacks are small fish that live in the same habitat. They have a complicated structure of feathery gills to obtain oxygen. Water is pushed over the gills by muscular action.

a Explain why the amoeba can obtain sufficient oxygen for respiration by simple diffusion across its outer surface but the stickleback requires a special structure.

b Explain how the gills and the circulating blood will increase the diffusion of oxygen into the cells of the stickleback.

AQA Examination-style questions

1 The diagrams show a typical plant, animal and bacterial cell.

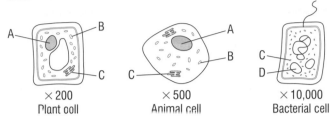

×200
Plant cell

×500
Animal cell

×10,000
Bacterial cell

Figure 1

a Name the structures A, B, C, and D. (4)

b Describe the function of the nucleus in cells. (2)

c Which parts of a bacterial cell carry out the same function as the nucleus does in plant and animal cells? (2)

d Calculate the length of each cell in μm.
($1\,\mu$m $= 0.001$ mm)

Use the formula: length on diagram = real length × magnification
i Plant cell = ... μm
ii Animal cell = ... μm
iii Bacterial cell = ... μm (3)

e Ribosomes make protein molecules for the cell.

Suggest two possible uses for these protein molecules. (2)

f Mitochondria release energy for the cell to use.

Suggest why there are no mitochondria in bacterial cells. (1)

2 The two plant cells below are very different because they have been specialised to carry out different functions.

Root hair cell

Mesophyll cell

Figure 2

a Describe the function of each cell. (5)

b *In this question you will be assessed on using good English, organising information clearly and using specialist terms where appropriate.*

Compare and contrast the structures of these two cells in relation to their function. (QWC) (6)

3 The plant in pot A has been adequately watered and is healthy. The plant in pot B has not been given enough water and is wilting.

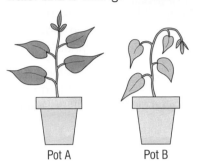

Pot A   Pot B

Figure 3

a Draw and label a stem cell from the plants in pot A and pot B.

Use the correct term to describe the state of each cell. (4)

b Explain in detail why the plant in pot A remains upright while the plant in pot B does not. (3)

4 Some scientists wish to grow mouse skin cells in tissue culture. They know that the tissue culture liquid must have the same concentration of salts and sugars as the cytoplasm of the cell.

They made solutions at four different concentrations and added some mouse skin cells.

After 24 hours they removed some cells and observed them under a microscope.

The table below shows the results.

Test number	1	2	3	4	Control
Concentration of salts in mol/dm³	0.24	0.26	0.28	0.30	Fresh cell from mouse
Appearance of cells					

a Name the term given to a solution that has the same concentration as the contents of the cells. (1)

b Which concentration of salts is suitable for the tissue culture liquid? (1)

c The concentration in test 1 is not suitable as it has damaged the cells.

Explain why the solution in test 1 has damaged the cells.

In this question you will be assessed on using good English, organising information clearly and using specialist terms where appropriate. (QWC) (6)

B2.1

Cell division, growth and differentiation

∞ **links**

For more information on alleles, look at 10.5 'Inheritance in action'.

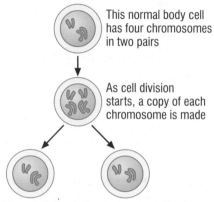

This normal body cell has four chromosomes in two pairs

As cell division starts, a copy of each chromosome is made

The cell divides in two to form two daughter cells. Each daughter cell has a nucleus containing four chromosomes identical to the ones in the original parent cell.

Figure 1 Two identical cells are formed by the simple division that takes place during mitosis. This cell is shown with only two pairs of chromosomes rather than 23.

New cells are needed for an organism, or part of an organism, to grow. They are also needed to replace cells that become worn out and to repair damaged tissue. However, the new cells must have the same genetic information as the originals so they can do the same job.

Each of your cells has a nucleus that contains chromosomes. Chromosomes carry the genes that contain the instructions for making both new cells and all the tissues and organs needed to make an entire new you.

A gene is a small packet of information that controls a characteristic, or part of a characteristic, of your body. It is a section of DNA. Different forms of the same gene are known as **alleles**. Different alleles of the same gene may result in different characteristics. For example, there is a gene which determines whether or not you have dimples: one allele gives dimples, another allele gives no dimples. The genes are grouped together on chromosomes. A chromosome may carry several hundred or even thousands of genes.

You have 46 chromosomes in the nucleus of your body cells. They are arranged in 23 pairs. One of each pair is inherited from your father and one from your mother. Your sex cells (gametes) have only one of each pair of chromosomes.

Mitosis

The cell division in normal body cells produces two identical cells and is called **mitosis**. As a result of mitosis, all your body cells have the same chromosomes. This means they have the same genetic information. Mitosis produces the additional cells needed for growth or replacement.

In asexual reproduction, the cells of the offspring are produced by mitosis from the cells of their parent. This is why they contain exactly the same alleles as their parent with no genetic variation.

How does mitosis work? Before a cell divides, it produces new identical copies of the chromosomes in the nucleus. Then the cell divides once to form two genetically identical cells (see Figure 1).

In some parts of an animal or plant, cell division like this carries on rapidly all the time. Your skin is a good example. You constantly lose cells from the skin's surface, and make new cells to replace them. In fact, about 300 million body cells die every minute, so mitosis is very important.

Practical

Observing mitosis

View a special preparation of a growing root tip under a microscope. You should be able to see the different stages of mitosis as they are taking place. Use Figure 2 for reference.

● Describe your observations of mitosis.

Differentiation

In the early development of animal and plant embryos, the cells are unspecialised. Each one of them (known as a **stem cell**) can become any type of cell that is needed.

In many animals, the cells become specialised very early in life. By the time a human baby is born, most of its cells are specialised. They will all do a particular job, such as liver cells, skin cells or muscle cells. They have differentiated. Some of their genes have been switched on and others have been switched off.

This means that when, for example, a muscle cell divides by mitosis, it can only form more muscle cells. So, in a mature (adult) animal, cell division is mainly restricted. It is needed for the repair of damaged tissue and to replace worn out cells, because in most adult cells, differentiation has already occurred. Specialised cells can divide by mitosis, but they only form the same sort of cell. Therefore, growth stops once the animal is mature. Some differentiated cells, such as blood and skin cells, cannot divide and so **adult stem cells** replace dead or damaged cells.

In contrast, most plant cells are able to differentiate all through their lives. Undifferentiated cells are formed at active regions of the stems and roots known as the meristems. In these areas, mitosis takes place almost continuously.

Plants keep growing all through their lives at these 'growing points'. The plant cells produced don't differentiate until they are in their final position in the plant. Even then, the differentiation isn't permanent. You can move a plant cell from one part of a plant to another. There it can redifferentiate and become a completely different type of cell. You can't do that with animal cells – once a muscle cell, always a muscle cell.

Producing identical offspring is known as **cloning**. We can produce huge numbers of identical plant clones from a tiny piece of leaf tissue. This is because, in the right conditions, a plant cell will become unspecialised and undergo mitosis many times. Each of these undifferentiated cells will produce more cells by mitosis. Given different conditions, these will then differentiate to form a tiny new plant. The new plant will be identical to the original parent.

It is difficult to clone animals because animal cells differentiate permanently, early in embryo development. The cells can't change back. Animal clones can only be made by cloning embryos in one way or another, although adult cells can be used to make an embryo.

Summary questions

1 Explain what is meant by the terms chromosome, gene and allele.

2 a Explain why the chromosome number must stay the same when the cells divide to make other normal body cells.
  b Explain clearly what happens during mitosis and why it is so important in the body.

3 a What is differentiation and why is it important in living organisms?
  b How does differentiation differ in animal and plant cells?
  c Explain how this difference affects the cloning of plants and animals.

⚭ links

You will learn more about the results of differentiation in 2.5 'Tissues and organs'.

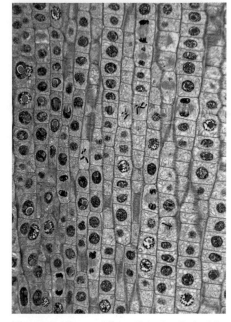

Figure 2 The undifferentiated cells in this onion root tip are dividing rapidly. You can see mitosis taking place, with the chromosomes in different positions as the cells divide.

Examiner's tip

Cells produced by mitosis are genetically identical.

Key points

- In body cells, chromosomes are found in pairs.

- Body cells divide by mitosis to produce more identical cells for growth, repair and replacement, or in some cases asexual reproduction.

- In plant cells, mitosis takes place throughout life in the meristems found in the shoot and root tips.

- Most types of animal cell differentiate at an early stage of development. Many plant cells can differentiate throughout their life.

B2.2

Cell division in sexual reproduction

Learning objectives

After this topic, you should know:

- how cells divide by meiosis to form gametes

- how sexual reproduction gives rise to variation.

Mitosis takes place all the time, in tissues all over your body. Yet there is another type of cell division that takes place only in the reproductive organs of animals and plants. In humans, this is the ovaries and the testes. **Meiosis** results in sex cells, called **gametes**, with only half the original number of chromosomes.

Meiosis

The female gametes, or **ova**, are made in the ovaries. The male gametes, or sperm, are made in the testes.

The gametes are formed by meiosis. In meiosis, the chromosome number is reduced by half in the following way:

- When a cell divides to form gametes, the chromosomes (the genetic information) are copied so there are four sets of chromosomes instead of the normal two sets. This is very similar to mitosis.

- The cell then divides twice in quick succession to form four gametes, each with a single set of chromosomes (see Figure 1).

Each gamete that is produced is slightly different from all the others. They contain random mixtures of the original chromosome pairs. This introduces variety.

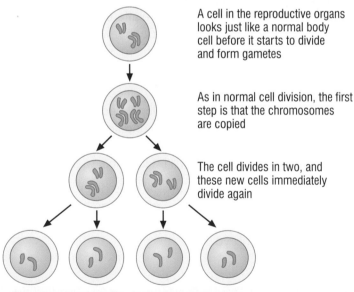

A cell in the reproductive organs looks just like a normal body cell before it starts to divide and form gametes

As in normal cell division, the first step is that the chromosomes are copied

The cell divides in two, and these new cells immediately divide again

This gives four sex cells, each with a single set of chromosomes – in this case two instead of the original four

Figure 1 The formation of sex cells in the ovaries and testes involves meiosis to halve the chromosome number. The original cell is shown with only two pairs of chromosomes, to make it easier to follow what is happening.

??? Did you know ... ?

The testes can produce around 400 million sperm by meiosis every 24 hours. Only one sperm is needed to fertilise an egg, but each sperm needs to travel 100 000 times its own length to reach the ovum, and less than one in a million make it.

Fertilisation

More variety is added when fertilisation takes place. Each sex cell has a single set of chromosomes. When two sex cells join during fertilisation, the single new cell formed has a full set of chromosomes. In humans, the egg cell (ovum) has 23 chromosomes and so does the sperm. When they join together, they produce a single new body cell with 46 chromosomes in 23 pairs – the correct number of chromosomes for all humans.

The combination of genes on the chromosomes of every newly fertilised ovum is unique. Once fertilisation is complete, the unique new cell begins to divide by mitosis to form a new individual. This will continue long after the fetus is fully developed and the baby is born.

In fact, about 80% of fertilised eggs never make it to become a live baby – about 50% never even implant into the lining of the womb.

Variation

The differences between asexual and sexual reproduction are reflected in the different types of cell division involved.

- In asexual reproduction, the offspring are produced as a result of mitosis from the parent cells. So, they contain exactly the same chromosomes and the same genes as their parents. There is no variation in the genetic material.
- In sexual reproduction, the gametes are produced by meiosis in the sex organs of the parents. This introduces variety as each gamete is different. Then, when the gametes fuse, one of each pair of chromosomes, and so one of each pair of genes, comes from each parent.

The combination of genes in the new pair of chromosomes will contain alleles from each parent. This also helps to produce variation in the characteristics of the offspring.

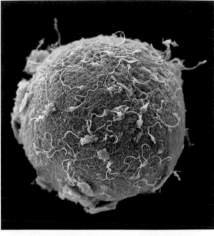

Figure 2 At the moment of fertilisation, the chromosomes of the two gametes are combined. The new cell has a complete set of chromosomes, like any other body cell. This new cell will then grow and reproduce by mitosis to form a new individual.

Examiner's tip

Learn to spell mitosis and meiosis.
Remember their meanings:
Mitosis – **m**aking **i**dentical **t**wo.
Meiosis – **m**aking **e**ggs (and sperm).

Summary questions

1 a How many pairs of chromosomes are there in a normal human body cell?
  b How many chromosomes are there in a human sperm cell?
  c How many chromosomes are there in a fertilised human egg cell?

2 Sexual reproduction results in variety. Explain clearly exactly how this comes about.

3 a What is the name of the special type of cell division that produces gametes from ordinary body cells? Describe clearly what happens to the chromosomes in this process.
  b Where in your body would this type of cell division take place?
  c Explain why this type of cell division is so important in sexual reproduction.

Key points

- Cells in the reproductive organs divide by meiosis to form the gametes (sex cells).
- Body cells have two sets of chromosomes; gametes have only one set.
- In meiosis, the genetic material is copied and then the cell divides twice to form four gametes, each with a single set of chromosomes.
- Sexual reproduction gives rise to variety because genetic information from two parents is combined.

B2.3

Stem cells

Learning objectives

After this topic, you should know:

● how stem cells are different from other body cells

● why scientists hope it will be possible to use stem cells to treat a number of health problems.

The function of stem cells

An egg and sperm cell fuse to form a **zygote**, a single new cell. That cell divides and becomes a hollow ball of cells – the embryo. The inner cells of this ball are the stem cells. Stem cells differentiate to form the specialised cells of your body that make up your various tissues and organs. They will eventually produce every type of cell in your body.

Even when you are an adult, some of your stem cells remain. Your bone marrow is a good source of stem cells. Scientists now think there may be a tiny number of stem cells in most of the different tissues in your body. This includes your blood, brain, muscle and liver.

Many of your differentiated cells can divide to replace themselves. However, some tissues cannot do this. The stem cells can stay in these tissues for many years. They are only needed if the cells are injured or affected by disease. Then they start dividing to replace the different types of damaged cell.

Using stem cells

Many people suffer and even die because parts of their body stop working properly. For example, spinal injuries can cause paralysis. That's because if the spinal nerves are damaged, they do not repair themselves. Millions of people would benefit if we could replace damaged body parts.

In 1998, there was a breakthrough. Two American scientists managed to culture human **embryonic stem cells**. These were capable of forming other types of cell.

Scientists hope that the embryonic stem cells can be encouraged to grow into almost any different type of cell needed in the body. For example, scientists in the USA have grown nerve cells from embryonic stem cells. In rats, these have been used to reconnect damaged spinal nerves. The rats regained some movement of their legs. In 2010, the first trials using nerve cells grown from embryonic stem cells in humans were carried out. The nerve cells were injected into the spinal cords of patients with new, severe spinal cord injuries. These first trials were to make sure that the technique is safe. The scientists and doctors hope it will not be long before they can use stem cells to help people who have been paralysed walk again.

We might also be able to grow whole new organs from embryonic stem cells. These could then be used in transplant surgery (see Figure 1). Scientists in Edinburgh have already grown functioning kidney structures using stem cells from amniotic fluid.

Doctors in the USA and the UK are carrying out trials to see if embryonic stem cells can be used to treat common causes of blindness. They have to discover first if it is safe to inject stem cells into the eyes, and then find out whether the stem cells can restore sight. Conditions from infertility to dementia could eventually be treated using stem cells.

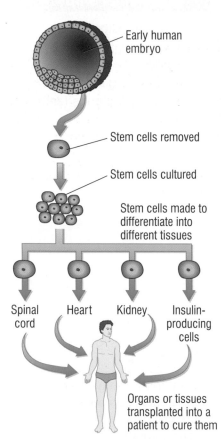

Early human embryo

Stem cells removed

Stem cells cultured

Stem cells made to differentiate into different tissues

Spinal cord   Heart   Kidney   Insulin-producing cells

Organs or tissues transplanted into a patient to cure them

Figure 1 This shows one way in which scientists hope embryonic stem cells might be formed into adult cells and used as human treatments in the future

Problems with stem cells

Many embryonic stem cells come from aborted embryos. Others come from spare embryos in fertility treatment. This raises ethical issues. There are people, including many religious groups, who feel this is wrong. They question the use of a potential human being as a source of cells, even to cure others. Some people feel that, as the embryo cannot give permission, using it is a violation of its human rights.

In addition, progress in developing therapies using stem cells has been relatively slow, although in fact scientists have been working with them for less than 20 years. There is some concern that embryonic stem cells might cause cancer if they are used to treat sick people. This has certainly been seen in mice. Furthermore, making stem cells is slow, difficult, expensive and hard to control.

The future of stem cell research

Scientists have found embryonic stem cells in the umbilical cord blood of newborn babies and even in the amniotic fluid that surrounds the fetus as it grows. These may help to overcome some of the ethical concerns.

Scientists are also finding ways of growing the **adult stem cells** found in bone marrow and some other tissues. So far, they can only develop into a limited range of cell types. However, this is another possible way of avoiding the controversial use of embryonic tissue. Adult stem cells have been used successfully to treat some forms of heart disease and to grow some new organs such as **tracheas** (windpipes).

The area of stem cell research known as **therapeutic cloning** could be very useful. However, it is proving very difficult. It involves using cells from an adult to produce a cloned early embryo of themselves. This would provide a source of perfectly matched embryonic stem cells. In theory, these could then be used to grow new organs for the original donor. The new organs would not be rejected by the body because they have been made from the body's own cells.

Most people remain excited by the possibilities of embryonic stem cell use in treating many diseases. At the moment, after years of relatively slow progress, hopes are high again that stem cells will change the future of medicine. We don't know how many of these hopes will be fulfilled; only time will tell.

Figure 2 In 2010, Ciaran Finn-Lynch was the first child to be given a life-saving new windpipe grown using his own stem cells. His recovery wasn't easy, but a year later he was back at school.

Summary questions

1 a What is the difference between a stem cell and a normal body cell?
  b What are the different types of stem cells?

2 a What are the advantages of using stem cells to treat diseases?
  b Suggest three areas where the use of stem cells could provide valuable medical treatments.
  c Explain how successful stem cell treatments have been so far.

3 a What are the difficulties with stem cell research?
  b How are scientists hoping to overcome the ethical objections to using embryonic stem cells in their research?

Key points

- Embryonic stem cells (from human embryos) and adult stem cells (from adult bone marrow) can be made to differentiate into many different types of cell.

- Stem cells have the potential to treat previously incurable conditions. We may be able to grow nerve cells to cure paralysis or whole new organs for people who need them.

B2.4

Cell growth and cancer

The cells in your body divide on a regular basis to bring about growth. They divide in a set sequence, known as the **cell cycle**, which involves several different stages. A tumour forms when control of this sequence is lost and the cells grow in an abnormal, uncontrolled way.

The cell cycle

The cell cycle in normal, healthy cells follows a regular pattern:

- there is a period of active cell division, when mitosis takes place and the number of cells increases
- this is followed by a long period of non-division called interphase. During this time, the cells get bigger, increase their mass, carry out normal cell activities and replicate their DNA ready for the next division.

The length of the cell cycle varies considerably. It can take less than 24 hours, or it can take several years, depending on which cells are involved and at which stage of life. The cell cycles are very short during the development of the embryo and fetus, when new cells are being made all the time. They remain fairly rapid during childhood, but the cell cycle slows down once **puberty** is over and the body is adult. However, even in adults, the cell cycle in some tissues of the body continues to turn over fairly fast. These are the regions where there is continued growth or a regular replacement of cells, such as the hair follicles, the skin, the blood and the lining of the digestive system.

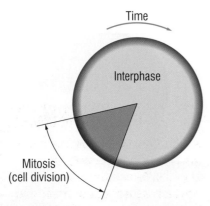

Figure 1 The cell cycle. In rapidly growing tissue, interphase may only be a few hours, but in adult animals it can last for years

Tumour formation

Tumour cells do not respond to the normal mechanisms that control the cell cycle. They divide rapidly with very little non-dividing time for growth in between each division. This results in a mass of abnormally growing cells called a **tumour**, which invades surrounding tissues (see Figure 2).

Benign tumours grow in one place and do not invade other tissues. This does not mean that they do not cause any health problems – a benign tumour can grow very large very quickly, and if it causes pressure or damage to an organ, this can be life-threatening. For example, benign tumours on the brain can be very dangerous because there is no extra space for them to grow into.

Malignant tumours can spread around the body, invading healthy tissue. A malignant tumour is often referred to as **cancer**. The initial tumour may split up, releasing small clumps of cells into the bloodstream or lymph system. They circulate and are carried around the body where they may lodge in another organ of the body. Then they continue their uncontrolled division and form secondary tumours. Cancer cells not only divide more rapidly than normal cells, they also live longer. The growing tumour often completely disrupts normal tissues and, if left untreated, will often kill the organism. Because of the way malignant tumours spread (**metastase**), it can be very difficult to treat them.

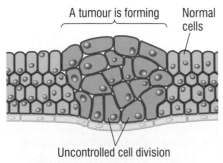

Figure 2 A tumour forms when there is uncontrolled cell division

The causes of cancer

What causes the cell cycle to become uncontrolled and triggers the formation of tumours? Scientists don't know all of the answers, but some of the causes of tumours are well known.

● Most cancers are the result of mutations – changes in the genetic material of the cells. Chemicals such as asbestos and the tar found in tobacco smoke can cause mutations that trigger the formation of tumours. Cancer-causing chemicals such as these are known as **carcinogens**.

● **Ionising radiation**, such as UV light and X-rays, can also interrupt the normal cell cycle and cause tumours to form. For example, melanomas (see Figure 3) appear when there is uncontrolled growth of pigment-forming cells in the skin as a result of exposure to UV light from the sun.

● About 15% of human cancers are caused by virus infections. For example, cervical cancer is almost always the result of infection by the human papilloma virus. This is why young girls in the UK are now routinely vaccinated against the virus.

?? Did you know ... ?

The two main ways of treating cancer at the moment are:
● **radiotherapy**, when the cancer cells are destroyed by targeted doses of radiation
● **chemotherapy**, where chemicals are used to either stop the cancer cells dividing or to make them 'self-destruct'.

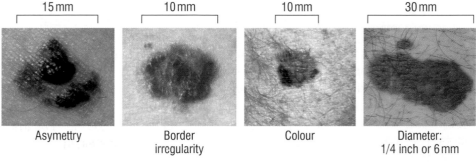

15 mm	10 mm	10 mm	30 mm
Asymettry	Border irregularity	Colour	Diameter: 1/4 inch or 6 mm

Figure 3 Melanomas look like moles on the skin, but they are malignant tumours triggered by exposure to UV radiation. Over 2000 people a year die from melanomas in the UK alone, so it is important to know the signs to look out for.

?? Did you know ... ?

Around 35 000 people die every year from lung cancer, and about 90% of those tumours develop as a result of breathing in the carcinogens in cigarette smoke.

Summary questions

1 a What is the cell cycle?
 b Explain how and why you would expect the length of the cell cycle to vary:
  i between an early embryo in the first days after fertilisation and a 5-year-old child
  ii between a 13-year-old student and a 70-year-old adult.

2 a What is a tumour?
 b Explain the difference between a benign tumour and a malignant tumour.
 c Why can both types of tumour cause serious health problems?

3 One of the most common methods of treating cancers is chemotherapy. The chemotherapy drugs often affect other parts of the body, particularly the hair follicles, the skin cells, the cells lining the stomach and the blood cells.
 a How do the drugs used in chemotherapy work?
 b Why do you think that healthy hair, skin, blood and stomach lining cells are particularly badly affected by the drugs used to treat cancer?

Key points

● Tumours result from the abnormal, uncontrolled growth of cells.

● Benign tumours form in one place and do not spread to other tissues.

● Malignant tumours invade healthy tissue and may spread to other healthy tissues in the bloodstream to form secondary tumours.

● Tumours can be caused by a number of factors, including chemical carcinogens and ionising radiation.

B2.5

Tissues and organs

Large **multicellular organisms** have to overcome the problems linked to their size. They develop different ways of exchanging materials. During the development of a multicellular organism, cells **differentiate**. They become specialised to carry out particular jobs. For example, in animals, muscle cells have a different structure to blood cells and nerve cells. In plants, the cells where photosynthesis takes place are very different to root hair cells.

However, the adaptations of multicellular organisms go beyond specialised cells. Similar specialised cells are often found grouped together to form a tissue.

Tissues

A **tissue** is a group of cells with similar structure and function working together. **Muscular tissue** can contract to bring about movement. **Glandular tissue** contains secretory cells that can produce and release substances such as enzymes and hormones. **Epithelial tissue** covers the outside of your body as well as your internal organs.

Plants have tissues too. **Epidermal tissues** cover the surfaces and protect them. **Palisade mesophyll** contains lots of chloroplasts and can carry out photosynthesis, while **spongy mesophyll** has some chloroplasts for photosynthesis but also has big air spaces and a large surface area to make the diffusion of gases easier. **Xylem** and **phloem** are the transport tissues in plants. They carry water and dissolved mineral ions from the roots up to the leaves and dissolved food from the leaves around the plant.

Figure 1 Muscle tissue contracts to move your skeleton around

Organs

Organs are made up of tissues. One organ can contain several tissues, all working together. For example, the stomach is an organ involved in the digestion of your food. It contains:

- muscular tissue, to churn the food and **digestive juices** of the stomach together
- glandular tissue, to produce the digestive juices that break down food
- epithelial tissue, which covers the inside and the outside of the organ.

⦾ links

For more information on specialised cells, look back at 2.1 'Cell division, growth and differentiation'.

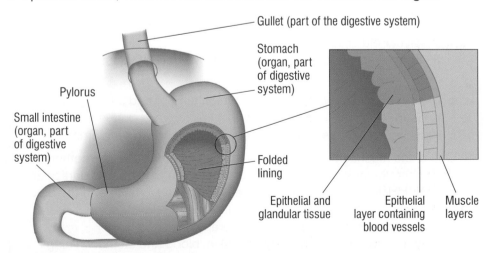

Figure 2 The stomach contains several different tissues, each with a different function in the organ

The pancreas is an organ that has two important functions. It makes hormones to control our blood sugar, as well as some of the enzymes that digest our food. It contains two very different types of tissue to produce these different secretions.

Plant organs

Animals are not the only organisms to have organs – plants do too.

Plants have differentiated cells that form specialised tissues. Within the body of a plant, tissues such as the palisade and spongy mesophyll, xylem and phloem are arranged to form organs. Each organ carries out its own particular functions.

Plant organs include the leaves, stems and roots, each of which has a very specific job to do (see Figure 3).

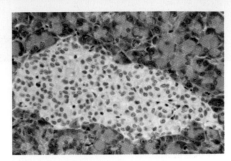

Figure 4 The pancreas showing endocrine and exocrine tissue

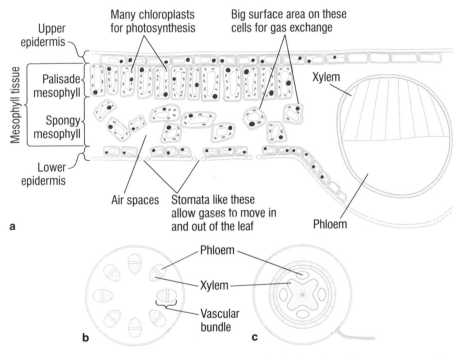

Many chloroplasts for photosynthesis

Big surface area on these cells for gas exchange

Upper epidermis

Mesophyll tissue

Palisade mesophyll

Spongy mesophyll

Lower epidermis

Xylem

Air spaces

Stomata like these allow gases to move in and out of the leaf

Phloem

a

Phloem

Xylem

Vascular bundle

b

c

Figure 3 Plants have specific tissues to carry out particular functions. They are arranged in organs such as the **a** leaf, **b** stem and **c** roots.

To summarise, whether in a plant or an animal, an organ is a collection of different tissues working together to carry out important functions for the organism.

∞ **links**

You can find out more about the structure of the leaf in 9.4 'Exchange in plants'.

??? Did you know ... ?

Some trees, such as the giant redwood, have trunks over 40 m tall. A plant cell is about 100 μm long. So the plant organ is 400 000 times bigger than the individual cells.

??? Did you know ... ?

A human liver cell is about 10 μm (1 × 10^{-5} m) in diameter. A human liver is about 22 cm across. It contains a lot of liver cells!

Summary questions

1 **a** What is a tissue?
    b What is an organ?

2 For each of the following, state whether they are a specialised cell, a tissue or an organ. Explain your answer.
    a Sperm
    b Kidney
    c Stomach

3 **a** Explain how the tissues in a leaf are arranged to form an effective organ for photosynthesis.
    b Explain how the stomach is adapted for its role in the digestion of food.

Key points

- A tissue is a group of cells with similar structure and function.

- Organs are made of tissues. One organ may contain several types of tissue.

- Animal organs include the stomach and heart.

- Plant organs include stems, roots and leaves.

B2.6 Organ systems

Learning objectives

After this topic, you should know:

- what makes up an organ system

- the main organs of the digestive system.

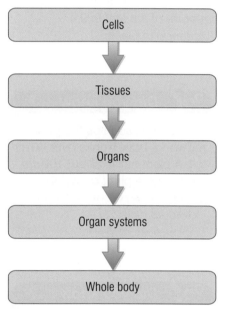

Figure 1 Larger multicellular organisms have many levels of organisation

A whole multicellular organism is made up of a number of **organ systems** working together. Organ systems are groups of organs that all work together to perform a particular function. The way one organ functions often depends on other organs in the system. The human digestive system is a good example of an organ system.

The digestive system

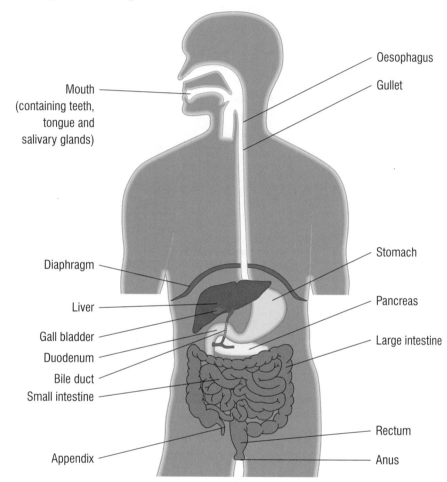

Figure 2 The main organs of the human digestive system

The digestive system of humans and other mammals exchanges substances with the environment. The food you take in and eat is made up of large **insoluble molecules**. Your body cannot absorb and use these molecules. They need to be broken down or digested to form smaller, soluble molecules that can then be absorbed and used by your cells. This process of digestion takes place in your **digestive system**, one of the major organ systems of the body.

The digestive system is a **muscular tube** that squeezes your food through it. It starts at one end with your mouth, and finishes at the other with your anus. The digestive system contains many different organs. There are glands such as the **pancreas** and **salivary glands**. These glands make and release digestive juices containing **enzymes** to break down your food.

The stomach and the small intestine are the main organs where food is digested. Enzymes break down the large insoluble food molecules into smaller, soluble ones.

Your small intestine is also where the soluble food molecules are absorbed into your blood. Once there, they get transported in the bloodstream around your body. The small intestine is adapted to have a very large surface area because it is covered in villi. This greatly increases diffusion and active transport from the gut to the blood.

?? Did you know ...?

The digestive system is between 6 and 9 m long. That is about 9 million times longer than an average human cell!

The muscular walls of the gut squeeze the undigested food onwards into your large intestine. This is where water is absorbed from the undigested food into your blood. The material left forms the faeces. Faeces are stored and then pass out of your body through the rectum and anus back into the environment.

Other organs associated with the digestive system include the liver. The liver is a large organ that carries out many different functions in your body. The function linked to the digestive system is the production of bile, which helps in the digestion of lipids.

Other organ systems in the body include the circulatory system and the respiratory system. All of these systems have adaptations in some of their organs that make them effective as exchange surfaces. The same is true for plant organs, as you saw in 2.5 Tissues and organs.

⚭ links

You can remind yourself about the adaptations of the villi in the small intestine as an exchange surface in 1.8 'Exchange in the gut'.

⚭ links

You will find out more about the role of the liver and bile in the digestion of food in 5.7 'Making digestion efficient'.

Figure 3 The organs of a plant

Summary questions

1 Match each of the following organs to its correct function.

A	Stem	1	Breaking down large insoluble molecules into smaller soluble molecules
B	Root	2	Photosynthesising in plants
C	Small intestine for absorption	3	Providing support in plants
D	Leaf	4	Anchoring plants and obtaining water and minerals from soil

2 Explain the difference between organs and organ systems, giving two examples.

3 Using the human digestive system as an example, explain how the organs in an organ system rely on each other to function properly.

Key points

- Organ systems are groups of organs that perform a particular function.

- The digestive system in a mammal is an example of a system where substances are exchanged with the environment.

Summary questions

1 a What is mitosis?

   b Explain, using diagrams, what takes place when a cell divides by mitosis.

   c Mitosis is very important during the development of a baby from a fertilised egg. It is also important all through life. Why?

2 What is meiosis and where does it take place?

3 a Why is meiosis so important?

   b Explain, using labelled diagrams, what takes place when a cell divides by meiosis.

4 a What are stem cells?

   b It is hoped that many different medical problems may be cured using stem cells. Explain how this might work.

   c There are some ethical issues associated with the use of embryonic stem cells. Explain the arguments both for and against their use.

5 Figure 1 is an MRI scan that clearly shows a brain tumour.

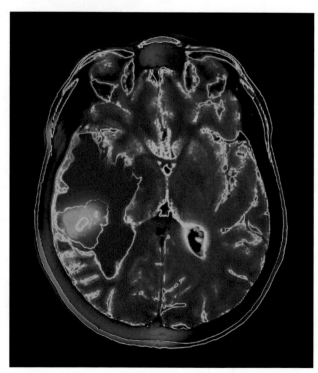

Figure 1

   a What is a tumour?

   b This could be a benign or a malignant tumour. Explain the similarities and differences in the effect of the diagnosis on the situation for the patient.

6 Plants have specialised cells, tissues and organs, just as animals do.

   a Give **three** examples of plant tissues.

   b What are the main plant organs and what do they do?

   c Which plant tissues are found in all of the main plant organs and why?

7

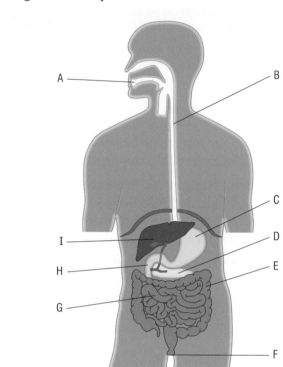

Figure 2

   a What is an organ system?

   b Make a table and name the parts of the human digestive system labelled A–I in Figure 2. For each organ, give a function in the digestive system as a whole.

   c Select **two** examples of individual tissues that you would find in an organ of the digestive system and explain how they are specialised for their role.

8 A man had small cell cancer, which is a tumour of the lungs. It spread rapidly to his liver and bones forming secondary tumours. This made it difficult to treat and after three years he died.

   a What is a tumour?

   b Is small cell lung cancer a benign or a malignant tumour? Give a reason for your answer.

   c How did the tumour cells spread to his liver and his bones?

   d Suggest what might have caused the first tumour to grow in the man's lung.

AQA Examination-style questions

1 List A contains words about genetic information in cells. List B contains explanations of the words.

Match each word in list A with the correct explanation in list B.

List A	List B
Chromosome	a different form of one gene
Allele	a cell with a single set of chromosomes
Gene	a structure carrying a large number of genes
Nucleus	a section of genetic material coding for one characteristic
Gamete	a cell with pairs of chromosomes
	the part of a cell that contains the genetic material

(5)

2 Cells from organism Z have three pairs of chromosomes.

a Complete stages C and D of the diagram below, to show the chromosomes at each stage of meiosis.

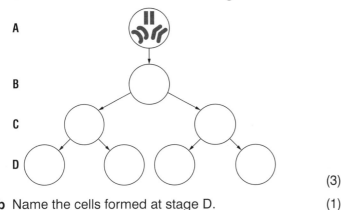

(3)

b Name the cells formed at stage D. (1)

c Complete the diagram below to show a cell from organism Z, which has been formed by mitosis.

(1)

3 The numbers **i** to **v** represent stages in the life cycle of a sunflower plant.

i Pollen grains from one sunflower fuse with the ova of another sunflower at fertilisation.

ii A fertilised ovum develops into a seed.

iii The seed germinates. It develops a radical (early root) and a plumule (early shoot).

iv The seed grows a shoot and a single root.

v The shoot develops into a stem and leaves. The single root forms a complex root system.

a Put a number from the stages above in each box to represent the stage at which you would find:

Differentiated cells	
Cells with a single set of chromosomes	
Undifferentiated cells	
Cells dividing rapidly by mitosis	
An embryo	

(5)

b The following words describe the organisation within a plant or animal:

ORGAN CELL ORGANISM TISSUE ORGAN SYSTEM

Rearrange these words in increasing order of complexity. (2)

c Use words from the list above to describe each of these parts of the sunflower plant.
i phloem
ii stem
iii root hair
iv water transport system
v sunflower plant

d Explain why the flowers grown from the sunflower seed may vary in colour from the sunflower flower that produced the seeds. (2)

4 A couple have a son with a rare and fatal genetic disorder. Doctors have advised the couple that the only chance of curing him is to create several embryos by in-vitro fertilisation and hope that one, without the defective gene, will be a tissue-type match. They will be able to use stem cells from the matching embryo to grow new healthy tissue to replace the defective tissue in their son. They may also be able to choose an unaffected embryo to be implanted in the mother's womb to produce a healthy brother or sister for their child.

a Explain why the doctors need stem cells and not body cells to grow the new tissue for their son. (3)

b The doctors advise the couple to see a counsellor before making a decision.

Explain the medical, social and ethical issues the counsellor might discuss with the couple to help them make a decision about whether they should go ahead with this treatment or not.

In this question you will be assessed on using good English, organising information clearly and using specialist terms where appropriate. (QWC) (6)

B3.1

Carbohydrates, lipids and proteins

Carbohydrates, lipids and proteins are the main compounds that make up the structure of a cell. They are vital components in the balanced diet of any organism which cannot make its own food. Carbohydrates, lipids and proteins are all large molecules that are often made up of smaller molecules joined together.

Carbohydrates

Carbohydrates provide us with energy. They contain the chemical elements carbon, hydrogen and oxygen.

All carbohydrates are made up of units of sugar.

● Some carbohydrates contain only one unit of sugar. The best known of these single sugars is glucose, $C_6H_{12}O_6$. Other carbohydrates are made up of two sugar units joined together, for example sucrose, the compound we call 'sugar' in everyday life. These small carbohydrates are referred to as simple sugars.

● **Complex carbohydrates** such as starch and cellulose are made up of long chains of simple sugar units bonded together (see Figure 1). They are made in a reaction in which a water molecule is released when the bond between sugar units is formed (a condensation reaction).

Carbohydrate-rich foods include bread, potatoes, rice and pasta. Much of the carbohydrate food you take into your body will be broken down to form glucose. The glucose is used in cellular respiration to provide energy for your cells. Carbohydrates in the form of cellulose are a very important support material in plants.

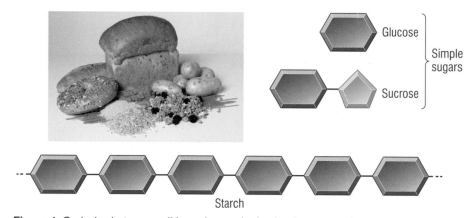

Figure 1 Carbohydrates are all based on a single simple sugar unit

Lipids

Lipids are fats (solids) and oils (liquids). They are the most efficient energy store in your body and an important source of energy in your diet. Combined with other molecules, lipids are very important in your cell membranes, as hormones and in your nervous system. Like carbohydrates, lipids are made up of carbon, hydrogen and oxygen. All lipids are insoluble in water.

Lipids are made up of three molecules of fatty acids joined to a molecule of glycerol (see Figure 2). The glycerol is always the same, but the fatty acids vary. It is the different fatty acids that cause some lipids to be solid fats and others to be liquid oils. Lipid-rich food includes all the oils, such as olive oil and corn oil, as well as butter, margarine, cheese and cream.

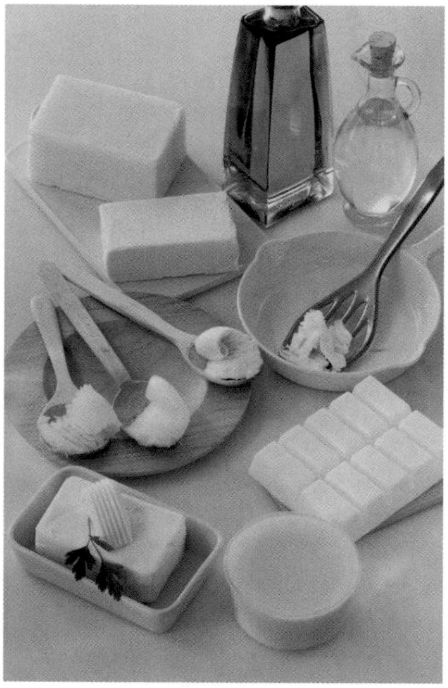

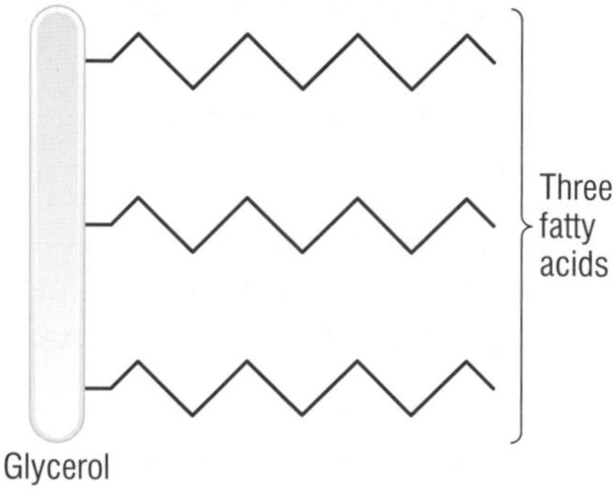

Glycerol

Three fatty acids

Figure 2 It is the combination of fatty acids joined to the glycerol molecule that affect the melting point of a lipid

Proteins

Proteins are used for building up the cells and tissues of your body as well as all your enzymes. They are made up of the elements carbon, hydrogen, oxygen and nitrogen. Protein-rich foods include meat, fish, pulses and cheese.

A protein molecule is made up of long chains of small units called **amino acids** (see Figure 3). These amino acids are joined together into long chains by special peptide links. Different arrangements of the various amino acids give you different proteins.

Figure 3 Amino acids are the building blocks of proteins. They can join in an almost endless variety of ways to produce different proteins.

The long chains of amino acids that make up a protein are folded, coiled and twisted to make specific 3-D shapes. It is these specific shapes that enable other molecules to fit into the protein. The bonds that hold the proteins in these 3-D shapes are very sensitive to temperature and pH, and can easily be broken. If this happens, the shape of the protein is lost and it may not function any more in your cells. The protein is **denatured**.

Proteins carry out many different functions in your body. They act as:

- structural components of tissues such as muscles and tendons
- hormones such as insulin
- antibodies, which destroy pathogens and are part of the immune system
- enzymes, which act as catalysts in the cells.

Summary questions

1 **a** What is a protein?
   b How are proteins used in the body?

2 Describe the main similarities and differences between the three main groups of chemicals (carbohydrates, proteins and lipids) in the body.

3 How would you test a food sample to see if it contained:
   a starch?
   b lipids?

4 **a** Explain why lipids can be either fats or oils.
   b Explain how simple sugars are related to complex carbohydrates.

Practical

Food tests

You can identify the main food groups using standard food tests.

- *Carbohydrates*: Iodine test turns solution from yellowy-red to blue-black if starch is present; Benedict's test turns solution from blue to brick red on heating if a simple reducing sugar such as glucose is present.
- *Protein*: Biuret test turns solution from blue to purple if protein is present.
- *Lipids*: The ethanol (highly flammable, harmful) test gives a cloudy white layer if a lipid is present.

Safety: Wear eye protection.

Key points

- Carbohydrates are made up of units of sugar.

- Simple sugars are carbohydrates that contain only one or two sugar units; complex carbohydrates contain long chains of simple sugar units bonded together.

- Lipids consist of three molecules of fatty acids bonded to a molecule of glycerol.

- Protein molecules are made up of long chains of amino acids joined by peptide links.

- Proteins act as structural components of tissues, as hormones, as antibodies and as enzymes.

B3.2

Catalysts and enzymes

After this topic, you should know:

- what a catalyst is

- how enzymes work as biological catalysts.

In everyday life, we control the rates of chemical reactions all the time. For example, you increase the temperature of your oven to speed up chemical reactions when you cook. You place food in your fridge to slow down reactions that cause food to go off.

Sometimes we use special chemicals known as **catalysts** to speed up reactions. A catalyst speeds up a chemical reaction, but it is not used up in the reaction. You can use a catalyst over and over again. For example, manganese(IV) oxide (MnO_2) catalyses the breakdown of hydrogen peroxide into oxygen and water.

Enzymes – biological catalysts

In your body, chemical reaction rates are controlled by enzymes. These are special biological catalysts that speed up reactions.

Enzymes are large protein molecules. The long chains of amino acids are folded to produce a molecule with a specific shape. This special shape allows other molecules (substrates) to fit into the enzyme protein. We call this part of the enzyme molecule its **active site**. The shape of an enzyme is vital for the enzyme's function (the way it works).

Enzymes are involved in:

- building large molecules from lots of smaller ones

- changing one molecule into another

- breaking down large molecules into smaller ones.

Enzymes do not change a reaction in any way – they just make it happen faster. Different enzymes catalyse (speed up) specific types of reaction. In your body you need to build large molecules from smaller ones, such as making glycogen from glucose or proteins from amino acids. You need to change certain molecules into different ones, for example one sugar into another, such as glucose to fructose, and you need to break down large molecules into smaller ones, such as breaking down insoluble food molecules into small soluble molecules, such as glucose. All these reactions are speeded up using enzymes.

Each of your cells can have a hundred or more chemical reactions going on within it at any one time. Each of the different types of reaction is controlled by a different specific enzyme. Enzymes deliver the control that makes it possible for your cell chemistry to work without one reaction interfering with another.

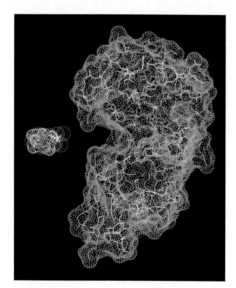

Figure 1 Enzymes are made up of chains of amino acids folded together to make large complex molecules, as you can see in this computer-generated image

 Did you know … ?

For chemicals to react, they need to collide with sufficient energy to break the chemical bonds that hold the molecules together. Enzymes lower the energy needed to break the bonds, which is how they speed up the reactions (because a higher proportion of molecules have sufficient energy to react).

Practical

Breaking down hydrogen peroxide

You can investigate the impact of both an inorganic catalyst and an enzyme on the breakdown of 20 'vol' hydrogen peroxide solution into oxygen and water using:

a manganese(IV) oxide, and **b** raw liver (which contains the enzyme catalase).

Your liver plays an important role in your body by breaking down toxins (poisons). Hydrogen peroxide is a poisonous compound that is often a waste product of reactions in cells. It is important that it is broken down into harmless oxygen and water quickly, before it causes any damage.

You can determine the rate of the reaction by measuring the volume of oxygen produced over time. A simple way to do a quick comparison between the catalyst and the enzyme is to add a drop of washing-up liquid to the hydrogen peroxide. Add the catalyst or the enzyme (the liver) and measure how quickly the foam produced by the bubbles of gas rises up the test tube!

- Describe your observations and interpret the graph (Figure 2).

Safety: Wear eye protection.
20 'vol' hydrogen peroxide – irritant.
Manganese(IV) oxide – harmful.

Figure 2 The decomposition of hydrogen peroxide to oxygen and water goes much faster using a catalyst like manganese(IV) oxide. Raw liver contains the enzyme catalase, which speeds up the same reaction.

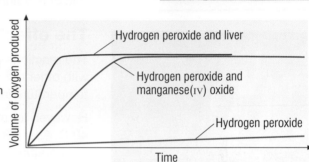

How do enzymes work?

The substrate (reactant) of the reaction to be catalysed fits into the active site of the enzyme. You can think of it like a lock and key. Once it is in place, the enzyme and the substrate bind together.

The reaction then takes place rapidly and the products are released from the surface of the enzyme (see Figure 3). Remember that enzymes can join small molecules together as well as break up large ones.

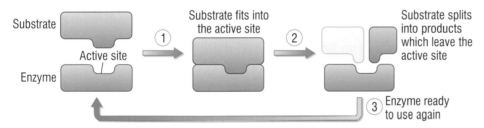

Figure 3 Enzymes act as catalysts using the 'lock-and-key' mechanism shown here

Key points

- Catalysts increase the rate of chemical reactions without changing chemically themselves.

- Enzymes are biological catalysts.

- Enzymes are proteins. The amino acid chains are folded to form the active site, which matches the shape of a specific substrate.

- The substrate binds to the active site and the reaction is catalysed by the enzyme.

Summary questions

1 Give a definition of the following terms:
   a catalyst   **b** enzyme   **c** active site.

2 **a** What are enzymes made of?
   b Explain carefully how enzymes act to speed up reactions in your body.

3 **a** Give **three** clear examples of the type of reactions that are catalysed by enzymes.
   b Explain the importance of enzymes within cells.

B3.3 Factors affecting enzyme action

A container of milk left at the back of your fridge for a week or two will be disgusting. The milk will go off as enzymes in bacteria break down the protein structure.

Leave your milk in the sun for a day and the same thing happens – but much faster. Temperature affects the rate at which chemical reactions take place, even when they are controlled by biological catalysts.

Biological reactions are affected by the same factors as any other chemical reactions. These factors include concentration, temperature and surface area. However, in living organisms, an increase in temperature only increases the rate of reaction up to a certain point.

The effect of temperature on enzyme action

The reactions that take place in cells happen at relatively low temperatures. As with other reactions, the rate of enzyme-controlled reactions increases as the temperature increases.

However, for most organisms this is only true up to temperatures of about 40°C. After this, the protein structure of the enzyme is affected by the high temperature. The long amino acid chains begin to unravel, and as a result, the shape of the active site changes. The substrate will no longer fit in the active site. We say the enzyme has been denatured. It can no longer act as a catalyst, so the rate of the reaction drops dramatically. Most human enzymes work best at 37°C, which is human body temperature.

Without enzymes, none of the reactions in your body would happen fast enough to keep you alive. This is why it is so dangerous if your temperature goes too high when you are ill. Once your body temperature reaches about 41°C, your enzymes start to be denatured and you will soon die.

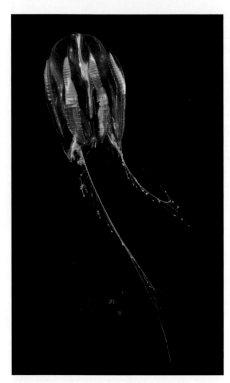

Figure 1 The magical light display of this/these comb jellies is caused by the action of an enzyme called luciferase

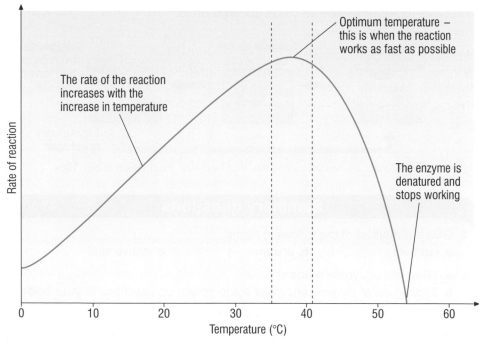

Figure 2 The rate of an enzyme-controlled reaction increases as the temperature rises – but only until the protein structure of the enzyme breaks down

Effect of pH on enzyme action

The shape of the active site of an enzyme comes from forces between the different parts of the protein molecule. These forces hold the folded chains in place. A change in the pH affects these forces. That's why it changes the shape of the molecule. As a result, the specific shape of the active site is lost, so the enzyme no longer acts as a catalyst.

Different enzymes work best at different pH levels. A change in the pH can stop them working completely.

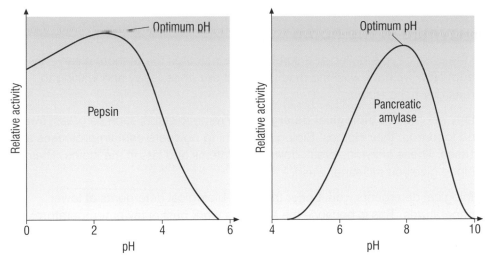

Figure 3 These two digestive enzymes need very different pH levels to work at their maximum rate. Pepsin is found in the stomach, along with hydrochloric acid, while pancreatic amylase is in the first part of the small intestine along with alkaline bile.

The digestive enzymes

Most of your enzymes work *inside* the cells of your body, controlling the rate of the chemical reactions. Your digestive enzymes are different. They work *outside* your cells. They are produced by specialised cells in glands (such as the salivary glands and pancreas), and in the lining of your gut. The enzymes then pass out of these cells into the gut itself, where they come into contact with food molecules.

Your food is made up of large, insoluble molecules that your body cannot absorb. They need to be broken down or **digested** to form smaller, soluble molecules that can be absorbed and used by your cells. It is this chemical breakdown of your food which is controlled by digestive enzymes.

Different areas of the digestive system have different pH levels which allow the enzymes in that region to work as efficiently as possible. For example, the mouth and small intestine are slightly alkaline, while the stomach has a low, acidic pH value.

Summary questions

1 Explain carefully, with the help of diagrams, how temperature affects enzyme-controlled reactions and why.

2 Look at Figure 3.
   a At which pH does pepsin work best?
   b At which pH does amylase work best?
   c What happens to the activity of the enzymes as the pH increases?
   d Explain why this change in activity happens.

⚬⚬ **links**

You have already discovered many of the different organs in the human digestive system in 2.5 'Tissues and organs' and 2.6 'Organ systems'.

Examiner's tip

Enzymes aren't killed (they are molecules, not living things themselves) – so make sure that you use the term 'denatured'.

Key points

- Enzyme activity is affected by temperature and pH.

- High temperatures denature the enzyme, changing the shape of the active site.

- pH can affect the shape of the active site of an enzyme and make it work very efficiently or stop it working.

- Digestive enzymes are produced by specialised cells in glands and in the lining of the gut. These enzymes work outside the body cells in the gut itself.

B3.4 Making use of enzymes

After this topic, you should know:

- how enzymes are used in the home and in industry.

Practical

Investigating biological washing powder

Weigh a chunk of cooked egg white and leave it in a strong solution of biological washing powder.

- What do you think will happen to the egg white?
- How can you measure how effective the protease enzymes are?
- How could you investigate the effect of surface area on enzyme action?

Figure 1 Biological detergents come in many different forms

Safety: Disposable plastic gloves available.

Enzymes were first isolated from living cells in the 19th century. Ever since then, people have found more and more ways of using them in industry. Some microorganisms produce enzymes that pass out of the cells and are easy for us to use, for example digestive enzymes. In other cases, such as in the production of human insulin, we use the whole microorganism.

Enzymes in the home

In the past, people boiled and scrubbed their clothes to get them clean – by hand! Now we have washing machines and enzymes ready and waiting to break down the stains.

Many people use **biological detergents** to remove stains such as grass, sweat and food from their clothes. Biological washing powders contain proteases and lipases. These enzymes break down the proteins and fats in the stains. They help to give you a cleaner wash.

Biological detergents work better than non-biological detergents at lower temperatures. This is because the enzymes work best at lower temperatures – they are denatured if the water is too hot. Therefore, they use a lot less energy than non-biological detergents. This is good for the environment and cheaper for the consumer.

It isn't just washing powders that use enzymes. Dishwasher detergents also contain enzymes that break down cooked-on proteins like eggs, which are often hard to remove.

Enzymes in industry

Pure enzymes have many uses in industry.

- **Proteases** (enzymes that digest protein) are used to make baby foods. They 'predigest' some of the protein in the food. When babies first begin to eat solid foods, they are not very good at digesting it. Treating the food with protease enzymes makes it easier for a baby's digestive system to cope with it. It is easier for them to get the amino acids they need from their food.
- **Carbohydrases** (enzymes that work on carbohydrates) are used to break down starch into sugar (glucose) syrup. We use huge quantities of sugar syrup in food production. You will see it on the ingredients labels on all sorts of foods. Starch is made by plants such as corn and it is very cheap. Using enzymes to convert this plant starch into sweet sugar provides a cheap source of sweetness for food manufacturers. It is also important for the process of making fuel (ethanol) from plants.
- Sometimes the glucose syrup made from starch is passed through another process that uses a different set of enzymes. The enzyme **isomerase** is used to change glucose syrup into **fructose syrup**. Glucose and fructose contain exactly the same amount of energy (1700 kJ or 400 kcal per 100 g). However, fructose is much sweeter than glucose, so much smaller amounts are needed to make food taste sweet. Fructose is widely used in 'slimming' foods because the food tastes sweet but contains fewer calories.

Figure 2 Learning to eat solid food isn't easy. Having some of it predigested by protease enzymes can make it easier to get the amino acids you need to grow.

Figure 3 Some people are always trying to lose weight. Enzyme technology is used to convert more and more glucose syrup into fructose syrup to make so-called 'slimming' foods.

The advantages and disadvantages of using enzymes

In industrial processes, many of the reactions need high temperatures and pressures to make them go fast enough to produce the products needed. This requires expensive equipment and a lot of energy.

Enzymes can solve industrial problems such as these. They catalyse reactions at relatively low temperatures and normal pressures. Enzyme-based processes are therefore often fairly cheap to run.

One problem with enzymes is that they are denatured at high temperatures, so the temperature must be kept down (usually below 45 °C). The pH also needs to be kept within carefully controlled limits that suit the enzyme. It costs money to control these conditions.

Many enzymes are also expensive to produce. Whole microorganisms are relatively cheap, but need to be supplied with food and oxygen and their waste products removed. They use some of the substrate to grow more microorganisms. Pure enzymes use the substrate more efficiently, but they are also more expensive to produce.

Summary questions

1 List three enzymes and the ways in which we use them in the food industry.

2 Biological washing powders contain enzymes in tiny capsules. Explain why:
   a they are more effective than non-biological powders at lower temperatures
   b they may be less effective at high temperatures.

3 Explain the role of microorganisms in providing industrial enzymes and discuss the advantages and disadvantages of using enzymes in industry.

Key points

● Some microorganisms produce enzymes that pass out of the cells and can be used in different ways.

● People use biological detergents to remove stains from their clothes. They may contain proteases and lipases.

● Proteases, carbohydrases and isomerase are all used in the food industry.

Summary questions

1 a What is the difference between a simple sugar and a complex carbohydrate?

b Why are carbohydrates so important in the body?

c Explain carefully how you would test for a simple sugar such as glucose and a complex carbohydrate such as starch.

2 a Compare a lipid with a complex carbohydrate and a protein. Explain the main differences between the different groups of molecules.

b Lipids can be solids or liquids.
  i What are the names given to solid and liquid lipids?
  ii Explain how the different types of lipids are formed.

3

Enzyme   Substrate

Figure 1

a Describe the structure of a protein.

b Draw diagrams based on Figure 1 to help you, explain how an enzyme catalyses a reaction.

c Using your knowledge of the structure of a protein molecule, explain why pH and temperature can affect the way a protein carries out its function in a cell.

4 The results in these tables come from a student who was investigating the breakdown of hydrogen peroxide using manganese(IV) oxide and grated raw potato.

Table 1 Using manganese(IV) oxide

Temperature (°C)	Time taken (s)
20	106
30	51
40	26
50	12

Table 2 Using raw grated potato

Temperature (°C)	Time taken (s)
20	114
30	96
40	80
50	120
60	no reaction

a Draw a graph of the results using manganese(IV) oxide.

b What do these results tell you about the effect of temperature on a catalysed reaction? Explain your observation.

c Draw a graph of the results when raw grated potato was added to the hydrogen peroxide.

d What is the name of the enzyme found in living cells that catalyses the breakdown of hydrogen peroxide?

e What does this graph tell you about the effect of temperature on an enzyme-catalysed reaction?

f Why does temperature have this effect on the enzyme-catalysed reaction but not on the reaction catalysed by manganese(IV) oxide?

g How could you change the second investigation to find the temperature at which the enzyme works best?

5 Read the piece of text below and make a table to summarise the pros and cons of using enzymes in washing powders.

For many people, biological washing powders have lots of benefits. Children can be messy eaters and their clothes get lots of mud and grass stains as well. Many of the stains that adults get on their clothes – sweat, food and drink – are biological too. So these enzyme-based washing powders are effective and therefore widely used.

Biological powders have another advantage. They are very effective at cleaning at low temperatures. Therefore they use a lot less electricity than non-biological detergents. That's good for the environment and cheaper for the consumer.

However, when biological detergent was first manufactured, many factory staff developed allergies. They were reacting to enzyme dust in the air – proteins often trigger allergies. Some people using the powders were affected in the same way. But there was a solution – the enzymes were put in tiny capsules and then most of the allergy problems stopped.

Unfortunately, it got bad publicity, which some people still remember. However, research (based on 44 different studies) was published by the British Journal of Dermatology in 2008. This showed that biological detergents do not seem to be a major cause of skin problems.

Some people worry about all the enzymes going into our rivers and seas from biological detergents. The waste water from washing machines goes into the sewage system. Also, the low temperatures used to wash with biological detergents may not be as good at killing pathogens on the clothes.

AQA Examination-style questions

1 The diagrams represent large molecules found in our body.

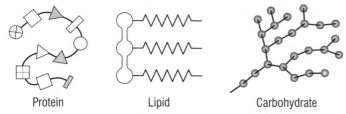

Protein   Lipid   Carbohydrate

a Name the small molecules represented by these symbols:

i   ii   iii   iv   (4)

b Enzymes are proteins.

  i What is an enzyme? (1)

  ii Explain how the specific shape of an enzyme is essential for it to work. (3)

  iii Give the term used to describe an enzyme that has lost its specific shape. (1)

  iv Name **two** factors that can cause an enzyme to lose its shape. (2)

c Name **three other** types of proteins found in the body. Describe the function of each type of protein. (6)

2 Enzymes have many uses in the home and in industry.

a Which type of organisms are used to produce these enzymes? (1)

b Babies may have difficulty digesting proteins in their food. Baby-food manufacturers use enzymes to 'pre-digest' the protein in baby food to overcome this difficulty.

Copy and complete the following sentences.

  i Proteins are 'pre-digested' using enzymes called .... (1)

  ii This pre-digestion produces .... (1)

c A baby-food manufacturer uses enzyme V to pre-digest protein.

He tries four new enzymes – W, X, Y and Z – to see if he can reduce the time taken to pre-digest the protein.

The graph shows the time taken for the enzymes to completely pre-digest the protein. The manufacturer uses the same concentration of enzyme and the same mass of protein in each experiment.

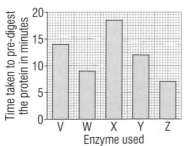

  i How long did it take enzyme V to predigest the protein? (1)

  ii Which enzyme would you advise the baby food manufacturer to use?

    Give a reason for your answer. (2)

  iii State two other factors that should be controlled in the baby-food manufacturer's investigations. (2)

3 A manufacturer of slimming foods is investigating carbohydrases from different microorganisms. Iodine solution is a pale golden brown, transparent solution. Starch reacts with iodine to form a dark blue mixture.

The mixture of starch and iodine solution is placed in a colorimeter, which measures the percentage of light passing through the mixture.

a Explain why less light passes through the mixture when the starch is more concentrated. (1)

b The manufacturer adds carbohydrases, **A**, **B** and **C**, to starch in flasks at 40 °C. Every minute a sample of the mixture is added to iodine solution and placed in the colorimeter. The graph below shows these results.

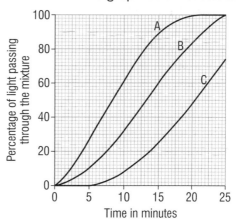

Suggest why the amount of light passing through the mixture containing carbohydrase A did not change after 20 minutes. (1)

c Explain why the manufacturer carried out the investigation at 40 °C. (2)

d Carbohydrases convert starch into glucose. To complete the manufacture of the slimming food the glucose should be converted into fructose.

Explain why fructose, rather than glucose, is used in slimming foods. (2)

Breathing and gas exchange in the lungs

After this topic, you should know:

- the structure of your respiratory system
- how you move air into and out of your lungs
- how gases are exchanged in the alveoli of your lungs.

For a gas exchange system to work efficiently, you need a steep concentration gradient. Humans are like many big, complex mammals in that they move air in and out of their lungs regularly. By changing the composition of the air in the lungs, they maintain a steep concentration gradient for both oxygen diffusing into and carbon dioxide diffusing out of the blood. This is known as ventilating the lungs or **breathing**. It takes place in a specially adapted **respiratory (breathing) system**.

The respiratory system

Your lungs are found in your chest, or **thorax**, and are protected by your bony ribcage. They are separated from the digestive organs beneath (in your **abdomen**) by the **diaphragm**. The diaphragm is a strong sheet of muscle. The job of your breathing system is to move air in and out of your lungs. The lungs provide an efficient surface for gas exchange in the alveoli (see Figure 1).

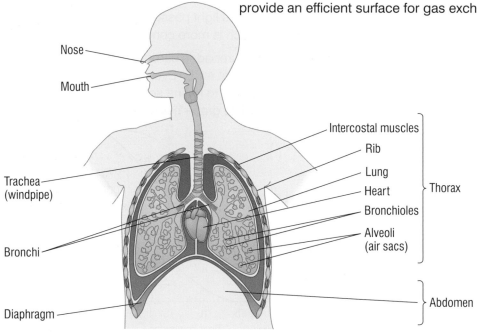

Figure 1 The breathing system supplies your body with vital oxygen and removes waste carbon dioxide

links

You can find out more about diffusion and concentration gradients in 1.4 'Diffusion'.

Table 1 The composition of inhaled and exhaled air (~ means approximately)

Atmospheric gas	% of air breathed in	% of air breathed out
nitrogen	~80	~80
oxygen	20	~16
carbon dioxide	0.04	~4

Moving air in and out of the lungs

Ventilation of the lungs is brought about by movements of your ribcage and diaphragm. You can see and feel the movements of your ribcage, but not of the diaphragm.

When you breathe in, your **intercostal muscles** contract, and this pulls your ribs upwards and outwards. At the same time, your diaphragm muscles contract, which flattens your diaphragm from its normal domed shape. These two movements *increase* the volume of your thorax. Because the same amount of gas is now inside a much bigger space, the pressure inside your thorax drops. Pressure inside the thorax is now lower than the pressure of air outside your body. As a result, air moves into your lungs, pushed in by atmospheric pressure.

When the intercostal muscles relax, your ribs drop down and in again. When the diaphragm relaxes, it curves back up into your thorax, resuming its domed shape. As a result, the volume of your thorax gets smaller again. This increases the pressure inside the chest so the air is squeezed and forced out of the lungs. That's how you breathe out (see Figure 2).

When you breathe in, oxygen-rich air moves into your lungs. This maintains a steep concentration gradient with the blood. As a result, oxygen continually diffuses into your bloodstream through the gas exchange surfaces of your alveoli. Breathing out removes carbon dioxide-rich air from the lungs. This maintains a concentration gradient so carbon dioxide can continually diffuse out of the bloodstream into the air in the lungs.

Adaptations of the alveoli

Your lungs are specially adapted to make gas exchange more efficient. They are made up of clusters of alveoli which provide a very large surface area. This is important in order to achieve the most effective diffusion of oxygen and carbon dioxide.

The alveoli also have a rich supply of blood **capillaries**. This maintains a concentration gradient in both directions – the blood coming to the lungs is always relatively low in oxygen and high in carbon dioxide compared to the inhaled air.

As a result, gas exchange takes place along the steepest concentration gradients possible. This makes the exchange rapid and effective. The layer of cells between the air in the lungs and the blood in the capillaries is also very thin. This allows diffusion to take place over the shortest possible distance.

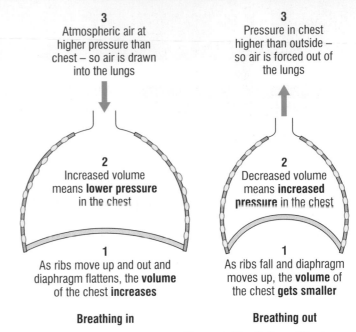

3
Atmospheric air at higher pressure than chest – so air is drawn into the lungs

2
Increased volume means **lower pressure** in the chest

1
As ribs move up and out and diaphragm flattens, the **volume** of the chest **increases**

Breathing in

3
Pressure in chest higher than outside – so air is forced out of the lungs

2
Decreased volume means **increased pressure** in the chest

1
As ribs fall and diaphragm moves up, the **volume** of the chest **gets smaller**

Breathing out

Figure 2 Ventilation of the lungs

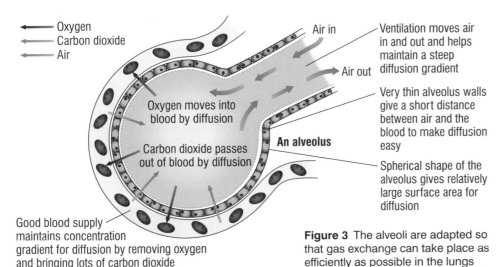

Oxygen
Carbon dioxide
Air

Air in
Air out

Oxygen moves into blood by diffusion

Carbon dioxide passes out of blood by diffusion

An alveolus

Good blood supply maintains concentration gradient for diffusion by removing oxygen and bringing lots of carbon dioxide

Ventilation moves air in and out and helps maintain a steep diffusion gradient

Very thin alveolus walls give a short distance between air and the blood to make diffusion easy

Spherical shape of the alveolus gives relatively large surface area for diffusion

Figure 3 The alveoli are adapted so that gas exchange can take place as efficiently as possible in the lungs

??? Did you know …?

If all the alveoli in your lungs were spread out flat, they would have a surface area about the size of a tennis court.

Summary questions

1 Explain clearly how air is moved into and out of your lungs.

2 What is meant by the term gaseous exchange and why is it so important in your body?

3 a Draw a bar chart to show the difference in composition between the air you breathe in and the air you breathe out (use Table 1 on page 44).
   b People often say we breathe in oxygen and breathe out carbon dioxide. Use your bar chart to explain why this is wrong.
   c Explain how your respiratory system is adapted to make gaseous exchange as efficient as possible.

Key points

● The lungs are in your thorax. They are protected by your ribcage and separated from your abdomen by the diaphragm.

● The intercostal muscles contract to move your ribs up and out and flatten the diaphragm, increasing the volume of your thorax. The pressure decreases and air moves in to your lungs.

● The intercostal muscles relax and the ribs move down and in, and the diaphragm domes up, decreasing the volume of your thorax. The pressure increases and air is forced out of your lungs.

● The alveoli provide a very large surface area and a rich supply of blood capillaries. This means gases can diffuse into and out of the blood as efficiently as possible.

B4.2 Artificial breathing aids

Learning objectives

After this topic, you should know:

- different ways in which people can be helped to breathe if their lungs become damaged or diseased.

Did you know ... ?

Nowadays, we are all vaccinated against polio and it has almost been wiped out worldwide.

A healthy person breathes automatically 24 hours a day, whether they are awake or asleep. However, this spontaneous breathing can be lost if someone is paralysed in an accident or by disease. This means the person can no longer stimulate the intercostal muscles and diaphragm to contract and relax.

There are a number of artificial aids for supporting or taking over breathing that have saved countless lives. Mechanical ventilation systems work in two main ways – **negative pressure** and **positive pressure**.

Negative pressure ventilators

Negative pressure ventilators cause air to be drawn into the lungs, and it is then exhaled passively as the chest collapses down.

Polio is a disease that can leave people paralysed and unable to breathe. To keep polio sufferers alive until their bodies recovered, an external negative pressure ventilator was developed. This was commonly known as the iron lung.

The patient lay in a metal cylinder with their head sticking out and a tight seal around the neck. Air was pumped out of the chamber, lowering the pressure inside to form a **vacuum**. As a result, the chest wall of the patient moved up. This increased the volume and decreased the pressure inside the chest. So air from the outside was drawn into the lungs, just like normal breathing.

The vacuum then switched off automatically and air moved back into the chamber, increasing the pressure. The ribs moved down, lowering the volume and increasing the pressure inside the thorax. This forced air out of the lungs.

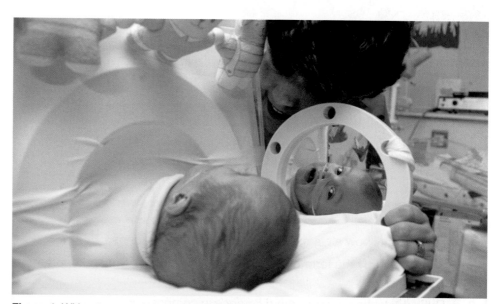

Figure 1 Without a negative pressure ventilator to draw air into its lungs, this child would have died

A more modern version, called the 'shell', is a mini-cylinder that fits just around the chest so it is much easier for the patient to use. These symptoms were used mainly with paralysed patients. However, negative pressure ventilation is not used much anymore. It has been overtaken by positive pressure systems.

Positive pressure breathing

A positive pressure ventilator forces a carefully measured 'breath' of air into the lungs under a positive pressure. It's a bit like blowing up a balloon. Once the lungs have been inflated, the air pressure stops. The lungs then deflate as the ribs move down again, forcing the air back out of the lungs.

Positive pressure ventilation can be used in patients with many different problems.

● It can be given using a simple face mask or by a tube going into the **trachea**. Positive pressure bag ventilators are held and squeezed by doctors or nurses in emergency treatments. They are very simple and temporary but can save lives.

● Full-scale positive pressure ventilating machines can keep patients alive through major surgery. They can also help people who are paralysed to survive for years.

One of the big benefits of positive pressure ventilation is that patients do not have to be placed inside an iron lung machine. The equipment can be used at home and the patient can move about. Another benefit is that patients can have some control over the machine. Modern systems can link a ventilator with computer systems, which help patients manage their own breathing much more easily.

For many years, positive pressure ventilation involved inserting a tube down the trachea of the patient, often through an incision in the neck. However, the more recent development of effective masks that cover just the mouth or the mouth and nose has greatly improved the quality of life for patients who need positive pressure ventilation for part of the day or all the time.

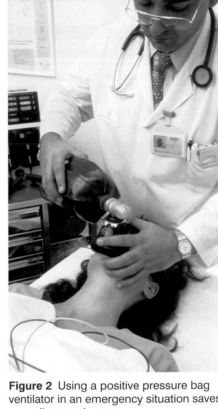

Figure 2 Using a positive pressure bag ventilator in an emergency situation saves many lives each year

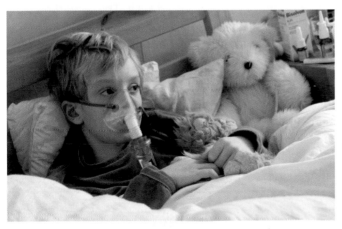

Figure 3 Positive pressure ventilators using a facial mask are now widely used both for patients who struggle to get enough oxygen and for those who cannot breathe unaided

Summary questions

1 Why would someone who becomes paralysed through an accident or disease need a mechanical ventilation system?

2 a How does an external negative pressure aid to breathing work?
  b How does this compare to the natural breathing process?
  c What are the main disadvantages of a negative pressure ventilator?

3 a Explain how a positive pressure ventilation system works.
  b How does this compare to the natural breathing process?
  c What are the main advantages and disadvantages of positive pressure breathing systems?

Key points

● Different types of artificial breathing aids have been developed over the years to help people when they become paralysed by accident or disease and cannot ventilate their lungs.

● The different methods have advantages and disadvantages.

B4.3 Aerobic respiration

Learning objectives

After this topic, you should know:

- the chemistry of aerobic respiration
- where aerobic respiration takes place in your cells.

One of the most important enzyme-controlled processes in living things is aerobic respiration. It takes place all the time in plant and animal cells.

Your digestive system, lungs and circulation all work to provide your cells with the glucose and oxygen they need for respiration.

During aerobic respiration, glucose (a sugar) reacts with oxygen. This reaction releases energy that your cells can use. This energy is vital for everything that goes on in your body.

Carbon dioxide and water are produced as waste products of the reaction. We call the process aerobic respiration because it uses oxygen from the air.

Aerobic respiration can be represented by the equation:

glucose + oxygen → carbon dioxide + water (+ energy)

$$C_6H_{12}O_6 + 6O_2 \rightarrow 6CO_2 + 6H_2O \text{ (+ energy)}$$

??? Did you know ... ?

The average energy needs of a teenage boy are around 11 510 kJ of energy every day – but teenage girls only need 8830 kJ a day. This is partly because, on average, girls are smaller than boys, but it is also because boys have more muscle cells, which means more mitochondria demanding fuel for aerobic respiration.

Practical

Investigating respiration

Animals, plants and microorganisms all respire. It is possible to show that cellular respiration is taking place. You can either deprive a living organism of the things it needs to respire, or show that waste products are produced from the reaction.

Depriving a living thing of food and/or oxygen would kill it. This would be unethical. So we concentrate on the products of respiration. Carbon dioxide is the easiest to identify. We can also measure the energy released to the surroundings.

Limewater goes cloudy when carbon dioxide bubbles through it. The higher the concentration of carbon dioxide, the quicker the limewater goes cloudy. This gives us an easy way of showing that carbon dioxide has been produced. We can also look for a rise in temperature to show that energy is being released during respiration.

- Plan an ethical investigation into aerobic respiration in living organisms.

Mitochondria – the site of respiration

Aerobic respiration involves lots of chemical reactions. Each reaction is controlled by a different enzyme. Most of these reactions take place in the mitochondria of your cells.

Mitochondria are tiny rod-shaped parts (organelles) that are found in almost all plant and animal cells as well as in fungi and algal cells. They have a folded inner membrane that provides a large surface area for the enzymes involved in aerobic respiration.

The number of mitochondria in a cell shows you how active the cell is.

Outer membrane

Folded inner membrane gives a large surface area where the enzymes which release cellular respiration are found

Figure 1 Mitochondria are the powerhouses that provide energy for all the functions of your cells

Reasons for respiration

Respiration releases energy from the food we eat so that our cells can use it.

- Living cells need energy to carry out the basic functions of life. They build up large molecules from smaller ones to make new cell material. Much of the energy released in respiration is used for these 'building' activities (synthesis reactions). Energy is also used to break down larger molecules to smaller ones, both during digestion and within the cells themselves.

- In animals, energy from respiration is used to make muscles contract. Muscles are working all the time in your body. Even when you sleep, your heart beats, you breathe and your gut churns. All muscular activities use energy.

- Mammals and birds maintain a constant internal body temperature almost regardless of the temperature of their surroundings. Doing this uses energy from respiration. So on cold days you will use energy to keep warm, while on hot days you use energy to sweat and keep your body cool.

- In plants, the energy from respiration is used to move mineral ions such as nitrates from the soil into root hair cells. It is also used to convert sugars, nitrates and other nutrients into amino acids, which are then built up into proteins.

Figure 2 When the weather is cold, birds like this robin use up a lot of energy from respiration just to keep warm. Giving them extra food supplies during the winter can therefore mean the difference between life and death.

◯◯ links

You can find out more about active transport and the movement of mineral ions into root hair cells in 1.6 'Active transport', about the use of energy in Chapter 16 'Energy and biomass in food chains and natural cycles', and about heat production and temperature control in 7.6 'Controlling body temperature'.

Examiner's tip

Make sure you know the word equation and balanced symbol equation for aerobic respiration. Remember that aerobic respiration takes place in the mitochondria.

Summary questions

1 a Give a word equation for respiration.
   b Give the chemical equation for respiration.
   c Why do muscle cells have many mitochondria while fat cells have very few?

2 You need a regular supply of food to provide energy for your cells. If you don't get enough to eat, you become thin and stop growing. You don't want to move around and you start to feel cold.
   a What are the three main uses of the energy released in your body during aerobic respiration?
   b How does this explain the symptoms of starvation described above?

3 Plan an experiment to show that: **a** oxygen is taken up, and **b** carbon dioxide is released, during aerobic respiration.

Key points

- Aerobic respiration involves chemical reactions that use oxygen and sugar and release energy.

- Most of the reactions in aerobic respiration take place inside the mitochondria.

- The energy released during respiration is used for many crucial life processes such as synthesis reactions for growth, active transport, movement, digestion, circulation and, in mammals and birds, maintaining a steady body temperature.

B4.4

The effect of exercise on the body

Learning objectives

After this topic, you should know:

- how your body responds to the increased demands for glucose and oxygen during exercise.

Your muscles use a lot of energy. They move you around and help support your body against gravity. Your heart is made of muscle and pumps blood around your body. The movement of food along your gut depends on muscles too.

Muscle tissue is made up of protein fibres that contract when they are supplied with energy from respiration. Muscle fibres need a lot of energy to contract. They contain many mitochondria to carry out aerobic respiration and supply the energy needed.

Muscle fibres usually occur in big blocks or groups known as muscles, which contract to cause movement. They then relax, which allows other muscles to work.

Your muscles also store glucose as the carbohydrate **glycogen**. Glycogen can be converted rapidly back to glucose to use during exercise. The glucose is used in aerobic respiration to provide the energy to make your muscles contract:

$$\text{glucose} + \text{oxygen} \rightarrow \text{carbon dioxide} + \text{water } (+ \text{ energy})$$
$$C_6H_{12}O_6 + 6O_2 \rightarrow 6CO_2 + 6H_2O \ (+ \text{ energy})$$

Figure 1 All the work done by your muscles is based on these special protein fibres, which use energy from respiration to contract

The response to exercise

Even when you are not moving about, your muscles use up a certain amount of oxygen and glucose. However, when you begin to exercise, many muscles start contracting harder and faster. As a result, they need more glucose and oxygen to supply their energy needs. During exercise the muscles also produce increased amounts of carbon dioxide. This needs to be removed for muscles to keep working effectively.

During exercise, when muscular activity increases, several changes take place in your body:

- Your heart rate increases and the arteries supplying blood to your muscles dilate (widen). These changes increase the blood flow to your exercising muscles. This in turn increases the rate of supply of oxygen and glucose to the muscles. It also increases the rate that carbon dioxide is removed from the muscles.

 Did you know … ?

The maximum rate to which you should push your heart is usually calculated as approximately 220 beats per minute minus your age. When you exercise, you should ideally get your heart rate into the range between 60 per cent and 90 per cent of your maximum.

- Your breathing rate increases and you breathe more deeply. This means you breathe more often and also bring more air into your lungs each time you breathe in. The rate at which oxygen is brought into your body and picked up by your red blood cells is increased, and this oxygen is carried to your exercising muscles. It also means that carbon dioxide can be removed more quickly from the blood in the lungs and breathed out.
- Glycogen stored in the muscles is converted back to glucose, to supply the cells with the fuel they need for increased cellular respiration.

In this way, the heart rate and breathing rate increase during exercise to supply the muscles with what they need and remove the extra waste produced. Cellular respiration increases to supply the muscle cells with the energy they need to contract during exercise. The increase in your breathing and heart rate is to keep up with the demands of the cells.

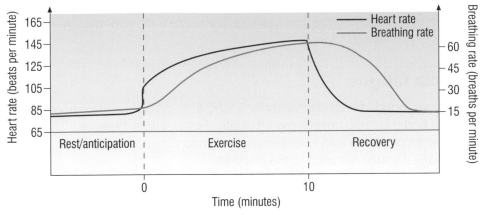

Figure 2 The changes measured in the heart and breathing rate before, during and after a period of exercise

	Unfit person	**Fit person**
Amount of blood pumped out of the heart during each beat at rest (cm³)	64	80
Volume of the heart at rest (cm³)	120	140
Resting breathing rate (breaths/min)	14	12
Resting pulse rate (beats/min)	72	63

Figure 3 The heart and lung functions change during exercise whether you are fit or not

Summary questions

1. **a** What is glycogen?
   b Why do you think that muscles contain a store of glycogen but most other tissues of the body do not?

2. Using Figure 2 and Figure 3, describe the effect of exercise on the heart rate and the breathing rate of a fit person and explain fully why these changes happen.

3. Plan an investigation into the fitness levels of your classmates. Describe how you might carry out this investigation and explain what you would expect the results to be.

Key points

- The energy that is released during respiration is used to enable muscles to contract.

- When exercising your muscles, you need an increased supply of glucose and oxygen and you produce more carbon dioxide to be removed.

- Body responses to exercise include:
  - an increase in the heart rate, in the breathing rate and in the depth of breathing
  - glycogen stores in the muscles are converted to glucose for cellular respiration
  - the blood flow to the muscles increases.

- These responses act to increase the rate of supply of glucose and oxygen to the muscles and the rate of removal of carbon dioxide from the muscles.

B4.5 Anaerobic respiration

Learning objectives

After this topic, you should know:

- why less energy is released by anaerobic respiration than by aerobic respiration

- what is meant by an oxygen debt

- that anaerobic respiration takes place in lots of different organisms, including bacteria and fungi.

Figure 1 Training hard is the simplest way to avoid anaerobic respiration. When you are fit, you can get oxygen to your muscles and remove carbon dioxide more efficiently.

Your everyday muscle movements use energy released by aerobic respiration. However, when you exercise hard, your muscle cells may become short of oxygen. Although you increase your heart and breathing rates, sometimes the blood cannot supply oxygen to the muscles fast enough. When this happens, the muscle cells can still get energy from glucose. They use **anaerobic respiration**, which takes place without oxygen.

In anaerobic respiration, the glucose is not broken down completely. It produces **lactic acid** instead of carbon dioxide and water, and releases a smaller amount of energy for the cells.

If you are fit, your heart and lungs will be able to keep a good supply of oxygen going to your muscles while you exercise. If you are unfit, your muscles will run short of oxygen much sooner.

Muscle fatigue

Using your muscle fibres vigorously for a long time can make them become fatigued and they stop contracting efficiently. For example, repeated movements can soon lead to anaerobic respiration in your muscles – particularly if you're not used to the exercise.

One cause of this muscle fatigue is the build up of lactic acid, made by anaerobic respiration in the muscle cells. Blood flowing through the muscles eventually removes the lactic acid.

Anaerobic respiration is not as efficient as aerobic respiration because the glucose molecules are not broken down completely. Since the breakdown of glucose is incomplete, far less energy is released than during aerobic respiration.

The end product of anaerobic respiration is lactic acid and this leads to the release of a small amount of energy, instead of the carbon dioxide and water plus lots of energy released by aerobic respiration.

Anaerobic respiration:

$$\text{glucose} \rightarrow \text{lactic acid (+ energy)}$$
$$C_6H_{12}O_6 \rightarrow 2C_3H_6O_3 \text{ (+ energy)}$$

Oxygen debt

If you have been exercising hard, you often carry on puffing and panting for some time after you stop. The length of time you remain out of breath depends on how fit you are. So why do you carry on breathing faster and more deeply when you have stopped using your muscles?

The waste lactic acid you produce during anaerobic respiration is a problem. You cannot simply get rid of lactic acid by breathing it out as you can with carbon dioxide. As a result, when the exercise is over, lactic acid has to be broken down to produce carbon dioxide and water. This needs oxygen.

The amount of oxygen needed to break down the lactic acid to carbon dioxide and water is known as the **oxygen debt**.

Practical

Making lactic acid

Repeat a single action many times. For example, you could step up and down, lift a weight or clench and unclench your fist. You will soon feel the effect of a build up of lactic acid in your muscles.

- How can you tell when your muscles have started to respire anaerobically?

After a race, your heart rate and breathing rate stay high to supply the extra oxygen needed to pay off the oxygen debt. The bigger the debt (the larger the amount of lactic acid), the longer you will puff and pant!

Oxygen debt repayment:

lactic acid + oxygen → carbon dioxide + water

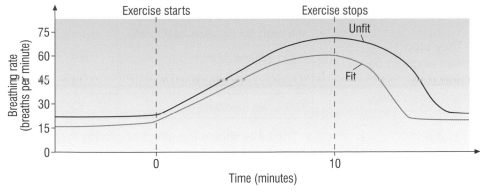

Figure 2 Everyone gets an oxygen debt if they exercise hard, but if you are fit you can pay it off faster

Anaerobic respiration in other organisms

Human beings and other animals are not the only living organisms that can respire anaerobically. Plants and microorganisms can also respire without oxygen. However, when plant cells respire anaerobically they do not form lactic acid – they form ethanol and carbon dioxide. Some microorganisms form lactic acid during anaerobic respiration – the bacteria used to form yoghurts, for example. Other microorganisms, such as yeast, form ethanol and carbon dioxide. People have made use of this for thousands of years in the production of alcoholic drinks.

$$glucose \rightarrow ethanol + carbon\ dioxide$$
$$C_6H_{12}O_6 \rightarrow 2C_2H_5OH + 2CO_2$$

Figure 3 Anaerobic respiration in yeast cells produces ethanol and carbon dioxide

Summary questions

1 If you exercise very hard or for a long time, your muscles begin to ache and do not work so effectively. Explain why.

2 If you exercise vigorously, you often puff and pant for some time after you stop. Explain what is happening.

3 a What is anaerobic respiration?
   b Explain how anaerobic respiration differs between animals, plants and yeast. In each case, give the word and balanced symbol equations for what is happening and explain the benefits to the organism of being able to respire in this way.

Key points

- If muscles work hard for a long time, they become fatigued and don't contract efficiently. If they don't get enough oxygen, they will respire anaerobically.

- Anaerobic respiration is respiration without oxygen. When this takes place in animal cells, glucose is incompletely broken down to form lactic acid.

- The anaerobic breakdown of glucose releases less energy than aerobic respiration.

- After exercise, oxygen is still needed to break down the lactic acid that has built up. The amount of oxygen needed is known as the oxygen debt.

- Anaerobic respiration in plant cells and some microorganisms results in the production of ethanol and carbon dioxide.

Summary questions

1 a How are the lungs adapted to allow the exchange of oxygen and carbon dioxide between the air and the blood?

b How is air moved in and out of the lungs and how does this ventilation of the lungs make gaseous exchange more efficient?

2 Some people suffer from sleep apnoea. They stop breathing in their sleep, which disturbs them and can be dangerous. A nasal intermittent positive pressure ventilation system can be used to help them sleep safely through the night.

a What is a positive pressure ventilation system?

b Explain how a positive pressure ventilation system differs from normal breathing.

c What are the advantages of a system like this over a negative pressure ventilation system?

3 Some students investigated the process of cellular respiration. They set up three vacuum flasks. One contained live, soaked peas. One contained dry peas. One contained peas which had been soaked and then boiled. They took daily observations of the temperature in each flask for a week. The results are shown in the table.

Day	Room temperature (°C)	Temperature in flask A containing live, soaked peas (°C)	Temperature in flask B containing dry peas (°C)	Temperature in flask C containing soaked, boiled peas (°C)
1	20.0	20.0	20.0	20.0
2	20.0	20.5	20.0	20.0
3	20.0	21.0	20.0	20.0
4	20.0	21.5	20.0	20.0
5	20.0	22.0	20.0	20.0
6	20.0	22.2	20.0	20.5
7	20.0	22.5	20.0	21.0

a Plot a graph to show these results.

b Explain the results in flask A containing the live, soaked peas.

c Why were the results in flask B the same as the room temperature readings?

d Why was the room temperature in the lab recorded every day?

e Look at the results for flask C.
i Why is the temperature at 20 °C for the first five days?
ii After five days the temperature increases. Suggest **two** possible explanations for why the temperature increases.

4 It is often said that taking regular exercise and getting fit is good for your heart and your lungs.

	Before getting fit	After getting fit
Amount of blood pumped out of the heart during each beat (cm³)	64	80
Heart volume (cm³)	120	140
Breathing rate (breaths/min)	14	12
Pulse rate (beats/min)	72	63

a The table shows the effect of getting fit on the heart and lungs of one person. Display this data in four bar charts.

b Use the information on your bar charts to help you explain exactly what effect increased fitness has on:
i your heart
ii your lungs.

5 a What is aerobic respiration?

b What is anaerobic respiration?

c How does anaerobic respiration differ between a human being and a yeast cell?

d What is meant by the term 'oxygen debt'?

e Explain the difference in the responses of a fit and an unfit individual to exercise in terms of their muscles, heart and lung function and oxygen debt.

6 Athletes want to be able to use their muscles aerobically for as long as possible when they compete. They train to develop their heart and lungs. Many athletes also train at altitude. There is less oxygen in the air so your body makes more red blood cells, which helps to avoid oxygen debt. Some athletes remove some of their own blood, store it and then just before a competition transfuse it back into their system. This is called blood doping and it is illegal. Other athletes use hormones to stimulate the growth of extra red blood cells. This is also illegal.

a Why do athletes want to be able to use their muscles aerobically for as long as possible?

b How does developing more red blood cells by training at altitude help athletic performance?

c How does blood doping help performance?

d Explain in detail what happens to the muscles if the body cannot supply glucose and oxygen quickly enough when they are working hard.

AQA Examination-style questions

1 Figure 1 is a diagram of the human respiratory system.

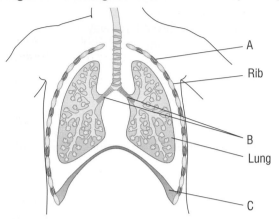

Figure 1

a Names the structures A, B and C. (3)

b Describe the sequence of events which occurs so that air is drawn into the lungs during inhalation. (5)

2 Figure 2 shows an alveolus and a blood capillary.

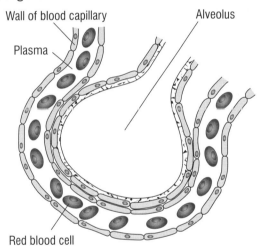

Figure 2

a Give **two** features seen in the diagram which increase the diffusion of oxygen from the air in the alveolus into the blood. Explain how each feature increases the rate of diffusion. (4)

b A steep diffusion gradient also increases the rate of oxygen diffusion. Give **two** ways in which a steep diffusion gradient is maintained between the air in the alveolus and the blood in the capillary. (2)

c A constant supply of oxygen is required for all body cells for aerobic respiration.

  i Complete the word and symbol equations for aerobic respiration.

    .... + oxygen →carbon dioxide + ...

    .... + $6O_2$ → CO_2 + ... (4)

  ii Name the cell parts where aerobic respiration take place. (1)

  iii Muscle cells contain a large number of these cell parts. Why? (2)

3 *In this question you will be assessed on using good English, organising information clearly and using specialist terms where appropriate.*

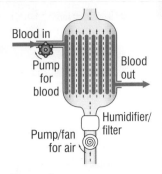

Figure 3

Figure 3 shows a design for an artificial lung.

Many people with lung disease are confined to a wheelchair or are unable to do much exercise. Scientists hope that a portable artificial lung, the size of a spectacle case, can be developed. This device might replace the need for lung transplants and allow patients to live a normal life.

When scientists design an artificial lung, what features of a normal lung must they copy? Suggest the advantages of the artificial lung compared with a lung transplant. (QWC) (6)

4 Yeast is used to make bread. Sealed inside the dough the yeast cells must respire anaerobically.

a Write the word equation for the anaerobic respiration in yeast cells. (3)

b Suggest which product of anaerobic respiration is causing the dough to rise. Give a reason. (2)

c Food scientists investigated the anaerobic respiration of yeast in bread dough. They made a dough mixture and divided it into five measuring cylinders. They placed each measuring cylinder at a different temperature for 15 minutes.

The table shows their results.

Temperature of measuring cylinder in °C	0	20	40	60	80
Volume of dough in cm^3 at 0 minutes	22	21	21	22	21
Volume of dough in cm^3 at 15 minutes	22	27	44	23	21

  i Suggest the best temperature to leave bread dough to rise before it is baked. (1)

  ii Use scientific knowledge and understanding to explain why the investigation gave the results seen in the table. (5)

B5.1 The circulatory system and the heart

∞ **links**

To find out more about how digested food gets into the transport system, see 1.8 'Exchange in the gut'.

To find out more about how oxygen and carbon dioxide enter or leave the blood, see 4.1 'Breathing and gas exchange in the lungs'.

To learn how oxygen is used in the cells and how carbon dioxide is produced, read 4.3 'Aerobic respiration'.

You are made up of billions of cells, and most of them are a long way from a direct source of food or oxygen. This means that direct diffusion is not enough in multicellular organisms such as humans when the surface area to volume ratio is small. A **transport system** is vital to carry the substances needed from where they come into your body (for example the digestive system, the lungs) to the cells where they are needed. So, a transport system is needed to supply your body cells with glucose and oxygen for respiration, and to remove the waste materials that are the by-products of respiration. This is the function of your **blood circulation system**. It has three parts:

● the **blood vessels** (the tubes that carry blood around your body)
● the **heart** (which pumps the blood around your body)
● the **blood** (the liquid that carries substances around your body).

A double circulation

You have two transport systems, called a **double circulation** system.

● One transport system carries blood from your heart to your lungs and back again. This allows oxygen and carbon dioxide to be exchanged with the air in the lungs.

● The other transport system carries blood to all other organs of your body and back again to the heart.

A double circulation like this is vital in warm-blooded, active animals such as humans. It makes our circulatory system very efficient. Fully **oxygenated** blood returns to the heart from the lungs. This blood can then be sent off to different parts of the body at high pressure, so more areas of your body can receive fully oxygenated blood quickly.

In your circulatory system, **arteries** carry blood away from your heart to the organs of the body. Blood returns to your heart in the **veins**. The two are linked by systems of tiny blood vessels called capillaries.

The heart as a pump

Your heart is the organ that pumps blood around your body. It is made up of two pumps (for the double circulation) that beat together about 70 times each minute. The walls of your heart are almost entirely muscle. This muscle is supplied with oxygen by the **coronary arteries**.

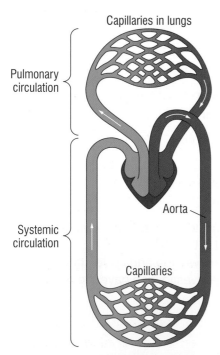

Figure 1 The two separate circulation systems supply the lungs and the rest of the body

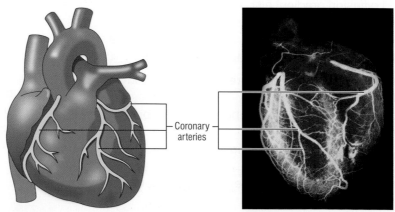

Figure 2 The muscles of the heart work hard so they need a good supply of oxygen and glucose. This is supplied by the blood in the coronary arteries.

The structure of the human heart is perfectly adapted for pumping blood to your lungs and your body. The two sides of the heart fill and empty at the same time. This gives a strong, coordinated heartbeat.

Blood enters the top chambers of your heart (the **atria**). The blood coming into the right atrium from the **vena cava** is **deoxygenated** blood from your body. The blood coming into the left atrium in the **pulmonary vein** is oxygenated blood from your lungs. The atria contract together and force blood down into the **ventricles**. Valves close to stop the blood flowing backwards out of the heart.

● The ventricles contract and force blood out of the heart.
● The right ventricle forces deoxygenated blood to the lungs in the **pulmonary artery**.
● The left ventricle pumps oxygenated blood around the body in a big artery called the **aorta**.

As the blood is pumped into the pulmonary artery and the aorta, valves close to prevent backflow of the blood to the heart. They make sure the blood flows in the right direction.

The muscle wall of the left ventricle is noticeably thicker than the wall of the right ventricle. This allows the left ventricle to develop much more pressure than the right. This higher pressure is needed as the blood leaving the left ventricle travels through the arterial system all over your body, while the blood leaving the right ventricle moves only through the pulmonary arteries to your lungs.

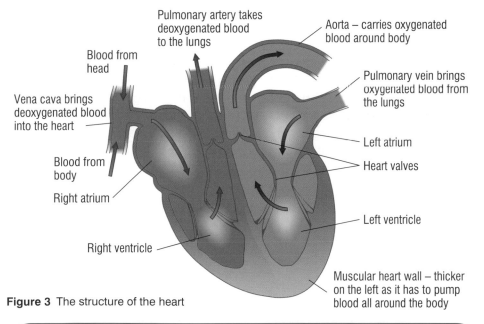

Pulmonary artery takes deoxygenated blood to the lungs

Aorta – carries oxygenated blood around body

Blood from head

Vena cava brings deoxygenated blood into the heart

Pulmonary vein brings oxygenated blood from the lungs

Blood from body

Left atrium

Heart valves

Right atrium

Left ventricle

Right ventricle

Muscular heart wall – thicker on the left as it has to pump blood all around the body

Figure 3 The structure of the heart

Summary questions

1 Explain carefully why people need a blood circulation system.
2 Blood in the arteries is usually bright red because it is full of oxygen. This is not true of the blood in the pulmonary arteries. Why not?
3 Make a flowchart showing the route of a unit of blood as it passes through the heart and the lungs in a double circulation system.
4 **a** Describe how the heart pumps blood around the body.
   b Explain the importance of the following in making the heart an effective pump in the circulatory system of the body:
   i heart valves   **ii** coronary arteries
   iii the thickened muscular wall of the left ventricle.

B5.2

Helping the heart

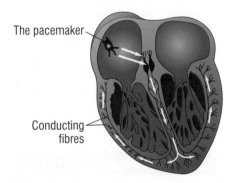

Figure 1 The pacemaker region of the heart, which controls the basic rhythm of your heart

The pacemaker

Conducting fibres

When you are an adult, your heart has a natural resting rhythm of around 70 beats a minute. If you are really fit, your resting heart rate will be slower – around 60 beats a minute.

You don't have to think about making your heart beat regularly. Your resting heart rate is controlled by a group of cells found in the right atrium of your heart that act as a **pacemaker**. They produce a regular electrical signal that spreads through the heart and makes it contract. This pacemaker area is known as the **sinoatrial node**.

Artificial pacemakers

If the natural pacemaker stops working properly, this can cause serious problems. If the heart beats too slowly, the person affected will not get enough oxygen. If the heart beats too fast, it cannot pump blood properly.

Problems with the rhythm of the heart can often be solved using an **artificial pacemaker**. This is an electrical device used to correct irregularities in the heart rate, which is implanted into your chest. Artificial pacemakers only weigh between 20 and 50 g, and they are attached to your heart by two wires. The operation to install the pacemaker is often carried out while you are still awake.

The artificial pacemaker sends strong, regular electrical signals to your heart that stimulate it to beat properly. Modern pacemakers are often very sensitive to what your body needs. So, if your heart is beating regularly on its own then the pacemaker does not send signals, but if your rhythm goes wrong then the pacemaker kicks in and keeps the heart beating smoothly. Some artificial pacemakers can even detect when you are active and breathing faster and will stimulate your heart to beat faster while you exercise.

If you have a pacemaker fitted, you will need regular medical check-ups throughout your life. However, most people feel that this is a small price to pay for the increase in the quality and length of life that a pacemaker brings.

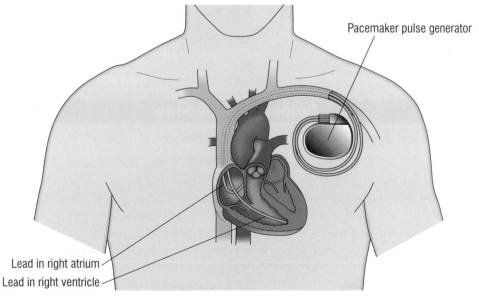

Pacemaker pulse generator

Lead in right atrium

Lead in right ventricle

Figure 2 An artificial pacemaker is positioned under the skin of the chest with wires running to the heart itself

Artificial hearts

Sometimes an artificial pacemaker to keep the heart beating steadily is not enough to restore health. For many different reasons, people can need a new heart. New technologies can help us overcome even the worst of problems. When people need a heart transplant, they have to wait for a donor heart that is a tissue match. However, there are never enough hearts to go around. Many people die before they get a chance to have a new heart.

For years, scientists have been developing artificial hearts. They have developed temporary hearts that can support your natural heart until it can be replaced. However, replacing your heart permanently with a machine is still a long way off.

Since 2004, about 1000 people worldwide have been fitted with a completely artificial heart. These artificial hearts need a lot of machinery to keep them working. Most patients have to stay in hospital until they have their transplant.

In 2011, 40-year-old Matthew Green became the first UK patient to leave hospital and go home with a completely artificial heart. He carried the machine operating the heart in a backpack! There is always a risk of the blood clotting in the artificial heart, which can kill the patient. Yet this new technology gives people a chance to live a relatively normal life while they wait for a heart transplant.

Artificial hearts can also be used to give a diseased heart a rest, so that it can recover. Patients have a part or whole artificial heart implanted that removes the strain of keeping the blood circulating for a few weeks or months. However, the resources needed to develop artificial hearts and the cost of each one means they are not yet widely used in patients.

Figure 3 This amazing artificial heart uses air pressure to pump blood around the body

links

You can find out more about heart disease on 5.3 'Keeping the blood flowing'.

Figure 4 Matthew Green on a walk with his family. His artificial heart is being carried by his wife.

Key points

- The resting heart rate is controlled by a group of cells in the right atrium that form a natural pacemaker.

- Artificial pacemakers are electrical devices used to correct irregularities in the heart rhythm.

- Artificial hearts are occasionally used to keep patients alive while they wait for a transplant, or for their heart to rest and recover.

Summary questions

1 How is the heartbeat controlled in a healthy adult heart?

2 Explain how problems in the rhythm of the heart might be overcome using an artificial pacemaker.

3 What are the main uses and limitations of artificial hearts?

4 Discuss some scientific and social arguments for and against the continued development of artificial hearts.

B5.3

Keeping the blood flowing

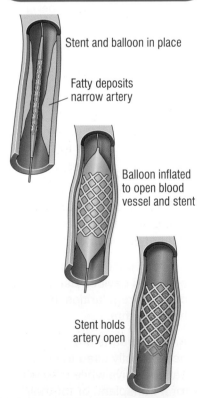

Stent and balloon in place

Fatty deposits narrow artery

Balloon inflated to open blood vessel and stent

Stent holds artery open

Figure 2 A stent being positioned in an artery

The blood vessels

Blood is carried around your body in three main types of blood vessels, each adapted for a different function.

- Your arteries carry blood away from your heart to the organs of your body. This blood is usually bright-red oxygenated blood. The arteries stretch as the blood is forced through them and go back into shape afterwards. You can feel this as a pulse where the arteries run close to the skin's surface (for example, at your wrist). Arteries have thick walls containing muscle and elastic fibres. As the blood in the arteries is under pressure, it is very dangerous if an artery is cut, because the blood will spurt out rapidly every time the heart beats.

- The veins carry blood from the organs towards your heart. This blood is usually low in oxygen and so is a deep purple-red colour. Veins do not have a pulse. They have much thinner walls than arteries and often have **valves** to prevent the backflow of blood as it returns to the heart.

- Throughout the body, capillaries form a huge network of tiny vessels linking the arteries and the veins. Capillaries are narrow with very thin walls. This enables substances, such as oxygen and glucose, to easily diffuse out of your blood and into your cells. The substances produced by your cells, such as carbon dioxide, pass easily into the blood through the walls of the capillaries.

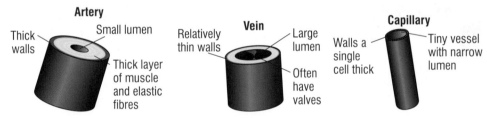

Artery
Thick walls
Small lumen
Thick layer of muscle and elastic fibres

Vein
Relatively thin walls
Large lumen
Often have valves

Capillary
Walls a single cell thick
Tiny vessel with narrow lumen

Figure 1 The three main types of blood vessels

Problems with blood flow through the heart

The coronary arteries that supply blood to the heart muscle can become narrow as you age. They also get narrower when fatty deposits build up on the lining of the vessel. This is known as **coronary heart disease**. If the flow of blood through the coronary arteries is restricted in this way, an insufficient supply of oxygen reaches your heart muscle. This can cause pain, a heart attack and even death.

Doctors often solve the problem of coronary heart disease with **stents**. A stent is a metal mesh that is placed in the artery. A tiny balloon is inflated to open up the blood vessel and the stent at the same time. The balloon is deflated and removed but the stent remains in place, holding the blood vessel open. As soon as this is done, the blood in the coronary artery flows freely. Doctors can put a stent in place without a general anaesthetic.

It isn't only coronary arteries that can narrow and cause problems. Stents can be used to open up an artery and improve blood flow almost anywhere in the body. Many stents now also release drugs to prevent the blood from clotting. However, there are some questions about the costs and benefits of this treatment. Some studies suggest that the benefits to the patient do not justify the additional expense of the drugs.

Doctors can also carry out bypass surgery. In this operation, they replace the narrow or blocked coronary arteries with bits of veins from other parts of the body. This works for badly blocked arteries where stents cannot help. This surgery is expensive and involves a general anaesthetic.

Leaky valves

Another problem with the blood flow through the heart itself comes from faulty **valves**. The heart valves keep the blood flowing in the right direction. These valves have to withstand a lot of pressure, so over time they may weaken and start to leak or become stiff and not open fully. When this happens, the heart does not work as well. The person affected can become very breathless and they will eventually die if the problem is not solved.

Doctors can operate on the heart and replace the faulty valve. Mechanical valves are made of materials such as titanium and polymers. They last a very long time. However, with a mechanical valve you have to take medicine for the rest of your life to prevent your blood from clotting around it.

Biological valves are based on valves taken from animals such as pigs or cattle, or sometimes from human donors. These work extremely well and the patient does not need any medication. However, they only last about 12–15 years.

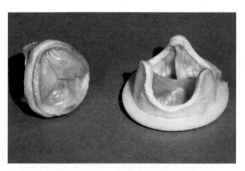 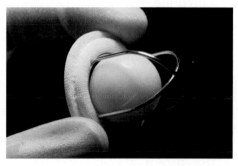

Figure 3 Both biological (left) and mechanical (right) heart valves work very well. They each have advantages and disadvantages for the patient.

Summary questions

1 Describe the following blood vessels:
   a artery,
   b vein,
   c capillaries.

2 a Draw a diagram that explains the way the arteries, veins and capillaries are linked to each other and to the heart.
   b Label the diagram and explain what is happening in the capillaries.

3 a What is a stent?
   b Make a table to show the advantages and disadvantages of using a stent to improve the blood flow through the coronary arteries compared with bypass surgery.

4 a Explain why a valve that does not close properly causes major problems in the heart.
   b Describe how mechanical and biological replacement heart valves can be used to solve the problems, and discuss the advantages and disadvantages of each type.

Key points

- Blood flows around the body via the blood vessels. The main types of blood vessels are arteries, veins and capillaries.

- Substances diffuse in and out of the blood in the capillaries.

- Stents can be used to keep narrowed or blocked arteries open.

- Heart valves keep the blood flowing in the right direction.

- Damaged heart valves can be replaced by biological or mechanical valves.

B5.4 — Transport in the blood

Your blood is a unique fluid based on a liquid called **plasma**. Plasma carries **red blood cells**, **white blood cells** and **platelets** suspended in it. It also carries many dissolved substances around your body.

?? Did you know … ?

The average person has between 4.7 and 5.0 litres of blood.

The blood plasma as a transport medium

Your blood plasma is a yellow liquid. The plasma transports all of your blood cells and some other substances around your body.

● Waste carbon dioxide produced in the organs of the body is carried to the lungs in the plasma, for expiration.

● **Urea** is carried to your kidneys. Urea is a waste product formed in your liver from the breakdown of proteins. It travels dissolved in the plasma from the liver to the kidneys. In the kidneys, the urea is removed from your blood to form **urine**.

● All the small, soluble products of digestion pass into the blood from your small intestine. These food molecules are carried in the plasma around your body to the other organs and individual cells.

Red blood cells

The red blood cells pick up oxygen from your lungs. They carry the oxygen to the organs, tissues and cells where it is needed. These blood cells have adaptations that make them very efficient at their job:

● They have a very unusual shape – they are **biconcave discs**. This means they are concave (pushed in) on both sides. This gives the cells an increased surface area to volume ratio over which the diffusion of oxygen can take place.

● Red blood cells are packed full of a special red **pigment** called **haemoglobin** that can carry oxygen.

● They do not have a nucleus. This makes more space to pack in molecules of haemoglobin.

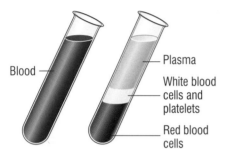

Blood — Plasma, White blood cells and platelets, Red blood cells

Figure 1 The main components of blood. The red colour of your blood comes from the red blood cells.

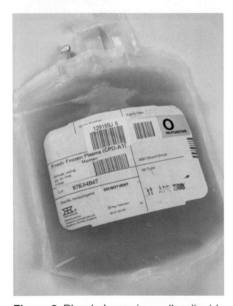

Figure 2 Blood plasma is a yellow liquid that transports everything you need – and need to get rid of – around your body

?? Did you know … ?

There are more red blood cells than any other type of blood cell in your body – about 5 million in each cubic millimetre of your blood.

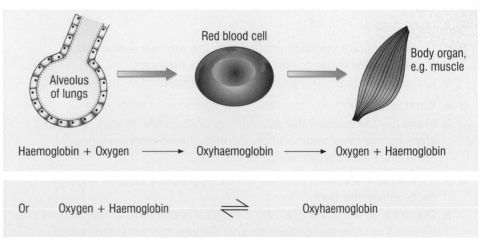

Alveolus of lungs → Red blood cell → Body organ, e.g. muscle

Haemoglobin + Oxygen ⟶ Oxyhaemoglobin ⟶ Oxygen + Haemoglobin

Or   Oxygen + Haemoglobin ⇌ Oxyhaemoglobin

Figure 3 The reversible reaction between oxygen and haemoglobin makes life as we know it possible by carrying oxygen to all the places where it is needed

In the lungs where there is a high concentration of oxygen, haemoglobin reacts with oxygen to form bright red **oxyhaemoglobin**. In other organs, where the concentration of oxygen is lower, the oxyhaemoglobin splits up. It forms purple-red haemoglobin and oxygen, which diffuses into the cells where it is needed.

White blood cells

White blood cells are much bigger than the red blood cells and there are fewer of them. They have a nucleus and form part of the body's defence system against harmful microorganisms. Some white blood cells (lymphocytes) form antibodies against microorganisms. Some form antitoxins against poisons made by microorganisms. Yet others (phagocytes) engulf and digest invading bacteria and viruses.

Platelets

Platelets are small fragments of cells that have no nucleus. They are very important in helping the blood to clot at the site of a wound. Blood clotting is a series of enzyme-controlled reactions that result in the change of fibrinogen into fibrin. This produces a network (or web) of protein fibres. The fibres then capture lots of red blood cells and more platelets to form a jelly-like clot. This stops you bleeding to death. The clot dries and hardens to form a scab. The scab protects the new skin as it grows and stops bacteria getting into your body through the wound.

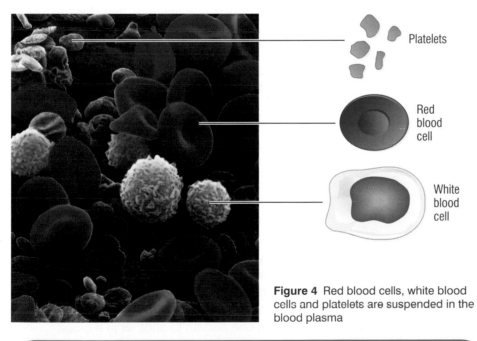

Platelets

Red blood cell

White blood cell

Figure 4 Red blood cells, white blood cells and platelets are suspended in the blood plasma

Key points

- Your blood plasma, and the blood cells suspended in it, transport dissolved food molecules, carbon dioxide and urea.

- Your red blood cells carry oxygen from your lungs to the organs of the body.

- Red blood cells are adapted to carry oxygen by being biconcave, which provides a bigger surface area, by containing haemoglobin, and by having no nucleus so more haemoglobin can fit in.

- White blood cells are part of the defence system of the body.

- Platelets are cell fragments involved in the clotting of the blood.

- Blood clotting involves a series of enzyme-controlled reactions that turn fibrinogen to fibrin to form a network of fibres and a scab.

Summary questions

1 State three functions of the blood.

2 a Why is it not accurate to describe the blood as a red liquid?
  b What actually makes the blood red?
  c Give three important functions of blood plasma.

3 Explain carefully the main ways in which the blood helps you to avoid infection, including a description of the parts of the blood involved.

B5.5

The immune system and blood groups

Learning objectives

After this topic, you should know:

● how antigens and antibodies are involved in the main human blood groups

● why blood typing and tissue matching are so important in transplant surgery.

⊂⊃ links

You can read more about the structure of proteins in 3.1 'Carbohydrates, lipids and proteins'.

Donor	Recipient			
	A	**B**	**AB**	**O**
A	✓	✗	✓	✗
B	✗	✓	✓	✗
AB	✗	✗	✓	✗
O	✓	✓	✓	✓

(✓ = blood compatible; ✗ = blood incompatible and a transfusion would fail)

Figure 1 Mixing the wrong blood groups can cause clotting and be fatal

Every cell has proteins on its surface called **antigens**. The combination of antigens on your cells is unique to you. It will be different to the antigens on anyone else's cells, unless you have an identical twin. The antigens on the microorganisms that get into your body are also different to the ones on your own cells. Your **immune system** recognises these different antigens.

White blood cells are large blood cells that have a nucleus. Some of your white blood cells make **antibodies** which attach to 'foreign' antigens. They either destroy the cells carrying the antigens, or enable other white blood cells to engulf and digest them.

Antigens and human blood groups

A number of different antigens are found specifically on the surface of the red blood cells. They give us the different human blood groups. There are several different blood grouping systems, but the best known is the ABO system. This has four different blood groups – **A**, **B**, **AB** and **O**. In this system there are two possible antigens on the red blood cells – antigen **A** and antigen **B**. There are also two possible antibodies in your plasma – antibody **a** and antibody **b**. These antibodies are there all the time; that is, they are not made in response to a particular antigen.

Table 1 shows the combinations of antibodies and antigens that give the four ABO blood groups.

Table 1 The ABO compatibility table

Blood group	Antigen on red blood cells	Antibody in plasma
A	A	b
B	B	a
AB	A and B	None
O	None	a and b

If blood from different groups is mixed, there may be a reaction between the antigen and the complementary antibody. This causes the blood cells to **agglutinate** (stick together). This means they cannot work properly and clog up capillaries or even larger vessels. In a healthy person this is not important, since everyone keeps their blood in their own circulatory system. However, if someone loses a lot of blood as a result of an accident or an operation, then blood may need to be given from one person to another in a blood transfusion.

Before a transfusion, it is vital that the blood groups of both the donor and the recipient are known, so that the right blood can be given to prevent agglutination. The blood containing a particular antigen must not be mixed with blood containing the matching antibody. This is why blood group O is so useful – because the cells have no antigens it does not react with any blood antibodies. It is the universal donor and can be given to anyone. Other blood groups have to be matched more carefully (see Figure 1). Blood typing before a blood transfusion is vital because an error can be fatal.

Antigens and organ transplants

In an organ transplant, a diseased organ is replaced with a healthy one from a **donor**. The donor is often someone who has died suddenly in an accident or following a stroke or heart attack. However, for some organs such as the kidney, a living donor is sometimes used. Successful organ transplants can restore the recipient to health and allow them to lead an almost completely normal life.

The biggest problem in an organ transplant is that the antigens on the surface of the donor organ are different to those of the **recipient** – the person who needs the new organ. The recipient makes antibodies that will attack the antigens on the donor organ. This may result in the rejection and destruction of the new organ.

There are a number of ways of reducing the risk of a transplanted organ being rejected.

- The match between the antigens of the donor and the recipient is made as close as possible. For example, you can use a donor heart from someone with the same blood group and with a 'tissue type' as close as possible to the recipient.

- The recipient is treated with drugs that suppress their immune system (**immunosuppressant drugs**) for the rest of their lives. This helps to prevent the rejection of their new organ. Immunosuppressant drugs are improving all the time, so the need for a really close tissue match is becoming less important.

- The disadvantage of taking immunosuppressant drugs is they prevent patients from dealing effectively with infectious diseases. So they have to take great care if they become ill in any way, which is a small price to pay for a new working organ.

- Transplanted organs don't last forever, although survival times are increasing as immunosuppressant drugs get better. Eventually, the donor organ will also start to fail and then the patient will need another transplant.

In general, even with modern immunosuppressant drugs, a good tissue match makes a transplant more likely to succeed. This is why artificial hearts (see page 59) and dialysis machines (see page 87) are needed to help people survive until a donated organ becomes available.

Figure 2 Harry Reyhing had a heart transplant. Drugs prevent his body from rejecting the foreign antigens.

Key points

- Antigens are proteins on the surface of cells.

- There are four ABO blood groups – A, B, AB and O. These are based on the type of antigens on the surface of red blood cells and the type of antibodies in the blood plasma.

- In organ transplants, a diseased organ is replaced with a healthy one from a donor. The recipient's antibodies may attack the antigens on the donor organ as they do not recognise them.

- To prevent rejection of the transplanted organ, a donor organ with a similar tissue type to the recipient is used and immunosuppressant drugs are given that suppress the immune response.

Summary questions

1 State the difference between an antigen and an antibody.

2 a Explain why someone with blood group O is particularly welcome as a blood donor.
   b Explain why there can be problems when a person of blood group O needs a blood transfusion.

3 Why is tissue typing so important before a successful heart transplant?

4 Explain the main advantages and disadvantages of using a transplant to replace a damaged heart rather than an artificial organ.

B5.6 The digestive system

Learning objectives

After this topic, you should know:

● how the food you eat is digested in your body

● the role played by the different parts of the digestive system

● the different digestive enzymes.

The food you take in and eat is made up of large insoluble molecules, including starch (a carbohydrate), proteins and fats. Your body cannot absorb and use these molecules, so they need to be broken down or digested to form smaller, soluble molecules. These can then be absorbed in your small intestine and used by your cells. This process of digestion takes place in your digestive system.

The digestive system

The digestive system starts at one end with your mouth and finishes at the other end with your anus. It is made up of many different organs, as you saw in Figure 2 on page 30. There are also glands such as the pancreas and the salivary glands that make and release digestive juices containing enzymes to break down your food.

◯◯ links

For information on the structure of the digestive system, look back to 2.5 'Tissues and organs' and 2.6 'Organ systems'.

The stomach and the small intestine are the main organs where food is digested. Enzymes break down the large insoluble food molecules into smaller, soluble ones.

Your small intestine is also where the soluble food molecules are absorbed into your blood. The digested food molecules are small enough to pass freely through the walls of the small intestine into the blood vessels by diffusion. They move in this direction because there is a very high concentration of food molecules in the gut and a much lower concentration in the blood. They move into the blood down a steep concentration gradient. Some substances are also moved from the gut into your blood by active transport. The villi and the microvilli greatly increase the surface area of the small intestine so that the absorption of digested food is very efficient. Once there, they get transported in the bloodstream around your body.

The muscular walls of the gut squeeze the undigested food onwards into your large intestine. This is where water is absorbed from the undigested food into your blood. The material that remains makes up the bulk of your faeces. Faeces are stored and then pass out of your body through the anus back into the environment.

◯◯ links

For more information on moving substances in and out of cells, see 1.4 'Diffusion', 1.5 'Osmosis' and 1.6 'Active transport'. For more information on the adaptations of the gut for absorption, see 1.8 'Exchange in the gut'.

Examiner's tip

Learn the names of the parts of the digestive system. Make sure you know the difference between the larger, lobed liver and the thinner 'leaf-like' pancreas.

⁇ Did you know ... ?

When Alexis St Martin suffered a terrible gunshot wound in 1822, Dr William Beaumont managed to save his life. However, Alexis was left with a hole (or fistula) from his stomach to the outside world. Dr Beaumont then used this hole to find out what happened in Alexis's stomach as he digested food!

Digestive enzymes

Most of your enzymes work *inside* the cells of your body, controlling the rate of the chemical reactions. Your digestive enzymes are different. They work *outside* your cells. They are produced by specialised cells in glands (such as your salivary glands and your pancreas), and in the lining of your gut.

The enzymes then pass out of these cells into the gut itself. Your gut is a hollow, muscular tube that squeezes your food. It helps to break up your food into small pieces with a large surface area for your enzymes to work on. It mixes your food with your digestive juices so that the enzymes come into contact with as much of the food as possible. The muscles of the gut move your food along from one area to the next.

Digesting carbohydrates

Enzymes that break down carbohydrates are called carbohydrases. Starch is one of the most common carbohydrates that you eat. It is broken down into sugars in your mouth and small intestine. This reaction is catalysed by an enzyme called **amylase**.

Amylase is produced in your salivary glands, so the digestion of starch starts in your mouth. Amylase is also made in the pancreas and the small intestine. No digestion takes place inside the pancreas. All the enzymes made there flow into your small intestine, where most of the starch you eat is digested.

Figure 1 Scientists produce artificial fistulas in animals such as cows so they can investigate the process of digestion in more detail. The cows lead a relatively normal life, eating, calving and being milked as usual.

Digesting proteins

The breakdown of protein foods such as meat, fish and cheese into amino acids is catalysed by protease enzymes. Proteases are produced by your stomach, your pancreas and your small intestine. The breakdown of proteins into **amino acids** takes place in your stomach and small intestine.

Digesting fats

The lipids (fats and oils) that you eat are broken down into **fatty acids** and **glycerol** in the small intestine. The reaction is catalysed by **lipase** enzymes, which are made in your pancreas and your small intestine. Again, the enzymes made in the pancreas are passed into the small intestine.

Once your food molecules have been completely digested into soluble glucose, amino acids, fatty acids and glycerol, they leave your small intestine. They pass into your bloodstream to be carried around the body to the cells that need them.

Examiner's tip

Learn three examples of digestive enzyme reactions.

Amylase   Starch → sugars

Protease Protein → amino acids

Lipase   Lipids → fatty acids + glycerol

Practical

Investigating digestion

You can make a model gut using a special bag containing starch and amylase enzymes. When the enzyme has catalysed the breakdown of the starch, you can no longer detect the presence of starch inside the 'gut'.

● How can you test for starch?

Smaller molecules of sugar diffuse out of the gut. Test the water in the beaker for (reducing) sugar.

● How can you test for this?

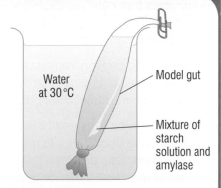

Water at 30 °C

Model gut

Mixture of starch solution and amylase

Figure 2 This apparatus provides you with a model of the gut. You can use it to investigate the effects of factors such as temperature and pH on how the gut enzymes work.

Key points

● Digestion involves the breakdown of large insoluble molecules into soluble substances that can be absorbed into the blood across the wall of the small intestine.

● Digestive enzymes are produced by specialised cells in glands and in the lining of the gut.

● Carbohydrases such as amylase catalyse the breakdown of carbohydrates such as starch to sugars.

● Proteases catalyse the breakdown of proteins to amino acids.

● Lipases catalyse the breakdown of lipids to fatty acids and glycerol.

Summary questions

1 Make a table that describes amylase, protease and lipase. For each enzyme, show where it is made, which reaction it catalyses and where it works in the gut.

2 Why is digestion of food so important? Explain your answer in terms of the molecules involved.

B5.7 Making digestion efficient

Learning objectives

After this topic, you should know:

- the roles of hydrochloric acid and bile in making digestion more efficient.

Practical

Breaking down protein

You can see the effect of acid on pepsin (the protease found in the stomach), quite simply. Set up three test tubes: one containing pepsin, one containing hydrochloric acid, and one containing a mixture of the two. Keep them at body temperature in a water bath. Add a similar-sized chunk of meat to all three of them. Set up a webcam and watch for a few hours to see what happens.

- What conclusions can you make?

Figure 1 These test tubes show clearly the importance of protein-digesting enzymes and hydrochloric acid in your stomach. Meat was added to each tube at the same time.

Safety: Wear eye protection (if HCl is stronger than 6.5 M then chemical splash proof eye protection would be needed).

Your digestive system produces many enzymes that speed up the breakdown of the food you eat. As your body is kept at a fairly steady 37 °C, your enzymes have an optimum temperature that allows them to work as fast as possible.

Keeping the pH in your gut at optimum levels isn't that easy, because different enzymes work best at different pH levels. For example, the protease enzyme found in your stomach works best in acidic conditions, while the proteases made in your pancreas need alkaline conditions to work at their best. So, your body makes a variety of different chemicals that help to keep conditions ideal for your enzymes all the way through your gut.

Changing pH in the gut

You have around 35 million glands in the lining of your stomach. These secrete pepsin, a protease enzyme, to digest the protein you eat. Pepsin works best in an acidic pH. So, your stomach also produces a relatively concentrated solution of hydrochloric acid from the same glands. In fact, your stomach produces around 3 litres of hydrochloric acid a day! This acid allows your stomach protease enzymes to work very effectively. It also kills most of the bacteria that you take in with your food.

Finally, your stomach also produces a thick layer of mucus. This coats your stomach walls and protects them from being digested by the acid and the enzymes

After a few hours – depending on the size and type of the meal you have eaten – your food leaves your stomach. It moves on into your small intestine. Some of the enzymes that catalyse digestion in your small intestine are made in your pancreas. Some are also made in the small intestine itself. They all work best in an alkaline environment.

The acidic liquid coming from your stomach needs to become an alkaline mix in your small intestine. In order that this can happen, your liver makes greeny-yellow alkaline liquid called **bile**. Bile is stored in your gall bladder until it is needed.

As food comes into the small intestine from the stomach, bile is squirted onto it through the bile duct. The bile neutralises the acid that was added to the food in the stomach. This provides the alkaline conditions necessary for the enzymes in the small intestine to work most effectively.

Altering the surface area

It is very important for the enzymes of the gut to have the largest possible surface area of food to work on. This is not a problem with carbohydrates and proteins. However, the fats that you eat do not mix with all the watery liquids in your gut. They stay as large globules (like oil in water) that make it difficult for the lipase enzymes to act.

This is the second important function of the bile: it **emulsifies** the fats in your food. This means bile physically breaks up large drops of fat into smaller droplets. This provides a much bigger surface area of fats for the lipase enzymes to act upon. The larger surface area helps the lipase chemically break down the fats more quickly into fatty acids and glycerol.

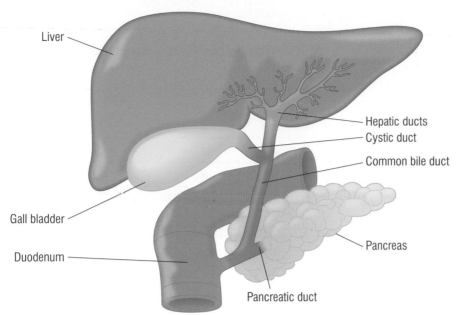

Liver

Hepatic ducts

Cystic duct

Common bile duct

Gall bladder

Pancreas

Duodenum

Pancreatic duct

Figure 2 Bile drains down small bile ducts in the liver. Most of it is stored in the gall bladder until it is needed.

Sometimes gall stones form and they can block the gall bladder and bile ducts. The stones can range from a few millimetres to several centimetres in diameter and can cause terrible pain. They can also stop bile being released onto the food and reduce the efficiency of digestion.

Figure 3 Gall stones can be very large and can cause extreme pain

Summary questions

1 Look at Figure 1 opposite and Figure 3 on page 39.
   a In what conditions does the protease from the stomach work best?
   b How does your body create the right pH in the stomach for this enzyme?
   c In what conditions do the proteases in the small intestine work best?
   d How does your body create the right pH in the small intestine for this enzyme?

2 Draw a diagram to explain how bile produces a big surface area for lipase to work on and explain why this is important.

3 Use everything you have learned about digestion to describe the passage of a meal containing bread, butter and egg through your digestive system from beginning to end.

Summary questions

1 Here are descriptions of three heart problems. In each case, use what you know about the heart and the circulatory system to explain the problems caused by the condition.

a The valve that stops blood flowing back into the left ventricle of the heart after it has been pumped into the aorta becomes weak and floppy and begins to leak.

b Some babies are born with a 'hole in the heart' – there is a gap in the central dividing wall of the heart. They may look blue in colour and have very little energy.

c The coronary arteries supplying blood to the heart muscle itself may become clogged with fatty material. The person affected may get chest pain when they exercise or even have a heart attack.

2 In each of the following examples, explain the effect on the blood and what this means to the person involved:

a an athlete goes and gives blood before running a race

b someone eats a diet low in iron.

3 If a patient has a blocked blood vessel, doctors may be able to open up the blocked vessels with a stent or replace the clogged up blood vessels with bits of healthy blood vessels taken from other parts of the patient's body.

Figure 1 shows you the results of these procedures in one group of patients after one year.

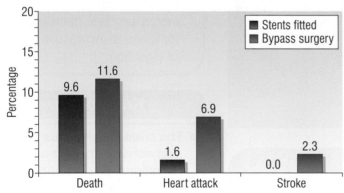

Figure 1

a What is a stent and how does it work?

b Which technique does the evidence suggest is the most successful for treating blocked coronary arteries? Explain your answer.

c What additional information would you need to decide whether this evidence was repeatable, reproducible and valid?

4 The following table shows the compatibility of ABO blood groups.

Donor	Recipient			
	A	**B**	**AB**	**O**
A	✓	✗	✓	✗
B	✗	✓	✓	✗
AB	✗	✗	✓	✗
O	✓	✓	✓	✓

a What is meant by compatibility of blood groups?

b Explain carefully the importance of blood group compatibility in:
i blood transfusions
ii organ transplants
and why in some ways compatibility can be more important in a blood transfusion than in an organ transplant.

5 Students investigated two protease enzymes, A and B. They added samples of A and B to test tubes containing solutions at a range of pH values. After 20 minutes they tested the activity of protease enzyme in each test tube.

The table shows their results.

pH of solution in test tube	2	4	6	8	10	12
Activity of enzyme A in arbitrary units	0	0	12	32	24	8
Activity of enzyme B In arbitrary units	26	20	6	0	0	0

a Name **two** variables that the students should have controlled in this investigation. (2)

b Give **one** way in which the students could have made this investigation more reliable. (1)

c What conclusions can the students make from these results about the enzymes A and B? (2)

d The students are told that the two enzymes are pepsin produced in the stomach and trypsin produced by the pancreas.

Suggest which letter represents pepsin and which letter represents trypsin. Give reasons for your answer. (4)

AQA Examination-style questions

1 Figure 1 shows a vertical section through the heart.

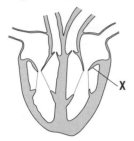

Figure 1

a Use words from the box to complete the sentences

aorta   left atrium   pulmonary artery   pulmonary vein   right atrium   vena cava

  i Blood returning from the body enters the .... of the heart.

  ii The heart pumps blood to the lungs via the ....

  iii Blood returns from the lungs to the heart via the

  ....

  iv The heart pumps blood to the rest of the body via the ....   (4)

b What is the function of the structure labelled **X** on the diagram?   (1)

c Patients with an irregular heartbeat may be fitted with a pacemaker.

Figure 2 shows an early type of pacemaker.

Figure 3 shows an X-ray of a modern pacemaker inserted under the skin of the thorax.

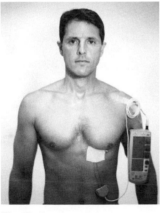

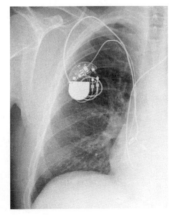

Figure 2   **Figure 3**

Suggest **two** advantages and **two** disadvantages of the modern pacemaker compared with the early type pacemaker.   (4)

2 Blood contains plasma, red blood cells, white blood cells and platelets.

a State the function of white blood cells.   (1)

b Give the function of platelets.   (1)

c Describe how oxygen is moved from the lungs to the tissues.   (3)

d Plasma transports dissolved substances from one part of the body to another. Name **two** of these substances. Explain where they are transported and why.   (4)

3 In organ transplants and blood transfusions, it is important to match the antigens on the donor's cells to the patient's cells.

a What is an antigen?   (1)

b Describe the **two** things that will be done to reduce the likelihood of a new organ being rejected after transplanting.   (2)

c A girl with blood group A requires an emergency blood transfusion after an accident. Name the blood groups that could be given to her safely and explain why.   (4)

4 Figure 4 shows the digestive system.

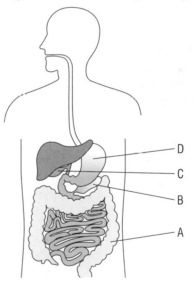

Figure 4

a **i** Name the parts A, B, C and D.   (4)

    ii Use the letters A, B, C and D from the diagram to complete the follow sentences.
Part .... churns the food by muscular action.
Fats are emulsified by bile from part ....
Protease enzymes are produced by parts .... and

    ....
Water is reabsorbed in part ....   (5)

b *In this question you will be assessed on using good English, organising information clearly and using specialist terms where appropriate.*

Describe the role of digestive enzymes in breaking down large insoluble food molecules into small soluble molecules that can be absorbed.   (QWC) (6)

Responding to change and receptors

After this topic, you should know:

- why you need a nervous system

- how receptors enable you to respond to changes in your surroundings.

Figure 1 Your body is made up of millions of cells that have to work together. Whatever you do with your body, whether it's walking to school or playing on the computer, your movements need to be coordinated.

You need to know what is going on in the world around you. Your **nervous system** makes this possible. It enables you to react to your surroundings and coordinate your behaviour.

Your nervous system carries electrical signals (**impulses**) that travel fast – between 1 and 120 metres per second. This means you can react to changes in your surroundings very quickly.

The nervous system

As with all living things, you need to avoid danger, find food and, eventually, find a mate! This is where your nervous system comes into its own. Your body is particularly sensitive to changes in the world around you. Any changes (known as **stimuli**) are picked up by cells called **receptors**.

Receptor cells, such as the light receptor cells in your eyes, are similar to most animal cells. They have a nucleus, cytoplasm and a cell membrane. These receptors are usually found clustered together in special **sense organs**, such as your eyes and your skin. You have many different types of sensory receptor (see Figure 2).

?? Did you know ... ?

Some male moths have receptors so sensitive they can detect the scent of a female several kilometres away and follow the scent trail to find her!

Figure 2 This fennec fox relies on its sensory receptors to detect changes in the environment

How your nervous system works

Once a sensory receptor detects a stimulus, the information (sent as an electrical impulse) passes along special cells called **neurones**. These are usually found in bundles of hundreds or even thousands of neurones known as **nerves**.

The impulse travels along the neurone until it reaches the **central nervous system**, or CNS. The CNS is made up of the brain and the spinal cord. The cells that carry impulses from your sense organs to your central nervous system are called **sensory neurones**.

Your brain gets huge amounts of information from all the sensory receptors in your body. It coordinates the response to the information, and sends impulses out along special cells. These cells, called **motor neurones**, carry information from the CNS to the rest of your body. They carry impulses to make the right bits of your body – the **effector organs** – respond.

Effector organs are muscles or glands. Your muscles respond to the arrival of impulses by contracting. Your glands respond by releasing (secreting) chemical substances, for example your salivary glands produce and release extra saliva when you smell food cooking.

The way your nervous system works can be summed up as:

receptor → **sensory neurone** → **coordinator (CNS)** → **motor neurone** → effector

Sensory nerves carry impulses to the CNS.
The information is processed and impulses are
sent out along motor nerves to produce an action.

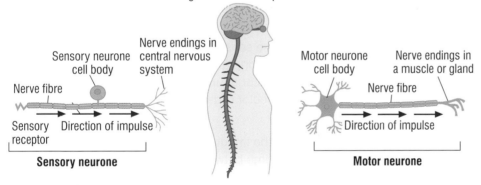

Figure 3 The rapid responses of our nervous system allow us to respond to our surroundings quickly – and in the right way!

Summary questions

1 **a** What is the main function of the nervous system?
  b What is the difference between a neurone and a nerve?
  c What is the difference between a sensory neurone and a motor neurone?

2 Make a table to show the different types of sense receptor. For each one, give an example of the sort of things it responds to, for instance touch receptors respond to an insect crawling on your skin.

3 Explain what happens in your nervous system when you see a piece of fruit, pick it up and eat it.

Key points

- The nervous system uses electrical impulses to enable you to react quickly to your surroundings and coordinate what you do.

- Cells called receptors detect stimuli (changes in the environment).

- Impulses from receptors pass along sensory neurones to the brain or spinal cord (CNS). The brain coordinates the response, and impulses are sent along motor neurones from the brain (CNS) to the effector organs.

B6.2

Reflex actions

Learning objectives

After this topic, you should know:

● what reflexes are

● why reflexes are important in your body.

Practical

The stick-drop test

A couple of ways in which you can investigate how quickly nerve impulses travel in your body are:

● using either stop clocks or ICT to measure how quickly you catch a metre rule

● standing in a circle holding hands with your eyes closed and measuring how long it takes a hand squeeze to pass around the circle.

Examiner's tip

Make sure you are clear about the link between 'motor' and movement. Motor neurones stimulate the muscles to contract.

Think 'motor cars move'!

Your nervous system lets you take in information from your surroundings and respond in the right way. However, some of your responses are so fast that they happen without giving you time to think.

When you touch something hot, or sharp, you pull your hand back before you feel the pain. If something comes near your face, you blink. Automatic responses like these are known as **reflexes**.

What are reflexes for?

Reflexes are very important both for human beings and for other animals. They help you to avoid danger or harm because they happen so fast. There are also lots of reflexes that take care of your basic body functions. These functions include breathing and moving food through your gut.

Reflexes do not involve the conscious areas of your brain. It would make life very difficult if you had to think consciously about those things all the time – and it would be fatal if you forgot to breathe!

How do reflexes work?

Reflex actions often involve just three types of neurone. These are:

● sensory neurones

● motor neurones

● relay neurones – these connect a sensory neurone and a motor neurone, and are found in the CNS.

An electrical impulse passes from the sensory receptor along the sensory neurone to the CNS. It then passes along a relay neurone (usually in the spinal cord) and straight back along the motor neurone. From there, the impulse arrives at the effector organ. The effector organ will be a muscle or a gland. We call this a **reflex arc**.

The key point in a reflex arc is that the impulse bypasses the conscious areas of your brain. The result is that the time between the stimulus and the reflex action is as short as possible.

How synapses work

Your neurones are not joined up directly to each other. There are junctions between them called **synapses** which form physical gaps between the neurones. The electrical impulses travelling along your neurones have to cross these synapses. They cannot leap the gap. Look at Figure 1 to see what happens next.

The reflex arc in detail

Look at Figure 2. It shows what would happen if you touched a hot object.

● When you touch the object, a receptor in your skin is stimulated. An electrical impulse from a receptor passes along a sensory neurone to the central nervous system – in this case, the spinal cord.

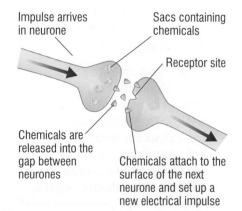

Impulse arrives in neurone

Sacs containing chemicals

Receptor site

Chemicals are released into the gap between neurones

Chemicals attach to the surface of the next neurone and set up a new electrical impulse

Figure 1 When an impulse arrives at the junction between two neurones, chemicals called neurotransmitters are released that cross the synapse and arrive at receptor sites on the next neurone. This starts up a new electrical impulse in the next neurone.

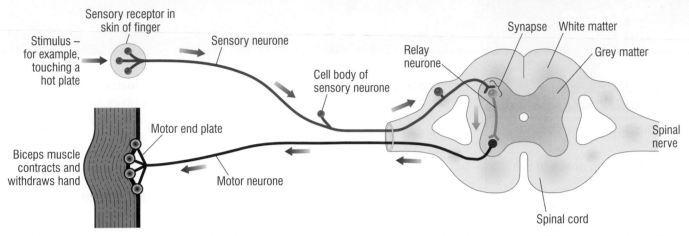

Figure 2 The reflex action that moves your hand away from something hot can save you from being burned. Reflex actions are quick and automatic; you do not think about them.

- When an impulse from the sensory neurone arrives at the synapse with a relay neurone, a neurotransmitter is released which acts as a chemical messenger. This chemical crosses the synapse to the relay neurone where it sets off a new electrical impulse that travels along the relay neurone. The diffusion of the neurotransmitter across the synapse is slower than the electrical impulse in the neurones, but it makes it possible for the impulse to cross the gap between them.

- When the impulse reaches the synapse between the relay neurone and a motor neurone returning to the arm, another neurotransmitter is released. Again, the chemical crosses the synapse and starts a new electrical impulse travelling down the motor neurone to the effector. When the impulse reaches the effector organ, it is stimulated to respond. In this example, the impulses arrive in the muscles of the arm, causing them to contract. This action moves the hand rapidly away from the source of pain. If the effector organ is a gland, it will respond by releasing (secreting) chemical substances.

The reflex pathway is not very different from a normal conscious action. However, in a reflex action the coordinator is a relay neurone either in the spinal cord or in the unconscious areas of the brain. The whole reflex is very fast indeed.

An impulse also travels up the spinal cord to the conscious areas of your brain. You know about the reflex action, but only after it has happened.

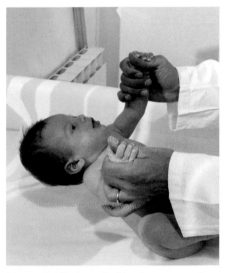

Figure 3 Newborn babies have a number of special reflexes that disappear as they grow. This grasp reflex is one of them.

Examiner's tip

Learn the reflex pathway off by heart.

Stimulus → receptor → sensory neurone → relay neurone → motor neurone → effector → response.

Summary questions

1 a Why are reflexes important?
   b Why is it important that reflexes don't go to the conscious areas of your brain?

2 Explain why some actions such as breathing and swallowing are reflex actions, while others such as speaking and eating are under your conscious control.

3 Draw a flowchart to explain what happens when you step on a pin. Make sure you include an explanation of how a synapse works.

Key points

- Some responses to stimuli are automatic and rapid and are called 'reflex actions'. They involve sensory, relay and motor neurones.

- Reflex actions control everyday bodily functions, such as breathing and digestion, and help you to avoid danger.

- There are gaps between neurones called synapses. The release of chemicals into the synapse allows the impulse to cross from one neurone to another.

B6.3

The brain

Learning objectives

After this topic, you should know:

- what the main areas of the brain do

- how scientists find out about the structure and functions of the brain.

∞ **links**

You can find out more about the pituitary gland and one of the hormones it produces in 7.3 'The human kidney'.

You can learn more about thermoregulation in 7.6 'Controlling body temperature'.

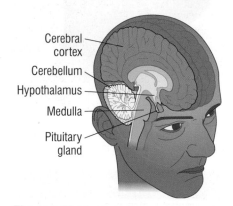

Cerebral cortex
Cerebellum
Hypothalamus
Medulla
Pituitary gland

Figure 1 The brain is very complex and coordinates and controls much of our behaviour

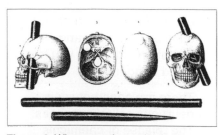

Figure 2 When people survive brain injuries, such as the terrible damage done to the skull of Phineas Gage, this gives scientists and doctors an insight into the function of the damaged areas of the brain

Information from sensory receptors all over your body feeds into your brain. In the brain this information is processed and then impulses are sent out along the motor nerves that coordinate your responses to all the different situations you meet. Your brain doesn't simply control simple actions, such as reaching out to pick up a book or walking along the corridor. It also controls complex behaviour and is responsible for your thoughts and feelings.

Scientists are finding out more about the brain all the time, but it is still in many ways a mystery.

The structure of the brain

Your brain is kept protected inside the bones of your skull, and is encased in membranes called the meninges.

 Did you know … ?

It is the meninges membranes that become infected and inflamed if you have meningitis.

The brain itself has a texture rather like set yoghurt. It is made up of millions of interconnected neurones, which are arranged to form different regions. The different regions of the brain carry out different functions. For example:

- The **cerebral cortex** is concerned with consciousness, intelligence, memory and language.
- The **cerebellum** is concerned mainly with coordinating muscular activity and balance.
- The **medulla** is concerned with unconscious activities, such as controlling the heartbeat, the movements of the gut and breathing.
- The **hypothalamus** is involved in the regulation of many body functions, such as thermoregulation.
- The **pituitary gland** produces chemical messages called **hormones** which control lots of reactions in the body.

Finding out about the brain

Since the brain is inside the skull, it has not been easy to find out exactly how a living brain works. Scientists have been able to map the regions of the brain and link different regions to particular functions using a number of different techniques.

Studying people with brain damage

Over many years, it has been possible to discover the role of different areas of the brain when people suffer from brain damage.

One dramatic example is that of Phineas Gage. When he was 25 years old, an explosives accident blew a piece of iron over a metre long and about 3 cm in diameter through his skull. The metal entered his skull through his left cheekbone and exited out the top of his head. Although he survived for the next 13 years, Gage's personality and behaviour changed drastically.

He had been hard working, reliable and polite, but became wild, unreliable and abusive, almost unrecognisable from the man he had been. It has subsequently been found that parts of Gage's cerebral cortex had been blown away, including the area that controls social inhibitions.

Electrically stimulating different parts of the brain

If scientists expose the brain by removing the top of the skull, they can stimulate different areas and see what effect this has. This type of work has been done on animals and on people during brain surgery (because there are no sensory nerve endings in the brain, brain surgery is usually done on conscious patients). So, for example, scientists have shown that there is an area of the brain associated with thirst – if it is stimulated, an animal will drink even if it is well hydrated. In the same way, human patients can experience hunger, anger, fear, thirst and other sensations simply because the relevant area of their brain is stimulated.

MRI scans

In recent years, scientists have been able to develop a much better understanding of how the brain works as a result of new ways of taking images of the brain in living people. For example, if someone develops a tumour in their brain, or has a stroke, this will affect their behaviour. An MRI (magnetic resonance imaging) scan will show exactly which area of the brain is affected. This enables scientists to link the loss of a certain function, such as speech or control of movement on one side of the body, with damage to a particular region of the brain.

The most recent MRI scanners can take images as someone carries out a simple task. For example, scientists can **monitor** which areas of the brain are active when you look at pictures of people you know compared with pictures of strangers.

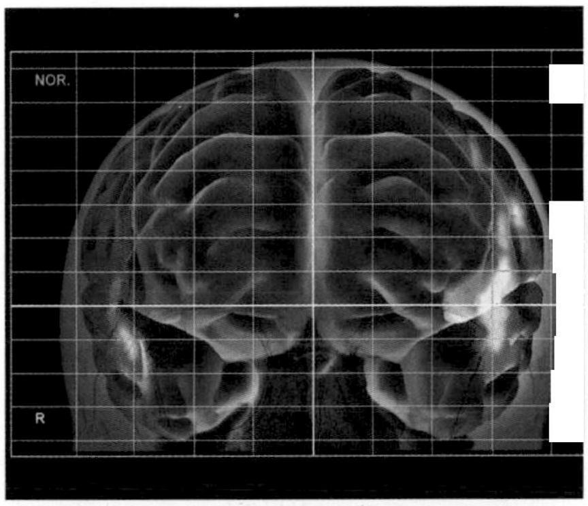

Figure 3 This special MRI scan shows the areas of your brain that are active as you are reading, so these areas of your cerebral cortex are working right now!

Examiner's tip

Remember what each part of the brain controls:
- Cerebral cortex – memory and thought
- Cerebellum – movement
- Medulla – heartbeat and breathing.

Summary questions

1 a What is the brain made of?
  b Why is the brain so important?

2 a The cerebral cortex, the cerebellum and the medulla are regions of the brain that each have very different functions. Explain the functions of each of these brain regions.
  b The cerebral cortex is bigger in animals such as apes than it is in mice and rats. It is even bigger in human beings. Suggest why these differences are seen.

3 Describe three ways in which scientists can find out about the functions of the different areas of the brain. Discuss the usefulness of each of them.

Key points

- The brain is made of billions of interconnected neurones that control complex behaviour.
- It has different regions, for example the cerebral cortex, the cerebellum and the medulla, that each have different functions.
- Scientists map regions of the brain to their functions by studying patients with brain damage, by electrically stimulating different areas of the brain and by using MRI scanning techniques.

Summary questions

1 This question is about animal responses. Match up the beginnings and ends of the sentences:

a Many processes in the body …	**A** … effector organs.
b The nervous system allows you …	**B** … secreted by glands.
c The cells which are sensitive to light …	**C** … to react to your surroundings and coordinate your behaviour.
d Hormones are chemical substances …	**D** … are found in the eyes.
e Muscles and glands are known as …	**E** … are known as nerves.
f Bundles of neurones …	**F** … are controlled by hormones.

2 a What is the job of your nervous system?

b Where in your body would you find nervous receptors which respond to:

i light? **ii** sound? **iii** heat? **iv** touch?

c Draw and label a simple diagram of a reflex arc. Explain carefully how a reflex arc works and why it allows you to respond quickly to danger.

3

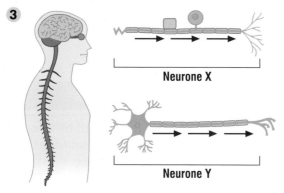

Figure 1

a What is the difference between neurone X and neurone Y?

b What is the difference between a neurone and a nerve?

c Draw and label a synapse.

d Describe how a nerve impulse passes across a synapse and explain their importance in the nervous system.

4

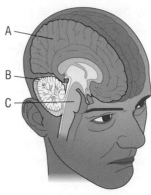

Figure 2

a A patient who suffered an injury to region C of their brain in an accident died. Explain why this damage was fatal.

b A patient had a disease that destroyed part of brain area B. Describe what symptoms you might expect this person to show and explain why.

c If a patient suffers an injury to area A of their brain, it is not easy to predict what effect this will have on them. Explain why.

5 Scientists could initially only map regions of the brain using brains taken from dead bodies. The first MRI scans took images of the brain at a given moment when the patient was lying still within the MRI scanner. Modern MRI technology allows images to be taken of the brain as it carries out particular tasks.

Explain how each of these techniques has helped scientists to understand how the brain works.

AQA Examination-style questions

1 The diagram shows a vertical section through the head, showing the brain.

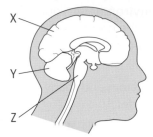

a Use words from the box to name the structures labelled **X**, **Y** and **Z** on the diagram.

> *cerebral cortex   cerebellum   medulla*
> *spinal cord   synapse*

X ....

Y ....

Z .... (3)

b One method of mapping brain function is to observe changes in body functions following a stroke.
  i Give two other methods of mapping brain function.
  1 ....
  2 .... (2)
  ii Give one way in which disruption of the blood supply to part **Y** might affect the functioning of the body. (1)

2 A man touches a hot saucepan and immediately his hand pulls away as a reflex action.

a Complete the pathway below showing a reflex action.

stimulus → .... → sensory neurone → .... →
.... → effector → .... (4)

b Name the stimulus and effector in this reflex action.

Stimulus: ....   Effector: .... (2)

c The impulse is transferred from one neurone to the next across a synapse.
  i Describe how the electrical impulse in a neurone is passed across a synapse. (2)
  ii Where in the nervous system are synapses located? (1)

d The nerve pathway from the hand to the spinal cord and back to the effector is 1.2 metres long. The time it takes for the impulse to reach the effector is 0.02 seconds. Calculate the speed of the impulse. (2)

3 A group of students were investigating the knee jerk reflex. They wanted to find out how the speed of the hammer affected the distance the lower leg moved.

The diagram shows how the experiment was set up.

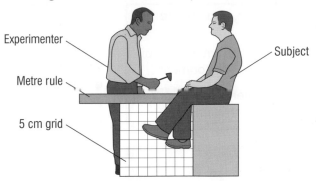

Each trial was recorded on a video. A frame was taken every 33 milliseconds. The video was then played using single-frame advance. The number of frames for the hammer to move to the knee was found. The faster the speed, the smaller was the number of frames. The video was also used to find the distance moved by the toe.

In each trial, the experimenter held the hammer 20 cm from the subject's knee and then hit the subject's tendon. For each trial the experimenter used the hammer at a different speed.

The table shows some of the results.

Trial number	1	2	3	4	5	6	7	8	9	10
Distance hammer moved to knee in cm	20	20	20	20	20	20	20	20	20	20
Number of frames it took the hammer to move to the knee	15	14	12	10	9	8	7	6	2	2
Distance moved by toe in cm	0	0	5	5	4	10	10	10	10	10

a From the table, identify the independent variable, the dependent variable and a control variable. (3)

b Give **two** advantages of using a video to make the measurements. (2)

c Suggest how the accuracy of this experiment could have been improved. (1)

d Draw a conclusion from the results of the experiment. (2)

B7.1   Principles of homeostasis

Figure 1 Everything you do from eating a meal to running a marathon affects your internal environment

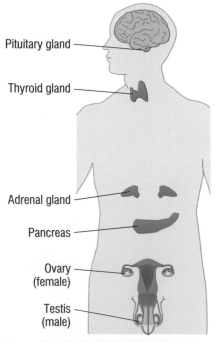

Pituitary gland

Thyroid gland

Adrenal gland

Pancreas

Ovary (female)

Testis (male)

Figure 2 Hormones act as chemical messages. They are made in glands in one part of the body, but have an effect somewhere else.

The conditions inside your body are known as its **internal environment**. Your organs cannot work properly if this keeps changing. Many of the processes that go on inside your body aim to keep everything as constant as possible. This balancing act is called **homeostasis**.

Homeostasis involves your nervous system, your hormone system and many of your body organs. Internal conditions that are controlled include:

- temperature
- the water content of the body
- the ion content of the body
- blood glucose levels.

⃝⃝ links

For more information on the nervous system, including control systems and receptors, look back to 6.1 'Responding to change and receptors'.

How hormones work

Hormones are chemical substances that coordinate many body processes. Special endocrine glands make and secrete (release) these hormones into your blood. The hormones are then carried around your body to their target organs in the bloodstream. Hormones regulate the functions of many organs and cells. They can act very quickly, but often their effects are quite slow and long lasting. A number of hormones are important in the processes of homeostasis.

Controlling water and ions

Water moves in and out of your body cells by osmosis. How much it moves depends on the concentration of mineral ions (such as those in salt) and the amount of water in your body. If too much water moves into or out of your cells, they can be damaged or destroyed.

⃝⃝ links

You can find out more about osmosis in 1.5 'Osmosis'.

You take water and minerals into your body as you eat and drink. You lose water as you breathe out, and in your sweat. You lose salt in your sweat as well. You also lose water and salt in your urine, which is made in your **kidneys**.

Your kidneys can change the amount of salt and water lost in your urine, depending on your body conditions. They help to control the balance of water and mineral ions in your body. The concentration of the urine produced by your kidneys is controlled by both nerves and hormones.

So, for example, imagine drinking a lot of water all in one go. Your kidneys will remove the extra water from your blood and you will produce lots of very pale urine.

Controlling temperature

It is vital that your deep **core body temperature** is kept at 37 °C. At this temperature, your enzymes work best. At only a few degrees above or below normal body temperature, the reactions in your cells no longer work at the ideal speed and you may die.

Your body controls your temperature in several ways. For example, you can sweat to cool down and shiver to warm up. Sweating causes the body to cool down because energy from the body is used to evaporate the water in sweat. Your nervous system is essential in coordinating the way your body responds to changes in temperature.

Once your body temperature drops below 35 °C, you are at risk of dying from **hypothermia**. Several hundred old people die from the effects of cold each year, as do a number of young people who get lost on mountains or try to walk home in the snow after a night out.

If your body temperature goes above about 40–42 °C, your enzymes and cells don't work properly. This means that you may die of heat stroke or heat exhaustion.

Figure 3 You can change your behaviour to help control your temperature, for example by adding extra clothing or turning up the heating when it's really cold, or wearing less or lighter clothing when it is hot

> ### Examiner's tip
>
> Sweating affects both temperature AND water content of the body.
> It cools the body by using heat energy from the skin to evaporate the water.

Controlling blood sugar

When you digest a meal, lots of glucose (simple sugar) passes into your blood. Left alone, your blood glucose levels would keep changing. The levels would be very high straight after a meal, but very low again a few hours later. This would cause chaos in your body.

However, the concentration of glucose in your blood is kept constant by hormones made in your pancreas. This means your body cells are provided with the constant supply of energy that they need.

Summary questions

1 **a** Define a hormone.
   b How does coordination and control by hormones differ from coordination and control by the nervous system?

2 Why is it important to control:
   a water levels in the body?
   b the body temperature?
   c glucose (sugar) levels in the blood?

3 **a** Look at the marathon runners in Figure 1. List the ways in which running is affecting their:
   i water balance
   ii ion balance
   iii temperature.
   b It is much harder to run a marathon in a costume than in running clothes. Explain why this is.

Key points

- Homeostasis is the process by which automatic control systems, including your nervous system, your hormones and your body organs, maintain almost constant conditions.

- Homeostasis is important because the body cells need almost constant conditions to work properly.

- Humans need to maintain a constant internal environment, controlling levels of water, ions and blood glucose as well as temperature.

B7.2

Removing waste products

For your body to work properly, the conditions surrounding your millions of cells must stay as constant as possible. On the other hand, almost everything you do tends to change things. For example:

- as you move you produce energy that warms the body
- as you respire you produce waste
- when you digest food you take millions of molecules into your body.

Yet somehow you keep your internal conditions constant within a very narrow range through homeostasis. Many of the functions in your body help to keep your internal environment as constant as possible. Now you are going to find out more about some of them.

Figure 1 The internal conditions of the human body hardly vary despite our surroundings

Removing waste products

No matter what you are doing, the cells of your body are constantly producing waste products. These are products of the chemical reactions that take place in the cells. The more extreme the conditions you put yourself in, the more waste products your cells make.

There are two main poisonous waste products – carbon dioxide and urea. They cause major problems for your body if their levels are allowed to build up.

Carbon dioxide

Carbon dioxide is produced during respiration. Every cell in your body respires, and so every cell produces carbon dioxide. It is vital that you remove this carbon dioxide because dissolved carbon dioxide produces an acidic solution. This would affect the working of all the enzymes in your cells.

The carbon dioxide moves out of the cells into your blood. Your bloodstream carries it back to your lungs. Almost all of the carbon dioxide is removed from your body via your lungs when you breathe out. The air you breathe in contains only 0.04% carbon dioxide. However, the air you breathe out contains about 4% carbon dioxide.

links

Find out more about the removal of carbon dioxide from the body in 4.1 'Breathing and gas exchange in the lungs'.

Urea

The other main waste product of your body is urea.

When you eat more protein than you need, or when body tissues are worn out, the extra protein has to be broken down. Amino acids cannot be used as fuel for your body. Your **liver** removes the amino group from the amino acids by a process called deamination. This forms ammonia, which is then converted into urea to be excreted.

The rest of the amino acid molecule can then be used in respiration or to make other molecules. The urea passes from the liver cells into your blood.

Urea is poisonous and if the levels build up in your blood, this will cause a lot of damage. Fortunately the urea is filtered out of your blood by your kidneys. It is then passed out of your body in your urine, along with any excess water and salt.

Functions of the liver

Your liver is a large reddish-brown organ that carries out many different functions in your body. Liver cells grow and regenerate themselves very rapidly. A number of the functions of the liver are involved in homeostasis, such as:

- deamination of excess amino acids to form urea (see above)
- detoxifying poisonous substances, such as the ethanol in alcoholic drinks, and passing the breakdown products into the blood so they can be excreted in the urine via the kidneys
- breaking down old, worn out red blood cells and storing the iron until it is needed to synthesise more red blood cells.

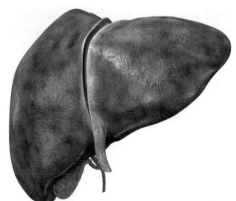

Figure 2 Your liver weighs about 1.5 kg and plays a vital role in removing poisons from your body

⬭ links

For information on osmosis, look back to 1.5 'Osmosis'.
For information on body temperature, see 7.6 'Controlling body temperature'.
For information on controlling glucose levels, see 7.7 'Controlling blood glucose'.

Did you know …?

The average person produces up to 900 litres of urine a year!

Examiner's tip

Don't confuse *urea* and *urine*. Urea is a waste molecule made in the liver, carried to the kidneys in the blood, and excreted in the urine.

Summary questions

1 There are two main waste products that have to be removed from the human body – carbon dioxide and urea. For each waste product, describe:
   a how it is formed
   b why it has to be removed
   c where it is removed from the body.

2 a What is urea?
   b Explain how the liver is involved in the production of urea.
   c Why is the liver sometimes described as an organ of homeostasis?

3 Draw a spider diagram with the word 'homeostasis' in the centre. Make as many links in the diagram as you can. Label the links made.

Key points

- Carbon dioxide is produced during respiration and leaves the body via the lungs when you breathe out.

- Urea is produced by your liver as excess amino acids are broken down, and is removed by your kidneys in the urine.

The human kidney

B7.3

Learning objectives

After this topic, you should know:

● why your kidneys are so important and how they work

● the importance of the hormone ADH in water balance.

Did you know ... ?

All the blood in your body passes through your kidneys about once every five minutes. Your kidneys filter about 180 litres of water out of your blood during the day. About 99% of it is returned straight back into your blood. So, on average, you produce about 1800 cm³ of urine a day. Urine trickles into your bladder where it is stored. When the bladder is full, you will feel the need to empty it. Water, glucose, urea and salt are all colourless, but your urine is yellow. This is the result of **urobilins** – yellow pigments that come from the breakdown of haemoglobin from old red blood cells in your liver. They are excreted by your kidneys in the urine along with everything else.

Examiner's tip

Understand that ALL small molecules are filtered in the kidney, but the useful ones such as glucose are reabsorbed. Only large molecules such as proteins cannot be filtered.

⚭ links

For information on diffusion, look back to 1.4 'Diffusion'.

For information on active transport, see 1.6 'Active transport'.

Your kidneys are one of the main organs that help to maintain homeostasis. They keep the conditions inside your body as constant as possible.

What are the functions of your kidneys?

Your kidneys are involved in excretion – the removal of waste products. They filter poisonous urea out of your blood. It is removed from the body in your urine, which is produced constantly by your kidneys and stored temporarily in your **bladder**. Your urine also contains excess mineral ions and water not needed by your body. The exact quantities vary depending on what you have taken in and given out.

The kidneys and water balance in the body

Your kidneys are also important for homeostasis in the water balance of your body. You gain water when you drink and eat. You lose water constantly from your lungs. The water evaporates into the air in your lungs and is breathed out. Whenever you exercise or get hot, you sweat more and lose more water.

So how do your kidneys balance all these changes? If you are short of water, your kidneys conserve it. You produce very little urine and most of the water is saved for use in your body. If you drink too much water then your kidneys produce lots of urine to get rid of the excess.

The ion concentration of your body is very important. You take in mineral ions with your food, so the amount you take in varies.

Some are lost through your skin when you sweat. Again, your kidneys are most important in keeping a mineral ion balance. They remove excess mineral ions and excrete them in your urine.

How do your kidneys work?

Your kidneys filter your blood. Glucose, mineral ions, urea and water all move out of your blood into the kidney tubules. They move by diffusion down a concentration gradient.

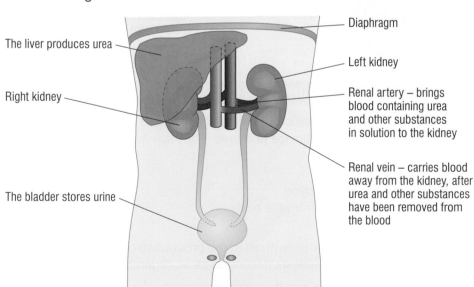

Figure 1 The kidney is a very important organ of homeostasis. It controls the balance of water and mineral ions in the body and gets rid of urea.

The blood cells and large molecules such as proteins are left behind. They are too big to pass through the membrane of the tubule.

All of the glucose is reabsorbed back into the blood by active transport. However, the amount of water and dissolved mineral ions that are reabsorbed varies. It depends on what is needed by your body. This is known as **selective reabsorption**. The amount of water reabsorbed into the blood is controlled by a very sensitive feedback mechanism (see below).

ADH and water balance

The amount of water in the blood is maintained at an almost constant level by a **negative feedback system** involving the hormone **ADH**. ADH is secreted by the pituitary gland in the brain.

Receptor cells in the brain detect the concentration of solutes in the blood plasma. If the blood becomes too concentrated, the pituitary gland releases lots of ADH into the blood. This affects the kidneys so they reabsorb much more water. This results in a relatively small volume of very concentrated urine and the concentration of solutes in the blood returns to normal levels.

On the other hand, if the solute concentration becomes too dilute, less ADH is released into the blood. Less water is reabsorbed in the kidneys, so you produce a large volume of dilute urine and the blood solute concentration returns back to normal.

Urea is lost in your urine. However, some of it leaves the kidney tubules and moves back into your blood. The urea moves back into the blood by diffusion down a concentration gradient.

On a hot day, if you drink little and exercise a lot, you will lose a lot of water in your sweat and produce very little urine. This will be concentrated and relatively dark yellow. On a cool day, if you drink a lot of liquid and do very little, you will produce a lot of dilute, almost colourless urine (see Figure 2).

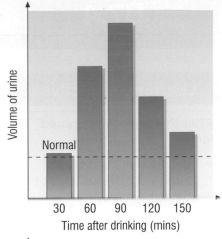

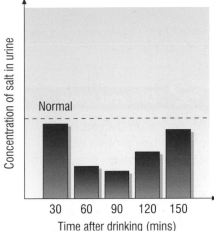

Figure 2 These data show how your kidneys respond when you drink a lot. They show the volume of urine produced and the concentration of salt in the urine after a student drank a large volume of water.

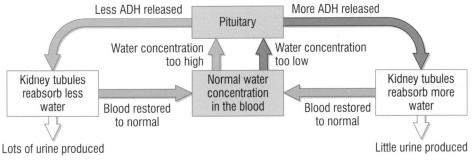

Figure 3 The concentration of the blood – and the amount of urine you produce – is controlled by the hormone ADH

Summary questions

1 a What is the function of the kidneys?
  b How do the kidneys carry out their job?

2 Why do your kidneys work hard after you have eaten a lot of processed food?

3 Explain how ADH stimulates your kidneys to maintain the water balance of your blood on:
  a a cool day when you stayed inside and drank lots of cups of tea
  b a hot sports day when you ran three races and had forgotten your drink bottle.

Key points

- The kidneys are important for excretion and homeostasis.

- A healthy kidney produces urine by filtering the blood. It then reabsorbs *all* of the glucose, plus any mineral ions and water needed by your body.

- Excess mineral ions and water, along with urea, are removed in the urine.

- The water balance of the blood is maintained by the hormone ADH, which changes the amount of water reabsorbed by the kidney.

B7.4 Dialysis – an artificial kidney

Learning objectives

After this topic, you should know:

- how dialysis can be used to carry out the function of damaged kidneys.

Your kidneys can be damaged and destroyed by infections. Some people have a genetic problem that means their kidneys fail. In others, the kidneys are damaged during an accident. Whatever the cause, untreated failure of both of your kidneys can lead to death. Toxins, such as urea, build up in the body and the salt and water balance of your body is not maintained, which can cause the cells to be damaged by osmosis.

Dialysis

For centuries, kidney failure meant certain death. Today, there are two effective methods of treating this problem:

- We can carry out the function of the kidney artificially using **dialysis**.
- We can replace the failed kidneys with a healthy one in a **kidney transplant**.

The machine that carries out the functions of the kidney is known as a **dialysis machine**. It relies on the process of dialysis to clean the blood. In a dialysis machine, a person's blood leaves their body and flows between partially permeable membranes. On the other side of these membranes is the dialysis fluid. The dialysis fluid contains the same concentration of useful substances as the blood of a healthy person.

If your kidneys don't work, the concentrations of urea and mineral ions build up in the blood. Treatment by dialysis restores the concentrations of these dissolved substances to normal levels. Then, as you carry on with normal life, urea and other waste substances build up again. So dialysis has to be repeated at regular intervals.

It takes around eight hours for dialysis to be complete. So people with kidney failure have to remain attached to a dialysis machine for hours several times a week. They also have to manage their diets carefully. This helps keep their blood chemistry as stable as possible so that they can lead a normal life between sessions.

??? Did you know ... ?

Someone on dialysis has to control their protein intake carefully between sessions to keep urea levels as low as possible. They also have to control the amount of salt they eat as their kidneys cannot get rid of any excess. However, for the first few hours of dialysis, they can eat what they like because the machine is balancing the water and salt levels of their blood.

How dialysis works

During dialysis, it is vital that patients lose the excess urea and mineral ions that have built up in the blood. It is equally important that they do not lose useful substances from their blood, such as glucose and some mineral ions.

The loss of these substances is prevented by the careful control of the dialysis fluid. The dialysis fluid contains the same concentration of glucose and mineral ions as the blood of a person without kidney disease. This ensures there is *no net* movement of glucose and useful mineral ions out of the blood. As the dialysis fluid contains normal plasma levels of mineral ions, any excess ions are removed from the blood. The excess ions move out by diffusion down a concentration gradient.

In contrast, the dialysis fluid contains no urea. This makes a steep concentration gradient from the blood to the fluid. As a result, much of the urea leaves the blood. The whole process of dialysis depends on diffusion down concentration gradients, which have to be maintained by the flow of fluid. There is no active transport.

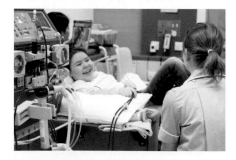

Figure 1 A dialysis machine. These 'artificial kidneys' not only save lots of lives, they allow sufferers from kidney failure to lead relatively full, active lives.

⊂⊃ links

For information on diffusion, look back to 1.4 'Diffusion'.

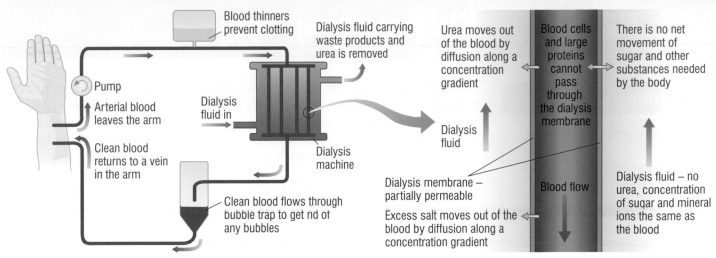

Figure 2 A dialysis machine relies on simple diffusion to clean the blood, removing the waste products that would damage the body as they build up

Many people go to hospital to receive dialysis. However, in 1964 home dialysis machines were made available for the first time. They are big and expensive but they enable some people to have dialysis at home. There is even a form of dialysis which takes place inside the body cavity, so the patient does not have to be connected to a machine while the dialysis takes place.

Dialysis has some disadvantages. You have to follow a very carefully controlled diet. You also have to spend regular, long sessions connected to a dialysis machine. You have only a relatively short time when the balance of chemicals in your blood is at the right level and so you may feel tired and unwell as the next dialysis session approaches. Over many years, the balance of substances in the blood can become more difficult to control, no matter how careful the dialysis. Even so, for many people with kidney failure, dialysis keeps them alive. Fortunately, in dialysis we have relatively successfully copied the action of the kidney in the body.

Summary questions

1 a Why is kidney failure such a threat to life?
  b On what process does dialysis depend?

2 Produce a flowchart to explain how a dialysis machine works.

3 a Why do people with kidney failure have to control their intake of protein and salt?
  b Why can patients with kidney failure eat and drink what they like during the first few hours of dialysis?

4 a Explain the importance of dialysis fluid containing no urea and normal plasma levels of salt, glucose and mineral ions.
  b Both blood and dialysis fluid are constantly circulated through the dialysis machine. Explain why the constant circulation of dialysis fluid is so important.

Examiner's tip

Look at as many different examples of dialysis diagrams as you can. Identify the membrane. Be clear about what diffuses through the membrane. What is in the dialysis fluid?

Key points

- People suffering from kidney failure may be treated by regular sessions on a kidney dialysis machine or by having a kidney transplant.

- In a dialysis machine, the concentration of dissolved substances in the blood is restored to normal levels.

- The levels of useful substances in the blood are maintained, while urea and excess mineral ions pass out from the blood into the dialysis fluid.

B7.5 Kidney transplants

Learning objectives

After this topic, you should know:

● what is involved in a kidney transplant

● how the problems of rejection can be solved.

⊂⊃ links

For information on antigens, see 8.3 'Immunity'.

Diseased kidneys can be replaced in a kidney transplant using a single healthy kidney from a donor. The donor kidney is joined to the blood vessels in the groin of the patient (the recipient). If all goes well, the donor kidney will function normally to clean and balance the blood. One kidney can balance your blood chemistry and remove your waste urea for a lifetime.

The rejection problem

The main problem with transplanting a kidney is that the new kidney comes from a different person. The antigens (proteins on the cell surface) of the donor organ will be different to those of the recipient (person who needs the new kidney). There is a risk that the antibodies of the immune system of the recipient will attack the antigens on the donor organ. This results in rejection and destruction of the donated kidney.

There are a number of ways of reducing the risk of rejection. The match between the antigens of the donor and the recipient is made as close as possible. For example, we can use a donor kidney with a 'tissue type' very similar to the recipient (from people with the same blood group).

The recipient is given drugs to suppress their **immune response** (immunosuppressant drugs) for the rest of their lives. This helps to prevent the rejection of their new organ. Immunosuppressant drugs are improving all the time. Nowadays the need for a really close tissue match is getting less important.

The disadvantage of taking immunosuppressant drugs is that they prevent the patients from dealing effectively with infectious diseases. This means they have to take great care if they become ill in any way. However, most people feel this is worth it for a new, working kidney.

Transplanted organs don't last forever. The average transplanted kidney works for around nine years, although some last much longer. Once the organ starts to fail, the patient has to return to dialysis. Then they have to wait until another suitable kidney is found.

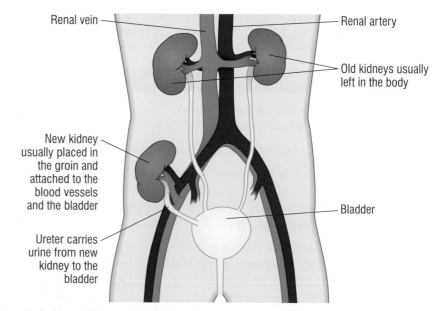

??? Did you know ... ?

In 2011, scientists grew functioning embryonic kidney tissue from stem cells. The hope is that in the future whole new kidneys can be grown – perhaps even without the antigens that trigger the immune reaction, so that patients don't even need to take immunosuppressant drugs.

Renal vein — Renal artery

Old kidneys usually left in the body

New kidney usually placed in the groin and attached to the blood vessels and the bladder

Bladder

Ureter carries urine from new kidney to the bladder

Figure 1 A donor kidney takes over the functions of failed kidneys, which are usually left in place

Dialysis or transplant?

Dialysis is much more readily available than donor organs, so it is there whenever kidneys fail. It enables people with kidney failure to lead a relatively normal life. However, you are tied to a special diet and regular sessions on the machine. Long-term dialysis is much more expensive than a transplant, and eventually dialysis causes serious damage to the body.

If you receive a kidney transplant, you are free from the restrictions that come with regular dialysis sessions. You can eat and drink what you want. An almost completely normal life is the dream of everyone waiting for a kidney transplant.

The disadvantages of transplants are mainly to do with the risk of rejection.

- You have to take medicine every day of your life in case the kidney is rejected. However, as better immunosuppressant drugs are developed, the dose and impact of these drugs is reduced.
- You also need regular check-ups to see if your body has started to reject the new organ.
- However, the biggest disadvantage is that you may never get the chance of a transplant at all.

The main source of kidneys is from people who die suddenly. The deaths are often from road accidents or from strokes and heart attacks. In the UK, organs can be taken from people if they carry an organ donor card or are on the online donor register. Alternatively, a relative of someone who has died suddenly can give their consent.

There are never enough donor kidneys to go around. Many of us do not register as donors. What's more, as cars become safer, fewer people die in traffic accidents. This is very good news, but it means there are fewer potential donors. At any one time there are thousands of people having kidney dialysis. Most would love to have a kidney transplant but never get the opportunity.

In 2008–9, 2497 people in the UK had kidney transplants. However, by the end of 2009 there were still almost 7000 people on dialysis waiting for a kidney. There are increasing numbers of live donor transplants, where a family member of someone with a tissue match donates a kidney.

links

For information on stem cell research, look back to 2.3 'Stem cells'.

Figure 2 This young person has been given a new lease of life by a kidney transplant. A lack of donors means not everyone who suffers from kidney failure is so lucky.

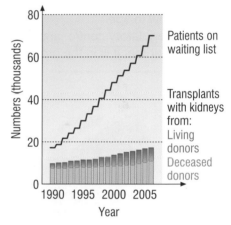

Figure 3 This graph shows how the gap between people needing a kidney and available organs is getting bigger in the USA, even with the increase in living donors. The same pattern is seen in most other countries, including the UK.

Summary questions

1. **a** How does someone with a kidney transplant overcome the problems of kidney failure?
   b There is one situation where there is no risk of rejection between the donor and the recipient. Suggest what that might be and explain how it works.

2. Sometimes a live donor – usually a close family member – will donate a kidney. These transplants have a higher rate of success than normal transplants from dead, unrelated donors.
   a Suggest two reasons why live transplants from a close family member have a higher success rate than normal transplants.
   b Why do you think that live donor transplants are relatively rare?

3. Produce a table to compare the advantages and disadvantages of treating kidney failure with dialysis or with a kidney transplant. Which treatment do you think is preferable and why?

Key points

- In a kidney transplant, a healthy kidney from a donor replaces the function of the diseased or damaged kidney.

- To try and prevent rejection of the donor kidney, the tissue types of the donor and the recipient are matched as closely as possible. Immunosuppressant drugs are also used.

B7.6 Controlling body temperature

Figure 1 People in different parts of the world live in conditions of extreme heat and extreme cold and still maintain a constant internal body temperature

Wherever you go and whatever you do, your body temperature needs to stay around 37 °C. This is the temperature at which your enzymes work best. Your skin temperature can vary enormously without problems. It is the temperature deep inside your body, known as the core body temperature, which must be kept stable.

At only a few degrees above or below normal body temperature, your enzymes don't function properly. Many things can affect your internal body temperature, including:

- energy produced in your muscles during exercise
- fevers caused by disease
- the external temperature rising or falling.

Basic temperature control

You can change your clothing, light a fire, and turn on the heating or air-conditioning to help control your body temperature. However, it is your internal control mechanisms that are most important.

Control of your core body temperature relies on the **thermoregulatory centre** in the hypothalamus of your brain. This centre contains receptors that are sensitive to temperature changes in the blood flowing through the brain itself.

Extra information comes from the temperature receptors in the skin. These send impulses to the thermoregulatory centre, giving information about the skin temperature. The receptors are so sensitive they can detect a difference in temperature as small as 0.5 °C.

If your temperature starts to go up, your sweat glands release more sweat, which cools the body down. Sweating also results in you losing water and mineral ions. Therefore you need to drink more to replace the water and ions you have lost. Your skin also looks redder as more blood flows through it, cooling you down.

If your temperature starts to go down, you will look pale as less blood flows through your skin. This means you lose less energy.

Cooling the body down

If you get too hot, your enzymes denature and can no longer catalyse the reactions in your cells. When your core body temperature begins to rise, impulses are sent from the thermoregulatory centre to the body so more energy is released to cool you down:

- The blood vessels that supply your surface skin capillaries dilate (open wider). This is called vasodilation and it lets more blood flow through the capillaries. Your skin flushes, so you lose more heat energy by radiation.

- Your rate of sweating goes up so your sweat glands are producing more sweat. This extra sweat cools your body down as its water evaporates from your skin, taking heat energy from the blood. In humid weather when the water in sweat does not evaporate it is much harder to keep cool.

As you lose more water through sweating when it is hot or you are exercising hard, it is important to take in more fluid through your drink and/or food to balance this loss.

Keeping warm

It is just as dangerous for your core temperature to drop as it is for it to rise. If you get very cold, the rate of the enzyme-controlled reactions in your cells falls too low. When this happens, you don't release enough energy and your cells begin to die. If your core body temperature starts to fall, impulses are sent from your thermoregulatory centre to the body to conserve energy and reduce heat loss.

- The blood vessels that supply your skin capillaries constrict (close up) to reduce the flow of blood through the capillaries. This vasoconstriction reduces the energy released by radiation through the surface of the skin.
- Sweat production is reduced. Less water in sweat evaporates so less heat energy is released.
- Your muscles contract and relax rapidly, causing you to shiver. These muscle contractions need lots of respiration, which releases more energy. This raises your body temperature. As you warm up, the shivering stops.

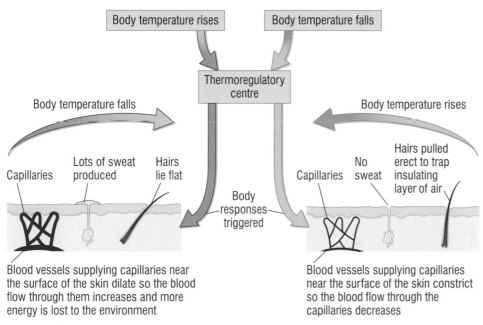

Figure 2 Changes in your core body temperature set off automatic responses to oppose the changes and maintain a steady internal environment

links

For more on enzyme reactions, see 3.3 'Factors affecting enzyme action'.

Examiner's tip

NEVER say that capillaries dilate or constrict. They are not able to do this as they have no muscle cells! Instead, it is the blood vessels supplying the capillaries that dilate or constrict.
Also blood vessels NEVER move! Either more blood flows in vessels near the skin surface, or more blood flows in the vessels lower down.

Key points

- Your body temperature is monitored and controlled by the thermoregulatory centre in your brain.

- Your body responds to cool you down or warm you up if your core body temperature changes, so it is maintained at around 37°C.

- The blood vessels that supply the capillaries in the skin dilate and constrict to control the blood flow to the surface.

- Heat energy is released through the evaporation of water in sweat from the surface of the skin to cool the body down.

- Shivering involves contraction of the muscles that releases energy from respiration to warm the body.

Summary questions

1 a Why is it so important to maintain a body temperature of about 37°C?
  b Explain why it is so important that the core body temperature does not rise above around 40°C or fall much below 35°C.

2 Explain the role of:
  a the thermoregulatory centre in the brain, and
  b the temperature sensors in the skin in maintaining a constant core body temperature.

3 Explain how the body responds to both an increase and a decrease in core temperature to return its temperature to normal levels.

B7.7

Controlling blood glucose

It is essential that your cells have a constant supply of the glucose they need for respiration. To achieve this, one of your body systems controls your blood sugar levels to within very narrow limits.

Insulin and the control of blood glucose levels

When you digest a meal, large amounts of glucose pass into your blood. Without a control mechanism, your blood glucose levels would vary significantly. They would range from very high after a meal to very low several hours later – so low that cells would not have enough glucose to respire.

This situation is prevented by your pancreas. The pancreas is a small pink organ found under your stomach. It constantly monitors and controls your blood glucose concentration using two hormones. The best known of these is **insulin**.

When your blood glucose concentration rises after you have eaten a meal, insulin is released. Insulin allows glucose to move from the blood into your cells where it is used. Soluble glucose is also converted to an insoluble carbohydrate called glycogen. Insulin controls the storage of glycogen in your liver and muscles. This glycogen can be converted back into glucose when it is needed. As a result, your blood glucose stays stable within a narrow range of concentrations.

When the glycogen stores in the liver and muscles are full, any excess glucose is converted into lipids and stored. If you regularly take in food which results in more glucose than can be stored as glycogen, you will gradually store more and more lipids and may eventually become **obese**.

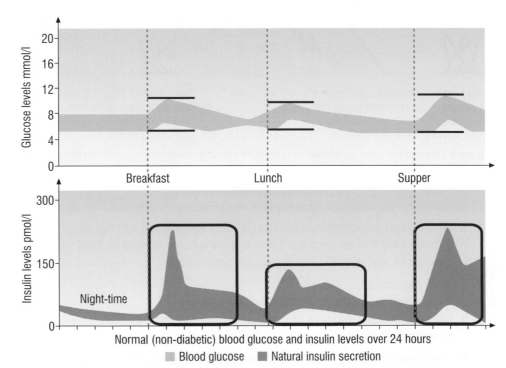

Figure 1 Insulin is secreted from the pancreas after meals to keep your blood glucose stable within narrow limits

Glucagon and control of blood glucose levels

The control of your blood sugar doesn't just involve insulin. When your blood glucose concentration falls below the ideal range, the pancreas secretes **glucagon**. Glucagon makes your liver break down glycogen, converting it back into glucose. In this way, the stored glucose is released back into the blood.

By using two hormones and the glycogen store in your liver, your pancreas keeps your blood glucose concentration fairly constant. It does this using feedback control, which involves switching between the two hormones.

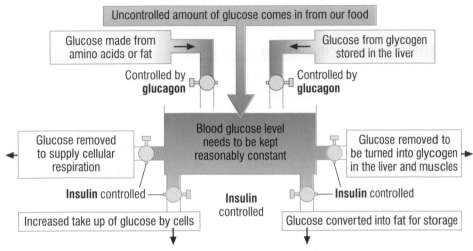

Figure 2 This model of your blood glucose control system shows the blood glucose as a tank. It has both controlled and uncontrolled inlets and outlets. In every case, the control is given by the hormones insulin and glucagon.

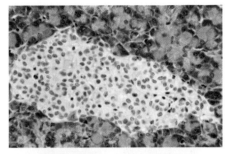

Figure 3 Part of the pancreas. The tissue stained red makes digestive enzymes while the central yellow area contains the cells that make insulin.

What causes diabetes?

If your pancreas does not make enough (or any) insulin, your blood glucose concentration is not controlled. You have **type 1 diabetes**.

Without insulin your blood glucose levels get very high after you eat. Eventually your kidneys excrete glucose in your urine. You produce lots of urine and feel thirsty all the time. Without insulin, glucose cannot get into the cells of your body, so you lack energy and feel tired. You break down fat and protein to use as fuel instead, so you lose weight. Type 1 diabetes usually starts in young children and teenagers, and there seems to be a genetic element to the development of the disease.

Type 2 diabetes is another, very common type of diabetes. It gets more common as people get older and is often linked to obesity, lack of exercise or both. There is also a strong genetic tendency to develop type 2 diabetes. In type 2 diabetes, the pancreas still makes insulin, although it may make less than your body needs. Most importantly, your body cells stop responding properly to the insulin you make. In countries such as the UK and the USA, levels of type 2 diabetes are rising rapidly as the populations become more obese.

Key points

● Your blood glucose concentration is monitored and controlled by your pancreas.

● The pancreas produces the hormone insulin, which allows glucose to move from the blood into the cells and to be stored as glycogen in the liver and muscles.

● The pancreas also produces glucagon, which allows glycogen to be converted back into glucose and released into the blood.

● In type 1 diabetes, the blood glucose may rise to fatally high levels because the pancreas does not secrete enough insulin.

● In type 2 diabetes, the body stops responding to its own insulin.

Summary questions

1 Define the following words: hormone, insulin, diabetes, glycogen.

2 a Explain how your pancreas keeps the blood glucose levels of your body constant.

 b Why is it so important to control the level of glucose in your blood?

3 Explain the difference between type 1 and type 2 diabetes.

B7.8

Treating diabetes

Learning objectives

After this topic, you should know:

- how the treatment of diabetes has developed over time

- the differences in the way type 1 and type 2 diabetes are treated.

Figure 1 The treatment of type 1 diabetes involves regular blood glucose tests and insulin injections to keep the blood glucose levels constant

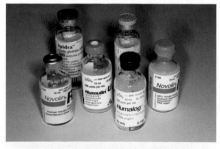

Figure 2 Treatments such as human insulin allow a person to manage type 1 diabetes and live with it, but they do not cure the condition

Before there was any treatment for diabetes, people would waste away. Eventually they would fall into a coma and die.

The treatment of diabetes has developed over the years and continues to improve today. There are now some very effective ways of treating people with diabetes, although over the long term, even well-managed diabetes may cause problems with the circulatory system, the kidneys or the eyesight.

Treating type 1 diabetes

If you have type 1 diabetes, you need replacement insulin before meals. Insulin is a protein that would be digested in your stomach, so it is usually given as an injection to get it into your blood.

This injected insulin allows glucose to be taken into your body cells and converted into glycogen in the liver. This stops the concentration of glucose in your blood from getting too high. Then, as the blood glucose levels fall, the glycogen is converted back to glucose. As a result, your blood glucose levels are kept as stable as possible.

If you have type 1 diabetes, you also need to be careful about the levels of carbohydrate you eat. You need to have regular meals. Like everyone else, you need to exercise to keep your heart and blood vessels healthy. However, taking exercise needs careful planning to keep your blood sugar levels steady and your cells supplied with glucose as your cells respire more rapidly to produce the energy needed for your muscles to work.

Insulin injections treat diabetes successfully but they do not cure it. Until a cure is developed, someone with type 1 diabetes has to inject insulin every day of their life.

Using insulin from other organisms

In the early 1920s, Frederick Banting and Charles Best made some dogs diabetic by removing their pancreases. Then they gave them extracts of pancreas taken from other dogs. We now know these extracts contained insulin. Banting and Best realised that extracts of animal pancreas could keep people with diabetes alive. Many dogs died in the search for a successful treatment. However, the lives of millions of people have been saved over the years since.

For years, insulin from pigs and cows was used to treat diabetics, although there were problems. Animal insulin is not identical to human insulin and the supply depended on how many animals were killed for meat. So sometimes there was not enough insulin to go around.

In recent years, genetic engineering has been used to develop bacteria that can produce pure human insulin. This is genetically identical to natural human insulin and the supply is constant. This is now used by most people with type 1 diabetes. However, some people do not think this type of interference with genetic material is ethical.

Ways of delivering the insulin are changing too. More and more people with diabetes wear a pump that delivers insulin automatically all the time, although the individual still has to carry out lots of blood tests to make sure their glucose levels are correct.

Curing type 1 diabetes

Scientists and doctors want to find a treatment that means people with diabetes never have to take insulin again. However, so far none of them is widely available.

- Doctors can transplant a pancreas successfully. However, the operations are quite difficult and rather risky. These transplants are still only carried out on a few hundred people each year in the UK. There are 250 000 people in the UK with type 1 diabetes and there are simply not enough donors available. What's more, the patient exchanges one sort of medicine (insulin) for another (immunosuppressants).
- Transplanting the pancreatic cells that make insulin from both dead and living donors has been tried, with very limited success so far.

In 2005, scientists produced insulin-secreting cells from embryonic stem cells and used them to cure diabetes in mice. In 2008, UK scientists discovered a completely new technique. Using genetic engineering, they turned mouse pancreas cells that normally make enzymes into insulin-producing cells. Other groups are using adult stem cells from diabetic patients to try the same idea.

Scientists hope that eventually they will be able to genetically engineer faulty human pancreatic cells so they work properly. Then they will be able to return them to the patient with no rejection issues. It still seems likely that the easiest cure will be to use stem cells from human embryos that have been specially created for the process. However, for some people, this is not ethically acceptable.

Much more research is needed. However, scientists hope that before too long, type 1 diabetes will be an illness we can cure rather than simply treat and manage.

Treating type 2 diabetes

If you develop type 2 diabetes, which is linked to obesity, lack of exercise and old age, you can often deal with it without needing to inject insulin. Many people can restore their normal blood glucose balance by taking three simple steps:

- eating a balanced diet with carefully controlled amounts of carbohydrates
- losing weight
- doing regular exercise.

If this doesn't work there are drugs that:

- help insulin work better on the body cells
- help your pancreas make more insulin
- reduce the amount of glucose you absorb from your gut.

Only if all of these treatments do not work will you end up having insulin injections.

Type 2 diabetes usually affects older people. However, it is becoming more and more common in young people who are very **overweight**.

links

For information on embryonic stem cells, look back to 2.3 'Stem cells'.

Figure 3 Losing weight and taking exercise seem simple ways to overcome type 2 diabetes. However, some people object to being given this advice and ignore it until they need medication to control the diabetes.

Key points

- In the past, there was no effective treatment for diabetes and people with the condition eventually died.
- Today, type 1 diabetes may be controlled by injecting insulin, careful diet control and exercise.
- Type 2 diabetes is often treated by careful attention to diet and taking more exercise. If this doesn't work, drugs may be needed.
- Currently, a variety of different methods are being used or developed to treat diabetes using genetic engineering and stem cell techniques.

Summary questions

1 It is a common misconception that diabetes is treated only by using insulin injections.
   a Explain why this is not always true for people with type 1 diabetes.
   b Explain why treatment with insulin injections is relatively uncommon for people with type 2 diabetes.
2 a Compare modern insulin treatment with the original insulin used to treat diabetics and evaluate the two treatments.
   b Transplanting a pancreas to replace natural insulin production seems to be the ideal treatment for type 1 diabetes. Compare this treatment with insulin injections and explain why it is not more widely used.

Summary questions

1 **a** What is homeostasis?

b Write a paragraph explaining why control of the conditions inside your body is so important.

2 **a** Negative feedback is involved in many different aspects of homeostasis. Draw a clear diagram showing how feedback systems are important in the control of:
  i water balance in the body
  ii temperature control in the body
  iii control of the blood sugar in the body.

b Draw a diagram to summarise the general principles of feedback control in the body.

3 In August 2003 a heat wave hit Europe. The graph shows the effect it had on the number of deaths in Paris.

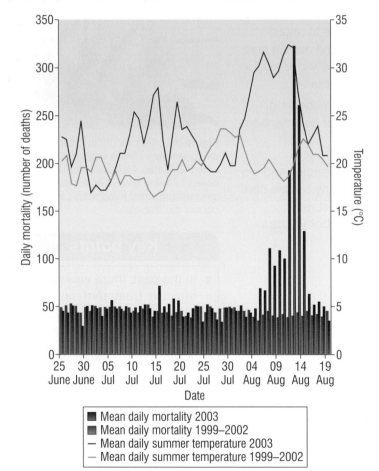

Figure 1

a What effect did the Paris heat wave have on deaths in the city?

b From the data, what temperature begins to have an effect on the death rate?

c Explain why more people die when conditions are very hot.

4 The graph shows the blood glucose levels of a non-diabetic person and someone with type 1 diabetes managed with regular insulin injections. They both eat at the same times.

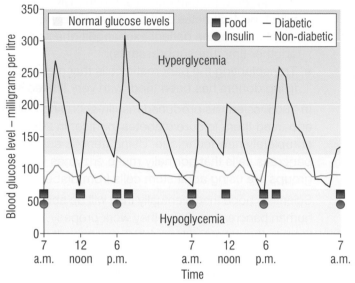

Figure 2

Use this graph to help you answer the questions below:

a What happens to the blood glucose levels in both individuals after eating?

b What is the range of blood glucose concentration of the normal subject?

c What is the range of blood glucose concentration of the person with diabetes?

d The graph shows the effect of regular insulin injections on the blood glucose level of someone with diabetes. Why are the insulin injections so important to their health and wellbeing? What does this data suggest are the limitations of insulin injections?

e People with diabetes have to monitor the amount of carbohydrate in their diet. Explain why.

AQA Examination-style questions

1 The body is coordinated by detecting stimuli in the environment, processing this information and responding to it.

   a Complete the sequence to show the parts involved.

      .... → coordination centre → ....   (2)

   b A dog responds to stimuli.

     Write down the name of the organ which detects:

     i chemical substances ....
     ii sound and body movements ....
     iii light ....
     iv pressure ....   (4)

   c Describe the **two** ways in which coordination centres can send information to initiate a response.   (2)

2 Automatic control systems in the body keep conditions inside the body relatively constant.

   a Name this process.   (1)

   b Give **three** examples of internal conditions that are controlled automatically.   (3)

   c Name the organ of the body which contains:
     i the thermoregulatory centre
     ii receptors for blood glucose.   (2)

3 A walker falls through thin ice into very cold water.

   The walker's core body temperature falls. He may die of hypothermia (when core body temperature falls too low).

   a i Which part of the brain monitors the fall in core body temperature?   (1)
     ii How does this part of the brain detect the fall in core body temperature?   (2)

   b While in the water the walker begins to shiver. Shivering helps to stop the core body temperature falling too quickly. Explain how.   (2)

   c The walker had been drinking alcohol. Alcohol causes changes to the blood vessels supplying the skin capillaries, making the skin look red.
     i Describe the change to the blood vessels.   (1)
     ii The walker is much more likely to die of hypothermia than someone who has not been drinking alcohol. Explain why.   (2)

4 The kidney is the main organ involved in regulating the amount of water in the body.

   a Describe how the blood is filtered in the kidney so that waste molecules can be excreted in the urine, but useful molecules are not.   (4)

   b The volume of urine excreted depends on the concentration of water in the blood.
     i Where is the water content of the blood monitored?   (1)
     ii Name the hormone that acts on the kidney to control how much water is excreted.   (1)
     iii Name the gland that releases this hormone.   (1)

   c *In this question you will be assessed on using good English, organising information clearly and using specialist terms where appropriate.*

   On a very hot day, a builder starts work. After one hour he becomes very thirsty. He visits the toilet and passes a small volume of concentrated urine. He drinks two large bottles of water and feels much better. Half an hour later he visits the toilet again and passes a large volume of dilute urine.

   Use the words named in part b to explain how the builder's body has responded to the water content of his blood since he started work.   (QWC) (6)

B8.1 Pathogens and disease

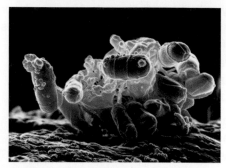

Figure 1 Many bacteria are very useful to humans but some, such as these *E. coli*, are pathogens and cause disease

⊂⊃ links

Find out more about the structure of bacteria by looking back to 1.2 'Bacteria and yeast'.

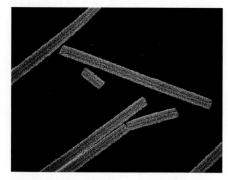

Figure 2 These tobacco mosaic viruses cause disease in plants

⊂⊃ links

For more information on bacteria that are resistant to antibiotics, see 8.5 'Changing pathogens'.

Infectious diseases are found all over the world, in every country. Some infectious diseases are fairly mild, such as the common cold and tonsillitis. Others are known killers, such as tetanus, influenza and HIV/Aids.

An infectious disease is caused by a **microorganism** entering and attacking your body. People can pass these microorganisms from one person to another. This is what we mean by **infectious**.

Microorganisms that cause disease are called **pathogens**. Common pathogens are bacteria and viruses. Pathogens can attack all sorts of different organisms, including plants.

The differences between bacteria and viruses

Bacteria are single-celled living organisms that are much smaller than animal and plant cells.

Although some bacteria cause disease, many are harmless and some are really useful to us. We use them to make food like yoghurt and cheese, to treat sewage and to make medicines. Bacteria are important both in the environment, as decomposers, and in your body.

Pathogenic bacteria are the minority – but they are significant because of the major effects they can have on individuals and society.

??? Did you know ... ?

Scientists estimate that most people have between 1 and 2 kg of bacteria in their guts, made up of around 500 different species.

Viruses are even smaller than bacteria. They usually have regular shapes. Viruses cause diseases in every type of living organism, from people to bacteria.

How pathogens cause disease

Once bacteria and viruses are inside your body, they reproduce rapidly. This is how they make you ill.

- Bacteria divide rapidly by splitting in two (called binary fission). They often produce toxins (poisons) which affect your body. Sometimes they directly damage your cells.
- Viruses take over the cells of your body as they reproduce, damaging and destroying the cells. They very rarely produce toxins.

Common disease symptoms are a high temperature, headaches and rashes. These are caused by the damage and toxins produced by the pathogens. The symptoms also appear as a result of the way your body responds to the damage and toxins.

You catch an infectious disease when you pick up a pathogen from someone else who is infected with the disease.

Understanding infections

Pathogens have caused infectious diseases in human beings for many thousands of years. People have been writing about diseases such as tuberculosis, smallpox and plague throughout recorded history. However, although people have recognised the symptoms of infectious diseases for many centuries, it is only in the last 150–200 years that we have really understood the causes of these diseases and how they are spread.

It has been the work of people such as Ignaz Semmelweis and Louis Pasteur that has helped us reach the understanding of pathogens that we have today.

The work of Ignaz Semmelweis

Semmelweis was a doctor in the mid-1850s. At the time, many women in hospital died from childbed fever a few days after giving birth. However, no one knew what caused it.

Semmelweis noticed that his medical students went straight from dissecting a dead body to delivering a baby without washing their hands. The women delivered by medical students and doctors rather than midwives were much more likely to die. Semmelweis wondered if they were carrying the cause of disease from the corpses to their patients.

When another doctor died from symptoms identical to childbed fever after cutting himself while working on a body, Semmelweis became convinced that the fever was caused by some kind of infectious agent. He therefore insisted that his medical students wash their hands before delivering babies. Immediately, fewer mothers died from the fever. However, other doctors were very resistant to Semmelweis's ideas.

Other discoveries

Also in the mid- to late 19th century:

- Louis Pasteur showed that microorganisms caused disease. He also developed vaccines to prevent the spread of diseases such as anthrax and rabies.
- Joseph Lister started to use antiseptic chemicals to destroy pathogens before they caused infection in operating theatres.
- As microscopes improved, it became possible to see pathogens ever more clearly too. This helped convince people that they were really there!

Understanding how infectious diseases are spread from one person to another makes it possible for us to take a number of measures to prevent their spread.

Figure 3 We are still discovering more about the role of pathogens in disease. Barry Marshall won a Nobel Prize in 2005 after a long battle to convince other doctors and scientists that most stomach ulcers are actually caused by a bacterium called *Helicobacter pylori*.

Examiner's tip

Remember the ways to stop spreading infections in hospitals:
- more hand-washing
- greater use of disinfectants
- better cleaning.

Summary questions

1 a What causes infectious diseases?
   b How do viruses differ from bacteria in the way they cause disease?
   c How do pathogens make you ill?

2 Give five examples of things we now know we can do to reduce the spread of pathogens to lower the risk of disease, e.g. hand-washing in hospitals.

3 Explain carefully why you think it took so long for people to recognise the causes of the infectious diseases that have caused illness and death in human populations for many thousands of years.

Key points

- Infectious diseases are caused by microorganisms called pathogens, such as bacteria and viruses.

- Bacteria and viruses reproduce rapidly inside your body. Bacteria can produce toxins that make you feel ill.

- Viruses damage your cells as they reproduce. This can also make you feel ill.

B8.2

Defence mechanisms

Learning objectives

After this topic, you should know:

- how your body stops pathogens getting in

- how your white blood cells protect you from disease.

There are a number of ways in which pathogens spread from one person to another. The more pathogens that get into your body, the more likely it is that you will get an infectious disease.

- **Droplet infection:** When you are ill, you expel tiny droplets full of pathogens from your breathing system when you cough, sneeze or talk. Other people breathe in the droplets, along with the pathogens they contain, so they pick up the infection, for example flu (influenza), tuberculosis or the common cold.

Figure 1 Droplets carrying millions of pathogens fly out of your mouth and nose at up to 100 miles an hour when you sneeze

- **Direct contact:** Some diseases such as impetigo and sexually transmitted diseases such as genital herpes are spread by direct contact of the skin.

- **Contaminated food and drink:** Eating raw, undercooked or contaminated food or drinking water containing sewage can spread disease such as diarrhoea, cholera or salmonellosis. You get these by taking large numbers of microorganisms straight into your gut.

- **Through a break in your skin:** Pathogens such as HIV/AIDS or hepatitis can enter your body through cuts, scratches and needle punctures.

When people live in crowded conditions with no sewage treatment, infectious diseases can spread very rapidly.

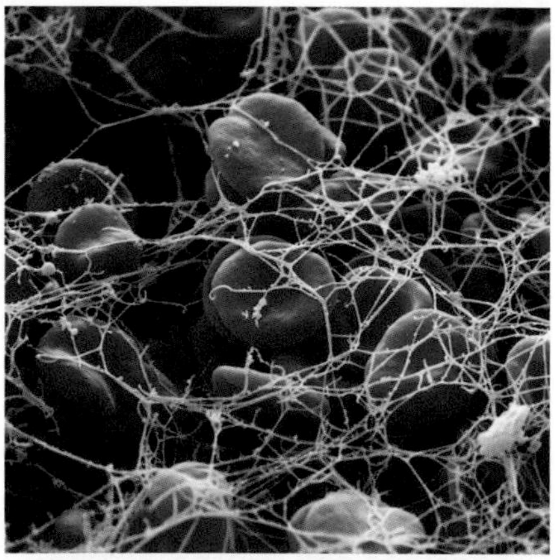

Preventing microorganisms getting into your body

Each day, you come across millions of disease-causing microorganisms. Fortunately, your body has several ways of stopping these pathogens getting inside.

- Your skin covers your body and acts as a barrier. It prevents bacteria and viruses from reaching the tissues beneath that can be infected.

- If you damage or cut your skin, you bleed. Your blood quickly forms a clot, which dries into a scab. The scab forms a seal over the cut, stopping pathogens getting in through the wound.

- Your breathing system could be a weak link in your body defences. Every time you breathe you draw air, which is full of pathogens, into the airways of the lungs. However, your breathing system produces sticky liquid, called mucus. This mucus covers the lining of your lungs and tubes, such as the bronchi and bronchioles. It traps the pathogens. The mucus is then moved out of your body or swallowed down into your gut where the acid destroys the microorganisms.

- In the same way, the stomach acid destroys most of the pathogens you take in through your mouth.

Figure 2 When you get a cut, the platelets in your blood set up a chain of events to form a clot that dries to a scab. This stops pathogens from getting into your body. It also stops you bleeding to death.

∞ links

To find out more about your blood and clotting, see 5.4 'Transport in the blood'.

How white blood cells protect you from disease

In spite of your body's defence mechanisms, some pathogens still get inside your body. Once there, they will meet your second line of defence – the white blood cells of your immune system.

The white blood cells help to defend your body against pathogens in several ways.

Table 1 Ways in which your white blood cells destroy pathogens and protect you against disease

Role of white blood cell	How it protects you against disease
Ingesting microorganisms	Some white blood cells ingest (take in) pathogens, digesting and destroying them so they can't make you ill.
Producing antibodies Antibody Antigen Bacterium White blood cell Antibody attached to antigen	Some white blood cells produce special chemicals called antibodies. These target particular bacteria or viruses and destroy them. You need a unique antibody for each type of pathogen. Once your white blood cells have produced antibodies once against a particular pathogen, they can be made very quickly if that pathogen gets into the body again.
Producing antitoxins Antitoxin molecule Toxin and antitoxin joined together Toxin molecule Bacterium	Some white blood cells produce antitoxins. These counteract (cancel out) the toxins (poisons) released by pathogens.

?? Did you know …?

Mucus produced from your nose turns green when you have a cold. This happens because some white blood cells contain green-coloured enzymes. These white blood cells destroy the cold viruses and any bacteria in the mucus of your nose when you have a cold. The dead white blood cells, along with the dead bacteria and viruses, are removed in the mucus, making it look green.

Summary questions

1 **a** What are the four main ways in which diseases are spread?
  b For each method, explain how the pathogens are passed from one person to another.

2 Certain diseases mean you cannot fight infections very well. Explain why the following symptoms would make you less able to cope with pathogens.
  a Your blood won't clot properly.
  b The number of white cells in your blood falls.

3 Here are three common things we do. Explain carefully how each one helps to prevent the spread of disease.
  a Washing your hands before preparing a salad.
  b Throwing away tissues after you have blown your nose.
  c Making sure that sewage does not get into drinking water.

4 Explain in detail how the white blood cells in your body work.

Key points

- Your body has several methods of defending itself against the entry of pathogens. These include the skin, the mucus of the breathing system and the clotting of the blood.

- Your white blood cells help to defend you against pathogens by ingesting them, making antibodies and making antitoxins.

B8.3 Immunity

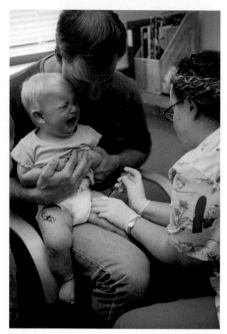

Figure 1 No one likes having a vaccination very much – but they save millions of lives around the world every year!

Every cell has unique proteins on its surface called antigens. The antigens on the microorganisms that get into your body are different to the ones on your own cells. Your immune system recognises they are different.

Your white blood cells then make specific antibodies, which join up with the antigens and destroy that particular pathogen.

Some of your white blood cells (the memory cells) 'remember' the right antibody needed to destroy a particular pathogen. If you meet that pathogen again, they can make the same antibody very quickly. So you become immune to disease.

The first time you meet a new pathogen you get ill because there is a delay while your body sorts out the right antibody needed. The next time, you completely destroy the invaders before they have time to make you feel unwell.

Vaccination

Some pathogens, such as meningitis, can make you seriously ill very quickly. In fact, you can die before your body manages to make the right antibodies. Fortunately, you can be protected against many of these serious diseases by **immunisation** (also known as **vaccination**).

Immunisation involves giving you a **vaccine**. A vaccine is usually made of a dead or inactivated form of the disease-causing microorganism. It works by stimulating your body's natural immune response to invading pathogens.

A small amount of dead or inactive pathogen is introduced into your body. This gives your white blood cells the chance to develop the right antibodies against the pathogen without you getting ill.

Then, if you meet the live pathogens, your white blood cells can respond rapidly. They can make the right antibodies just as if you had already had the disease, so that you are protected against it.

We use vaccines to protect us against both bacterial diseases, such as tetanus and diphtheria, and viral diseases such as polio, measles and mumps. For example, the MMR vaccine protects against measles, mumps and rubella. Vaccines have saved millions of lives around the world. One disease – smallpox – has been completely wiped out by vaccinations. Doctors hope polio will also disappear in the next few years.

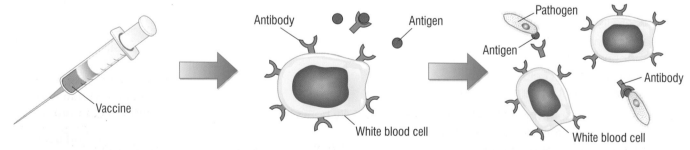

Small amounts of dead or inactive pathogen are put into your body, often by injection.

The antigens in the vaccine stimulate your white blood cells into making antibodies. The antibodies destroy the antigens without any risk of you getting the disease.

You are immune to future infections by the pathogen. That's because your body can respond rapidly and make the correct antibody as if you had already had the disease.

Figure 2 This is how vaccines protect you against dangerous infectious diseases

Herd immunity

If a large proportion of the population is immune to a disease, the spread of the pathogen is very much reduced. This is known as **herd immunity**. If, for any reason, the number of people taking up a vaccine falls, the disease can reappear. This is what happened in the UK in the 1970s when there was a scare about the safety of whooping cough vaccine. Vaccination rates fell from over 80% to around 30%. In the following years, thousands of children got whooping cough again and a substantial number died. Yet the vaccine was as safe as any medicine – and when people eventually realised this and enough children were vaccinated for herd immunity to be effective again, cases of the disease and deaths quickly decreased once more.

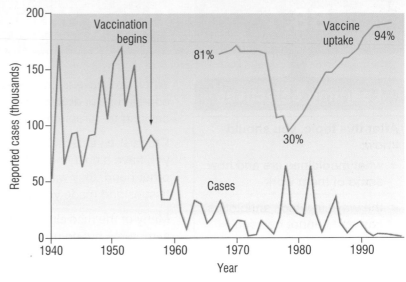

Figure 3 Graph showing the effect of the whooping cough scare on both uptake of the vaccine and the number of cases of the disease (Source: Open University)

No medicine is completely risk free. Very rarely, a child will react badly to a vaccine with tragic results. Making the decision to have your baby immunised can be difficult. Yet because vaccines are so successful, we rarely see the terrible diseases they protect us against. A hundred years ago, nearly 50% of all deaths of children and young people were caused by infectious diseases. The development of antibiotics and vaccines means that now only 0.5% of all deaths in the same age group are due to infectious disease. Many children were also left permanently damaged by serious infections. Parents today are often aware of the very small risks from vaccination – but sometimes forget about the terrible dangers of the diseases we vaccinate against.

Society needs as many people as possible to be immunised against as many diseases as possible to keep the pool of infection in the population very low. On the other hand, there is a remote chance that something may go wrong with a vaccination. For the great majority, vaccination is the best option both for the child and for society.

Examiner's tip

High levels of antibodies do not stay in your blood forever – immunity is the ability of your white blood cells to produce the right antibodies quickly if you are re-infected by a disease as a result of the memory cells.

Key points

- The white blood cells of your immune system produce antibodies to destroy particular pathogens. Your body will then respond rapidly to future infections by the same pathogen by making the correct antibody very rapidly. In this way, you become immune to the disease.

- You can be immunised against a disease by introducing small amounts of dead or inactive pathogens into your body.

- We can use vaccinations to protect against both bacterial and viral pathogens.

Summary questions

1 a What is an antigen?
  b What is an antibody?
  c Give an example of one bacterial and one viral disease which you can be immunised against.

2 Explain carefully, using diagrams if they help you:
  a how the immune system of your body works
  b how vaccines use your natural immune system to protect you against serious diseases.

3 Explain why vaccines can be used against both bacterial and viral diseases.

B8.4 Using drugs to treat disease

When you have an infectious disease, you generally take medicines that contain useful **drugs**. Often the medicine doesn't affect the pathogen that is causing the problems – it just eases the symptoms and makes you feel better.

Drugs such as aspirin and paracetamol are very useful as painkillers. When you have a cold, they will help relieve your headache and sore throat. On the other hand, they will have no effect on the viruses that have entered your tissues and made you feel ill.

Many of the medicines you can buy at a chemists or supermarket relieve your symptoms but do not kill the pathogens, so they do not cure you any faster. You have to wait for your immune system to overcome the pathogens.

Antibiotics

Drugs that make us feel better are useful, but what we really need are drugs that can cure us. We use antiseptics and disinfectants to kill bacteria outside the body, but they are far too poisonous to use inside your body – they would kill you and your pathogens at the same time!

The drugs that have really changed the way we treat infectious diseases are antibiotics. These are medicines that can work inside your body to kill the bacteria that cause diseases.

Discovering penicillin

In the early 20th century, doctors and scientists were on the lookout for chemicals which might kill bacteria and so cure some of the terrible infectious diseases of the day. In 1928, Alexander Fleming was growing lots of bacteria on agar plates to investigate them. Fleming was rather careless, and his lab was quite untidy. He often left the lids off his plates for a long time and forgot about experiments he had set up!

After one holiday, Fleming saw that lots of his culture plates had mould growing on them. He noticed a clear ring in the jelly around some of the spots of mould. Something had killed the bacteria covering the jelly.

Fleming saw how important this was. He called the mould 'penicillin'. He worked hard to extract a juice from the mould, but he couldn't get much penicillin and he couldn't make it survive, even in a fridge. So Fleming couldn't prove an extract of the mould would actually kill bacteria and make people better. By 1934, he gave up on penicillin and went on to do different work.

About 10 years after penicillin was first discovered, Ernst Chain and Howard Florey set about trying to find better ways of extracting penicillin from the mould so they could use it on people. They gave some penicillin they extracted to a man dying of a blood infection. The effect was amazing and he recovered until the penicillin ran out. Florey and Chain even tried to collect unused penicillin from the patient's urine, but in spite of this he died.

Chain and Florey kept working and eventually they managed to make penicillin on an industrial scale, producing enough antibiotic to supply the demands of the Second World War. We have used it as a medicine ever since.

Figure 1 Taking a painkiller will make this baby feel better, but he will not actually get well any faster as a result

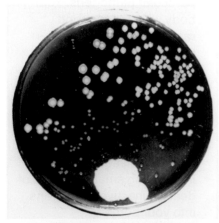

Figure 2 Alexander Fleming was on the lookout for something that would kill bacteria. Because he noticed the effect of this mould on his cultures, millions of lives have been saved around the world.

How antibiotics work

Antibiotics such as penicillin work by killing the infective bacteria that cause disease while they are inside your body. They damage the bacterial cells without harming your own cells. They have had an enormous effect on our society. We can now cure bacterial diseases that killed millions of people in the past.

If you need antibiotics, you usually take a pill or syrup, but if you are very ill antibiotics may be fed straight into your bloodstream so they reach the pathogens in your cells as quickly as possible. Some antibiotics kill a wide range of bacteria. Others are very specific and only work against very specific bacteria. It is very important that the right antibiotic is chosen and used.

Unfortunately, antibiotics are not the complete answer to the problem of infectious diseases. They have no effect on diseases caused by viruses. The problem with viral pathogens is that they reproduce inside the cells of your body. It is extremely difficult to develop drugs that kill the viruses without damaging the cells and tissues of your body at the same time.

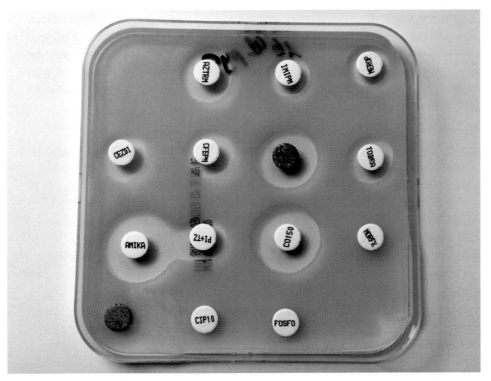

Figure 3 Penicillin was the first antibiotic. Now we have many different ones which kill different types of bacterium. Here, several different antibiotics are being tested.

Key points

- Some medicines relieve the symptoms of disease but do not kill the pathogens which cause it.
- Antibiotics cure bacterial diseases by killing the bacteria inside your body.
- Antibiotics do not destroy viruses because viruses reproduce inside the cells. It is difficult to develop drugs that can destroy viruses without damaging your body cells.

Summary questions

1 What is the main difference between drugs such as paracetamol and drugs such as penicillin?

2 a How did Alexander Fleming discover penicillin?
  b Why was it so difficult to make a medicine out of penicillin?
  c Who developed the industrial process that made it possible to mass-produce penicillin?

3 Explain why it is so much more difficult to develop medicines against viruses than it has been to develop antibacterial drugs.

B8.5   Changing pathogens

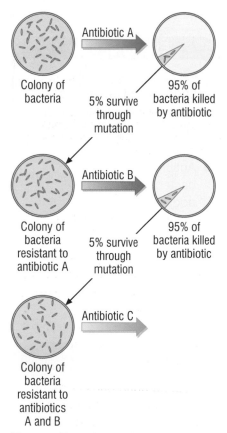

Figure 1 Bacteria can develop resistance to many different antibiotics in a process of natural selection, as this simple model shows

If you are given an antibiotic and use it properly, the bacteria that have made you ill are killed off. However, some bacteria develop resistance to antibiotics. They have a natural mutation (change in their genetic material) that means they are not affected by the antibiotic. These mutations happen by chance and they produce new strains of bacteria by **natural selection**.

More types of bacteria are becoming resistant to more antibiotics, so bacterial diseases are becoming more difficult to treat. Over the years, antibiotics have been used inappropriately and when they are not really needed. This increases the rate at which antibiotic-resistant strains have developed.

Antibiotic-resistant bacteria

Normally, an antibiotic kills the bacteria of a non-resistant strain. However, individual resistant bacteria survive and reproduce, so the population of resistant bacteria increases. Antibiotics may no longer be active against this new resistant strain of the pathogen. What is more, in some cases existing vaccines are no longer effective against the mutated, resistant pathogen. As a result, the new strain will spread rapidly because no one is immune to it and there is no effective treatment. This is what has happened with bacteria such as MRSA (see below).

To prevent more resistant strains of bacteria appearing:

● It is important not to overuse antibiotics. It's best to use them only when you really need them. For this reason, doctors no longer use antibiotics to treat non-serious infections such as mild throat or ear infections. Also, since antibiotics don't affect viruses, people should not demand antibiotics to treat an illness which their doctor thinks is caused by a virus.

● Some antibiotics treat very specific bacteria, while others treat many different types of bacteria. The right type of antibiotic must be used to treat each bacterial infection.

● It is also important that people finish their course of medicine every time. This is to make sure that even bacteria in the early stages of developing resistance are killed by the antibiotic.

Hopefully, steps like these will slow down the rate of development of resistant strains.

The MRSA story

Hospitals use a lot of antibiotics to treat infections. As a result of natural selection, some of the bacteria in hospitals are resistant to many antibiotics. This is what has happened with **MRSA**, the bacterium methicillin-resistant *Staphylococcus aureus*.

As doctors and nurses move from patient to patient, these antibiotic-resistant bacteria are spread easily.

MRSA alone now causes or contributes to over 1000 deaths every year in UK hospitals and care homes, yet a number of simple measures can reduce the spread of microorganisms such as MRSA.

- Antibiotics should only be used when they are really needed.
- Specific bacteria should be treated with specific antibiotics.
- Medical staff should wash their hands with soap and water or alcohol gel between patients and wear disposable clothing or clothing that is regularly sterilised.
- Hospitals should have high standards of hygiene so they are really clean.
- Patients who become infected with antibiotic-resistant bacteria should be looked after in isolation from other patients.
- Visitors to hospitals and care homes should wash their hands as they enter and leave.

Simple commonsense measures such as these can have a considerable effect on reducing deaths from antibiotic-resistant bacteria.

Medicines for the future

In recent years, doctors have found strains of bacteria that are resistant to even the strongest antibiotics. When that happens, there is nothing more that antibiotics can do for a patient and he or she may well die. Scientists are constantly looking for new antibiotics. However, it isn't easy to find chemicals that kill bacteria without damaging human cells.

Penicillin and several other antibiotics are made by moulds. Scientists are collecting soil samples from all over the world to try and find another mould to produce a new antibiotic to kill antibiotic-resistant bacteria such as MRSA. They are also spreading the search much wider than moulds. For example, crocodiles have teeth full of rotting meat, live in dirty water and fight a lot, but the terrible bites they inflict on each other do not become infected. Scientists have extracted peptides from crocodile and alligator blood which seem to act as antibiotics and hope to turn them into human medicines.

Similarly:
- Scientists are analysing the protective slime that covers fish. They have isolated proteins with antibiotic properties in the slime, which may be useful.
- Scientists in Germany and Australia have found that certain types of honey (used since the time of the Ancient Egyptians to help heal wounds) have antibiotic properties that kill many bacteria, including MRSA. Doctors are using manuka honey dressings to treat infected wounds.

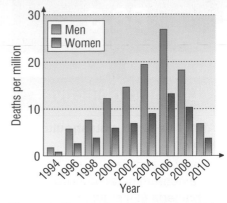

Figure 2 The number of deaths in which MRSA played a part, 1993–2010 (Source: Office for National Statistics)

Figure 3 Scientists are looking throughout the natural world for new antibiotics – including investigations into crocodile blood

Key points

- Mutations of pathogens produce new strains.
- Antibiotics kill the non-resistant strain of bacteria, but individual resistant pathogens survive and reproduce, so the population of the resistant strain increases by natural selection.
- Existing antibiotics and vaccines may not be effective against the new resistant strain.
- To prevent the problem getting worse, it is important not to overuse antibiotics, to use the correct antibiotics and to complete each course of medicine.
- The development of antibiotic resistance means new antibiotics must be developed.

Summary questions

1 Make a flowchart to show how bacteria develop resistance to antibiotics.

2 a Is MRSA a bacterium or a virus?
  b How does MRSA illustrate the importance of not using antibiotics too frequently or when they are not really necessary?

3 Use Figure 2 to help you answer these questions.
  a How could you explain the increase in deaths linked to MRSA?
  b Suggest reasons for the difference in deaths from MRSA in men and women.
  c Deaths from MRSA and other hospital-acquired infections are falling. How could you explain this fall, which is still continuing in most places?

B8.6

Growing and investigating bacteria

Learning objectives

After this topic, you should know:

- how to grow an uncontaminated culture of bacteria in the lab

- how uncontaminated cultures are used

- why bacteria are cultured at lower temperatures in schools than in industry.

??? Did you know ... ?

You are surrounded by disease-causing bacteria all the time. If you cultured bacteria at 37 °C (human body temperature) there would be a very high risk of growing some dangerous pathogens.

To find out more about microorganisms, we need to culture them. This means we grow very large numbers of them so that we can see all of the bacteria (the colony) as a whole. Many microorganisms can be grown in the laboratory. This helps us to learn more about them. We can find out what nutrients they need to grow and investigate which chemicals are best at killing them. Bacteria are the most commonly cultured microorganisms.

Growing microorganisms in the lab

To culture (grow) microorganisms, you must provide them with everything they need. This means giving them a liquid or gel containing nutrients – a **culture medium**. This contains carbohydrate as an energy source, various minerals, a nitrogen source so they can make proteins and sometimes other chemicals. Most microorganisms also need warmth and oxygen to grow.

You usually provide the nutrients in **agar** jelly. Hot agar containing all the nutrients your bacteria will need is poured into a Petri dish. It is then left to cool and set before you add the microorganisms.

You must take great care when you are culturing microorganisms. The bacteria you want to grow may be harmless. However, there is always the risk that a **mutation** (a change in the DNA) will take place and produce a new and dangerous pathogen.

You also want to keep the pure strains of bacteria you are culturing free from any other microorganisms. Such contamination might come from your skin, the air, the soil or the water around you. Investigations need uncontaminated cultures of microorganisms. Whenever you are culturing microorganisms, you must carry out strict health and safety procedures to protect yourself and others.

Growing useful organisms

You can prepare an uncontaminated culture of microorganisms in the laboratory by following a number of steps.

Step 1:

The Petri dishes on which you will grow your microorganisms must be sterilised before using them. The nutrient agar, which will provide their food, must also be sterilised. This kills off any unwanted microorganisms. You can use heat to sterilise glass dishes. A special oven called an autoclave is often used. It sterilises by using steam at high pressure. Plastic Petri dishes are often bought ready-sterilised. UV light or gamma radiation is used to kill the bacteria.

Figure 1 When working with the most dangerous pathogens, scientists need to be very careful. Sensible safety precautions are needed when working with microorganisms.

Examiner's tip

Make sure you understand that we sterilise solutions and equipment to kill all the bacteria already on them. Otherwise they would grow and contaminate the culture we are studying.

Step 2:

The next step is to **inoculate** the sterile agar with the microorganisms you want to grow.

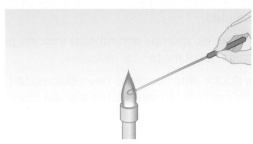

Sterilise the inoculating loop used to transfer micro-organisms to the agar by heating it until it is red hot in the flame of a Bunsen and then letting it cool. Do not put the loop down or blow on it as it cools.

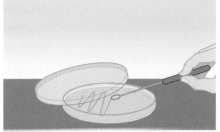

Dip the sterilised loop in a suspension of the bacteria you want to grow and use it to make zigzag streaks across the surface of the agar. Replace the lid on the dish as quickly as possible to avoid contamination.

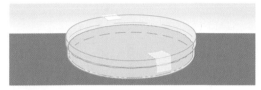

Fix the lid of the Petri dish with adhesive tape to prevent microorganisms from the air contaminating the culture – or microbes from the culture escaping. Do not seal all the way around the edge so oxygen can get into the dish preventing harmful anaerobic bacteria from growing.

The Petri dish should be stored upside down to stop condensation falling onto the agar surface and labelled.

Figure 2 Culturing microorganisms safely in the laboratory

Step 3:

Once you have inoculated your plates, the secured Petri dishes need to be incubated (kept warm) for several days so the microorganisms can grow (see Figure 3). In school and college laboratories, the maximum temperature at which cultures are incubated is 25 °C. This greatly reduces the likelihood that you will grow pathogens that might be harmful to people. In industrial conditions, bacterial cultures, for example insulin-producing GM bacteria, are often grown at higher temperatures to enable the microorganisms to grow more rapidly. A hospital lab would also incubate human pathogens at 37 °C, so they grow as fast as possible to be identified.

Summary questions

1 **a** Why do we culture microorganisms in the laboratory?
   b What is agar jelly and why is it so important in setting up bacterial cultures?

2 When you set up a culture of bacteria in a Petri dish (see Figure 3), you give the bacteria everything they need to grow as fast as possible. However, these ideal conditions do not last forever. What might limit the growth of the bacteria in a culture on a Petri dish?

3 **a** Why do we grow bacteria at 25 °C or below in the school lab when this is not their optimum temperature for growth?
   b Why are bacteria cultured at much higher temperatures in industrial plants?

Summary questions

1 Bacteria and viruses are very small.

   a How do they get into the body?

   b How do bacteria cause the symptoms of disease?

   c How do viruses make you ill?

2 a How are infectious diseases spread from one person to another?

   b What steps can individuals take to reduce the spread of infectious diseases from one person to another?

   c What steps can companies and organisations take to reduce the spread of infectious diseases between employees?

3 a Vancomycin is an antibiotic which doctors used for patients infected with MRSA and other antibiotic-resistant bacteria. Now they are finding some infections are resistant to vancomycin. Explain how this may have happened.

   b What can we do to prevent the problem of antibiotic resistance getting worse?

4 a How would you set up a culture of bacteria in a school lab?

   b Describe how you would test to find out the right strength of disinfectant to use to wash the school floors.

5 The body has a number of defences against pathogens. Some of them are very general and work against any pathogen that enters your body. Others are very specific to a particular pathogen.

Describe all of the ways in which the body defends you against pathogens causing disease in your body.

6 Vaccination uses your body's natural defence system to protect you against disease.

   a Explain how vaccination works.

   b Why are you vaccinated against some diseases and not others?

7 Measles is a disease that affects millions of people around the world. Approximately every three minutes, someone somewhere dies of measles – a total of 164 000 people each year. Others are left blind or brain damaged by the disease.

Mumps is another common infectious disease, which is usually relatively mild but can cause sterility in men, deafness and meningitis.

Rubella is a mild disease in adults but can cause big problems in the developing fetus if a pregnant woman becomes infected.

The MMR (measles, mumps and rubella) vaccine protects children against all of these viral diseases.

However, a doctor who has since been discredited and struck off the medical register started a scare story about the safety of the MMR vaccine. In spite of the fact that all the evidence shows that the MMR vaccine carries no more risk than any of the other commonly used vaccines, many people became worried and stopped having their children vaccinated. Use the graphs below to help you answer the following questions

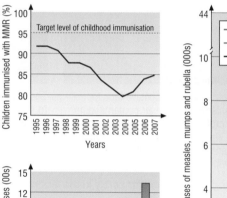

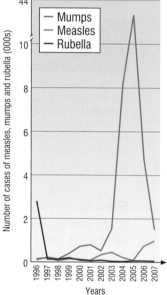

a Based on this evidence, when do you think the MMR scare story was published?

b What happened to the numbers of children infected with measles after the scare?

c What happened to the number of cases of mumps in 2005?

d Why did the numbers of cases of measles and mumps remain stable for several years after the numbers of children being vaccinated started to fall?

e In 2011, levels of uptake of the MMR vaccine were over 90% for children aged 5 years and under. The aim is to get levels up to 95% of the population as soon as possible.

   i Why is it important to get vaccination levels so high?

   ii Describe the pattern you would expect to see in the numbers of cases of measles and mumps over the next few years and explain your answer.

AQA Examination-style questions

1 Complete the following sentences:

a Microorganisms that cause infection are called .... (1)

b These microorganisms may be bacteria or .... (1)

c Bacteria may produce .... that make us feel ill. (1)

2 Polio is a disease caused by a virus. In the UK, children are given polio vaccine to protect them against the disease.

a Complete the sentences below.

i It is difficult to kill the polio virus inside the body because .... (1)

ii The vaccine contains an .... form of the polio virus. (1)

iii The vaccine stimulates the white blood cells to produce .... which destroy the virus. (1)

AQA, 2006

b Figure 1 shows the number of cases of polio in the UK between 1948 and 1968.

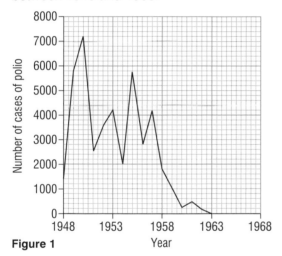

Figure 1

i In which year was the number of cases of polio highest? (1)

ii Polio vaccination was first used in the UK in 1955. How many years did it take for the number of cases of polio to fall to zero? (1)

iii There have been no cases of polio in the UK for many years. However, children are still vaccinated against the disease. Suggest one reason for this. (1)

3 Diphtheria was a common bacterial disease that killed many children before vaccination was introduced.

The Diphtheria bacteria produce a powerful toxin that damages the patient's cells.

a Diphtheria is spread by droplet infection. However, not all children who inhaled the bacteria developed the disease. Suggest reasons why. (4)

b Describe **three** ways in which the white blood cells would try to protect the body if the Diphtheria bacteria that were inhaled entered the patient's blood. (6)

4 The blood system supplies the body tissues with essential materials.

a Blood contains red blood cells, white blood cells and platelets.

i Give the function of white blood cells. (1)

ii Give the function of platelets. (1)

iii Figure 2 shows a magnified red blood cell.

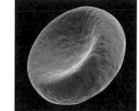

Figure 2

The average diameter of a real red blood cell is 0.008 millimetres. On the photograph, the diameter of the red blood cell is 100 millimetres. Use the formula below to calculate the magnification of the photograph.

diameter on photograph = real diameter × magnification

Magnification = ... (2)

iv Some blood capillaries have an internal diameter of approximately 0.01 millimetres. Use information given in part **4(a)(iii)** to explain why only one red blood cell at a time can pass through a capillary. (2)

v Red blood cells transport oxygen. Describe how oxygen is moved from the lungs to the tissues. (3)

b Two students did the same step-up exercise for 3 minutes.

One of the students was fit. The other student was unfit.

Figure 3 shows how the students' heart rate changed during the exercise and after the exercise.

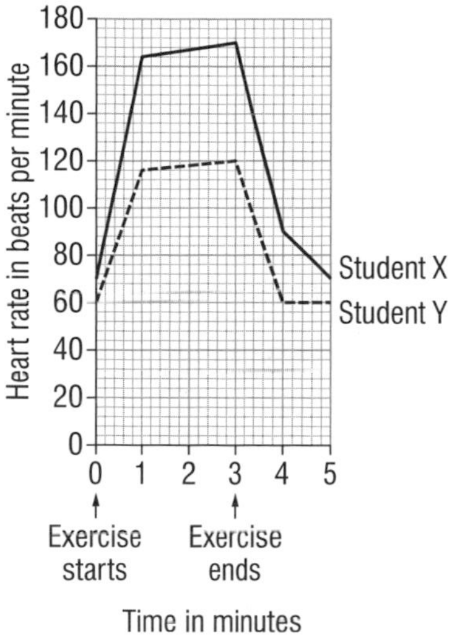

i Use the information in the graph to suggest which student was the fitter. Explain your choice. (3)

ii Explain the advantage to the students of the change in heart rate during exercise. (4)

Figure 3

B9.1 Photosynthesis

Examiner's tip

Learn the word and chemical equations for photosynthesis. Remember it needs light energy, which normally comes from the Sun.

Practical

Producing oxygen

You can show that a plant is photosynthesising by the oxygen it gives off as a by-product. Oxygen is a colourless gas, so it isn't easy to show it is being produced in land plants. However, if you use water plants such as *Cabomba* or *Elodea*, you can see and collect the bubbles of gas they give off when they are photosynthesising. The gas will relight a glowing splint, showing that it is rich in oxygen.

Figure 1 The oxygen produced during photosynthesis is vital for life on Earth. You can demonstrate that it is produced using water plants such as this *Cabomba*.

As with all living organisms, plants and algae need food to provide them with the energy for respiration, growth and reproduction. However, plants don't need to eat – they can make their own food by photosynthesis. This takes place in the green parts of plants (especially the leaves) when it is light. Algae can also carry out photosynthesis.

The process of photosynthesis

The cells in algae and plant leaves are full of small green parts called chloroplasts, which contain a green substance called chlorophyll. During photosynthesis, light energy is absorbed by the chlorophyll in the chloroplasts. This energy is then used to convert carbon dioxide from the air plus water from the soil into a simple sugar called **glucose**. The chemical reaction also produces oxygen gas as a by-product. The oxygen is released into the air, which we can then use when we breathe it in.

Photosynthesis can be summarised in the following equation:

$$\text{carbon dioxide} + \text{water} \xrightarrow{\text{light energy}} \text{glucose} + \text{oxygen}$$

$$6CO_2 + 6H_2O \xrightarrow{\text{light energy}} C_6H_{12}O_6 + 6O_2$$

Some of the glucose produced during photosynthesis is used immediately by the cells of the plant for respiration. However, a lot of the glucose is converted into insoluble starch and stored.

Practical

Testing for starch using iodine

Iodine solution is a yellow-brown liquid that turns blue-black when it reacts with starch. You can use this iodine test for starch to show that photosynthesis has taken place in a plant.

Practical

Testing for starch

To show that light is vital for photosynthesis to take place:

Take a leaf from a plant kept in the light and a plant kept in the dark for at least 24 hours. Leaves have to be specially prepared so the iodine solution can reach the cells. Just adding iodine solution to a leaf is not enough, because the waterproof cuticle keeps the iodine out so it can't react with the starch. Also, the green chlorophyll would mask any colour changes if the iodine did react with the starch. You therefore need to treat the leaves by boiling them in ethanol, to destroy the waxy cuticle and then to remove the colour. The leaves are then rinsed in hot water to soften them. After treating the leaves, add iodine solution to them both. Iodine solution turns blue-black in the presence of starch. The leaf that has been in the light will turn blue-black. The iodine solution on the leaf kept in the dark remains orange-red.

Safety: Take care when using ethanol. It is volatile, highly flammable and harmful. Always wear eye protection. No naked flames – use a hot water bath to heat ethanol.

Leaf adaptations

For photosynthesis to be successful, a plant needs plenty of carbon dioxide, light and water. The leaves of plants are perfectly adapted as organs of photosynthesis because:

- most leaves are broad, giving them a big surface area for light to fall on
- they contain chlorophyll in the chloroplasts to absorb the light energy
- they have air spaces that allow carbon dioxide to get to the cells, and oxygen to leave them by diffusion
- they have veins, which bring plenty of water in the xylem to the cells of the leaves and remove the products of photosynthesis in the phloem.

These adaptations mean the plant can photosynthesise as much as possible whenever there is light available.

Algae are aquatic so they are adapted to photosynthesising in water. They have a large surface area and absorb carbon dioxide dissolved in the water around them. The oxygen they produce also dissolves in the water around them as it is released.

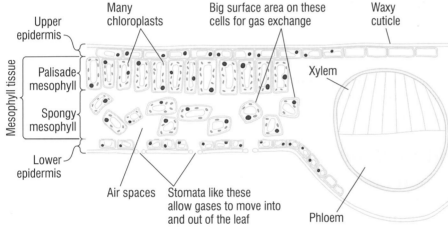

Figure 2 A section (slice) through a leaf showing the different tissues and how they are adapted for photosynthesis

??? Did you know …?

Every year, plants produce about 368 000 000 000 tonnes of oxygen, so there is plenty to go around!

Summary questions

1 a Where does a plant get the carbon dioxide and water that it needs for photosynthesis, and how does it get the light it needs?
   b Where do algae get carbon dioxide and water from?

2 Describe the path taken by a carbon atom as it moves from being part of the carbon dioxide in the air to being part of a starch molecule in a plant.

3 Explain carefully why a leaf from a plant kept in the light for 24 hours will turn iodine solution blue-black, whereas a leaf kept in the light for 24 hours and then in the dark for 24 hours has no effect on iodine solution.

∞ links

For more on the structure and function of plant cells, see 1.1 'Animal and plant cells'.

Examiner's tip

Practise labelling the parts and cells in the cross-section of a leaf, and be sure you know the function of each one.

Key points

- During photosynthesis, light energy is absorbed by chlorophyll in the chloroplasts of the green parts of the plant. It is used to convert carbon dioxide and water into sugar (glucose). Oxygen is released as a by-product.

- Photosynthesis can be summed up by the following word and symbol balanced equations:

$$\text{carbon dioxide} + \text{water} \xrightarrow[\text{energy}]{\text{light}} \text{glucose} + \text{oxygen}$$

$$6CO_2 + 6H_2O \xrightarrow[\text{energy}]{\text{light}} C_6H_{12}O_6 + 6O_2$$

- Leaves are well adapted to allow the maximum amount of photosynthesis to take place.

B9.2   Limiting factors

Learning objectives

After this topic, you should know:

- which factors limit the rate of photosynthesis in plants

- how we can use what we know about limiting factors to grow more food.

You may have noticed that plants grow quickly in the summer, yet they hardly grow at all in the winter. Plants need light, warmth and carbon dioxide if they are going to photosynthesise and grow as fast as they can. Sometimes any one or more of these things can be in short supply and limit the amount of photosynthesis a plant can manage. This is why they are known as **limiting factors**.

Light

The most obvious factor affecting the rate of photosynthesis is light intensity. If there is plenty of light, lots of photosynthesis can take place. In low light, photosynthesis will stop. Whatever the other conditions are around the plant. For most plants, the brighter the light, the faster the rate of photosynthesis.

Temperature

Temperature affects all chemical reactions, including photosynthesis. As the temperature rises, the rate of photosynthesis increases as the reaction speeds up. However, photosynthesis is controlled by enzymes. Most enzymes are destroyed (denatured) once the temperature rises to around 40–50 °C. So, if the temperature gets too high, the enzymes controlling photosynthesis are denatured and the rate of photosynthesis will fall.

Carbon dioxide levels

Plants need carbon dioxide to make glucose. The atmosphere is only about 0.04% carbon dioxide, which often limits the rate of photosynthesis. Increasing the carbon dioxide levels will increase the rate at which photosynthesis takes place.

On a sunny day, carbon dioxide levels are the most common limiting factor for plants. The carbon dioxide levels around a plant tend to rise at night, when the plant respires but doesn't photosynthesise. As light and temperature levels increase in the morning, the carbon dioxide around the plant is used up.

In a garden, woodland or field (rather than a lab or greenhouse where conditions can be controlled), light, temperature and carbon dioxide levels interact, and any one of them might be the factor that limits photosynthesis.

Making the most of photosynthesis

The more a plant photosynthesises, the more biomass it makes and the faster it grows. Farmers want their plants to grow as fast and as big as possible to make the best profit.

Out in the fields it is almost impossible to influence.

People can artificially control the environment of their plants using greenhouses or **polytunnels**. Most importantly, the atmosphere is warmer inside than out. This speeds up the rate of photosynthesis so plants grow faster, flower and fruit earlier and produce higher yields. You can also use greenhouses to grow fruit such as peaches and lemons which don't grow well outside in the UK.

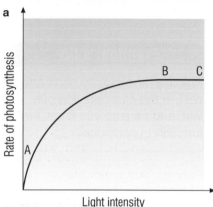

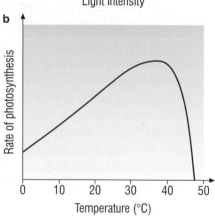

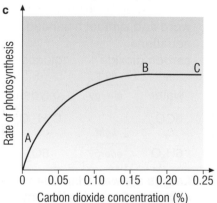

Figure 1 Light, temperature and carbon dioxide levels all affect the rate of photosynthesis in a plant

Controlling a crop's environment

Companies use big commercial greenhouses to control the temperature and the levels of light and carbon dioxide. The levels are varied to get the fastest possible rates of photosynthesis. For example:

- Carbon dioxide levels are increased during the day when light levels are at their highest, so they do not act as a limiting factor.
- The optimum temperature for enzyme activity is maintained all the time.
- Artificial lighting is used to prolong the hours of photosynthesis and to increase the light intensity.

As a result, the plants photosynthesise for as long as possible and grow increasingly quickly. Artificial lighting can be used to give year-round production by plants, and to grow plants out of their normal season or out of their normal habitat.

The greenhouses are huge and conditions are controlled using computer software. It costs a lot of money, but controlling the environment has many benefits. Turnover is fast, which means profits can be high. The crops are clean and unspoilt. There is no ploughing or preparing the land, and crops can be grown where the land is poor.

It takes a lot of energy to keep conditions in the greenhouses just right – but fewer staff are needed. Monitoring systems and alarms are vital in case things go wrong, but for plants grown in controlled greenhouse conditions, limiting factors are a thing of the past!

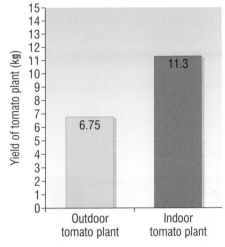

Figure 2 One piece of American research showed that the crop yield inside a greenhouse was almost double that of crops grown outdoors

Figure 3 Controlling the temperature, light and carbon dioxide level in a greenhouse removes limiting factors and enables farmers to grow the biggest crops possible in the shortest time

Summary questions

1. What are the **three** main limiting factors that affect the rate of photosynthesis in a plant?

2. **a** In each of these situations, **one** factor in particular is most likely to be limiting photosynthesis. In *each* case listed below, suggest which factor this is and explain why the rate of photosynthesis is limited.
   - **i** A wheat field first thing in the morning
   - **ii** The same field later on in the day
   - **iii** Plants growing on a woodland floor in winter
   - **iv** Plants growing on a woodland floor in summer

   b Why is it impossible to be certain which factor is involved in each of these cases?

3. Look at the graph **a** in Figure 1.
   - **a** Explain what is happening between points A and B on the graph.
   - **b** Explain what is happening between points B and C on the graph.
   - **c** Now look at graph **b** in Figure 1. Explain why it is a different shape to the other two graphs shown in Figure 1.

Key points

- The rate of photosynthesis may be limited by shortage of light, low temperature and shortage of carbon dioxide.

- We can artificially control the levels of light, temperature and carbon dioxide when growing crops in greenhouses to increase the rate of photosynthesis and so increase the yield of the crops.

B9.3 How plants use glucose

Figure 1 Worldwide, photosynthesis in algae produces more oxygen and biomass than photosynthesis in plants does – but we often forget all about them

?? Did you know ... ?

Some algal cells are very rich in oils. They are even being considered as a possible source of biofuels for the future.

⃝⃝ links

For more information on transport in plants, see 9.6 'Transport systems in plants'. For more on osmosis in plants, see 1.5 'Osmosis'.

Plants and algae make glucose when they photosynthesise. This glucose is vital for their survival. Some of the glucose produced during photosynthesis is used immediately by the plant and algal cells. They use it for respiration, to provide energy for cell functions such as growth and reproduction.

Using glucose

Plant cells and algal cells, like any other living cells, respire all the time. They use some of the glucose produced during photosynthesis as they respire. The glucose is broken down using oxygen to provide energy for the cells. Carbon dioxide and water are the waste products of the reaction. Chemically, respiration is the reverse of photosynthesis.

The energy released in respiration is used to build up smaller molecules into bigger molecules. Some of the glucose made in photosynthesis is changed into insoluble starch for storage (see below). Plants and algae also build up glucose into more complex carbohydrates such as cellulose. They use this to strengthen their cell walls.

Plants use some of the glucose from photosynthesis to make amino acids. They do this by combining sugars with **nitrate ions** and other **mineral ions** from the soil. These amino acids are then built up into proteins to be used in their cells (see below). This uses energy from respiration.

Algae also make amino acids. They do this by taking the nitrate ions and other materials they need from the water they live in.

Plants and algae also use glucose from photosynthesis and energy from respiration to build up fats and oils. These may be used in the cells as an energy store. They are sometimes used in the cell walls to make them stronger. In addition, plants often use fats or oils as an energy store in their seeds. Seeds provide lots of energy for the new plant as it germinates.

Starch for storage

Plants make food by photosynthesis in their leaves and other green parts, but it is needed all over the plant. It is moved around the plant in the phloem.

Plants convert some of the glucose produced in photosynthesis into starch to be stored. Glucose is soluble in water. If it were stored in plant cells, it could affect the way water moves into and out of the cells by osmosis. Lots of glucose stored in plant cells could affect the water balance of the whole plant.

Starch is insoluble in water, so it will have no effect on the water balance of the plant. This means that plants can store large amounts of starch in their cells.

Starch is the main energy store in plants and it is found all over a plant:

- Starch is stored in the cells of the leaves. It provides an energy store for when it is dark or when light levels are low.

- Starch is also kept in special storage areas of a plant. For example, many plants produce **tubers** and bulbs which are full of stored starch, to help them survive through the winter. We often take advantage of these starch stores, found in vegetables such as potatoes and onions, by eating them ourselves.

Making starch

The presence of starch in a leaf is evidence that photosynthesis has taken place. You can test for starch using the iodine solution test – see page 112 for details of how to treat the leaves so they will absorb the iodine. After this treatment, adding iodine will show you clearly if the leaf has been photosynthesising or not.

Safety: Take care when using ethanol. It is volatile, highly flammable and harmful. Always wear eye protection. No naked flames – use a hot water bath to heat ethanol.

Figure 2 The leaf on the right has been kept in the dark. Its starch stores have been used for respiration or moved to other parts of the plant. The leaf on the left has been in the light and been able to photosynthesise. The glucose has been converted to starch, which is clearly visible when it reacts with iodine and turns blue-black.

Minerals, proteins and carnivorous plants

Plants make amino acids and build them up into proteins. However, to make amino acids from the carbohydrates produced by photosynthesis, plants must take in nitrates from the soil. Very few plants can survive well if the soil they are growing in is low in minerals. For example, bogs are wet and their peaty soil has very few nutrients in it. This makes it a difficult place for plants to live.

Some carnivorous plants, such as the Venus flytrap and sundews, are especially adapted to live in nutrient-poor soil. They can survive because they obtain most of their nutrients from the animals such as insects that they catch.

The Venus flytrap has special 'traps' that contain sweet smelling nectar. They sit wide open showing their red insides. Insects are attracted to the colour and the smell. Inside the trap are many small, sensitive hairs. As the insect moves about to find the nectar, it will brush against these hairs. Once the hairs have been touched, the trap is triggered: it snaps shut and traps the insect inside.

Special enzymes then digest the insect inside the trap. The Venus flytrap uses the nutrients from the digested bodies of its victims in place of the nutrients that it cannot get from the poor bog soil in which it grows. After the insect has been digested, the trap reopens, ready to try again.

Sundews simply trap insects on their sticky hairs and digest them where they are held to make use of the valuable nitrates and other minerals.

Figure 3 The Venus flytrap – an insect-eating plant

Summary questions

1 List as many ways as possible in which a plant uses the glucose produced by photosynthesis.

2 a Why is some of the glucose made by photosynthesis converted to starch to be stored in the plant?
  b Where might you find starch in a plant?
  c How could you show that a potato is a store of starch?

3 Explain why relatively few plants grow successfully in bogs yet carnivorous plants are often found growing there.

B9.4

Exchange in plants

Learning objectives

After this topic, you should know:

- how the leaves of a plant are adapted for gaseous exchange

- how plant roots are adapted for the efficient uptake of water and mineral ions.

Animals aren't the only living organisms that need to exchange materials. Plants rely heavily on diffusion to get the carbon dioxide they need for photosynthesis. They use osmosis to take water from the soil and active transport to obtain mineral ions from the soil. Plants have adaptations that make these exchanges as efficient as possible.

Gas exchange in plants

Plants need carbon dioxide and water for photosynthesis to take place. They get the carbon dioxide they need by diffusion through their leaves. The flattened shape of the leaves increases the surface area for diffusion. Most plants have thin leaves. This means the distance the carbon dioxide has to diffuse from the outside air to the photosynthesising cells is kept as short as possible.

What's more, leaves have many air spaces in their structure. These allow carbon dioxide to come into contact with lots of cells and provide a large surface area for diffusion.

However, there is a problem: leaf cells constantly lose water by **evaporation**. If carbon dioxide could diffuse freely into and out of the leaves, water vapour would also be lost very quickly. Then the leaves – and the plant – would die.

⚭ **links**

For more on photosynthesis, look back to 9.1 'Photosynthesis'.

The leaf cells do not need carbon dioxide all the time. When it is dark, they don't need carbon dioxide to diffuse in because they are not photosynthesising. When light is a limiting factor on the rate of photosynthesis, enough carbon dioxide is produced by respiration to supply the needs of photosynthesis. Yet, on bright, warm, sunny days, there is a high rate of photosynthesis and the plant needs a lot of carbon dioxide to come into the leaves by diffusion.

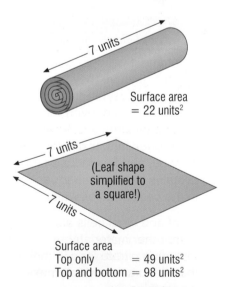

Figure 1 The wide, flat shape of most leaves greatly increases the surface area for collecting light and exchanging gases, compared with more cylindrical leaves

7 units

Surface area = 22 units^2

7 units

(Leaf shape simplified to a square!)

7 units

Surface area
Top only = 49 units^2
Top and bottom = 98 units^2

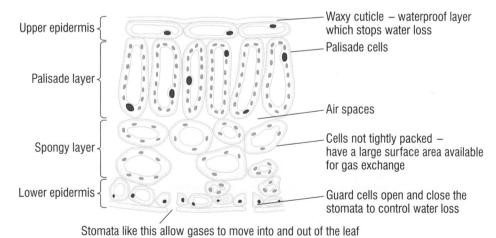

Upper epidermis

Palisade layer

Spongy layer

Lower epidermis

Waxy cuticle – waterproof layer which stops water loss

Palisade cells

Air spaces

Cells not tightly packed – have a large surface area available for gas exchange

Guard cells open and close the stomata to control water loss

Stomata like this allow gases to move into and out of the leaf

Figure 2 This cross-section of a leaf shows the arrangement of the cells inside. Lots of air spaces and short diffusion distances, which means that the carbon dioxide needed for photosynthesis reaches the cells as efficiently as possible.

Leaves are adapted to allow carbon dioxide in only when it is needed. They are covered with a waxy **cuticle**. This is a waterproof and gas-proof layer.

All over the leaf surface are small openings known as stomata. The stomata can be opened when the plant needs to allow air into the leaves. Carbon dioxide from the atmosphere diffuses into the air spaces and then into the cells down a concentration gradient. At the same time, oxygen produced by photosynthesis is removed from the leaf by diffusion into the surrounding air. This maintains a concentration gradient for oxygen from the cells into the air spaces of the leaf. The stomata can be closed the rest of the time to limit the loss of water.

The size of the stomata and their opening and closing is controlled by the **guard cells**.

Most of the water vapour lost by plants is lost from the leaves and most of this loss takes place by diffusion through the stomata when they are open. This is one of the main reasons why it is important that plants can close their stomata – to limit the loss of water vapour.

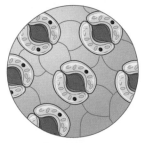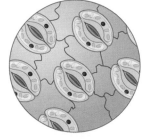

Figure 3 The size of the opening of the stomata is controlled by the guard cells. This in turn controls the carbon dioxide going into the leaf and water vapour and oxygen leaving it.

Open stomata   Closed stomata

Uptake of water and mineral ions in plants

Plant roots are adapted to take water and mineral ions from the soil as efficiently as possible. The roots themselves are thin, divided tubes with a large surface area. The cells on the outside of the roots near the growing tips have special adaptations that increase the surface area. These **root hair cells** have tiny projections from the cells which push out between the soil particles.

Water moves into the root hair cells by osmosis across the partially permeable root cell membrane. It then has only a short distance to move across the root to the xylem, where it is moved up and around the plant.

Plant roots are also adapted to take in mineral ions using active transport. They have plenty of mitochondria to supply the energy they need for this process. They also have all the advantages of a large surface area and the short pathways needed for the movement of water (see Figure 4).

??? Did you know … ?

Root hairs have an amazing effect – a 1 m^2 area of lawn grass has 350 m^2 of root surface area!

Summary questions

1 **a** What are stomata?
   b Describe their role in the plant.
   c How are they controlled?

2 How are plant roots adapted for the absorption of water and mineral ions?

3 Explain carefully how the adaptations of plants for the exchange of materials compare with human adaptations in the lungs and the gut.

⃝⃝ links

For more information on stomata, see 12.3 'Adaptations in plants'. For information on xylem, see 9.6 'Transport systems in plants'.

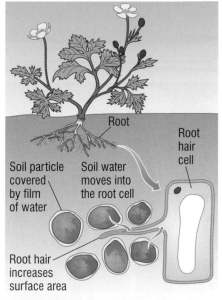

Figure 4 Many small roots, and the presence of microscopic root hairs on the individual root cells, increase diffusion of substances from the soil into the plant

Key points

- Plant leaves have stomata that allow the plant to obtain carbon dioxide from the atmosphere.

- Carbon dioxide enters the leaf by diffusion. Leaves have a flat, thin shape and internal air spaces to increase the surface area available for diffusion.

- Plants mainly lose water vapour from their leaves, and most of this loss takes place through the stomata.

- Most of the water and mineral ions needed by a plant are absorbed by the root hair cells, which increase the surface area of the roots.

B9.5 Evaporation and transpiration

Learning objectives

After this topic, you should know:

- what transpiration is

- the factors that affect how quickly plants transpire.

Figure 1 The transpiration stream in trees can pull litres of water many metres above the ground

The top of a tree may be many metres from the ground. Yet the leaves at the top need water just as much as those on the lower branches. So how do they get the water they need?

Water loss from the leaves

The stomata on the surface of plant leaves can be opened and closed by the guard cells that surround them. Plants open their stomata to take in carbon dioxide for photosynthesis. However, when the stomata are open, plants lose water vapour through them as well. The water vapour evaporates from the cells lining the air spaces and then passes out of the leaf through the stomata by diffusion. This loss of water vapour is known as **transpiration**.

As water evaporates from the surface of the leaves, more water is pulled up through the xylem to take its place. This constant movement of water molecules through the xylem from the roots to the leaves is known as the **transpiration stream**. It is driven by the evaporation of water from the leaves. So, anything that affects the rate of evaporation will affect transpiration.

The effect of the environment on transpiration

Anything that increases the rate of photosynthesis will increase the rate of transpiration. This occurs because more stomata are opened up to let in carbon dioxide. In turn, more water is lost by evaporation and then diffusion through the open stomata. So, warm, sunny conditions increase the rate of transpiration.

Conditions that increase the rate of evaporation and diffusion of water when the stomata are open will also make transpiration happen more rapidly. Hot, dry, windy conditions increase the rate of transpiration. Water evaporates more from the cells as the temperature increases, and diffusion also happens more quickly. Water vapour will diffuse more rapidly into dry air than into humid air, and windy conditions both increase the rate of evaporation and also maintain a steep concentration gradient from the inside of the leaf to the outside by removing water vapour as it diffuses out. So, each of these conditions individually increases the rate of transpiration, and combined they mean a plant will lose a lot of water in this way.

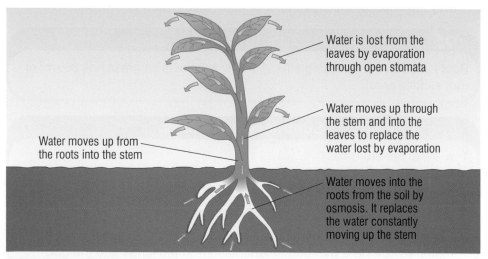

Water is lost from the leaves by evaporation through open stomata

Water moves up through the stem and into the leaves to replace the water lost by evaporation

Water moves up from the roots into the stem

Water moves into the roots from the soil by osmosis. It replaces the water constantly moving up the stem

Figure 2 The transpiration stream

Controlling water loss

Most plants have a variety of adaptations that help them to photosynthesise as much as possible while losing as little water as possible.

Most leaves have a waxy, waterproof layer (the cuticle) to prevent uncontrolled water loss. In very hot environments, the cuticle may be very thick and shiny. Most of the stomata are found on the underside of the leaves. This protects them from the direct light and energy of the Sun, and reduces the time they are open.

If a plant begins to lose water faster than it is replaced by the roots, it can take come drastic measures

- The whole plant may wilt. **Wilting** is a protection mechanism against further water loss. The leaves all collapse and hang down. This greatly reduces the surface area available for water loss by evaporation.
- The stomata close, which stops photosynthesis and risks overheating. However, this prevents most water loss and any further wilting.

The plant will remain wilted until the temperature drops, the sun goes in or it rains.

Examiner's tip

Remember that the transpiration stream is driven by the loss of water by evaporation out of the stomata.

Practical

Evidence for transpiration

There are a number of experiments which can be done to investigate the movement of water in plants by transpiration. Many of them use a piece of apparatus known as a potometer.

A potometer can be used to show how the uptake of water by the plant changes with different conditions. This gives you a good idea of the amount of water lost by the plant in transpiration. A potometer measures water uptake, which is almost the same as transpiration but not quite, as some of the water is used in metabolism (e.g. photosynthesis).

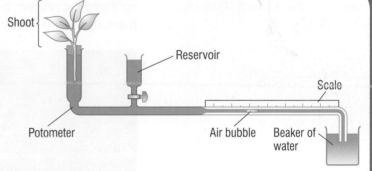

Figure 3 A potometer is used to show the water uptake of a plant under different conditions

Summary questions

1 a What is transpiration?
  b Describe how water moves up a plant in the transpiration stream.

2 a Which part of the leaves helps the plant to reduce water loss under normal conditions?
  b How will transpiration in a plant be affected if the top leaf surfaces are coated in petroleum jelly?
  c How will transpiration in a plant be affected if the bottom leaf surfaces are coated in petroleum jelly?
  d Explain the effect on transpiration of turning a fan onto the leaves of the plant.
  e What does a potometer actually measure?

3 Water lilies have their stomata on the tops of their leaves.
  a How will this affect transpiration in water lilies?
  b Explain how the plants will cope with this situation.

Key points

- The loss of water vapour from the surface of plant leaves is known as transpiration.
- Water is lost through the stomata, which open to let in carbon dioxide for photosynthesis.
- Transpiration is more rapid in hot, dry, windy or bright conditions.

B9.6 Transport systems in plants

∞ links

For information on phloem and xylem, look back to 2.5 'Tissues and organs'.

Plants make glucose (a simple sugar) by photosynthesis in the leaves and other green parts. This glucose is needed all over the plant. Similarly, water and mineral ions move into the plant from the soil through the roots, but they are needed by every cell of the plant. Water moves through the plant in the transpiration stream. Plants have two separate transport systems to move substances around their bodies.

Phloem – moving food

The phloem tissue transports the sugars made by photosynthesis from the leaves to the rest of the plant. This includes the growing areas of the stems and roots where the dissolved sugars are needed for making new plant cells. Food is also transported to the storage organs where it is needed to provide an energy store for the winter.

Phloem is a living tissue – the phloem cells are alive. The movement of dissolved sugars from the leaves to the rest of the plant is called **translocation**.

Greenfly and other aphids are plant pests. They stick their sharp mouthparts right into the phloem and feed on the sugary fluid. If too many of them attack a plant, they can kill it by taking all of the food.

Figure 1 Aphids take the liquid full of dissolved sugars directly from the phloem

Xylem – moving water and mineral ions

The xylem tissue is the other transport tissue in plants. It carries water and mineral ions from the soil around the plant to the stem and the leaves. Mature xylem cells are dead.

Practical

Evidence for movement through xylem

You can demonstrate the movement of water up the xylem by placing celery stalks in water containing a coloured dye. After a few hours, slice the stem in several places – you will see the coloured circles where the water and dye have been moved through the xylem.

In woody plants like trees, the xylem makes up the bulk of the wood and the phloem is found in a ring just underneath the bark. This makes young trees in particular very vulnerable to damage by animals: if a complete ring of bark is eaten, transport in the phloem stops and the tree will die.

Figure 2 Without protective collars on the trunks, deer would destroy the transport tissue of young trees like these and kill them before they could become established in the woodland

Why is transport so important?

It is vital to move the food made by photosynthesis around the plant – all the cells need sugars for respiration as well as for providing materials for growth. The movement of water and dissolved mineral ions from the roots is equally important – the mineral ions are needed for the production of proteins and other molecules within the cells.

The plant needs water for photosynthesis, when carbon dioxide and water combine to make glucose (plus oxygen). It also needs water to hold the plant upright. When a cell has plenty of water inside it, the vacuole presses the cytoplasm against the cell walls. This pressure of the cytoplasm against the cell walls gives support for young plants and for the structure of the leaves. For young plants and soft-stemmed plants – although not trees – this is the main method of support.

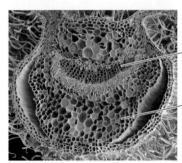

Phloem

Xylem

Figure 3 The phloem and xylem are arranged in vascular bundles in the stem

Key points

● Flowering plants have separate transport systems.

● Xylem tissue transports water and mineral ions from the roots to the stems and leaves.

● Phloem tissue transports dissolved sugars from the leaves to the rest of the plant, including the growing regions and storage organs.

Summary questions

1 a Why does a plant need a transport system?
  b Explain why a constant supply of sugar and water are so important to the cells of a plant.

2 Make a table to compare the xylem and phloem in a plant.

3 A local woodland trust has set up a scheme to put protective plastic covers around the trunks of young trees. Some local residents are objecting to this, saying it spoils the look of the woodland. Explain exactly why this protection is necessary and the impact it would have on the wood if the trees are not protected.

Plant responses

After this topic, you should know:

- how plants respond to light, gravity and moisture in their environment
- the role of the hormone auxin in the response of a plant to different stimuli.

Figure 1 Seedlings such as these show you clearly how plant shoots respond to light by growing towards it

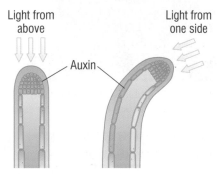

Light from above   Light from one side

Auxin

Figure 2 The response of shoots to unilateral light is the result of an uneven distribution of auxin. This causes uneven growth of the cells, resulting in a bend in the stem.

??? Did you know ...?

The first scientists to demonstrate the way the shoot of a plant responds to light from one direction were Charles Darwin and his son Francis.

It is easy to see how animals, including humans, take in information about the surroundings and then react to it. Yet plants also need to be coordinated. They are sensitive to light, water and gravity.

Plants are sensitive

When seeds are dispersed (spread), they may fall any way up in the soil. It is very important that when the seed starts to grow (germinate) the roots grow downwards into the soil, anchoring the seedling and keeping it stable. They can also take up the water and minerals needed for healthy growth.

At the same time, the shoots need to grow upwards towards the light so they can **photosynthesise** as much as possible.

Plant roots are sensitive to gravity and water. The roots grow towards moisture and in the direction of the force of gravity. Plant shoots are sensitive to gravity and light. The shoots grow towards light and against the force of gravity. This means that whichever way up the seed lands, the plant always grows the right way up!

Plant responses

Plant responses happen as a result of plant hormones which coordinate and control growth. These responses are easy to see in young seedlings, but they also happen in adult plants. For example, the stems of a houseplant left on a windowsill will soon bend towards the light.

The responses of plant roots and shoots to light, gravity and moisture are known as **tropisms** or tropic responses.

- The response of a plant to light is known as a **phototropism**.
- The response of a plant to gravity is called **gravitropism** (also known as geotropism).
- The response of a plant to moisture (water) is called **hydrotropism**.

The responses of plants to light and gravity are controlled by a hormone called **auxin**. The response happens because of an uneven distribution of this hormone in the growing shoot or root. This causes an unequal growth rate. As a result, the root or shoot bends in the right direction.

Phototropism can clearly be seen when a young shoot responds to light from one side only. The shoot will bend so it is growing towards the light. Auxin moves from the side of the shoot where the light is falling to the unlit side of the shoot. The cells on that side respond to the hormone by growing more – and so the shoot bends towards the light. Once light falls evenly on the shoot, the levels of auxin will be equal on all sides and so the shoot grows straight again.

Gravitropisms can be seen in roots and shoots. Auxin has different effects on root and shoot cells. High levels of auxin make shoot cells grow more but inhibit growth of root cells. This is why roots and shoots respond differently to gravity.

1 A normal young bean plant is laid on its side in the dark. Auxin is equally spread through the tissues.

Root   Shoot

Gravity   Gravity

2 In the root, more auxin gathers on the lower side.

In the shoot, more auxin gathers on the lower side.

3 The root grows *more* on the side with *least* auxin, making it bend and grow down towards the force of gravity. When it has grown down, the auxin becomes evenly spread again.

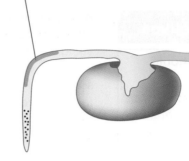

The shoot grows *more* on the side with *most* auxin, making it bend and grow up away from the force of gravity. When it has grown up, the auxin becomes evenly spread again.

Figure 3 Gravitropism in shoots and roots. The uneven distribution of the hormone auxin causes unequal growth rates, so the roots grow down and the shoots grow up.

Hydrotropism is an essential response in plant roots. Plants depend on water for photosynthesis and for the normal functioning of their cells. They also need water to enter the cells by osmosis and make them swollen so that the cytoplasm presses against the cell walls (this is known as turgor), which supports the soft tissues. Because water is taken into the plant by the roots, it is a key adaptation that roots respond positively and grow towards water. However, this tropism does not seem to be controlled by auxin levels and scientists are still investigating exactly how it works.

??? Did you know … ?

Research has shown that roots will grow down a moisture gradient in the laboratory. However, the exact mechanism of hydrotropism is not yet fully understood.

Practical

The effect of light on the growth of seedlings

You can investigate the effect of one-sided light on the growth of seedlings using a simple box with a hole cut in it and cress seedlings growing in a Petri dish.

Summary questions

1 Explain clearly why the tropic responses of shoots and roots are so important in the life of plants.

2 Explain using annotated diagrams how a plant shoot responds to gravity if it is laid down horizontally.

3 **a** In an experiment, a scientist covers the tips of half of the shoots with foil caps. First, both covered and normal shoots are exposed to light shining from directly above. Then they are given several days in a box with light shining from one side only. Explain carefully how you would expect the seedlings to respond.

   b What do you think would happen to the seedlings if the foil caps were removed half-way through the period of one-sided light? Explain your answer.

Examiner's tip

The action of auxin in gravitropism in shoots and roots is tricky! Unless you are sure about the difference, just say it causes unequal growth of cells on one side which causes the shoot or root to bend.

Key points

- Plants are sensitive to light, moisture and gravity.
- Plant responses to light and gravity are brought about by the plant hormone auxin.
- The responses of roots and shoots to stimuli of light and gravity are the result of the unequal distribution of auxin.
- Shoots grow towards light and against the force of gravity.
- Roots grow towards moisture and in the direction of the force of gravity.

B9.8 Making use of plant hormones

Learning objectives

After this topic, you should know:

● how we use plant growth hormones in agriculture and horticulture.

🔗 links

For information on plant growth hormones, look back at 9.7 'Plant responses'.

Auxin is one of the best known plant hormones, but there are a number of others. For example, gibberellins are another type of plant hormone that stimulates the growth of plant stems. People have found a number of ways in which we can use these natural hormones to help us grow plants more successfully, both for the garden (**horticulture**) and on farms to provide food (**agriculture**). We can use plant hormones to help plants to grow, but also to get rid of plants that we don't want (weeds).

Rooting hormones

Gardeners and horticulturists always want to make more plants. If you grow plants from seeds, there is always some variety in the offspring. By taking cuttings (a traditional form of artificial asexual reproduction or cloning), you can be sure of exactly what you are going to get.

When taking a cutting, you take a small piece of a stem and place it in specially prepared compost or soil. With luck, in time new roots will form at the base of the stem to form a complete new small plant. Rooting powders are available which contain the hormone auxin (also known as IAA). By dipping the cut end of a cutting into rooting powder, the chances of success are greatly increased because the hormone stimulates the growth of new roots and helps the cutting to grow into a new plant. This helps gardeners to have more success. More importantly, it helps commercial horticulturists produce huge numbers of successful cuttings to sell to the public for their gardens.

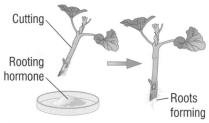

Gardeners and horticulturists rely on taking cuttings to produce lots of identical plants. Plant growth hormones are used as rooting powder. A little placed on the end of a cutting stimulates the growth of new roots and helps the cutting to grow into a new plant.

Figure 1 Hormone rooting powder greatly increases the chances of taking successful cuttings

Hormones as weed killers

Scientists have discovered that plant hormones such as auxin can be used to make effective weed killers. Auxin naturally stimulates growth in plants. If you spray auxin solution onto the leaves of plants, the hormone is absorbed. This extra auxin can send the plants into rapid, uncontrolled growth, which kills them.

Many cereal crops and grass are narrow-leaved plants (monocotyledonous plants, or monocots). Most weeds are broad-leaved plants (dicotyledonous plants, or dicots). The amount of hormone weed killer absorbed by a leaf depends largely on the surface area, so broad-leaved weeds absorb much more than narrow-leaved cereal or grass plants. As a result, the plants the farmer wants are mainly unaffected, but the broad-leaved weeds go into uncontrolled growth and die. Because these chemicals affect one type of plant and not another, they are known as selective **herbicides**.

Farmers around the world use hormone weed killers to kill off the weeds in cereal crops. This removes the competition for light and for minerals from the soil. Hormone weed killers are one of the reasons why the yield of cereal crops is now so much higher all across Europe. It means that more food is available at cheaper prices.

The hormones used in commercial weed killers are not natural hormones extracted from plants. They are synthetically made in chemical factories. These weed killers seem effective and safe. People use them on their lawns because the grass is not affected, but the weeds like dandelions and daisies are killed. Golf courses are kept weed-free in the same way.

Figure 2 Hormone-based weed killers help keep weeds in the garden under control

Practical

The effect of rooting compounds and weed killers on the growth of plants

You can investigate the effect of rooting hormone by taking some cuttings and growing half of them with rooting powder and half without.

You can investigate the effects of hormone weed killers by applying the correct dose to some grass or cereal plants and to some broad-leaved weeds and observing the effects on both.

Safety: Avoid breathing in dust and wear disposable gloves.

Figure 3 Hormone weed killers have helped improve the yield of important crops such as this spring barley

However, chemicals based on plant hormones (synthetic plant hormones) can cause serious problems. In the Vietnam War, one of these chemicals (Agent Orange) was sprayed on the forests. It works in the same way as natural plant hormones, and in high doses it strips all the leaves off the trees. This made it easier for American soldiers to find enemy fighters, but it caused terrible damage to the forests and hundreds of thousands of people were badly affected by the powerful chemicals. This includes many babies born with severe deformities, a problem that still continues today.

??? Did you know ... ?

Agent Orange has been used to destroy areas of the Amazon rainforest, particularly for the building of the Tucurui dam in Brazil.

Key points

- Plant growth hormones are widely used in horticulture as rooting hormones to increase the success of cuttings.

- Plant growth hormones are widely used in agriculture as weed killers, selectively killing broad-leaved weed plants.

Summary questions

1 a What is a plant hormone?
   b Explain how hormone rooting powders have made it easier for gardeners to propagate their own plants.

2 How can plant hormones kill plants?

3 Describe some of the ways in which synthetic plant hormones can be used to increase the food available to feed the world's growing population.

B9.9 Sexual reproduction in plants

Figure 1 Flowers may be beautiful – but they are simply the sex organs of plants!

Flowers are often very beautiful to look at and they may have a wonderful scent and be full of nectar. They produce the male and female gametes (sex cells), which must join for successful sexual reproduction in the plant.

The structure of a flower

Flowers are made up of a number of different parts. They all have different functions. For the female gametes to be fertilised by the male gametes, the pollen containing the male gamete must be transferred to the female sex organs. There are two main ways in which the pollen can be transferred – by insects (or other animals) or by the wind.

The main features of any flower are as follows:

● **Petals** – these may be large and brightly coloured to attract insects, or they may be small and green or brown if the plant is wind pollinated.

● **Sepals** – these are small, green, leaf-like structures that protect the flower when it is in bud.

● **Stamens** – these are the male parts of the flower. They are made up of the **anther**, which produces large quantities of small pollen grains containing the male gametes, and the **filament**, which attaches the anther to the flower.

● **Carpel** – this is the female part of the flower. It is made up of the **stigma**, where the pollen lands during pollination, the **style**, which transports the male sex cell to the ovary, and the **ovary**, which produces a small number of relatively large **ovules**, which are the female gametes. The ovary also often forms the fruit once the ovules are fertilised.

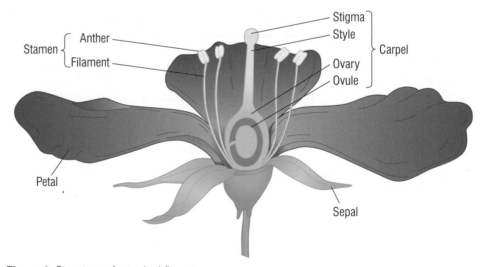

Figure 2 Structure of a typical flower

Pollination

Pollination is the process whereby the pollen grain is transferred from the anther of a flower to the stigma, often of another flower. Pollination is usually brought about by either insects or the wind. Flowers each have distinctive features which are adaptations for getting the male gametes close to the female gametes.

Feature	Insect pollinated flowers	Wind pollinated flowers
Petals	Large, brightly coloured; many are patterned to guide insects in	Small, usually brown or green
Scent	Often scented to attract insects	Not scented
Nectar	A sugary liquid made to attract insects	No nectar
Stigma	Found inside the petals so insects brush against it on way to nectar; may be sticky	Large, feathery; hangs outside the petals to collect pollen from the air; may be sticky
Anthers	Inside the petals so insects brush past on way to nectar	Hang outside petals so pollen blown away by wind
Pollen grains	Relatively few, large and sticky to attach onto the insects that visit the flower	Many, small and light to float easily in the wind

Did you know ... ?

The largest flower in the world grows in Indonesia. *Rafflesia arnoldii* grows up to 1 m across and weighs around 11 kg. It smells of rotting flesh to attract the flies which pollinate it.

The smallest flower belongs to *Wolffia globosa*. The whole plant is about 0.6 mm long and 0.3 mm wide!

Summary questions

1 a Describe the male and female sex organs of a typical flowering plant.
   b How do the male and female gametes differ in a typical flower?

2 What are the functions of the petals and the sepals in a flower?

3 a What is pollination?
   b Identify the **two** main ways in which pollination is brought about in flowering plants.
   c What features would you look for to help you decide how a particular plant is pollinated by the wind or by insects?

Key points

- Sexual reproduction in flowering plants involves the production of male and female gametes. The anther produces the male gametes (pollen) and the ovary produces the female gametes (ovules).

- The transfer of the male gametes to the female gamete is a process called pollination.

- The wind or insects can carry the pollen to the female sex organs during pollination.

- Flowers have distinctive adaptations to increase the likelihood of successful pollination taking place.

B9.10 Fertilisation and fruit formation

Learning objectives

After this topic, you should know:

- how the female gametes of flowers are fertilised

- how fruits and seeds develop.

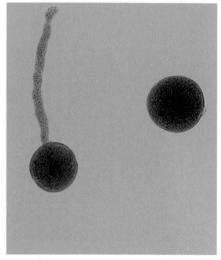

Figure 1 Pollen tubes grow out of pollen grains remarkably fast. You can watch them under the microscope.

The process of fertilisation is quite complex in plants because both gametes have more than one nucleus that must be joined. Once fertilisation is completed successfully, the ovules grow into seeds within a fruit, ready to be dispersed far and wide.

Fertilisation

Once a pollen grain arrives on the stigma of a flower, pollination has taken place. However, for fertilisation to occur, the male nuclei from the pollen grain have to travel all the way down the style and into the ovary to fuse with the nuclei in the ovule.

Both the pollen grain and the ovule have more than one nucleus. In the ovule, there is a nucleus that will go on to form the embryo in the seed (the **egg nucleus**) and nuclei that will form the food store for the developing embryo (the **endosperm nucleus**). All of the nuclei in the ovule have to fuse with **male nuclei** from the pollen grain before fertilisation is complete.

The pollen grain attaches to the top of the stigma in pollination. A special **pollen tube** then grows out of the pollen grain and down the style. The pollen tube grows into the ovary and into an ovule. The male nuclei from the pollen grain migrate (move) into the pollen tube and move down into the ovule. Here, one of the male nuclei from the pollen grain fertilises the egg nucleus in the ovule to form a zygote. Variety is introduced when the male and female nuclei fuse. The zygote grows and divides to develop into an embryo plant.

The other male nucleus fuses with two more female nuclei to form the endosperm nucleus. The fertilised endosperm nucleus and egg cell nucleus of the ovule give rise to a seed. The endosperm forms a food store, while the tissue that results from the female egg nucleus forms the embryo plant. If there are several ovules, most or all of them will be fertilised. As the seeds form, the ovary then grows into a fruit, which surrounds and protects the seeds.

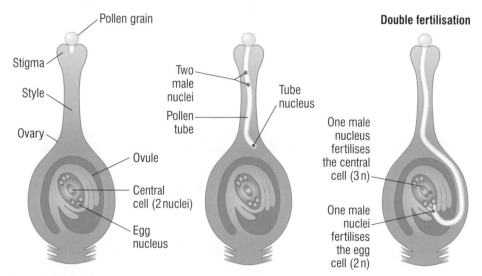

Figure 2 The fertilisation of the nuclei in the ovule by the pollen nuclei

Seed and fruit formation

The fertilised ovule forms a seed with the embryo plant and a food store contained within a tough outer coat called the testa. Some plants form single seeds, while others have many.

The fruit that forms is an adaptation to give the seed or seeds inside it the very best chance of surviving and growing into a new plant when conditions are right. The fruit is often involved in dispersing (spreading) the seeds as far away as possible from the parent plants, so they can grow without competition from the adult plants – or each other.

Some fruits become fleshy with stored food. They are eaten by animals or birds which carry the seeds away inside their gut and later deposit them in a pile of manure. Sometimes the ovary wall forms wings which enable the seeds to be carried by the wind. In other cases the ovary wall becomes very hard and tough, it may have hooks to attach it to the fur of animals or form an explosive pad which expels the seeds at speed. All of these fruit adaptations help to give the seeds the best possible opportunity to germinate and grow.

Figure 3 This familiar fruit is a tomato. You can see clearly the seeds inside the fleshy tissue of the ovary wall.

Summary questions

1 Explain carefully the difference between pollination and fertilisation in plants.

2 Make a flow diagram to show the events of fertilisation in sequence.

3 a Describe what happens in the ovary of a plant after the ovules have been fertilised.

 b Explain why the development of the ovary wall is important to successful sexual reproduction in plants.

4 Describe three different fruits and explain how they help in the dispersal of the seeds inside them.

Key points

- During fertilisation:
  - A pollen tube grows down the style to the ovary.
  - Nuclei pass from the pollen grain along the pollen tube and fuse with the nuclei in the ovule to fertilise it.
  - The resulting zygote develops into an embryo, which forms into a seed with a food store and a tough outer coat.
  - The ovary grows into a fruit, which surrounds the seed.

Summary questions

1 **a** Write the word and balanced symbol equations for photosynthesis.

b Much of the glucose made in photosynthesis is turned into an insoluble storage compound. What is this compound?

c

Year	Mean height of seedlings grown in 85% full sunlight (cm)	Mean height of seedlings grown in 35% full sunlight (cm)
2005	12	10
2006	16	12.5
2007	18	14
2008	21	17
2009	28	20
2010	35	21
2011	36	23

The figures in the table show the mean growth of two sets of oak seedlings. One set was grown in 85% full sunlight, the other set in only 35% full sunlight.

i Plot a graph to show the growth of both sets of oak seedlings.

ii Using what you know about photosynthesis and limiting factors, explain the difference in the growth of the two sets of seedlings.

2 Palm oil is made from the fruit of oil palms. Large areas of tropical rainforests have been destroyed to make space to plant these oil palms, which grow rapidly.

a Why do you think that oil palms grow rapidly in the conditions that support a tropical rainforest?

b Where does the oil in the oil palm fruit come from?

c What is it used for in the plant?

d How else is glucose used in the plant?

3 Compare the adaptations of plant leaves for the exchange of carbon dioxide, oxygen and water vapour with the adaptations of the roots for the absorption of water and mineral ions.

4 Figure 1 shows a series of experiments carried out on the first shoots of cereal plants. This experiment has been carried out by various scientists to investigate phototropisms – the response to light from one side only. Charles Darwin and his son Francis were the first scientists to carry out some of these investigations. They have been used to demonstrate that:

– the sensitivity to light comes from the tip of the shoot

– the response is the result of growth lower down the shoot

– the message is a chemical, hormonal one rather than an electrical impulse.

Look carefully at each of the diagrams A–G. Describe carefully what is happening and what this tells us about phototropisms.

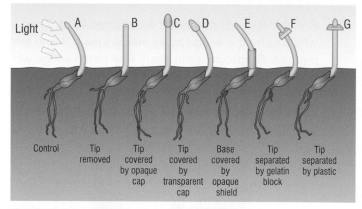

Figure 1 Experiments to investigate phototropism

5 **a** Describe the different features you would expect to see in a flower pollinated by the wind and a flower pollinated by insects.

b Explain the sequence of events that follow pollination and lead to the development of the seed and fruit.

6 This apparatus (known as a potometer) is often used to give an approximate measure of the transpiration taking place in the plant.

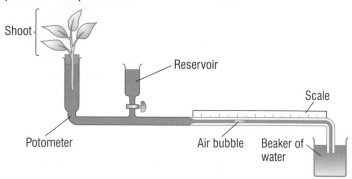

a What is transpiration?

b Explain carefully what a potometer measures and why it does NOT measure transpiration.

c Readings are taken using a potometer with plants in different conditions. Explain how and why you would expect the readings to vary from the normal control shoot if:

i a fan was set up to blow air over the plant

ii the underside of all the leaves was covered with petroleum jelly.

AQA Examination-style questions

1 a Complete the word equation for photosynthesis.

_____ + water $\xrightarrow{\text{(light energy)}}$ glucose + _____ (2)

b Geraniums are green plants that grow in gardens.

Where does the light energy for photosynthesis in the geranium come from? How does the geranium absorb this light energy? (3)

c On a frosty morning in December, the rate of photosynthesis in the geranium plant is very slow.

Suggest which factors may be limiting and why. (4)

d Some of the glucose produced by the geranium plant is used for respiration. Give **three** other ways in which the plant uses the glucose produced in photosynthesis. (3)

2 a Water and food molecules need to be transported around the plant. **List A** contains words about these processes. **List B** contains explanations. Link the words in list A with the correct explanation in list B.

List A	List B
Translocation	The using up of glucose in respiration
	The transport of water from roots to leaves.
Xylem	The evaporation of water.
Stomata	Openings in the lower surface of the leaf for gas exchange.
Phloem	The cells which transport sugars around the plant.
	The cells which transport water around the plant.
Transpiration stream	The movement of sugars from the leaves to other tissues.

(5)

b Water is needed for photosynthesis. Give two other essential roles for water within the plant. (2)

c Explain why plants take up larger amounts of water from the soil in hot, dry and windy conditions. (4)

d Describe the process by which root hairs take up mineral ions from the soil against a concentration gradient. (2)

e Why do plants need nitrate ions from the soil? (1)

3 Hormones control growth in plants.

a Give **two** uses of plant growth hormones in horticulture.

1 _____

2 _____ (2)

b A student grew a plant in an upright pot.

Later she put the pot in a horizontal position and left the plant in the dark for two days.

Figure 1 shows the potted plant after two days in the dark.

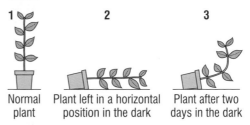

1 Normal plant **2** Plant left in a horizontal position in the dark **3** Plant after two days in the dark

Figure 1

Explain fully why the plant responded in this way. (4)

4 A farmer has decided to grow strawberry plants in polytunnels.

The tunnels are enclosed spaces with walls made of plastic sheeting. The farmer decides to set up several small polytunnels, as models, so he can work out the best conditions for the strawberry plants to grow. He needs help from a plant biologist who provides some data.

The data is shown in Figure 2.

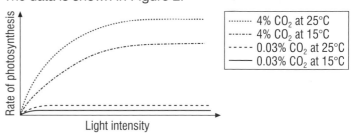

.... 4% CO_2 at 25°C
-·-·- 4% CO_2 at 15°C
- - - 0.03% CO_2 at 25°C
——— 0.03% CO_2 at 15°C

Figure 2

a _In this question you will be assessed on using good English, organising information clearly and using specialist terms where appropriate._

You are advising the farmer. Using all the information given, describe the factors the farmer should consider when building his model tunnels so he can calculate the optimal conditions for growing strawberry plants. (QWC) (6)

b Biologists often use models in their research. Suggest one reason why. (1)

AQA, 2007

B10.1 Inheritance

Variation and inheritance

Learning objectives

After this topic, you should know:

- how parents pass on genetic information to their offspring

- why we resemble our parents but are not identical to them

- where the genetic information is found in a cell

- how both genes and environmental causes influence the characteristics of individuals.

Figure 1 This mother cat and her kittens are not identical, but they are obviously related

⃝⃝ links

For more on how sexual reproduction gives rise to genetic variety, see 2.2 'Cell division in sexual reproduction' and 10.2 'Types of reproduction'.

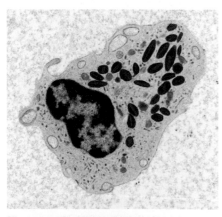

Figure 2 The DNA which carries the genetic information is found in the nucleus of a cell

Young animals and plants resemble their parents. For example, horses have foals, people have babies and chestnut trees produce conkers that grow into little chestnut trees. Many of the smallest organisms that live in the world around us are actually identical to their parents, so what makes us the way we are?

Why do we resemble our parents?

Most families have characteristics that we can see are clearly passed from generation to generation. Characteristics such as nose shape, eye colour and dimples are inherited. They are passed on to you from your parents.

Your resemblance to your parents is the result of information carried by genes. These are passed on to you in the sex cells (gametes) from which you developed. This genetic information determines what you will be like.

Chromosomes and genes

The genetic information is carried in the nucleus of your cells and is passed from generation to generation during reproduction. The nucleus contains all the plans for making and organising a new cell and a whole new organism.

Inside the nuclei of all your cells, there are thread-like structures called chromosomes. The chromosomes are made up of large molecules of a special chemical called DNA (deoxyribonucleic acid). This is where the genetic information – the coded information that determines inherited characteristics – is actually stored.

DNA is a long molecule made up of two strands that are twisted together to make a spiral. This is known as a double helix – imagine a ladder that has been twisted round.

⃝⃝ links

Find out more about DNA in 10.4 'From Mendel to modern genetics'.

Each different type of organism has a different number of chromosomes in their body cells. For example, humans have 46 chromosomes, potatoes have 48, and chickens have 78. Chromosomes always come in pairs. You have 23 pairs of chromosomes in all your normal body cells. You inherit half your chromosomes from your mother and half from your father.

Each of your chromosomes contains thousands of genes joined together. These are the units of inheritance.

Each gene is a small section of the long DNA molecule. Genes control what an organism is like. They determine its size, its shape and its colour. Genes work at the level of the molecules in your body to control the development of all the different characteristics you can see. They do this by controlling all the different proteins made in your body. This means genes determine which enzymes and other proteins are made in your body.

Examiner's tip

Make sure you know the difference:

One chromosome → many genes → lots of DNA.

Your chromosomes are organised so that both of the chromosomes in a pair carry genes controlling the same things. This means your genes also come in pairs – one from your father and one from your mother.

Some of your characteristics are decided by a single pair of genes. For example, there is one pair of genes which decides whether or not you will have dimples when you smile. However, most of your characteristics are the result of several different genes working together. For example, your hair and eye colour are both the result of several different genes.

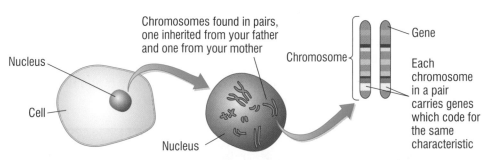

Figure 3 The relationship between a cell, the nucleus, the chromosomes and the genes

Similarities and differences

Although individuals of the same kind of organism have characteristics in common, they do not all look identical. This is partly due to the genes they have inherited (**genetic causes**). However, the conditions in which individuals develop also affects their characteristics. For example, genetically identical plants would grow differently if they were planted in a shady spot compared with bright sunshine. These external influences are known as **environmental causes**.

The differences in characteristics between most organisms of the same species are due to a combination of genetic and environmental causes.

Summary questions

1 a What is the basic unit of inheritance?
  b Offspring inherit information from their parents, but do not look identical to them. Why not?

2 a Why do chromosomes come in pairs?
  b Why do genes come in pairs?
  c How many genes do scientists think humans have?

3 a Most organisms from the same species would not look the same even if they were given identical growing conditions. Explain why.
  b If genetically identical organisms have the same growing conditions, they should look identical. Explain why.
  c In reality, even genetically identical organisms do not have exactly the same characteristics. Why is this?

 Did you know ...?

Although scientists have analysed the entire human genome (the total amount of genetic information in the chromosomes), they are still not sure exactly how many genes we have. At present, they think the human genome is made up of between 20 000 and 25 000 genes.

⊂⊃ links

To find out more about the effect of genetic and environmental factors on characteristics, see 10.3 'Genetic and environmental differences'.

Key points

- Parents pass on genetic information to their offspring in the sex cells (gametes).

- The genetic information is found in the nucleus of your cells. The nucleus contains chromosomes, and chromosomes carry the genes that control the characteristics of your body.

- Different genes control the development of different characteristics.

- Differences in the characteristics of individuals may be due to genetic causes, environmental causes or both.

B10.2 Types of reproduction

Learning objectives

After this topic, you should know:

● what a clone is and why asexual reproduction results in offspring that are identical to their parents

● how sexual reproduction produces variety

● the role of alleles in introducing variety.

Reproduction is essential to living things. It is during reproduction that genetic information is passed on from parents to their offspring. There are two very different ways of reproducing – **asexual reproduction** and **sexual reproduction**.

Asexual reproduction

Asexual reproduction only involves one parent. There is no joining of special sex cells (gametes) and there is no variety in the offspring.

Asexual reproduction gives rise to identical offspring known as **clones**. Their genetic material is identical both to the parent and to each other.

Asexual reproduction is very common in the smallest animals and plants, and in fungi and bacteria too. However, many larger plants, such as daffodils, strawberries and brambles, reproduce asexually too.

The cells of your body reproduce asexually all the time. They divide into two identical cells for growth and to replace worn-out tissues.

Figure 1 A mass of daffodils such as this can contain hundreds of identical flowers because they come from bulbs that reproduce asexually. They also reproduce sexually using their flowers.

Sexual reproduction

Sexual reproduction involves a male sex cell and a female sex cell from two parents. These two special sex cells (gametes) join together to form a zygote which goes on to develop into a new individual.

The offspring that result from sexual reproduction inherit genetic information from both parents. This means you will have some characteristics from both of your parents, but won't be identical to either of them. This introduces variety. The offspring of sexual reproduction show much more variation than the offspring from asexual reproduction.

● In plants, the gametes involved in sexual reproduction are found within ovules and pollen.

● In animals, they are called ova (eggs) and sperm.

Sexual reproduction is risky because it relies on the sex cells from two individuals meeting. However, it also introduces variety. That's why we find sexual reproduction in organisms ranging from single celled organisms to people.

∞ links

To find out more about sexual reproduction in plants, look back to 9.9 'Sexual reproduction in plants' and 9.10 'Fertilisation and fruit formation'.

Examiner's tip

Remember – in humans, the egg and sperm have 23 chromosomes, which is half the usual number. When they fuse at fertilisation, the zygote has 46 again.

Variation

Why is sexual reproduction so important? The variety it produces is a great advantage in making sure a species survives. Variety makes it more likely that at least a few of the offspring will have the ability to survive difficult conditions.

If you take a closer look at how sexual reproduction works, you can see how variation appears in the offspring.

Different genes control the development of different characteristics. Most things about you, such as your hair and eye colour, are controlled by several different pairs of genes. Each gene will have different forms, or alleles. Each allele will result in a different protein. A few of your characteristics are controlled by one single pair of genes, with just two possible alleles.

For example, there are genes that decide whether:
- your earlobes are attached closely to the side of your head or hang freely
- your thumb is straight or curved
- you have dimples when you smile
- you have hair on the second segment of your ring finger.

We can use these genes to help us understand how inheritance works.

Figure 2 Although this family group have some likenesses, the variety caused by the mixing of genetic information in the generations is clear

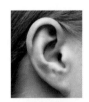

Figure 3 These are all human characteristics that are controlled by a single pair of genes. They can help us to understand how sexual reproduction introduces variety and how inheritance works.

You will get a random mixture of genetic information from your parents, which is why you don't look exactly like either of them!

Key points

- In asexual reproduction, there is no joining of gametes and only one parent. There is no genetic variety in the offspring.

- The genetically identical offspring of asexual reproduction are known as clones.

- In sexual reproduction, male and female gametes join. The mixture of genetic information from two parents leads to genetic variety in the offspring.

- The different forms of a gene are known as alleles.

Summary questions

1 Define the following:
   a asexual reproduction
   b sexual reproduction
   c gamete
   d variation.

2 Compare the advantages and disadvantages of sexual reproduction with asexual reproduction.

3 Some animals such as *Hydra* and some plants such as daffodils reproduce asexually and sexually.
   a How do daffodils reproduce i) asexually and ii) sexually?
   b How does this help to make *Hydra* and daffodils very successful organisms?
   c Explain the genetic differences between a *Hydra*'s sexually and asexually produced offspring.

Genetic and environmental differences

Learning objectives

After this topic, you should know:

- what makes you different from the rest of your family

- why identical twins are not exactly the same in every way.

Figure 1 However much this Chihuahua eats, it will never be as big as the Great Dane. It just isn't in the genes.

Figure 2 The differences in these wolves are partly genetic and partly down to their environment, from the milk they drank as pups to how good they are at finding and killing prey, and how fiercely they fight for a share of the meat

Have a look at the ends of your fingers and notice the pattern of your fingerprints. No one else in the world will have exactly the same fingerprints as you. Even identical twins have different fingerprints. What factors make you so different from other people?

Nature – genetic variety

The genes you inherit determine a lot about you. An apple tree seed will never grow into an oak tree. Environmental factors, such as the weather or soil conditions, do not matter – the basic characteristics of every species are determined by the genes they inherit.

Certain human characteristics are clearly inherited. Features such as eye colour, the shape of your nose and earlobes, your sex and dimples are the result of genetic information inherited from your parents. However, your genes are only part of the story.

Nurture – environmental variety

Some differences between you and other people are completely due to the environment you live in. For example, if a woman drinks heavily when she is pregnant, her baby may be very small when it is born and have learning difficulties. These characteristics would be a direct result of the alcohol that the fetus had to deal with as it developed. Also, you may have a scar as a result of an accident or an operation. Such characteristics are environmental, not genetic.

Genes certainly play a major part in deciding how an organism will look. However, the conditions in which it develops are important too. Genetically identical plants can be grown under different conditions of light or soil nutrients. The resulting plants do not look identical. For example, plants deprived of light, carbon dioxide or nutrients do not make as much food as plants with plenty of everything. The deprived plants will be smaller and weaker as they have not been able to fulfil their 'genetic potential'.

Combined causes of variety

Many of the differences between individuals of the same species are the result of both their genes and the environment. For example, you inherit your hair colour and skin colour from your parents. However, whatever your inherited skin colour, it will be darker if you live in a sunny environment. If your hair is brown or blonde, it will be lighter if you live in a sunny country.

Your height and weight are also affected by both your genes and the conditions in which you grow up. You may have a genetic tendency to be overweight. However, if you never have enough to eat, you will be underweight.

Investigating variety

It is quite easy to produce genetically identical plants to investigate variety. You can then put them in different situations to see how the environment affects their appearance. Scientists also use groups of animals that are genetically very similar to investigate variety. You cannot easily do this in a school laboratory.

The only genetically identical humans are identical twins who come from the same fertilised egg. Scientists are very interested in identical twins, to find out how similar they are as adults.

It would be unethical to take identical twins away from their parents and have them brought up differently just to investigate environmental effect. However, there are cases of identical twins who have been adopted by different families. Some scientists have researched these separated identical twins.

Often, identical twins look and act in a remarkably similar way. Scientists have measured features such as height, weight and IQ (a measure of intelligence). The evidence shows that human beings are just like other organisms. Some of the differences between us are mainly due to genetics and some are largely due to our environment.

In one study, scientists compared four groups of adults:
● identical twins brought up together
● separated identical twins
● non-identical, same sex twins brought up together
● same sex, non-twin siblings brought up together.

The differences between the pairs were measured. A small difference means the individuals in a pair are very alike. If there was a big difference between the identical twins, the scientists could see that their environment had more effect than their genes.

⊂⊃ links
For more information on producing genetically identical plants, see 11.1 'Cloning'.

Figure 3 Whether identical twins are brought up together or apart, they are often very similar but never exactly identical as adults. This is because their different environments will have made some subtle differences.

Table 1 Differences in pairs of adults

Measured difference in:	Identical twins brought up together	Identical twins brought up apart	Non-identical twins	Non-twin siblings
height (cm)	1.7	1.8	4.4	4.5
mass (kg)	1.9	4.5	4.6	4.7
IQ	5.9	8.2	9.9	9.8

Examiner's tip

Genes control the development of characteristics.
Characteristics may be changed by the environment.

Summary questions

1 The variety between organisms results from a combination of genetic and environmental causes. Explain why it can be very difficult to decide which has caused a particular difference between two similar organisms and why it is easier to investigate the cause of such differences in plants than it is in animals.

2 **a** Using the data from Table 1, explain which human characteristic appears to be mostly controlled by genes and which appears to be most affected by the environment.
b Why do you think non-twin siblings reared together were included in the study as well as twins reared together and apart?

3 You are given 20 pots containing identical cloned seedlings, all the same height and colour. Explain how you would investigate the effect of temperature on the growth of these seedlings compared to the impact of their genes.

Key points

● The different characteristics between individuals of a family or species may be due to genetic causes, environmental causes or a combination of both.

● Identical twins are clones who share the same genetic material, but even they will never be exactly identical due to differences in their environmental influences.

B10.4 From Mendel to modern genetics

Learning objectives

After this topic, you should know:

- that different forms of genes, called alleles, can be either dominant or recessive

- the importance of Gregor Mendel in developing our ideas about genetics

- how to construct simple genetic diagrams.

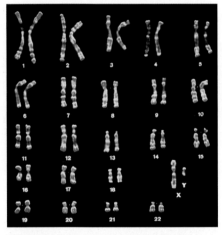

Figure 1 This special photo, called a karyotype, shows the 23 pairs of human chromosomes. You can see the XY chromosomes (bottom right), which tell you they are from a male.

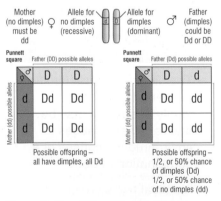

Figure 2 The different forms of genes, known as alleles, can result in the development of quite different characteristics. Genetic diagrams such as these Punnett squares help you explain what is happening and predict what the possible offspring might be like.

Most of your characteristics, such as your eye colour and nose shape, are controlled by a number of genes. However, some characteristics, such as dimples or having attached earlobes, are controlled by a single gene. Often, there are only two possible alleles for a particular feature. However, sometimes you can inherit one of a number of different possibilities.

We can make biological models that help us predict the outcome of any genetic cross.

How inheritance works

Humans have 23 pairs of chromosomes. In 22 cases, each chromosome in the pair is a similar shape. Each one has genes carrying information about the same things. One pair of chromosomes is different – these are the **sex chromosomes**. Two X chromosomes mean you are female; one X chromosome and a much smaller one, known as the Y chromosome, mean you are male.

The chromosomes you inherit carry your genetic information in the form of genes. Many of these genes have different forms, or alleles. Each allele codes for a different protein. The combination of alleles you inherit will determine your characteristics.

Picture a gene as a position on a chromosome. An allele is the particular form of information in that position on an individual chromosome. For example, the gene for dimples may have the dimple (D) or the no-dimple (d) allele in place. Because you inherit one allele from each parent, you will have two alleles controlling whether or not you have dimples.

Some alleles control the development of a characteristic even when they are only present on one of your chromosomes. These alleles are **dominant**, such as the alleles for dimples and dangly earlobes. We use a capital letter to represent dominant alleles, e.g. D. So, if you inherit DD or Dd from your parents, you will have dimples (or dangly earlobes).

Some alleles only control the development of a characteristic if they are present on both chromosomes – in other words, when no dominant allele is present. These alleles are **recessive**, such as the alleles for no dimples and attached earlobes. We use a lower case letter to represent recessive alleles, e.g. d. So, you would only show the characteristic of no dimples or attached earlobes if you have inherited two recessive alleles, e.g. dd.

We can use genetic diagrams such as a Punnett square (see Figure 2) to predict the outcome of different genetic crosses. These are biological models of how alleles are passed on from parents to offspring, and they are very useful for predicting the outcome of a particular genetic cross.

Genetic terms

Some words are useful when you are working with biological models such as Punnett squares or family trees:

- **Homozygous** – an individual with two identical alleles for a characteristic, e.g. **DD**, **dd**.

- **Heterozygous** – an individual with different alleles for a characteristic, e.g. **Dd**.

- **Genotype** – this describes the genetic makeup of an individual regarding a particular characteristic, e.g. **Dd** or **dd**.
- **Phenotype** – this describes the physical appearance of an individual regarding a particular characteristic, e.g. dimples or no dimples.

Mendel's discoveries and monohybrid inheritance

Until about 150 years ago, people had no idea how genetic information passed from one generation to the next. Today, we can predict the outcome of a single genetic cross. The man who first worked out these patterns was an Austrian monk called Gregor Mendel, who was born in 1822.

As Mendel worked in the monastery gardens he became fascinated by the peas growing there. He carried out some breeding experiments using peas. He used smooth peas, wrinkled peas, green peas and yellow peas for his work. Mendel cross-bred the peas and counted the different offspring carefully. He found that characteristics were inherited in clear and predictable patterns.

Mendel explained his results by suggesting there were separate units of inherited material. He realised that some characteristics were dominant over others and that they never mixed together. This was an amazing idea for the time when even chromosomes had not yet been discovered.

Mendel kept records of everything he did, and analysed his results. This was almost unheard of in those days. Eventually, in 1866, Mendel published his findings. He explained some of the basic laws of genetics using mathematical models in ways that we still use today; for example, the **monohybrid inheritance** in peas shown in Figure 3.

Mendel was ahead of his time. As no one knew about genes or chromosomes, people simply didn't understand his theories. Sixteen years after Mendel's death in 1884, his work was finally recognised. By 1900, people had seen chromosomes through a microscope. Other scientists discovered Mendel's papers and repeated his experiments. When they published their results, they gave Mendel the credit for what they observed.

From then on, ideas about genetics developed rapidly. It was suggested that Mendel's units of inheritance might be carried on the chromosomes seen under the microscope. In this way, the science of genetics as we know it today was born.

G = green (dominant), g = yellow (recessive)

	G	G
g	Gg	Gg
g	Gg	Gg

Parents GG × gg

Offspring 1 All green peas (Gg)

	G	g
G	GG	Gg
g	Gg	gg

Offspring 2 These green peas crossed: Gg × Gg

Genotype 1 GG: 2 Gg: 1 gg
Phenotype 3 green peas: 1 yellow pea

Figure 3 Gregor Mendel was the father of modern genetics. His work with peas was not recognised in his lifetime, but now we know just how right he was!

Key points

- In human body cells, the sex chromosomes determine whether you are female (XX) or male (XY).
- Some features are controlled by a single gene.
- Genes can have different forms called alleles.
- Some alleles are dominant and some recessive.
- We can construct genetic diagrams to predict characteristics.
- Gregor Mendel was the first person to suggest separately inherited factors, which we now call genes.

Summary questions

1 **a** What is meant by the term 'dominant allele'?
  b What is meant by the term 'recessive allele'?
  c Try and discover as many human characteristics as you can that are inherited on a single gene. Which alleles are dominant and which are recessive?

2 Draw a Punnett square similar to the ones in Figures 2 and 3 to show the possible offspring from a cross between two people who both have dimples and the genotype Dd.

3 **a** How did Mendel's experiments with peas convince him that there were distinct 'units of inheritance' that were not blended together in offspring?
  b Why didn't people accept Mendel's ideas when they were first published?
  c The development of the microscope played an important part in helping to convince people that Mendel was right. How?

B10.5

Inheritance in action

Learning objectives

After this topic, you should know:

- what DNA is

- how the information in the DNA results in different proteins in your body

- how family trees can be used with genetic diagrams to predict the outcome of genetic crosses.

The work of Gregor Mendel was just the start of our understanding of inheritance. Today, we know that our features are inherited on genes carried on the chromosomes found in the nuclei of our cells.

DNA – the molecule of inheritance

The chromosomes are made up of long molecules of a chemical known as **DNA** (deoxyribonucleic acid). These very long strands of DNA twist to form a double helix structure. Your genes are small sections of this DNA.

The DNA carries the instructions to make the proteins that form most of your cell structures. These proteins include the enzymes that control your cell chemistry. This is how the relationship between the genes and the whole organism builds up.

The genes make up the chromosomes in the nucleus of the cell. They control the proteins, which make up the different specialised cells that form tissues. These tissues then form organs and organ systems that make up the whole body. Different alleles of the same gene code for different proteins, which is why they end up coding for different characteristics.

The genetic code

The long strands of your DNA are made up of combinations of four different compounds called **bases** (see Figure 1). These are grouped into threes, and each group of three bases codes for a particular amino acid.

Each gene is made up of hundreds or thousands of these bases. The order of the bases controls the order in which the amino acids are assembled to produce a particular protein for use in your body cells. Each gene codes for a particular combination of amino acids, which make a specific protein. This is sometimes referred to as the 'one gene, one protein' principle.

A change or mutation in a single group of bases can be enough to change or disrupt the whole protein structure and the way it works.

Did you know ... ?

Unless you have an identical twin, your DNA is unique to you. The likelihood of two identical samples coming from different people is millions to one. Scientists have used this to develop **DNA fingerprinting**, a way of identifying people from tiny traces of skin cells or body fluids.

Examiner's tip

Three bases on DNA code for one amino acid. Amino acids are joined together to make a protein. It is the particular sequence of amino acids that gives each protein a specific shape and function.

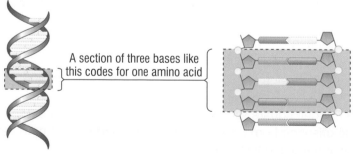

A section of three bases like this codes for one amino acid

Figure 1 DNA codes for the amino acids that make up the proteins that make up the enzymes that make each individual

More about genetic diagrams

Genetic diagrams that involve characteristics which are inherited on single genes are called monohybrid crosses. Mendel showed that the possible offspring of crosses between different types of individuals in monohybrid inheritance fall into clear patterns that you can learn and predict.

Look at the genetic diagrams in Figure 2 showing crosses involving dangly and attached earlobes, to see how the common patterns work out.

A = dangly earlobes   a = attached earlobes

Punnett square 1: homozygous dominant (AA) × homozygous recessive (aa)

	A	A
a	Aa	Aa
a	Aa	Aa

Genotype: all heterozygous Aa
Phenotype: all dangly earlobes

Punnett square 2: two heterozygous organisms (Aa) × (Aa)

	A	a
A	AA	Aa
a	Aa	aa

Genotype: 1 homozygous dominant: 2 heterozygous: 1 homozygous recessive
Ratio: 1 AA : 2 Aa : 1 aa
Phenotype: 3 dangly : 1 attached earlobes

Punnett square 3: heterozygous (Aa) × homozygous recessive (aa)

	A	a
a	Aa	aa
a	Aa	aa

Genotype: 2 heterozygous : 2 homozygous recessive
Ratio: Aa : aa
Phenotype: 1 dangly : 1 attached earlobes

Figure 2 You can use genetic diagrams to show the patterns of monohybrid inheritance

Family trees

You can trace genetic characteristics through a family by drawing a family tree (see Figure 3). Family trees show males and females and can be useful for tracing family likenesses. They can also be used for tracking inherited diseases, showing a physical characteristic or showing the different alleles people have inherited. Family trees can be used to work out where an individual is likely to be homozygous or heterozygous for particular alleles.

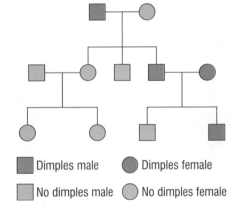

■ Dimples male   ● Dimples female
□ No dimples male   ○ No dimples female

Figure 3 A family tree to show the inheritance of dimples

Summary questions

1 Explain the saying 'One gene, one protein'.

2 The characteristic of having round peas or wrinkled peas is a monohybrid characteristic in peas. The allele for round peas is dominant to the allele for wrinkled peas.
   a Choose a suitable letter to represent the alleles for round and wrinkled peas.
   b What genotypes and phenotypes would you expect to see in the offspring if two heterozygous round pea plants are crossed? Use genetic diagrams to help show your answer.
   c What genotypes and phenotypes would you expect to see in the offspring if a heterozygous round pea plant is crossed with a wrinkled pea plant? Use genetic diagrams to help show your answer.

3 Copy the family tree shown in Figure 3. For each individual shown, write down their possible genotype. If there are two possibilities, put both down.

B10.6 Inherited conditions in humans

Learning objectives

After this topic, you should know:

● how the human genetic disorders polydactyly and cystic fibrosis are inherited

● how we can use a genetic diagram to predict the risk of a child inheriting a genetic disorder.

Not all diseases are infectious. Sometimes diseases are the result of a change in the bases or coding of our genes and can be passed on from parent to child. These types of diseases are known as **genetic disorders** or **inherited disorders**.

We can use our knowledge of dominant and recessive alleles to work out the risk of inheriting a genetic disorder.

Polydactyly

Sometimes babies are born with extra fingers or toes. This is called **polydactyly**. The most common form of polydactyly is caused by a dominant allele. It can be inherited from one parent who has the condition. People often have their extra digit removed, but some people live quite happily with them.

If one of your parents has polydactyly and is heterozygous, you have a 50% chance of inheriting the disorder. That's because half of their gametes will contain the faulty dominant allele. If they are homozygous, you will definitely have the condition.

Some dominant genetic disorders have a much more widespread effect on the way the body works than polydactyly. For example, Huntington's disease is a dominant genetic disorder that develops in middle age. It affects the nervous system and eventually leads to death.

Cystic fibrosis

Cystic fibrosis is a genetic disorder that affects many organs of the body, particularly the lungs and the pancreas. Over 8500 people in the UK have cystic fibrosis (CF).

Cystic fibrosis is a disorder of the cell membranes that means they are unable to move certain substances from one side to the other. As a result, the mucus made by cells in many areas of the body becomes very thick and sticky, which causes a number of different problems. Organs become clogged up by the thick, sticky mucus, which stops them working properly. The reproductive system is also affected, so many people with cystic fibrosis are infertile.

Treatment for cystic fibrosis includes physiotherapy and antibiotics to help keep the lungs clear of mucus and infections. The pancreas cannot make and secrete enzymes properly because the tubes through which the enzymes are released into the small intestine are blocked with mucus. Enzymes are used to replace the ones the pancreas cannot produce and to thin the mucus.

However, although treatments are getting better all the time, there is still no cure for the disorder.

Cystic fibrosis is caused by a recessive allele so it must be inherited from both parents. Children affected by cystic fibrosis are usually born to parents who do not suffer from the disorder. They have a dominant healthy allele, which means their bodies work normally. However, they also carry the recessive cystic fibrosis allele. Because it gives them no symptoms, they have no idea it is there. They are known as **carriers**.

In the UK, one person in 25 carries the cystic fibrosis allele. Most of them will never be aware of it. The only situation when it may become obvious is if they have children with a partner who also carries the allele. Then there is a 25% (one in four) chance that any child they have will be affected.

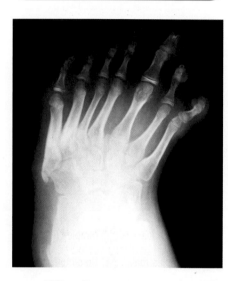

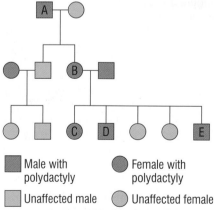

■ Male with polydactyly   ● Female with polydactyly

□ Unaffected male   ○ Unaffected female

Figure 1 Polydactyly is passed through a family tree by a dominant allele

links

You can find out more about how to construct and use genetic diagrams and the patterns of Mendelian inheritance in 10.4 'From Mendel to modern genetics' and 10.5 'Inheritance in action'.

The genetic lottery

When the genes from parents are combined, it is called a genetic cross. We can show this genetic cross using a genetic diagram. A genetic diagram gives us:

- the alleles for a characteristic carried by the parents (the genotype of the parents)
- the possible gametes which can be formed from these
- how these could combine to form the characteristic in their offspring. The possible genotypes of the offspring allow you to work out the possible phenotypes too.

When looking at the possibility of inheriting genetic disorders, it is important to remember that every time an egg and a sperm fuse it is down to chance which alleles combine. So, if two parents who are heterozygous for the cystic fibrosis allele have four children, there is a 25% chance (one in four) that each child will have the disorder. However, in fact all four children could have cystic fibrosis, or none of them might be affected. They might all be carriers, or none of them might inherit the faulty alleles at all (see Figure 3). It's all down to chance!

Curing genetic disorders

So far we have no way of curing genetic disorders. In some cases they are very minor, for example colour blindness and most cases of polydactyly. However, some genetic disorders are very serious and can even shorten lives. Scientists hope that **genetic engineering** could be the answer. It should be possible to cut out faulty alleles and replace them with healthy ones. They have tried this in people affected by cystic fibrosis. Unfortunately, so far they have not managed to cure anyone with an inherited, genetic disorder, but they remain very hopeful of this possibility.

P = dominant allele (polydactyly)

p = recessive allele (normal number of fingers and toes)

Parent with polydactyly (Pp)

	P	p
p	Pp	pp
p	Pp	pp

Normal parent (pp)

Genotype of offspring:
50% affected (Pp)
50% normal (pp)

Phenotype of offspring:

1/2, or 50% chance polydactyly
1/2, or 50% chance normal

Figure 2 A genetic diagram for polydactyly

C = dominant allele (normal metabolism)
c = recessive allele (cystic fibrosis)

Both parents are carriers, so (Cc)

	C	c
C	CC	Cc
c	Cc	cc

Genotype of offspring:
25% normal (CC)
50% carriers (Cc)
25% affected by cystic fibrosis (cc)

Phenotype of offspring:

3/4, or 75% chance normal
1/4, or 25% chance cystic fibrosis

Figure 3 A genetic diagram for cystic fibrosis

links

Learn more about how scientists can change the genes in the cells of an organism in 11.3 'Genetic engineering'.

Key points

- Some disorders are inherited.
- Polydactyly is caused by a dominant allele of a gene and can be inherited from either parent.
- Cystic fibrosis is caused by a recessive allele of a gene and so must be inherited from both parents.
- You can use genetic diagrams to predict how genetic disorders might be inherited and predict the inheritance of genetic disease.

Summary questions

1 a What is polydactyly?
  b Why can one parent with the allele for polydactyly pass the condition on to their children even though the other parent is not affected?
  c Look at the family tree in Figure 1. For each of the five people labelled A to E, give their possible alleles and explain your answers.

2 a Why are carriers of cystic fibrosis not affected by the disorder themselves?
  b Why must both of your parents be carriers of the allele for cystic fibrosis before you can inherit the disease?

3 A couple have a baby who has cystic fibrosis. Neither the couple, nor their parents, have any signs of the disorder.
  Draw genetic diagrams showing the possible genotypes of the grandparents and the parents to explain how this could happen.

More inherited conditions in humans

Learning objectives

After this topic, you should know:

- that some inherited conditions give heterozygous individuals protection against other diseases

- that some inherited conditions are the result of inheriting abnormal numbers of chromosomes rather than a fault in an individual gene.

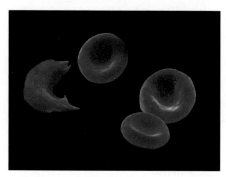

R = normal red blood cells (rbc)
r = sickle red blood cells

Parents are heterozygous carriers: Rr × Rr

	R	r
R	RR	Rr
r	Rr	rr

Offspring genotype:
1 homozygous dominant RR:
2 heterozygotes Rr:
1 homozygous recessive rr

Offspring phenotype:
1 normal rbc:
2 some normal, some sickle rbcs:
1 sickle-cell anaemia

Figure 1 The inheritance and effects of sickle-cell anaemia

There are many different genetic disorders, some of which are extremely rare with only a few families around the world affected. Others are relatively common. Some genetic disorders can even carry surprising advantages.

Sickle-cell anaemia

Sickle-cell anaemia is a genetic disorder that affects millions of people around the world. It affects the red blood cells that carry oxygen from your lungs to all the cells of your body. In sickle-cell anaemia, the red blood cells become sickle shaped. When this happens, they don't carry oxygen effectively and so you feel breathless, lack energy and are tired. Affected children often fail to grow. The sickle-shaped cells also block small blood vessels. This can cause great pain and death of the tissue leading to severe infections.

Sickle-cell anaemia causes the death of up to 2 million people a year. It is particularly common in people originating from Africa, the Mediterranean, India and Spanish-speaking areas of the Americas. Sickle-cell anaemia is caused by a recessive allele, so you need to inherit one from each parent before you are fully affected by the disease. However, even heterozygotes are partly affected and have some sickle cells in their blood.

In some ways, it is surprising that the sickle-cell allele survives and is so widespread as it has such a damaging impact on people who are homozygous. However, scientists have discovered that people who are heterozygous for sickle-cell disorder are less likely to get malaria than people who are homozygous for the dominant normal allele. Malaria is another killer disease which affects the lives of millions of people worldwide. It is caused by a **parasite** passed from the blood of one person to another by mosquito bites.

People who are heterozygous for sickle-cell anaemia have some problems with their blood cells and it seems this change in shape is enough to protect them against the malaria parasites. This gives them an advantage – and makes sure they survive to pass on their sickle-cell alleles to another generation. This means that sickle-cell disease persists at least partly because heterozygotes are protected against malaria. In parts of the world where there is no malaria, sickle-cell disease is very rare and usually only found in families who originate in malarial areas.

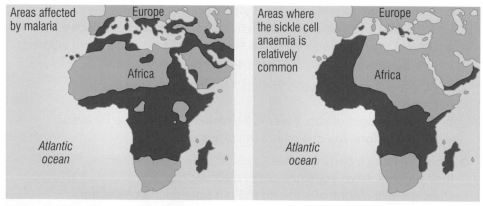

Figure 2 This diagram shows the distribution of malaria (left) and sickle-cell anaemia (right) in Africa

Whole chromosome disorders

Some inherited disorders are not the result of a change in a single gene. They are caused by the inheritance of abnormal numbers of chromosomes. As the cells divide by meiosis to form the gametes, sometimes things go wrong. One of the gametes may end up with too few chromosomes or with an extra chromosome. Often these gametes cannot survive, but sometimes they do.

One of the most common inherited conditions resulting from the inheritance of an abnormal number of chromosomes is Down's syndrome. This is caused by an extra copy of chromosome number 21, so the baby has 47 chromosomes instead of 46. This can cause a number of developmental problems in many different areas of the body, including the brain, the heart and the muscles.

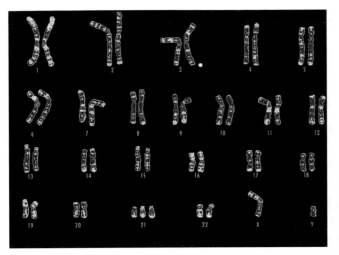 

Figure 3 Inheriting an extra chromosome can affect many systems in the body, which is seen clearly when someone is affected by Down's syndrome. Compare this karyotype with the normal human karyotype on page 140.

⊂⊃ links

To find out more about meiosis, look back to 2.2 'Cell division in sexual reproduction'.

Examiner's tip

Learn which type of genes cause genetic disorders.
Dominant: Polydactyly and Huntington's disease
Recessive: Cystic fibrosis and sickle-cell anaemia

Summary questions

1 a Sickle-cell anaemia is a recessive inherited disorder. Explain carefully what this means.
  b What are the main symptoms of sickle-cell anaemia? Explain how they are caused.

2 Using the letter R for the dominant normal allele and r for the recessive sickle-cell allele, carry out the following genetic crosses. For each cross state the likelihood of having a child with sickle-cell anaemia and a child carrying the sickle-cell allele.
  a One parent is homozygous dominant and the other is heterozygous.
  b Both parents are heterozygous.
  c One parent is homozygous dominant and the other has sickle-cell disease.

3 a What is Down's syndrome?
  b How does the inheritance of Down's syndrome differ from the inheritance of genetic disorders such as cystic fibrosis and sickle-cell anaemia?

Key points

- Sickle-cell anaemia is an inherited condition that affects the red blood cells and is caused by a recessive allele.

- Being heterozygous for the sickle-cell allele gives people some protection against malaria compared with people who are homozygous for the dominant normal allele.

- Some inherited conditions are caused by the inheritance of abnormal numbers of chromosomes. For example, Down's syndrome is caused by the presence of an extra chromosome.

Summary questions

1 If you dig up a strawberry plant, it will often have many other small strawberry plants attached to it.

   a How are these small plants produced?

   b What sort of reproduction is this?

   c Strawberry plants also produce seeds. How are these produced and what sort of reproduction is it?

   d How are the new plants that you would grow from seeds different from the new plants grown directly from the parent plant?

2 **a** What is a gamete?

   b How do the chromosomes in a gamete vary from the chromosomes in a normal body cell?

3 **a** What are chromosomes made of?

   b What is a gene?

   c Explain carefully how the information carried in a gene is expressed in the phenotype of an organism.

4 Explain what Mendel did, what was unusual about his work and why people initially rejected his ideas. What developments in scientific ideas and technology helped people eventually understand and accept Mendel's ideas?

5 Whether you have a straight thumb or a curved one is decided by a single gene with two alleles. The allele for a straight thumb, S, is dominant to the curved allele, s. Use this information to help you answer these questions.

   Josh has straight thumbs but Sami has curved thumbs. They are expecting a baby.

   a We know exactly what Sami's thumb alleles are. What are they and how do you know?

   b If the baby has curved thumbs, what does this tell you about Josh's thumb alleles? Draw and complete a Punnett square to show the genetics of your explanation.

   c If the baby has straight thumbs, what does this tell us about Josh's thumb alleles? Draw and complete a Punnett square to show the genetics of your explanation.

6 Amjid grew some purple-flowering pea plants from seeds he had bought at the garden centre. He planted them in his garden.

   Here are his results:

Seeds planted	247
Purple-flowered plants	242
White-flowered plants	1
Seeds not growing	4

   a How would you explain these results?

   b Amjid was interested in these plants, so he collected the seed from some of the purple-flowered plants and used them in the garden the following year. He made a careful note of what happened.

   Here are his results:

Seeds planted	406
Purple-flowered plants	295
White-flowered plants	102
Seeds not growing	6

   Amjid was slightly surprised. He did not expect to find that a third of his flowers would be white.

   i The purple allele (P) is dominant and the allele for white flowers (p) is recessive. Draw a genetic diagram that explains Amjid's numbers of purple and white flowers.

   ii How accurate were Amjid's results compared with the expected ratio?

   c Suggest another genetic cross that would confirm the genotype of the purple plants. Produce a genetic diagram to show the results you would expect.

7 Many human features are the result of different genes interacting, but there are some which are the result of monohybrid inheritance.

   a What is monohybrid inheritance?

   b What is meant by the terms 'dominant allele' and 'recessive allele'?

   c Describe two normal human characteristics inherited by monohybrid inheritance.

   d Cystic fibrosis is a disorder inherited on a recessive allele. Explain what this means and draw a genetic diagram to show how two healthy parents could have a child with cystic fibrosis.

   e Huntington's disease is a serious human genetic disorder carried on a dominant allele. The problems it causes do not show up until the person is middle aged. Draw a genetic diagram to show how an affected individual could pass this disease to their offspring.

AQA Examination-style questions

1 Complete the following sentences using words from the box.

> alleles   heterozygous   amino acid   genes   DNA
> skin   chromosomes   homozygous   gamete

a Inherited characteristics are controlled by .... made up of the chemical substance ....

b Human body cells have 46 ...., but the .... cells have only 23.

c Different forms of one gene are called ....

d If an individual inherits two different forms of one gene they are .... for that gene, but if they have two of the same form of the gene they are .... for the gene.   (7)

2 A teacher wanted to grow new geranium plants to use for an investigation in science. She took five identical cuttings and planted them in identical pots of compost.

She gave the five pots to different students to take home for the long summer holiday.

a What type of reproduction is taking cuttings?   (1)

b The parent plant produced red flowers. What colour flowers will the cuttings produce? Why?   (2)

c When the plants were returned after the holiday, they were different heights and had different numbers and sizes of leaves. Names two factors that may have caused this variation.   (2)

d The teacher wanted to use these plants as she said it would make the investigation more reliable than buying five new plants. Suggest reasons why.   (2)

3 Complete the passage by inserting the correct scientific term in each space provided.

A gene is a small section of the chemical .... Each gene codes for the synthesis of a specific .... made up of .... joined in the correct sequence. The .... is made up of long strands twisted into a .... shape. On these strands .... bases code for each ....   (7)

4 *In this question you will be assessed on using good English, organising information clearly and using specialist terms where appropriate.*

A class in school contained identical twin girls.

Twin A was 150 cm tall and weighed 51 kg. She had long blonde straight hair and blue eyes.

Twin B was 151 cm tall and weighed 63 kg. She had short, black curly hair and blue eyes.

Use your knowledge and understanding of inheritance and variation due to genetic and environmental factors to evaluate the characteristics seen in these two girls.   (QWC) (6)

5 The maps show the present distribution of malaria and the sickle-cell allele in Africa.

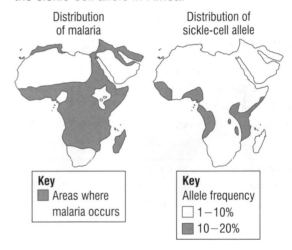

a Draw a genetic diagram to show how sickle-cell anaemia can be inherited from parents who do not have the condition. Use the following key to symbols for alleles:

Hb$_A$ Normal adult haemoglobin

Hb$_S$ Sickle-cell haemoglobin   (4)

b i Explain the link between sickle-cell anaemia, resistance to malaria and the frequency of the Hb$_S$ allele.   (3)

ii Select and evaluate the evidence from the maps that accounts for the distribution of the sickle-cell allele and the resistance to malaria in parts of Africa.   (2)

B11.1 Cloning

Learning objectives

After this topic, you should know:

- different ways of creating clones
- why clones are useful.

∞ links

For more information on taking plant cuttings, look back at 9.8 'Making use of plant hormones'.

Figure 1 Traditional methods of cloning plants by cuttings and grafting are still widely used

A **clone** is an individual that has been produced asexually and is genetically identical to the parent. Many plants reproduce naturally by cloning and this has been used by farmers and gardeners for many years.

Cloning plants

Taking cuttings is a form of artificial asexual reproduction or cloning that has been carried out for hundreds of years.

In recent years, scientists have come up with a more modern way of cloning plants called **tissue culture**. It is more expensive, but it allows you to make thousands of new plants from one tiny piece of plant tissue.

The first step is to use a mixture of plant hormones to make a small group of cells from the plant you want to clone and produce a big mass of identical plant cells called a **callus**.

Then, using a different mixture of hormones and conditions, you can stimulate each of these cells to form a tiny new plant. This type of cloning guarantees that you can produce thousands of offspring with the characteristics you want from one individual plant.

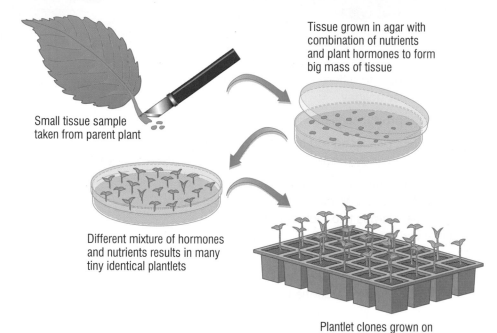

Small tissue sample taken from parent plant

Tissue grown in agar with combination of nutrients and plant hormones to form big mass of tissue

Different mixture of hormones and nutrients results in many tiny identical plantlets

Plantlet clones grown on

Figure 2 Tissue culture makes it possible to produce thousands of identical plants quickly and easily from one small tissue sample

Cloning animals

In recent years, cloning animals has become quite common in farming, particularly transplanting cloned cattle embryos. Cows normally produce only one or two calves at a time. If you use embryo cloning, your best cows can produce many more top-quality calves each year.

How does embryo cloning work? First, you give a top-quality cow fertility hormones so that it produces a lot of eggs. You then fertilise these eggs using sperm from a really good bull. Often, this is done inside the cow and the embryos that are produced are then gently washed out of her womb. Sometimes the eggs are collected and you add sperm in a laboratory to produce the embryos.

At this very early stage of development, every cell of the embryo can still form all of the cells needed for a new cow. This is because the cells have not become specialised. These cells can be split apart and then transplanted into host surrogate mothers. The split cells are effectively identical twins.

Cloning cattle embryos and transferring them to host cattle is skilled and expensive work. However, it is worth it because when using normal reproduction, a top cow might produce 8–10 calves during her working life. Using embryo cloning, the cow can produce 30 or more calves in a single year.

Cloning embryos means we can transport high-quality embryos all around the world. They can be carried to places where cattle with a high milk yield or lots of meat are badly needed for breeding with poor local stock. Embryo cloning is also used to make lots of identical copies of embryos that have been **genetically modified** to produce medically useful compounds.

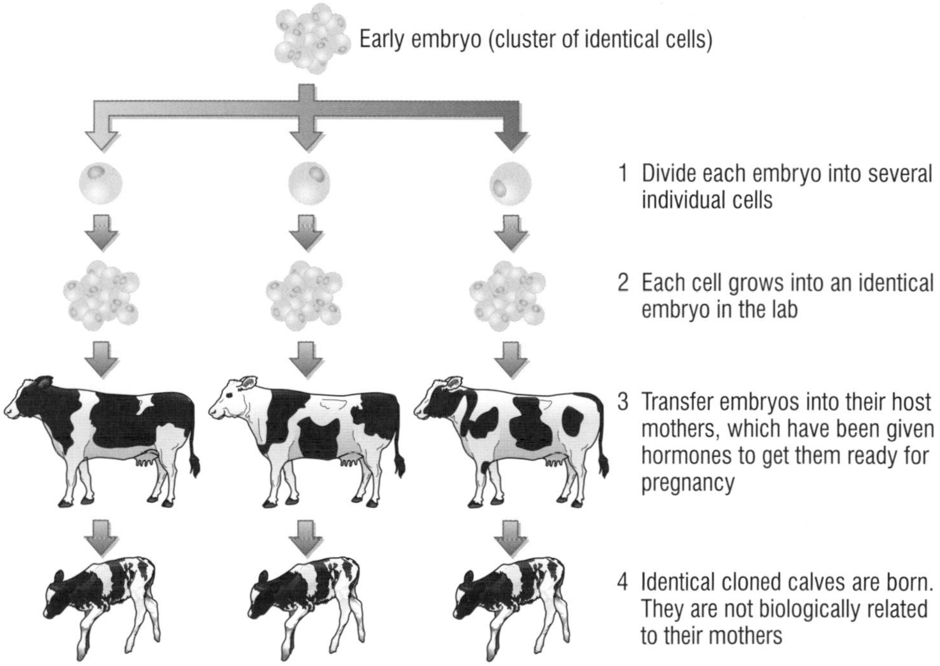

links
For more information on cloning embryos, see 11.2 'Adult cell cloning'.

Early embryo (cluster of identical cells)

1 Divide each embryo into several individual cells

2 Each cell grows into an identical embryo in the lab

3 Transfer embryos into their host mothers, which have been given hormones to get them ready for pregnancy

4 Identical cloned calves are born. They are not biologically related to their mothers

Figure 3 Cloning cattle embryos

Examiner's tip
Remember that clones have identical genetic information to each other and the single parent nucleus.

Key points

- A modern technique for cloning plants is tissue culture using small groups of cells taken from part of the original plant.

- Transplanting cloned embryos involves splitting apart cells from a developing animal embryo before they become specialised and then transplanting the identical embryos into host mothers.

- Animals and plants that are cloned are chosen because of their high quality, for example in terms of their resistance to disease or high milk yield.

Summary questions

1 Define the following words:
   a cuttings
   b tissue cloning
   c asexual reproduction
   d embryo cloning.

2 a Cloning cattle embryos is very useful. Why?
   b Draw a flowchart to show the stages in the embryo cloning of cattle.
   c Suggest some of the economic and ethical issues raised by embryo cloning in cattle.

3 Make a table to compare the similarities and differences between tissue cloning in plants and embryo cloning in cattle.

B11.2

Adult cell cloning

Learning objectives

After this topic, you should know:

● how adult cell cloning is carried out.

Many small invertebrate animals such as hydra reproduce asexually in a way which is quite similar to plants. Even some reptiles can reproduce asexually with eggs that do not need to be fertilised. However, mammals never reproduce asexually. True cloning of large mammals, without sexual reproduction, has been a major scientific breakthrough. It is the most complicated form of asexual reproduction you can find.

Adult cell cloning

To clone a cell from an adult animal is easy. The cells of your body reproduce asexually all the time to produce millions of identical cells. However, to take a cell from an adult animal and make an embryo or even a complete identical animal is a very different thing.

When a new whole animal is produced from the cell of another adult animal, it is known as **adult cell cloning**. This is still relatively rare. You place the nucleus of one cell into the empty egg cell of another animal of the same species. Then you place the resulting embryo into the uterus of another adult female where it develops until it is born.

Here are the steps involved:

● The nucleus is removed from an unfertilised egg cell.

● At the same time, the nucleus is taken from an adult body cell, for example a skin cell of another animal of the same species.

● The nucleus from the adult cell is inserted in the empty egg cell.

● The new egg cell is given a tiny electric shock, which stimulates it to start dividing to form embryo cells. These contain the same genetic information as the original adult cell and the original adult animal.

● When the embryo has developed into a ball of cells, it is inserted into the womb of an adult female to continue its development.

Figure 1 Dolly the sheep was the first large mammal to be cloned from another adult mammal. She went on to have lambs of her own in the normal way.

Adult cell cloning has been used to produce a number of whole animal clones. The first large mammal ever to be cloned from the cell of another adult animal was Dolly the sheep, born in 1997.

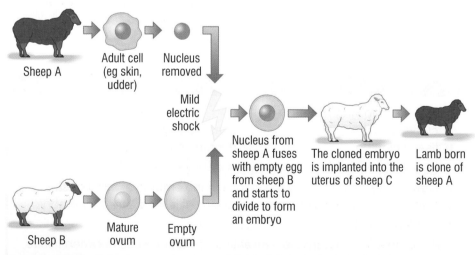

Figure 2 Adult cell cloning remains a very difficult technique, but scientists hope it may bring benefits in the future

When Dolly was produced, she was the only success from hundreds of attempts. The cloning technique is tricky and unreliable, but scientists hope that it will become easier in future.

The benefits and disadvantages of adult cell cloning

One big hope for adult cell cloning is that animals that have been genetically engineered to produce useful proteins in their milk can be cloned. This would give us a good way of producing large numbers of cloned, medically useful animals.

This technique could also be used to help save animals from extinction, or even bring back species of animals that died out years ago. The technique could be used to clone pets or prized animals, so that they continue even after the original has died. However, some people are not happy about this idea.

There are some disadvantages to this exciting science as well. Many people fear that the technique could lead to the cloning of human babies. This could be used to help infertile couples, but it could also be abused. This is not possible at the moment, but who knows what might be possible in the future?

Another problem is that modern cloning techniques produce lots of plants or animals with identical genes. In other words, cloning reduces variety in a population. This means the population is less able to survive any changes in the environment that might happen in the future. That's because if one of them does not contain a useful characteristic, none of them will.

In a more natural population, at least one or two individuals can usually survive change. They go on to reproduce and restock. This could be a problem in the future for cloned crop plants or for cloned farm animals.

Did you know ... ?

The only human clones alive at the moment are natural ones known as identical twins! However, the ability to clone mammals such as Dolly the sheep has led to fears that some people may want to have a clone of themselves produced – whatever the cost.

links

For more information on adult cell cloning, see 11.4 'Making choices about genetic technology'.

Summary questions

1 Produce a flowchart to show how adult cell cloning works.

2 Explain clearly the differences between natural mammalian clones (identical twins), embryo clones and adult cell clones.

3 What are the main advantages and disadvantages of the development of adult cell cloning techniques? How valid do you consider the main concerns expressed?

Key points

- In adult cell cloning, the nucleus of a cell from an adult animal is transferred to an empty egg cell from another animal. A small electric shock causes the egg cell to begin to divide and starts embryo development. The embryo is then placed in the womb of a third animal to develop.

- The animal that is born is genetically identical to the animal that donated the original adult cell.

B11.3 Genetic engineering

Learning objectives

After this topic, you should know:

- how genes are transferred from one organism to another in genetic engineering

- the potential benefits and problems associated with genetically modified crops.

What is genetic engineering?

Genetic engineering involves changing the genetic material of an organism using the following process:

- You take a gene from one organism and transfer it to the genetic material of a completely different organism. Enzymes are used to isolate and 'cut out' the required gene.
- The gene is then inserted into a vector using more enzymes. The vector is usually a bacterial plasmid or a virus.
- The vector is then used to insert the gene into the required cells, which may be bacteria, animal, fungi or plants.

So, for example, genes from the chromosomes of a human cell can be 'cut out' using enzymes and transferred to the cell of a bacterium. The gene carries on making a human protein, even though it is now in a bacterium.

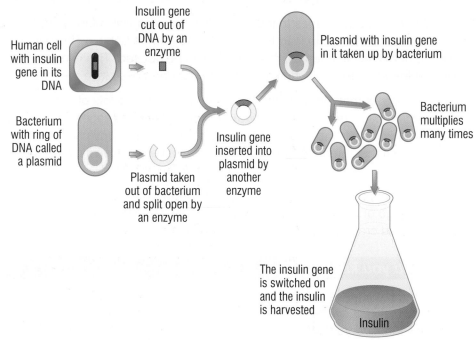

Figure 1 The principles of genetic engineering. A bacterial cell receives a gene from a human being so it makes a human protein – in this case, the human hormone insulin.

If genetically engineered bacteria are cultured on a large scale, they can make huge quantities of protein from other organisms. We now use them to make a number of drugs and hormones used as medicines, for example genetically engineered bacteria are used to make human insulin.

⚲ links

To find out more about the use of insulin to treat diabetes, see 7.8 'Treating diabetes'.

Examiner's tip

Cloning and genetic engineering are different! Learn the techniques for both processes.

Transferring genes to animal and plant cells

There is a limit to the types of proteins that bacteria are capable of making. As a result, genetic engineering has moved on. Scientists have found that genes from one organism can be transferred to the cells of another type of animal or plant at an early stage of their development. As the animal or plant grows, it develops with the new desired characteristics from the other organism. For example, glowing genes from jellyfish have been used to produce crop plants that glow in the dark when they are lacking in water. The farmer can then tell when the crops need irrigation.

Animals have been genetically engineered in a number of ways, but it is with plants that most progress has been made.

Genetically modified crops

Crops that have had their genes modified by genetic engineering techniques are known as **genetically modified crops (GM crops)**. Genetically modified crops often show increased yields. For example, genetically modified crops include plants that are resistant to attack by insects because they have been modified to make their own **pesticide**. This means that more of the crops survive to provide food for people. GM plants that are more resistant than usual to herbicides mean farmers can spray and kill weeds more effectively without damaging their crops. Again, this increases the crop yield.

Increasing crop yields is extremely important in providing food security for the world's human population, which is growing all the time. For example:

● Genetic engineering has resulted in many cereal plants with much shorter stems than the original plants. This means they are much less likely to be damaged by wind or storms – and so increases the yield.

● Recent work on rice plants has produced crops that can withstand being completely covered in water for up to three weeks during flooding and still produce a high yielding crop of rice. As more than 3.3 billion people worldwide rely on rice for a large proportion of their daily calorie intake, and climate change seems to be bringing much more severe flooding in many rice growing countries, genetic modifications such as these could literally save millions of people from starvation.

Sometimes genetically modified crops contain genes from a completely different species – such as the jellyfish genes added to crop plants described earlier. Sometimes genetic modification simply speeds up normal selective breeding, by taking a gene from another closely related plant and inserting it into the genome. This has been done in the example of the flood-resistant rice.

Figure 2 Rice is a vital staple food for millions of people. This genetically modified strain is still growing when traditional strains have been destroyed by prolonged flooding.

Summary questions

1 Early genetic engineering was carried out almost entirely in bacteria. Now many different species of animals and plants have been genetically engineered. Explain why it is important to be able to modify the genome of these different organisms.

2 Make a flowchart that explains the stages of transferring a gene for a shorter stem from one plant to another using a bacterial plasmid as a vector.

3 Give three examples of ways in which food crops have been genetically modified and explain how the change has increased the yield of the crop and why this is important.

Key points

● Genes can be transferred to the cells of animals and plants at an early stage of their development so they develop desired characteristics. This is genetic engineering.

● In genetic engineering, genes from the chromosomes of humans and other organisms can be 'cut out' using enzymes and transferred to the cells of bacteria and other organisms using a vector, which is usually a bacterial plasmid or a virus.

● Crops that have had their genes modified are known as genetically modified (GM) crops. GM crops often have improved resistance to insect attack or herbicides and generally produce a higher yield.

B11.4

Making choices about genetic technology

Learning objectives

After this topic, you should know:

- some of the concerns and uncertainties about the new genetic technologies such as cloning and genetic engineering.

Did you know ... ?

Short-stemmed GM crops, flood- and drought-resistant GM crops and others are already helping to solve the problems of world hunger.

⬭ links

You can find out more about GM crops in 11.3 'Genetic engineering'.

Did you know ... ?

A great deal of work is currently being done on the lungs of people with cystic fibrosis and children with SCID (severe combined immunodeficiency). There have been some successes in using gene therapy to cure SCID, although there were also major problems.

Figure 1 Yellow beta carotene is needed to make vitamin A in the body. The amount of beta carotene in golden rice and golden rice 2 is reflected in the depth of colour of the rice.

The benefits of genetic engineering and cloning are becoming more apparent all the time. However, there are some concerns about the use of these new technologies before we fully understand any long-term impact they may have on individuals or the environment.

Benefits of genetic engineering

People are already seeing many benefits from genetic engineering. Genetically engineered bacteria can make exactly the proteins we need, in exactly the amounts needed and in a very pure form. For example, pure human insulin is mass produced using genetically engineered bacteria.

Some of the advantages of genetic engineering are:

- improved growth rates of plants and animals
- increased food value of crops, as genetically modified (GM) crops usually have much bigger yields than ordinary crops
- crops can be designed to grow well in dry, hot or cold parts of the world
- crops can be engineered to produce plants that make their own pesticide or are resistant to herbicides used to control weeds.

Human engineering

One huge potential benefit of genetic engineering that has still to be fully realised is curing human genetic conditions. It might become possible to put 'healthy' genes into affected cells using genetic engineering, so the cells work properly. Perhaps the cells of an early embryo can be engineered so that the individual develops into a healthy person. If these treatments become possible, many people would have new hope of a normal life for themselves or their children. However, gene therapy in humans has a long way to go.

Concerns about genetic engineering

Genetic engineering is still a very new science, and no one can be sure what the long-term effects might be. For example, insects may become pesticide-resistant if they eat a constant diet of pesticide-forming plants.

Some people are concerned about the effect of eating GM food on human health. However, people eat a wide range of organisms with many different types of DNA every day as part of a normal diet, so this concern may well be unfounded. Others feel we have enough varieties of crop plants without using GM crops.

Another concern is that genes from genetically modified plants and animals might spread into the wildlife of the countryside. Some people are very anxious about the effect these GM organisms might have on populations of wild flowers and insects. GM crops are often made infertile, which means farmers in poor countries have to buy new seed each year. Many people are unhappy with this practice. If these infertility genes spread into wild populations, it could cause major problems in the environment – although scientists are working hard to prevent this.

Ever since genetically modified foods were first introduced, there has been controversy and discussion about them. For example, varieties of GM rice known as 'golden rice' and 'golden rice 2' have been developed. These varieties of rice produce large amounts of vitamin A. Up to 500 000 children go blind each year as a result of lack of vitamin A in their diets. In theory, golden rice offers a solution to this problem.

In fact, many people objected to the way trials of the rice were run and the cost of the product, even though the rice is fertile and farmers can grow their own after they buy the original seed. No golden rice is yet being grown in countries affected by vitamin A blindness, and children continue to go blind due to vitamin A deficiency.

However, the majority of plant scientists around the world believe that GM crops are the way forward in solving the problem of feeding the world's expanding population.

People might want to manipulate the genes of their future children. This may be to make sure they are born healthy, but there are concerns that people might want to use it to have 'designer' children with particular characteristics such as high intelligence. Genetic engineering raises issues for us all to think about.

Cloning pets

Cloning plants and even some animals is widely used, but cloning mammals has also led to some ethical issues. Most of the research into cloning had been focused on farm and research animals, but some companies are hoping to be able to clone people's dying or dead pets for them. It has already been shown that a successful clone can be produced from a dead animal, as beef from a slaughter house has been used to create a live cloned calf.

Cloning your pet won't be easy or cheap. The issue is: should people be cloning their dead cats and dogs when there are thousands of unwanted animals already in existence? Even if a favourite pet cat is cloned, it may look nothing like the original because the coat colour of many cats is the result of genes switching on and off at random in the skin cells. A cloned pet will develop and grow in a different environment to the original animal as well. This means other characteristics that are affected by the environment will probably be different too.

Figure 2 The cat on the left is Rainbow. The cat on the right is Cc, Rainbow's clone. Rainbow and Cc share the same DNA – but they don't look the same.

To some people these are exciting events. To others they are a waste of time, money and the lives of all the embryos that don't make it.

Figure 3 Lancelot Encore, a clone of a much-loved pet, with his owners and a portrait of the original dog

Summary questions

1 Describe the main advantages and disadvantages of genetically modifying plants.

2 People get very concerned about cloning. Do you think these fears are justified? Explain your answer.

3 Summarise the use of genetic engineering and cloning in the treatment of human diseases so far.

Key points

- Concerns about GM crops include the effects on populations of wild flowers and insects, and uncertainty about the effects of eating GM crops on human health.

Summary questions

1 Tissue culture techniques mean that 50 000 new raspberry plants can be grown from one old one instead of two or three by taking cuttings. Cloning embryos from the best bred cows means that they can be genetically responsible for 30 or more calves each year instead of two or three.

a How does tissue culture differ from taking cuttings?

b How can one cow produce 30 or more calves in a year?

c What are the similarities between cloning plants and cloning animals in this way?

d What are the differences in the techniques for cloning animals and plants?

e Why do you think there is so much interest in finding different ways to make the breeding of farm animals and plants increasingly efficient?

2 a Describe the process of adult cell cloning.

b There has been a great deal of media interest and concern about cloning animals, but very little about cloning plants. Why do you think there is such a difference in the way people react to these two different technologies?

3 Human growth is usually controlled by growth hormones produced by the pituitary gland in the brain. If you don't make enough hormones, you don't grow properly and remain very small. This condition affects 1 in every 5000 children. Until recently, the only way to get growth hormone was from the pituitary glands of dead bodies. Genetically engineered bacteria can now make plenty of pure growth hormone.

a Draw and label a diagram to explain how a healthy human gene for making growth hormone can be taken from a human chromosome and put into a working bacterial cell.

b What are the advantages of producing substances such as growth hormone using genetic engineering?

4 In 2003, two mules called Idaho Gem and Idaho Star were born in America. They were clones of a famous racing mule. They both seem very healthy. They were separated and sent to different stables to be reared and trained for racing. So far Idaho Gem has been more successful than his cloned brother, winning several races against ordinary racing mules. There is a third clone, Utah Pioneer, which has not been raced.

a The mules are genetically identical. How do you explain the fact that Idaho Gem has beaten Idaho Star in several races?

b Why do you think one of the clones is not being raced?

c The clones' progress is being carefully monitored by scientists. What type of data do you think will be available from these animals?

5 a What is meant by the term GM crops?

b Explain the main concerns of people about the use of GM crops around the world.

c Most plant scientists believe GM technology will be the key to producing enough food to feed the world population. How can it be used to do that?

d One concern people have about GM crops is that they might cross pollinate with wild plants. Scientists need to find out how far pollen from a GM crop can travel to be able to answer these concerns.

Describe how a trial to investigate this might be set up.

AQA Examination-style questions

1 a What is a clone? (1)

b Clones of plants can be created by taking small blocks of stem, leaf or root cells and growing them in a special medium. Name this type of cloning. (1)

c Animal clones can be created from embryos or by adult cell cloning. Briefly describe the steps in these two methods. (7)

d Suggest which method would be most suitable for creating a herd of cows giving high yields of milk. Give reasons for your choice. (4)

2 The use of cloned animals in food production is controversial.

It is now possible to clone 'champion' cows. Champion cows produce large quantities of milk.

a Describe how adult cell cloning could be used to produce a clone of a 'champion' cow. (4)

b Read the passage below about cloning cattle.

> The government has been accused of 'inexcusable behaviour' because a calf of a cloned American 'champion' cow has been born on a British farm. Campaigners say it will undermine trust in British food because the cloned cow's milk could enter the human food chain.

> However, supporters of cloning say that milk from clones and their offspring is as safe as the milk we drink every day.

> Those in favour of cloning say that an animal clone is a genetic copy. It is not the same as a genetically engineered animal. Opponents of cloning say that consumers will be uneasy about drinking milk from cloned animals.

Use the information in the passage and your own knowledge and understanding to evaluate whether the government should allow the production of milk from cloned 'champion' cows.

Remember to give a conclusion to your evaluation. (5)

AQA, 2006

3 Read the passage below. Use the information and your own knowledge to answer the questions.

> At one time, the boll weevil destroyed cotton crops. Farmers sprayed the crops with a pesticide.

> The weevil died out but another insect, the bollworm moth, became resistant to this pesticide.

> In the 1990s, large crops of the cotton plant were destroyed by the bollworm moth. The pesticides then used to kill the moth were expensive and very poisonous, resulting in deaths to humans.

> Scientists investigated alternative ways to control the bollworm moth. They found out that a type of bacterium produced a poison that killed bollworm larvae (grubs).

> A GM cotton crop plant was developed which produced the poison to kill bollworms. This proved to be very effective and farmers were able to stop using pesticide sprays.

> Now farmers have another problem. Large numbers of other insects have multiplied because they were not killed when the farmers stopped using pesticides. Some of these insects have started to destroy the GM cotton and farmers are beginning to use pesticides again!

a i Give **one** advantage of spraying crops with pesticides. (1)

ii Give **two** disadvantages of spraying crops with pesticides. (2)

iii Give **one** economic advantage of using GM cotton. (1)

iv Some people object to using GM crops. Suggest **one** reason why. (1)

b *In this question you will be assessed on using good English, organising information clearly and using specialist terms where appropriate.*

The GM cotton was genetically engineered to produce the same poison as the bacterium.

Describe fully how this is done. (QWC) (6)

B12.1 Adapt and survive

🔗 **links**

For more information on plant adaptation, see 12.3 'Adaptations in plants'.

Examiner's tip

Practise recognising plant and animal adaptations related to where they live. You may be asked to do this in your examination.

Figure 1 Mangroves are trees that live in soil with very little oxygen, often with their roots covered by salty water. They have special adaptations to get rid of the salt through their leaves, and roots which grow in the air to get oxygen.

🔗 **links**

For more information on animal adaptations, see 12.2 'Adaptations in animals'.

The variety of conditions on the surface of the Earth is huge. It ranges from hot, dry deserts to permanent ice and snow. There are deep, saltwater oceans and tiny freshwater pools. Whatever the conditions, almost everywhere on Earth you will find living organisms able to survive and reproduce.

Survive and reproduce

Living organisms need a supply of materials from their surroundings and from other living organisms so they can survive and reproduce successfully. What they need depends on the type of organism.

● Plants need light, carbon dioxide, water, oxygen and nutrients to produce glucose to give them the energy they need to survive.

● Animals need food from other living organisms, water and oxygen.

● Microorganisms need a range of things. Some are similar to plants, while some are similar to animals and some don't need oxygen or light to survive.

Living organisms have special features known as **adaptations**. These features make it possible for them to survive in their particular habitat, even when the conditions are very extreme.

Plant adaptations

Plants need to photosynthesise to produce the glucose needed for energy and growth. They also need to have enough water to maintain their cells and tissues. They have adaptations that enable them to live in many different places. For example, most plants get water and mineral nutrients from the soil through their roots.

Epiphytes are found in rainforests. They have adaptations which allow them to live high above the ground attached to other plants. They collect water and nutrients from the air and in their specially adapted leaves.

Some plant adaptations are all about reproduction. For example, the South African sausage tree (*Kigelia pinnata*) is one of a relatively small number of plants that rely on bats to pollinate their flowers. The flowers open at night, have a strong perfume and produce lots of nectar. They hang down below the branches and leaves which makes it as easy as possible for the bats to approach and feed from them – and at the same time transfer pollen from one flower to another on their fur.

Animal adaptations

Animals cannot make their own food – they have to eat plants or other animals. This type of feeding is known as heterotrophic. Many of the adaptations of animals help them to get the food they need. This means that you can tell what a mammal eats by looking at its teeth.

● **Herbivores** have teeth for grinding up plant cells.

● **Carnivores** have teeth adapted for tearing flesh or crushing bones.

Animals also often have adaptations to help them find and attract a mate.

Adapting to the environment

Some of the adaptations seen in animals and plants help them to survive in a particular environment. For example:

- Some sea birds get rid of all the extra salt they take in from the sea water by 'crying' very salty tears from a special salt gland.
- Animals that need to survive extreme winter temperatures often produce a chemical in their cells which acts as antifreeze. It stops the water in the cells from freezing and destroying the cell.
- Plants such as water lilies have lots of big air spaces in their leaves. This adaptation enables them to float on top of their watery environment and make food by photosynthesis.

Living in extreme environments

Organisms that survive and reproduce in the most difficult conditions are known as **extremophiles**. Many extremophiles are microorganisms. Microorganisms are found in more places in the world than any other living thing. These places range from ice packs to hot springs and geysers. Microorganisms have a range of adaptations which make this possible.

Some extremophiles live at very high temperatures. Bacteria known as thermophiles can survive at temperatures of over 45 °C and often up to 80 °C or higher. (In most organisms, their enzymes stop working at around 40 °C.) These extremophiles have specially adapted enzymes that do not denature and so work at these high temperatures. In fact, many of these organisms cannot survive and reproduce at lower temperatures.

Other bacteria have adaptations so they can grow and reproduce at very low temperatures, down to −15 °C. They are found in ice packs and glaciers around the world.

Most living organisms struggle to survive in a very salty environment because of the problems it causes with water balance. However, there are species of extremophile bacteria that can only live in extremely salty environments, such as the Dead Sea and salt flats. These bacteria have adaptations to their cytoplasm so that water does not move out of their cells into their salty environment. However, in ordinary sea water they would swell up and burst!

Figure 3 Black smoker bacteria live in deep ocean vents, 2500 m down, at temperatures of well over 100 °C, with enormous pressure, no light and an acid pH of about 2.8. They have adaptations to cope with some of the most extreme conditions on Earth.

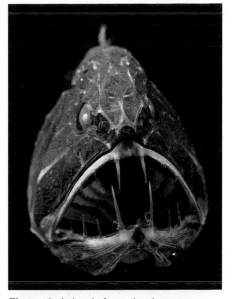

Figure 2 Animals from the deep oceans are adapted to cope with enormous pressure, no light and very cold, salty water. If these extremophiles are brought to the surface too quickly, they explode because of the rapid change in pressure.

Key points

- Organisms need a supply of materials from their surroundings and from other living organisms to survive and reproduce.
- Organisms, including microorganisms, have features (adaptations) that enable them to survive in the conditions in which they normally live.
- Extremophiles have adaptations that enable them to live in environments with extreme conditions of salt, temperature or pressure.

Summary questions

1 Describe what plants and animals need from their surroundings to survive and reproduce and explain the differences between them.

2 a What is an extremophile?
  b Give two examples of adaptations found in different extremophiles.

3 Explain what is meant by an adaptation and give three examples of adaptations in either animals or plants to a particular environment or way of life.

B12.2 Adaptations in animals

Learning objectives

After this topic, you should know:

- some of the ways in which animals are adapted to survive.

⬭⬭ **links**

You can see a diagram explaining surface area to volume ratio in 1.7 'Exchanging materials'.

Figure 1 The Arctic woolly bear moth caterpillar is adapted to survive up to 14 years of freezing and thawing before it becomes an adult moth

Animals have adaptations that help them to get the food and mates they need to survive and reproduce. They also have adaptations for survival in the conditions where they normally live. These include:

- structural adaptations, for example the shape or colour of the organism or part of the organism
- behavioural adaptations such as migration, basking, tool using
- functional adaptations related to processes such as reproduction and metabolism, for example delayed implantation of embryos or antifreeze in cells.

Animals in cold climates

To survive in a cold environment, you must be able to keep yourself warm. Animals which live in very cold places, such as the Arctic, are adapted to reduce the energy they lose from their bodies.

You lose body heat through your body surface (mainly your skin). The amount of energy you lose is closely linked to your surface area to volume ratio (SA:V). The larger the surface area to volume ratio, the larger the rate of energy loss.

The ratio of surface area to volume falls as objects get bigger. This is why mammals in a cold climate grow to a large size: it keeps their surface area to volume ratio as small as possible and so helps them retain their body heat. The surface area to volume ratio is very important when you look at the adaptations of animals that live in cold climates. It explains why so many Arctic mammals, such as seals, walruses, whales and polar bears, are relatively large.

Animals in very cold climates often have other adaptations too. The surface area of the thinly skinned areas of their bodies, like their ears, is usually very small. This reduces their energy loss.

Many Arctic mammals have plenty of insulation, both inside and out. Inside they have blubber (a thick layer of fat that builds up under the skin). On the outside they have a thick fur coat that provides very effective insulation. These adaptations really reduce the amount of energy lost through their skin.

The fat layer also provides a food supply. Animals often build up their fat in the summer. Then they can live off their body fat through the winter when there is almost no food.

Some Arctic animals can actually withstand freezing. The caterpillar of the Arctic woolly bear moth lives for about 14 years before it pupates and becomes a moth. For up to 10 months of every year it survives frozen, before waking up for the brief summer months when it feeds. The cells are protected from damage by a functional adaptation – they contain special antifreeze chemicals. Structural adaptations, such as the dark colour that absorbs energy from the sun and the long hairs that insulate the caterpillar and reduce energy loss during the brief Arctic summer, also help it to survive.

Camouflage

Camouflage is a form of structural adaptation that is important both to **predators** (so their prey doesn't see them coming) and to prey (so they can't be seen).

Examiner's tip

Remember that animals living in very cold conditions often have a low surface area to volume ratio. This means there is less area for heat loss. The opposite can be true in hot climates.

⁇ Did you know ... ?

Polar bears don't change colour. They have no natural predators on the land. They hunt seals all year round in the sea, where their white colour makes them less visible among the ice.

The colours that would camouflage an Arctic animal in summer against plants would stand out against the snow in winter. Many Arctic animals, including the Arctic fox, the Arctic hare and the stoat, therefore have grey or brown summer coats that change to pure white in the winter.

The colour of the coat of a lioness is another example of effective camouflage. The sandy brown colour matches perfectly with the dried grasses of the African savannah. Her colour hides the lioness from the grazing animals that are her prey.

The patterns on the wings of many moths make them almost invisible as they rest on lichen covered trees.

Surviving in dry climates

Dry climates are often also hot climates – like deserts. Deserts are very difficult places for animals to live. There is then scorching heat during the day, followed by bitter cold at night. Water is also in short supply. However, very cold climates can also be dry because the water is frozen and unavailable to plants and animals.

The biggest challenges if you live in a desert are:
● coping with the lack of water
● stopping your body temperature from getting too high.

Many desert animals are adapted to need little or nothing to drink. They get the water they need from the food they eat.

Mammals need to keep their body temperature the same all the time. So as the environment gets hotter, they have to find ways of keeping cool. Sweating means they lose water, which is not easy to replace in the desert.

Animals that live in hot conditions adapt their behaviour to keep cool. They are often most active in the early morning and late evening, when it is not so hot. During the cold nights and the hottest times of the day, they rest in burrows or shady areas where the temperature doesn't change much.

Many desert animals are quite small, so their surface area is large compared to their volume. This helps them to lose heat energy through their skin. They also often have large, thin ears to increase their surface area for losing energy.

Another adaptation of many desert animals is to have thin fur. Any fur they do have is fine and silky. They also have relatively little body fat stored under the skin. These features all make it easier for them to lose heat energy through the surface of the skin.

Figure 2 This moth in an English woodland needs to avoid the birds which might eat it, so camouflage is an important adaptation for survival

Figure 3 Bactrian camels have to survive extremes of both heat (38 °C) and cold (−29 °C) in the rocky deserts of East and Central Asia. Adaptations which help them survive include: a thick winter coat; very little sweating; tissues that can cope with big fluctuations in their core temperature; a large store of fat in the humps; the ability to take water from their food; drinking large amounts of water (around 135 litres) at a time when it becomes available.

Summary questions

1 **a** List the main problems that face animals living in cold conditions such as the Arctic.
   b List the main problems that face animals living in the desert.

2 Animals that live in the Arctic are adapted to keep warm through the winter. Describe three of these adaptations and explain how they work.

3 **a** Describe the visible adaptations of an elephant that enable it to keep cool in hot conditions.
   b Suggest other ways in which animals might be adapted to survive in hot, dry conditions.
   c Describe and explain at least **two** adaptations which enable marine mammals such as whales and seals to survive in the seas and oceans of the world.

Key points

● All living things have adaptations that help them to survive in the conditions where they live.

● Adaptations include:
   – structural adaptations such as the shape and colour of the organism
   – behavioural adaptations such as migration
   – functional adaptations of processes such as reproduction and metabolism.

B12.3 Adaptations in plants

Plants need light, water, space and nutrients to survive. There are some places where plants cannot grow. In deep oceans, no light penetrates and so plants cannot photosynthesise. In the icy wastes of the Antarctic, it is simply too cold for plants to grow.

Almost everywhere else, including the hot, dry areas of the world, you find plants growing. Without them there would be no food for animals. However, plants need water for photosynthesis and to keep their tissues supported. If a plant does not get the water it needs, it wilts and eventually dies.

Plants take in water from the soil through their roots. It moves up through the plant and into the leaves. There are small openings called stomata in the leaves of a plant. These open to allow gases in and out for photosynthesis and respiration. At the same time, water vapour is lost through the stomata by diffusion after it evaporates from the surface of the cells into the air spaces in the leaves.

The rate at which a plant loses water is linked to the conditions in which it grows. When a plant grows in hot and dry conditions, photosynthesis and respiration take place quickly. As a result, plants lose water vapour very quickly. Plants that live in very hot, dry conditions therefore need special adaptations to survive. Most plants either reduce their surface area so they lose less water or store water in their tissues, while some plants do both!

Changing surface area

When it comes to stopping water loss through the leaves, the surface area to volume ratio is very important to plants. A few desert plants have broad leaves with a large surface area. These leaves collect the dew that forms in the cold evenings. They then funnel the water towards their shallow roots.

Some plants in dry environments have curled leaves to reduce the surface area of the leaf. This also traps a layer of moist air around the leaf to reduce the amount of water the plant loses by evaporation.

Most plants that live in dry conditions have leaves with a very small surface area. This adaptation cuts down the area from which water can be lost. Some desert plants have small fleshy leaves with a thick cuticle to keep water loss down. The cuticle is a waxy covering on the leaf that stops water evaporating.

Some examples of plant adaptations are:

- Marram grass grows on sand dunes. It has tightly curled leaves to reduce the surface area for water loss so it can survive the dry conditions.
- Butcher's broom lives in shady, dry conditions under woodland trees and in hedgerows. To reduce water loss its 'leaves' are really flattened leaf-like bits of stem. Stems have far fewer stomata than true leaves, and so the butcher's broom loses very little water and can survive and reproduce in conditions where there is little competition from other species.

The best-known desert plants are the cacti. Their leaves have been reduced to spines with a very small surface area. This means that cacti only lose a tiny amount of water. Not only that, their sharp spines also discourage animals from eating them.

∞ **links**

To find out more about transport in plants and transpiration, look back to 9.5 'Evaporation and transpiration' and 9.6 'Transport systems in plants'.

Figure 1 The leaves of butcher's broom are really stems, not leaves. This adaptation reduces water loss so the plant can survive in the dry, shady conditions under big woodland trees.

∞ **links**

For information on surface area to volume ratio, look back at 12.2 'Adaptations in animals'.

Collecting water

Many plants that live in very dry conditions have specially adapted and very big root systems. They may have extensive root systems that spread over a very wide area, roots that go down a very long way, or both. These adaptations allow the plant to take up as much water as possible from the soil. For example, the mesquite tree has roots that grow as far as 50 m down into the soil.

Storing water

Some plants cope with dry conditions by storing water in their tissues. When there is plenty of water after a period of rain, the plant stores it. Some plants use their fleshy leaves to store water, while other plants use their stems or roots.

For example, cacti don't just rely on their spiny leaves to help them survive in dry conditions. The fat green body of a cactus is its stem, which is full of water-storing tissue. These adaptations make cacti the most successful plants in a hot, dry climate.

Figure 2 Plants such as this saguaro cactus and apple tree live in very different environments and have very different adaptations for maintaining their water balance

Did you know ... ?

After a storm, a large saguaro cactus in the desert can take in 1 tonne of water in a single day. Its adaptations for water conservation mean that it normally loses less than one glass of water a day even in the desert heat. A UK apple tree can lose a whole bath of water in the same amount of time!

Summary questions

1 a Why do plants need water?
  b How do plants get the water they need?

2 a How do plants lose water from their leaves?
  b Why does this make living in a dry place such a problem?

3 a Plants living in dry conditions have adaptations to reduce water loss from their leaves. Give three of these and explain how they work.
  b Preventing water loss from the leaves is not the only way plants can deal with dry conditions. Describe and explain three other adaptations seen in plants to help them survive in dry conditions.

Key points

- Plants lose water vapour from the surface of their leaves.

- Plant adaptations for surviving in dry conditions include reducing the surface area of the leaves, having water-storage tissues and growing extensive root systems.

B12.4

Competition in animals

Learning objectives

After this topic, you should know:

- why animals compete
- what makes an animal a successful competitor.

Did you know ...?

Competition between members of different species for the same resources is known as **inter-specific competition**.

Competition between members of the same species is known as **intra-specific competition**.

Figure 1 Some herbivores only feed on one particular plant, but this approach is risky. Pandas only eat bamboo, so they are vulnerable to competition from other animals that eat bamboo and to diseases that damage bamboo.

Figure 2 The dramatic colours of this Costa Rican strawberry poison dart frog are a clear warning to predators to keep well away

Animals and plants grow alongside lots of other living things. Some will be from the same species while others will be completely different. In any area there is only a limited amount of food, water and space, and a limited number of mates. As a result, living organisms have to compete for the things they need.

The best adapted organisms are those most likely to win the **competition** for resources. They will be most likely to survive and produce healthy offspring.

What do animals compete for?

Animals compete for many things, including:

- food
- **territory**
- mates.

Competition for food

Competition for food is very common. Herbivores sometimes feed on many types of plant, and sometimes on only one or two different sorts. Many different species of herbivores will all eat the same plants. Just think how many types of animals eat grass!

The animals that eat a wide range of plants are most likely to be successful. If you are a picky eater, you risk dying out if anything happens to your only food source. An animal with wider tastes will just eat something else for a while!

Competition is also common among carnivores. They compete for prey. Small mammals such as mice are eaten by animals such as foxes, owls, hawks and domestic cats. The different types of animals all hunt the same mice. So, the animals that are best adapted to finding and catching mice will be most successful.

Carnivores have to compete with their own species for their prey as well as with different species. Some successful predators are adapted to have long legs for running fast and sharp eyes to spot prey. These features will be passed on to their offspring.

Animals often avoid direct competition with members of other species when they can. It is the competition between members of the same species which is most intense.

Prey animals compete with each other too – to be the one that *isn't* caught! Their adaptations help prevent them becoming a meal for a predator. Some animals contain poisons that make anything that eats them sick or even kills them. Very often these animals also have bright warning colours so that predators quickly learn which animals to avoid. Poison arrow frogs are a good example (see Figure 2).

Competition for territory

For many animals, setting up and defending a territory is vital. A territory may simply be a place to build a nest, or it could be all the space needed for an animal to find food and reproduce. Most animals cannot reproduce successfully if they have no territory. So they will compete for the best spaces.

This helps to make sure they will be able to find enough food for themselves and for their young. For example, the number of territories of many small birds such as tits found in an area varies with the amount of food available. Many animals mark the boundaries of their territories to keep other competitors out. This is often done using urine or faeces to make a strong scented boundary.

Competition for a mate

Competition for mates can be fierce. In many species, the male animals put a lot of effort into impressing the females. The males compete in different ways to win the privilege of mating with a female.

In some species – such as deer, lions and elephant seals – the males fight between themselves. Then the winner gets to mate with several females.

Many male animals display to the females to get their attention. Some birds have spectacular adaptations to help them stand out. Male peacocks have the most amazing tail feathers. They use them for displaying to other males (to warn them off) and to females (to attract them). Birds of paradise also produce spectacular displays to attract a mate (see Figure 4).

What makes a successful competitor?

A successful competitor is an animal that is adapted to be better at finding food or a mate than the other members of its own species. It also needs to be better at finding food than the members of other local species. In addition, it must be able to breed successfully.

Many animals are successful because they avoid competition with other species as much as possible. They feed in a way that no other local animals do, or they eat a type of food that other animals avoid. For example, one plant can feed many animals without direct competition. While caterpillars eat the leaves, greenfly drink the sap, butterflies suck nectar from the flowers and beetles feed on pollen.

Figure 3 The territory of a gannet pair may be small, but without a space they cannot build a nest and reproduce

Figure 4 The male bird of paradise uses a very spectacular display to attract a more camouflaged female

Examiner's tip

Learn to look at an animal and spot the adaptations that make it a successful competitor.

Summary questions

1 a Animals that rely on a single type of food can easily become extinct. Explain why.
  b Give an example of animals competing with members of the same species for food.
  c Give an example of animals competing with members of other species for food.
  d Why is competition between members of the same species often more fierce than competition between different species?

2 a Give two ways in which animals compete for mates.
  b Suggest the advantages and disadvantages of the methods chosen in part **a**.

3 Explain some of the adaptations you would expect to find in the following organisms and the advantages they would give:
  a an animal that hunts small mammals such as mice and voles
  b an animal that eats grass
  c an animal that is hunted by many different predators
  d an animal that feeds on the tender leaves at the top of trees.

Key points

● Animals compete with each other for food, territories and mates.

● Animals have adaptations that make them successful competitors.

B12.5 | Competition in plants

Learning objectives

After this topic, you should know:

- what plants compete for
- how plants compete.

Practical

Investigating competition in plants

Carry out an investigation to look at the effect of competition on plants. Set up two trays of seeds – one crowded and one spread out. Then monitor the plants' height and wet mass (mass after watering). Keep all of the conditions – light level, the amount of water and nutrients available, and the temperature – exactly the same for both sets of plants. The differences in their growth will be the result of overcrowding and competition for resources in one of the groups.

The data shows the growth of tree seedlings. You can get results in days rather than months by using cress seeds.

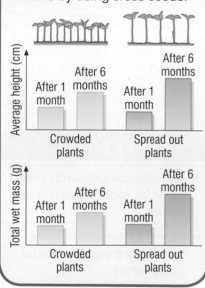

Plants compete fiercely with each other. They compete for:

- light for photosynthesis, to make food using energy from sunlight
- water for photosynthesis and to keep their tissues rigid and supported
- nutrients (minerals) from the soil so they can make all the chemicals they need in their cells
- space to grow, allowing their roots to take in water and nutrients and their leaves to capture light.

Why do plants compete?

As with animals, plants are in competition both with other species of plants and with their own species.

Big, tall plants such as trees take up a lot of water and nutrients from the soil. They also prevent light from reaching the plants beneath them. So the plants around them need adaptations to help them to survive.

When a plant sheds its seeds they might land nearby. Then the parent plant will be in direct competition with its own seedlings. As the parent plant is large and settled, it will take most of the water, nutrients and light. So the plant will deprive its own offspring of everything they need to grow successfully. The roots of some desert plants even produce a chemical that stops seeds from germinating, killing the competition even before it begins to grow!

Sometimes the seeds from a plant will all land close together, a long way from their parent. They will then compete with each other as they grow.

Coping with competition

Plants that grow close to other species often have adaptations which help them to avoid competition.

Small plants found in woodlands often grow and flower very early in the year. This is when plenty of light gets through the bare branches of the trees. The dormant trees take very little water out of the soil. The leaves shed the previous autumn have rotted down to provide nutrients in the soil. Plants such as snowdrops, anemones and bluebells are all adapted to take advantage of these things. They flower, set seeds and die back again before the trees are in full leaf.

Another way plants compete successfully is by having different types of roots. Some plants have shallow roots taking water and nutrients from near the surface of the soil, while other plants have long, deep roots that go far underground. In this way, both types of plants compete successfully for what they need without affecting the other.

Leguminous plants such as peas, beans and clover all have special bacteria living in nodules on their roots. These bacteria fix nitrogen from the air – in other words, they carry out chemical reactions that produce nitrates. Some of these nitrates are used by the plants for making amino acids, which in turn are used to build up proteins for growth. This gives the plants a real edge over competing species that have to take their nitrates from the soil.

If one plant is growing in the shade of another, it may grow taller to reach the light. It may also grow leaves with a bigger surface area to take advantage of all the light it does get. Plants may have adaptations such as tendrils or suckers that allow them to climb up artificial structures or large trees to reach the light.

Some plants are adapted to prevent animals from eating them. They may have thorns, like the African acacia or the blackberry, or they may make poisons that mean they taste very bitter or make the animals that eat them ill. Either way, these plants compete successfully because they are less likely to be eaten than other plants without these adaptations.

Spreading the seeds

To reproduce successfully, a plant has to avoid competition with its own seedlings for light, space, water and nutrients. Many plants use the wind to help them spread their seeds as far as possible. They produce fruits or seeds with special adaptations for flight to carry their seeds away. Examples of this are the parachutes of the dandelion 'clock' and the winged seeds of the sycamore tree.

Some plants use mini-explosions to spread their seeds. The pods dry out, twist and pop, flinging the seeds out and away. Gorse bushes and peas are examples of plants that use this method.

Juicy berries such as grapes and blackcurrants, and nuts such as hazelnuts and walnuts, are adaptations to tempt animals to eat them. The fruit is digested and the tough seeds are deposited well away from the parent plant in their own little pile of fertiliser!

Fruits that are sticky or covered in hooks, such as burrs, get caught up in the fur or feathers of a passing animal. They are carried around until they fall off hours or even days later.

Sometimes, the seeds of several different plants land on the soil and start to grow together. The plants that grow fastest will compete successfully against the slower-growing plants. For example:

- The plants that get their roots into the soil first will get most of the available water and nutrients.
- The plants that open their leaves fastest will be able to photosynthesise and grow faster still, depriving the competition of light.

Examiner's tip
Plants compete for space, light, water and mineral ions.
Animals compete for food, mates and territory.

Summary questions

1 a Suggest three ways in which plants can overcome the problems of growing in the shade of another plant.
  b How do snowdrops and bluebells grow and flower successfully in spite of living under large trees in woodlands?

2 a Why do so many plants have adaptations to make sure that their seeds are spread successfully?
  b Give three examples of successful adaptations for spreading seeds.

3 The dandelion is a successful weed. Carry out some research and evaluate the adaptations that make it a better competitor than many other plants on a school field.

Figure 1 Clover makes its own nitrates. This helps it to outcompete the grass, which has to take its minerals from the soil.

Figure 2 The light seeds and fluffy parachutes of dandelion mean they are spread widely and compete very successfully

Figure 3 Coconuts will float for weeks or even months on ocean currents, which can carry them hundreds of miles from competition with their parents – or any other coconuts!

Key points
- Plants often compete with each other for light, for space, for water and for nutrients (minerals) from the soil.
- Plants have many adaptations that make them good competitors.

B12.6 Adaptations in parasites

Some organisms have very special adaptations that enable them to live a very different way of life to most animals or plants. **Parasites** are organisms that are adapted for living in or on a host organism and feeding off it while it is still alive. The parasite gains an advantage, but the host is always harmed or damaged in some way. Parasites have adaptations so they can feed effectively. Depending on their way of life, they also have adaptations to prevent them being removed from the body of their host or attacked by the host immune system.

Fleas – external parasites

Fleas are parasitic insects that live among the hairs and suck the blood of their many mammalian hosts. They have specially adapted sharp mouthparts that make it possible for them to pierce the skin of their host and also suck the blood. Flea saliva contains a special chemical to stop the blood clotting as they drink it, which would block their mouthparts.

Fleas also have flattened bodies that enable them to move easily between the hairs on the body of a mammal such as a cat or a dog. Their flattened body also means that they are not easily dislodged from their host. They also have very hard bodies, so they are not damaged when the animal scratches at the itchy places caused by fleas. However, they also have very long and powerful hind legs, so they can jump from host to host. They can survive for weeks in the environment as adults and as eggs, and up to a year as a pupa.

Figure 1 Fleas are very well adapted to life as external parasites

Tapeworms – internal parasites

Tapeworms are parasitic flatworms that can grow many metres long. Tapeworms live in the intestines of their hosts, which include mammals, fish, birds and reptiles. They do not feed off the body of their host but deprive them of their digested food.

Tapeworms are specially adapted to survive in the gut. They have a head with fearsome looking hooks and/or suckers that is used to attach the tapeworm firmly to the gut wall. The rest of the body is made up of about a thousand very thin, flattened segments that produce many eggs every day. A tapeworm does not need a mate to fertilise the eggs. The eggs are eaten by another animal, such as a cow or a pig, and this is where they begin their life cycle.

Figure 2 The head of a human tapeworm is well adapted for holding on to the lining of your gut

Tapeworms do not have a gut so they have to absorb nutrients directly across their skin. Their long, flattened shape provides a large surface area so they can absorb ready digested, soluble food from their host. They also have a thick outer cuticle that protects them from the digestive enzymes of their host.

Two of the most common tapeworms that infect people are the beef tapeworm and the pork tapeworm. They get into our body from infected, undercooked meat. Problems arise when the tapeworm becomes too large and starts blocking your bowel or robbing the host of vital nutrients – very large tapeworms may cause deficiencies of vitamins such as vitamin B12 if left for too long.

Did you know … ?

The largest segments of a tapeworm are pushed further and further back until they break off and are passed out in the faeces, full of eggs.

A person with a single tapeworm would pass about 8 or 9 segments each day – and this would release about 750 000 eggs!

Plasmodium falciparum – the malaria parasite

Malaria is caused by the single-celled parasite *Plasmodium falciparum,* which has a very complicated life cycle. It spends part of its life cycle in a mosquito and part in the human body. The parasites are passed on to people when the female *Anopheles* mosquitoes take two blood meals from people before laying their eggs. Once inside the human body, the parasites damage your liver and your blood and cause serious disease symptoms including fevers, chills and exhausting sweats. However, people who are heterozygous for sickle-cell anaemia are protected from the worst effects of malaria.

There are several forms of the malarial parasite, and each form is adapted to survive in different places in different hosts:

- **Gametocytes** are the form of the parasite that infects mosquitoes, and this form reproduces sexually. The female mosquito takes them in when she feeds on the blood of someone infected with malaria. The gametocytes make their way to the salivary glands of the mosquito and change into a new form called sporozoites.

- **Sporozoites** are passed on to humans next time the mosquito takes a blood meal. The female injects saliva into the blood vessels of her host to prevent the blood from clotting as she feeds. Sporozoites enter the blood stream with the saliva and are carried in the blood to the liver where they enter the liver cells. In the liver cells, some of the sporozoites divide asexually to form thousands of merozoites, which is another form of the malaria parasite.

- The **merozoites** are released from the liver into the blood where they enter the red blood cells. Here, hidden from the immune system of the body, some of the merozoites become schizonts.

- After a time, the **schizonts** burst out of the red blood cells, destroying them and releasing more merozoites. It is the reaction of the body to this release of schizonts and the destruction of red blood cells that causes the terrible fever attacks that are seen when someone suffers from malaria.

- Some of the merozoites in the blood go into a stage of sexual reproduction and produce female gametocytes, which can then be transferred to the female mosquito when she bites, and so the whole cycle starts again.

links

You can find out more about the protective effect of sickle-cell anaemia in 10.7 'More inherited conditions in humans'.

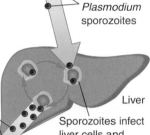

Sexual phase of *Plasmodium* life cycle takes place inside mosquito – gametes fuse to form zygotes, meiosis takes place, sporozoites are produced and migrate to salivary gland

Infected mosquito bites another human, injecting saliva that contains *Plasmodium* sporozoites

Female *Anopheles* mosquito bites a human infected with malaria and picks up *Plasmodium* gamete cells

Plasmodium sporozoites

Schizonts burst the red blood cells, releasing more merozoites that can infect further red blood cells. Some of these merozoites enter a sexual phase of reproduction and produce female gametocytes, which can be transferred to the mosquito when it bites.

Merozoites

Liver

Sporozoites infect liver cells and multiply asexually

Some merozoites form schizonts in red blood cells

Red blood cells

Infected liver cells burst, releasing *Plasmodium* cells called merozoites that infect red blood cells

Figure 3 *Plasmodium* is adapted to live both in mosquito guts and salivary glands and in human liver and blood cells at different times during its complex life cycle

Key points

- Parasites are adapted for living on or inside their hosts.

- Fleas are adapted to live among animal hair and take blood meals.

- Tapeworms are adapted for life inside the gut of their hosts.

- The malaria parasite has a number of different forms that are adapted to living in different regions of both mosquitoes and humans.

Summary questions

1 How are fleas adapted to be effective external parasites?

2 Explain carefully how a tapeworm is adapted to life inside the gut.

3 Malaria is very difficult to treat medically and scientists have still not developed a really effective vaccine against the disease. Explain why you think *Plasmodium* is such an effective parasite and why it is so difficult to develop medicines and vaccines against it.

Summary questions

1 Match the following words to their definitions:

a	competition	A	an animal that eats plants
b	carnivore	B	an area where an animal lives and feeds
c	herbivore	C	an animal that eats meat
d	territory	D	the way animals compete with each other for food, water, space and mates

2 Cold-blooded animals such as amphibians and reptiles do not control their own body temperature internally. They absorb energy from their surroundings and cannot move until they are warm.

a Why do you think that there are no frogs or snakes in the Arctic?

b What problems do you think reptiles face in desert conditions and what adaptations could they have to cope with them?

c Most desert animals are quite small. Explain how this adaptation helps them survive in the harsh conditions.

3 a What are the main problems for plants living in a hot, dry climate?

b Why does reducing the surface area of their leaves help plants to reduce water loss?

c Describe **two** ways in which the surface area of the leaves of some desert plants is reduced.

d Describe other plant adaptations for hot, dry conditions.

e Why are cacti such perfect desert plants?

4 Bamboo plants all tend to flower and die at the same time. Why is this such bad news for pandas, but doesn't affect most other animals?

5 a Why is competition between animals of the same species so much more intense than the competition between different species?

b How does marking out and defending a territory help an animal to compete successfully?

c What are the advantages and disadvantages for males of having an elaborate courtship ritual and colouration compared with fighting over females?

6 Use the bar charts from the practical activity on 12.5 to answer these questions.

a Describe what happens to the height of both sets of seedlings over the first six months and explain why the changes take place.

b The total wet mass of the seedlings after one month was the same whether or not they were crowded. After six months there was a big difference.
  i Why do you think both types of seedling had the same mass after one month?
  ii Explain why the seedlings that were more spread out each had more wet mass after six months.

c When scientists carry out experiments such as the one described, they try to use large sample sizes. Why?

d i Name a control variable mentioned in the practical.
  ii Why were other variables kept constant?

7

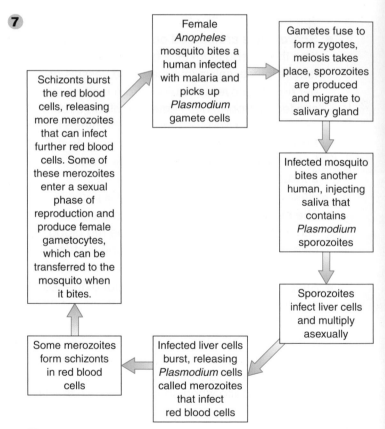

Figure 1

Using Figure 1 to help you, give a clear description of the life cycle of the *Plasmodium* parasite and how it is adapted to survive and be passed on.

AQA Examination-style questions

1 *In this question you will be assessed on using good English, organising information clearly and using specialist terms where appropriate.*

Elephants can survive in hot dry areas.

Explain how the large, thin ears, lack of a fat layer beneath the skin and fine bristles instead of fur helps the elephant to live in hot dry areas. Suggest why they move about and feed in the early morning and evening. (QWC) (6)

2 This is a photograph of a flea taken under a microscope. A flea is a parasite that lives in the fur of animals such as cats and dogs.

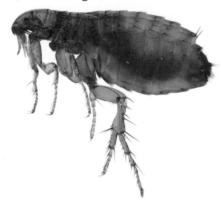

Suggest how each of the following adaptations helps the flea to survive in its habitat.

a No wings

b Piercing mouth parts

c Body flattened from side to side

d Hard external exoskeleton

e Long back legs with spring-like mechanism

f Covered in bristles and combs (6)

3 Gardeners may spray their vegetable plots with herbicide in the hope of growing bigger vegetables.

a What is a herbicide? (1)

b Explain, using your knowledge of competition in plants, how using a herbicide might increase the size of the vegetables. (5)

4 The gemsbok is a large herbivore living in dry desert regions of South Africa. It feeds on grasses that are adapted to the dry conditions by obtaining moisture from the air as it cools at night. The table below shows the water content of these grasses and the feeding activity of the gemsbok over a 24-hour period.

Time of day	% water content of grasses	% of gemsboks feeding
03.00	18	40
06.00	23	60
09.00	25	20
12.00	08	17
15.00	06	16
18.00	05	19
21.00	07	30
24.00	14	50

a i Name the independent variable investigated. (1)
ii Name a variable that should have been controlled. (1)

b How does the water content of the grasses change throughout the 24-hour period? (1)

c Between which recorded times are more than 30% of the gemsboks feeding? (1)

d Suggest **three** reasons why the gemsboks benefit from feeding at this time. (3)

AQA, 2008

B13.1   Organisms in their environment

Learning objectives

After this topic, you should know:

- the relationships within communities of living organisms

- the factors that affect the distribution of organisms in their natural environment.

In any habitat, you will find different distributions of living organisms. These organisms form communities, with the different animals and plants often dependent on each other:

- the animals eat the plants
- insects pollinate the plants
- animals eat other animals
- plants need the nutrients from animal droppings and decay
- different species compete with each other for the various resources, and within species animals and plants also compete for resources
- different communities exist close to each other and may overlap.

It is important that you understand the relationships within and between these communities. A number of environmental factors – both non-living (abiotic) and living (biotic) – affect organisms and how they are distributed in the environment.

∞ links

You can find out more about competition in 12.4 'Competition in animals' and 12.5 'Competition in plants'.

Figure 1 Snow leopards are one of the rarest big cats. They live in cold, high altitude environments where there are not many plants, and so there are very few herbivores for the snow leopards to hunt.

?? Did you know … ?

Reindeer live in cold environments where most of the plants are small because temperature and light levels limit growth. They eat grass, moss and lichen. Reindeer travel thousands of miles as they feed. They cannot get enough food to survive in just one area.

Factors affecting living organisms

Non-living factors that affect living organisms include the following:

Temperature

You have seen that temperature is a limiting factor on photosynthesis and therefore growth in plants. In cold climates, temperature is always a limiting factor. For example, the low temperatures, limited light levels and water, and harsh, windy conditions mean that Arctic plants are all small. This in turn affects the numbers of herbivores that can survive in the area, which affects the number of carnivores that can be supported within a community.

Availability of nutrients

The level of mineral ions, for example nitrate ions, has a considerable impact on the distribution of plants. Carnivorous plants such as Venus flytraps thrive where nitrate levels are very low because they can trap and digest animal prey. The nitrates they need are provided when they break down the animal protein. Most other plants struggle to grow in areas with low levels of mineral ions.

Amount of light

Light limits photosynthesis, so it also affects the distribution of plants and animals. Some plants are adapted to living in low light levels, for example they may have more chlorophyll or bigger leaves. So nettles growing in the shade of other bushes have leaves with a much bigger surface area than nettles growing in the open. However, most plants need plenty of light to grow well.

The breeding cycles of many animal and plant species are linked to light levels, only living and breeding where day length and light intensity are right for them.

Figure 2 The distribution of plants such as these sundews growing on a New Forest bog depends heavily on nutrient levels – they cannot compete in habitats with more nutrients in the soil

Availability of water

If there is no water, there will be little or no life. As a rule, plants and animals are relatively rare in a desert as the availability of water is limited. However, the distribution changes after it rains. A large number of plants grow, flower and set seeds very quickly while the water is available. These plants are eaten by many animals that move into the area to take advantage of them.

An excess of water also affects the distribution of organisms – only plants and animals with special adaptations can survive.

Availability of oxygen and carbon dioxide

The availability of oxygen has a huge impact on water-living organisms. Some invertebrates can survive in water with very low oxygen levels. However, most fish need a high level of dissolved oxygen. The distribution of land organisms is not affected by oxygen levels as oxygen levels in the air vary very little.

Carbon dioxide levels act as a limiting factor on photosynthesis and plant growth. They can also affect the distribution of organisms. For example, mosquitoes are attracted to the animals whose blood they feed on by high carbon dioxide levels. Plants are also more vulnerable to insect attacks in an area with high carbon dioxide levels.

The physical factors that affect the distribution of living organisms do not work in isolation. They interact to create unique environments where different animals and plants can live.

Living factors which affect living organisms include the following:

Availability of nesting sites, shelter and appropriate habitats

The environment where an animal lives – its habitat – has to provide what it needs to feed, reproduce successfully and shelter from the worst of the weather. If any of these factors is missing, the population of that animal in a community will fall. This is why certain animals are found in particular habitats – for example, sand martins need sandy cliffs or river banks to build their nests while woodpeckers need trees to provide both nest sites and a supply of food from the beetles under the bark. If these are not available, the birds do not nest.

Changes in the numbers or types of competitor organism

If a new predator comes into an area, this will affect the number of herbivores. This in turn will affect the numbers of the original carnivores, as there will be fewer prey animals available to feed their young. Similarly, the introduction of a new herbivore can drastically reduce the amount of plant material available for other animals. The introduction of the rabbit into Australia, for example, led to the extinction of a number of common species who simply could not compete with the grass-eating and breeding abilities of the rabbits.

Summary questions

1 What is a community of organisms?
2 What are the physical factors most likely to affect living organisms?
3 How do carnivorous plants survive in areas with very low levels of nitrate ions while other plants cannot grow there?
4 Explain how the limiting factors for photosynthesis – light, temperature and carbon dioxide levels – also affect the distribution of animals directly and indirectly.
5 Explain clearly how a new predator or a new carnivore can change the balance of organisms in a community and ultimately change the living organisms in an entire habitat.

⚭ links

To find out more about measuring oxygen levels in aquatic environments, see 13.4 'Measuring environmental change'.

⁇ Did you know ... ?

Scientists thought that all organisms, apart from specialised microorganisms, needed oxygen to live. Then, in 2010, multicellular organisms that do not need oxygen were discovered living deep under the Mediterranean sea. If more of these amazing organisms are found, our ideas of how oxygen affects the distribution of organisms will have to change.

Figure 3 This is one of the first known multicellular organisms that do not need oxygen to respire

Key points

- There are relationships both within and between communities of living organisms.

- Factors that may affect the distribution of living organisms include changes in:
  - the numbers or types of competitor organisms
  - temperature
  - nutrients
  - the amount of light
  - the availability of water
  - the availability of oxygen and carbon dioxide
  - the availability of nest sites, shelter and appropriate habitats.

Measuring the distribution of organisms

Learning objectives

After this topic, you should know:

- how you can measure the distribution of living things in their natural environment

- how finding the mean, median and mode can help you understand your data.

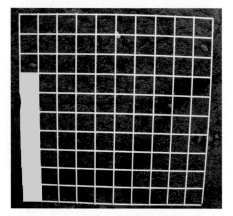

Figure 1 Using a quadrat to measure barnacles on a rocky shore

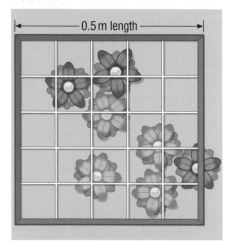

|← 0.5 m length →|

Figure 2 It doesn't matter if organisms partly covered by a quadrat are counted as in or out, as long as you decide and do the same each time. In this diagram of a quadrat, you have six or seven plants per 0.25 m² (that's 24 or 28 plants per square metre), depending on the way you count.

It is often important to show how a physical factor (or changes in a physical factor) affects the distribution of living organisms. To do this, you must be able to measure how those organisms are distributed in the first place.

Quadrats

The simplest way to sample an area (to count the number of organisms there) is to use a **quadrat**. A quadrat is usually a square frame made of wood or metal that you lay on the ground. This outlines your sample area.

A quadrat with sides 0.5 m long gives you a 0.25 m² sample area. Quadrats are used to investigate the size of a population of plants. They can also be used for animals that move very slowly, such as snails or sea anemones.

You use the same size quadrat every time, and sample as many areas as you can. This makes your results as valid as possible. **Sample size** is very important. You must choose your sample areas *at random*. This ensures that your results reflect the true distribution of the organisms and that any findings you make will be valid.

There are a number of ways to make sure that the samples you take are random. For example, the person with the quadrat closes their eyes, spins round, opens their eyes and walks 10 paces before dropping the quadrat. A random number generator is a more scientific way of deciding where to drop your quadrat.

You need to take a number of random readings and then find the **mean** number of organisms per m². This technique is known as **quantitative sampling**. You can use quantitative sampling to compare the distribution of the same organism in different habitats. You can also use it to compare the variety of organisms in a number of different habitats.

> ### 🖩 *Maths skills*
>
> #### Finding the range, the mean, the median and the mode
>
> A student takes 10 random 1 m² quadrat readings looking at the number of snails in a garden. The results are:
>
> | 4 | 4 | 3 | 4 | 5 | 2 | 6 | 5 | 4 | 3 |
> |---|---|---|---|---|---|---|---|---|---|
>
> The **range** of the data is the range between the minimum and maximum values – in this case from **2–6 snails per m²**.
>
> To find the **mean** distribution of snails in the garden, add all the readings together and divide by 10:
>
> 4 + 4 + 3 + 4 + 5 + 2 + 6 + 5 + 4 + 3 ÷ 10 = 40 ÷ 10 = **4 snails per m²**
>
> The **median** is the middle value when the numbers are put in order – in this case, the range is 2–6 snails per m² so the median is **4 snails per m²**.
>
> The **mode** is the most frequently occurring value – in this case, **4 snails per m²**.

Sampling is also used to measure changes in the distribution of organisms over time. You do this by repeating your measurements at regular time intervals. Finding the **range** of distribution and the **median** and **mode** of your data can also give you useful information.

Counting along a transect

Sampling along a **transect** is another useful way of measuring the distribution of organisms. There are different types of transect. A line transect is most commonly used.

Transects are not random. You stretch a tape between two points, for example up a rocky shore, across a pathway or down a hillside. This is often done where you suspect a change is linked to a particular abiotic factor. You sample the organisms along that line at regular intervals using a quadrat. This shows you how the distribution of organisms changes along that line. You can also measure some of the physical factors, such as light levels and soil pH, that might affect the growth of the plants along the transect.

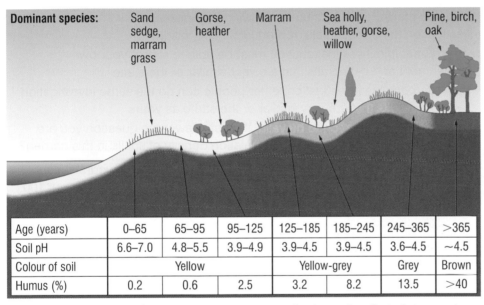

Dominant species: Sand sedge, marram grass | Gorse, heather | Marram | Sea holly, heather, gorse, willow | Pine, birch, oak

Age (years)	0–65	65–95	95–125	125–185	185–245	245–365	>365
Soil pH	6.6–7.0	4.8–5.5	3.9–4.9	3.9–4.5	3.9–4.5	3.6–4.5	~4.5
Colour of soil	Yellow			Yellow-grey		Grey	Brown
Humus (%)	0.2	0.6	2.5	3.2	8.2	13.5	>40

Figure 3 In this transect of some sand dunes, you can clearly see the effect of changes in the physical factors on the distribution of the plants

Figure 4 Carrying out a transect of a rocky shore

Summary questions

1 Explain how to use a quadrat to gain quantitative data on the distribution of organisms. What are the limitations of this technique?

2 a How can you make sure your sampling with a quadrat is random?
  b Why is it so important for samples to be random?
  c In a series of 10 random 1 m² quadrats, a class found the following numbers of dandelions: 6, 3, 7, 8, 4, 6, 5, 7, 9, 8. What is the mean density of dandelions per m² on the school field, the median value and the mode?

3 Explain the ways in which the information you get from quadrats and transects is similar and how it differs.

How valid is the data?

Environments are changing naturally all the time. For example, cliffs crumble, the flow of a river changes after a storm, a tree is killed by a lightning strike or an animal dies and provides a whole new rich environment for all the decomposers.

People also have an effect on the environment. This can be locally, such as dropping litter or building a new road, or on a worldwide scale, as with possible global warming and climate change.

A change in the distribution of living organisms can be evidence of a change in the environment. However, if you want to use this type of data as evidence for environmental change, it is important to use **repeatable**, **reproducible** and **valid** methods to collect your results.

Reproducible, valid and repeatable data

When you measure the distribution of living organisms, you want your investigation to be repeatable, reproducible and valid:

- in a repeatable investigation, you must be able to repeat your own experiment and get results that are very similar or the same

- in a reproducible investigation, other people can do the same investigation and get results that are very similar or the same as yours

- and for the investigation to be valid, it must answer the question you are asking, for example, what is the population density of snails in this garden?

One important factor is the size of your sample. If you do 10 quadrats, your data will not be as repeatable, reproducible or as valid as if you carry out 100 quadrats.

Your method of sampling must be appropriate. If you want to measure the distribution of plants in an area, random quadrats work well. If you want to measure change in distribution over a range of habitats, then a transect is a better technique to use.

If you are trying to measure change over time, you must be able to replicate your method every time you repeat your readings.

Changes in the distribution of a species are often used as evidence of environmental change. You must use a method of measuring that works regardless of who is collecting the data.

Controlling variables

When you are working in a laboratory, you can control as many of the **variables** as possible. Then you can repeat the investigation or other scientists can carry it out under the same conditions. This increases the likelihood that your results will be repeatable and reproducible.

In fieldwork, it is not possible to control all the variables of the natural environment. However, you can control some. For example, you can always measure at the same time of day, although you cannot control the weather or the arrival of different organisms.

You must be clear about the problems of collecting data if you want to use them as evidence of environmental change.

Figure 1 If you are trying to find evidence of environmental change in an area as big as this, it is important to use a method that is as valid as possible

A penguin case study

In the early 1980s, Dee Boersma noticed that the numbers of penguins in a breeding colony in Argentina were falling. In 1987 she set up a research project making a transect of the colony with 47 permanent stakes, 100 metres apart.

Every year, Dee counted the active nests within a 100 m² circle around 19 of the stakes. She surveyed the remaining sites less regularly. However, Dee found the same pattern everywhere – penguin numbers were falling.

What is causing these changes? Climate change seems to be significant:

● There have been several breeding seasons where unusually heavy rainfall has occurred. This has destroyed many nests and killed many chicks (see Figure 2).

● There have been changes in the numbers of small fish that the penguins eat. This is in response to changes in the water temperature. So there has been less food available in some years.

However, in biology things are rarely simple. The penguins are also affected by oil and waste from nearby shipping lanes. Around 20 000 penguins were killed by one major oil spill in 1991 alone. People catch the same small fish that the penguins feed on. Thousands of tourists visit the colony every year. They trample the area and cause stress to the birds.

Many factors, probably including climate change, are involved in the distribution changes of the penguins.

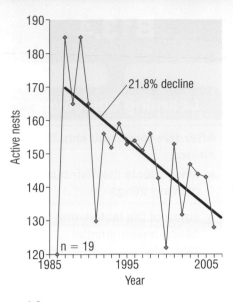

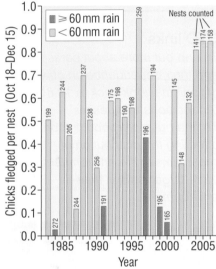

Figure 3 The penguin population at Punta Tombo fell by almost 22% between 1987 and 2006

Figure 2 Patagonian penguins reflect environmental change in a very sensitive way. These graphs, created using Dee Boersma's data, show clearly the effect of heavy rain on chick survival.

Summary questions

1 It is very important that the results of any scientific investigation into changes in animal distribution can be respected by the community of scientists involved. The data must be repeatable, reproducible and valid. Explain what is meant by these terms.

2 Look at Figure 2 and Figure 3 and the text above to help you answer this question.
  a When was the penguin population at Punta Tombo at its peak?
  b When was the population at its lowest? Suggest a reason for this.
  c How could Professor Boersma's data be used as evidence for environmental change?

3 Professor Boersma is widely respected in the scientific community. In what ways can you see that her data are repeatable, reproducible and valid?

Key points

● Different methods can be used to collect environmental data.

● Repeatability, reproducibility and validity must be considered carefully as it is difficult to control variables in fieldwork.

● Sample size is an important factor in the repeatability, reproducibility and validity of data.

B13.4

Measuring environmental change

Learning objectives

After this topic, you should know:

● what affects the distribution of living things

● some of the factors that cause environmental changes

● how environmental changes can be measured.

⛓ links

To find out more about parasites and their dependence on other organisms, look back to 12.6 'Adaptations in parasites'.

To find out more about factors affecting the distribution of organisms in the environment, see 13.1 'Organisms in their environment'.

Figure 1 The distribution of bullhorn acacia ants depends on where the swollen-thorn acacia trees grow

Have you noticed different types of animals and plants when you travel to different places? The distribution of living organisms depends on the environmental conditions and it varies around the world.

Factors affecting the distribution of organisms

Non-living factors have a big effect on where organisms live:

● The average temperature will have a huge impact on what can survive. You don't find polar bears in countries where the average temperature is over 20 °C, for example.

● The average rainfall also affects the distribution of both plants and animals. The plants that can grow in a rainforest with an almost constant amount of water are very different to the plants that grow in your garden or in a desert.

● Light, pH and the local climate all influence where living organisms are found.

● The distribution of different species of animals in water is closely linked to the oxygen levels. Salmon can only live in water with lots of dissolved oxygen, but bloodworms can survive in very low oxygen levels.

Living organisms also affect the distribution of other living organisms. So, for example, koala bears are only found where eucalyptus trees grow. Parasites such as tapeworms, fleas and *Plasmodia* only live where they can find a host.

One species of ant – the bullhorn acacia ant – eats nectar produced by the flowers of the swollen-thorn acacia tree. The ants hollow out the vicious thorns and live within them. So any animal biting the tree not only gets the sharp thorns, they get a mouthful of angry ants as well. The distribution of the ants depends on the trees.

Environmental changes

When the environment changes, this can cause a change in the distribution of living organisms in the area. Non-living factors often cause these changes in an environment.

The average temperature may rise or fall. The oxygen concentration in water may change. A change in the amount of sunlight, the strength of the wind or the average rainfall may affect an environment. Any of these factors can affect the distribution of living organisms.

Living factors can also cause a change in the environment where an organism lives, affecting distribution. A new type of predator may move into an area. A new disease-causing pathogen may appear and wipe out a species of animal or plant. Different plants may appear and provide food or a home for a whole range of different species.

Measuring environmental change

When an environment changes, the living organisms in it are also affected. If the change is big enough, the distribution of animals or plants in an area may change.

You can measure environmental change using non-living indicators. You can measure factors such as average rainfall, temperature, oxygen levels, pH and pollutant levels in water or the air, and much more. All sorts of different instruments are available to do these measurements. These range from simple rain gauges and thermometers to oxygen meters and dataloggers used in schools.

Different types of equipment have advantages and disadvantages. The simpler equipment is cheap and relatively easy to use, but often needs a lot of human input and it is easy to make errors when taking readings or for different people to read the equipment differently. Oxygen meters and dataloggers are more expensive, more likely to go wrong and depend on access to electricity and computers. However, they can take readings constantly or at regular intervals, and there is not 'experimenter error' in the way the readings are taken. If the instruments are well calibrated, the results recorded will be an accurate reflection of the changes in the factor being investigated.

You can also use the changing distribution of living organisms as an **indicator** of environmental change. Living organisms are particularly good as indicators of pollution.

Lichens grow on places such as rocks, roofs and the bark of trees. They are very sensitive to air pollution, particularly levels of sulfur dioxide in the atmosphere. When the air is clean, many different types of lichen grow. The more polluted the air, the fewer lichen species there will be. So a field survey on the numbers and types of lichen can be used to give an indication of air pollution. The data can be used to study local sites or to compare different areas of the country.

In the same way, you can use invertebrate animals as water pollution indicators. In general, the more polluted the water, the lower the oxygen levels will be. The cleaner the water, the more species you will find. Some species of invertebrates are only found in the cleanest waters. Others can be found even in very polluted waters. Counting the different types of species gives a good indication of pollution levels, and it can be used to monitor any changes and to build up a **biotic index of water cleanliness**.

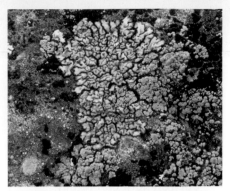

Figure 2 Lichens grow well where the air is clean. In an area polluted with sulfur dioxide, there would be fewer lichen species. So lichens are good indicators of pollution.

Practical

Indicators of pollution levels

Investigate both the variety of lichens in your local area and the number of invertebrate species in your local pond or stream. Then compare your data to national figures, to give you an idea of pollution levels in your area.

Safety: Follow safety advice for outside activities.

Examiner's tip

Examples of biological indicators of pollution are lichens for sulfur dioxide and number of invertebrate species for water pollution.
Examples of non-living indicators are oxygen, temperature and pH values.

Summary questions

1 Give examples of two living and two non-living factors that can change the distribution of living organisms in an environment and explain why they have this effect.

2 In the past, the River Thames has been very polluted. A lot of effort has been made to clean up the river and manage the sewage and pollution better. A regular survey is carried out of the species of living organisms at different places along the river. Explain why this type of survey is carried out and what it might show.

3 Give **three** different methods you could use to collect environmental data. For each method, comment on its repeatability, reproducibility and usefulness as a source of evidence of environmental change.

Key points

- The distribution of living things is affected by both living and non-living factors.

- Environmental changes can be measured using non-living indicators such as oxygen levels, temperature and rainfall.

- Living organisms can be used as indicators of environmental change and pollution; for example, lichens for air pollution, invertebrate animals for water pollution and dissolved oxygen levels.

B13.5 The impact of change

There are many different examples of the distribution of living organisms changing as the environment in which they live changes in different ways. For example, the distribution of birds across the UK is very susceptible to changes in temperature, as the story of the Dartford warbler demonstrates.

Changing birds of Britain

Temperatures in the UK seem to be rising. Many people like the idea as they think of summer barbeques and low heating bills. However, rising temperatures will have a big impact on many living organisms and we could see changes in the distribution of many species. Food plants and animals might become more common, or die out, in different conditions.

The Dartford warbler is a small brown bird that breeds mainly in southern Europe. A small population lived in Dorset and Hampshire. By 1963, two very cold winters left just 11 breeding pairs in the UK. However, temperatures have increased steadily since then. Dartford warblers are now found in Wales, the Midlands and East Anglia. If climate change continues, Dartford warblers could spread through most of England and Ireland. However, in Spain the numbers are dropping rapidly – by 25% in the last 10 years – as it becomes too warm.

Scientists can simulate the distribution of birds as the climate changes. They predict that by the end of the century, Spain could lose most of its millions of Dartford warblers.

By the end of this century, if climate change continues at its present rate, scientists predict that the range of the average bird species will move nearly 550 km north-east. About 75% of all the birds that nest in Europe are likely to have smaller ranges as a result, and many species will be lost from Europe completely or become extinct and be lost for good.

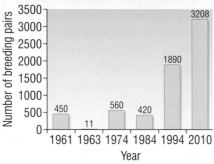

Figure 1 The Dartford warbler is becoming more common in the UK as average temperatures rise

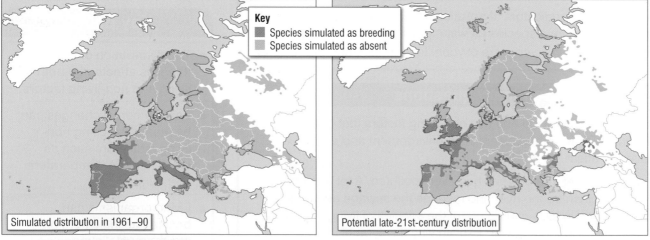

Simulated distribution in 1961–90

Potential late-21st-century distribution

Key
- Species simulated as breeding
- Species simulated as absent

Figure 2 The maps show how scientists think the distribution of European bird species might change in the future

Bluebells under threat

It isn't only animals that are affected by temperature changes. The bluebell woods which are so famous in the UK are also under threat.

Bluebells do well because they can develop leaves and flowers relatively early in the year when it is colder. This is before the leaves on the trees are fully opened and the more temperature-dependent ground plants such as cow parsley start growing. However, as springs are becoming warmer, the ground plants are growing earlier. They quickly get taller and grow more vigorously than the bluebells. Combined with problems of habitat loss, over-picking, trampling and cross-breeding with cultivated Spanish bluebells, our native bluebell woods may become a thing of the past.

No bees, no fruit?

All around the world, honey bees are disappearing. In the UK alone, around one in five bee hives has been lost in the last few years. In the United States, around 2 million colonies of bees were lost in 3 years. The bees had been struck down by a new, mystery disease called Colony Collapse Disorder or CCD. The bees either die, or simply fail to return to the hive. Without the mass of worker bees, those bees left in the hive quickly die.

Members of the British Beekeepers Association are alarmed. They say that if hives continue to be lost at the same rate, there will be no honey bees left in Britain by 2018. You might think that having fewer bees doesn't really matter – it just means honey is more expensive to buy. In fact, bees are vital in plant ecology. Honey bees pollinate flowers as they collect the nectar. Without them, flowers are not pollinated and fruit does not form – so we would have no apples, raspberries, cucumbers, strawberries, peaches … the list goes on and on. There would be cereal crops, because they are pollinated by the wind, but not much else.

No one yet fully understands what is happening to the bees and changing their distribution. Scientists think that viral diseases, possibly spread by a parasitic mite, are a major cause. So living factors – the agents of disease – are causing a major change in the environment of the honey bee. This in turn is affecting their distribution.

Other living and non-living factors affecting the environment have also been suggested. Flowering patterns are changing as temperatures vary with climate change. This may affect the food supply of the bees. Farmers spray chemicals that may build up in the bees. Some people have even suggested that mobile phones affect the bees' navigation system.

Research is continuing all over the world. Disease-resistant strains of bees are being bred. Collecting the evidence to show exactly what environmental change is affecting the honey bee population is proving difficult. Yet there is a little good news – UK numbers have recovered slightly as more people have started keeping bees.

Figure 3 Bluebells are beautiful, but are losing ground to more vigorous plants as the temperature rises earlier in the year

??? Did you know … ?

In China, many apple orchards have to be pollinated by hand because there are no longer any bees to visit the flowers and carry pollen from one flower to another.

Figure 4 Honey bees are vital pollinators. Bee-pollinated fruits are worth about £50 billion of trade every year.

Key points

- Both living and non-living factors can cause changes in the environment.

- Changes in the environment can affect the distribution of living organisms.

- Examples of the effects of environmental changes on the distribution of living organisms include the changes in the distribution of a number of British and European birds and plants in response to rising temperatures, and the fall in the honey bee population as a result of new disease and possible climate change.

Summary questions

1 Using the information on this spread, what aspect of climate change seems to be linked to a change in the distribution of British birds?

2 Many changes in the distribution of organisms are **multifactorial**. The loss of bluebells from our native woods is an example of this. What do you think multifactorial means, and what factors are affecting the distribution of bluebells in the UK?

3 a Why is the loss of honey bees so important?
   b List the main suggested causes for the decline of the honey bee.
   c Why is it important to find out whether the environmental cause of the problem is a living or non-living factor?

Summary questions

1 Suggest how each of the following factors affect the distribution of living organisms in an environment. In each case, try to give a plant and an animal example.

  a Availability of nesting sites or sheltered areas

  b Availability of nutrients

  c Temperature

  d Amount of light

2 Students carried out an investigation into the distribution of worm casts in different areas of the school grounds – heavily trampled areas of a path across the games field and a well-composted flower-bed. They took nine 0.25 m² quadrat readings at random in each area. The results are given opposite:

Trampled area	Flowerbed
4	6
3	7
7	5
4	8
5	9
2	9
2	6
0	10
4	4

  a Why is it important that the quadrats are done at random?

  b Describe a method students could use to ensure the quadrats are done at random.

  c Explain what is meant by the mean, the median and the mode of a data set.

  d For each set of results, give the mean, the median and the mode of the data.

  e What do the results suggest about the distribution of worms in an environment?

  f Describe how you might make the data produced in this investigation more repeatable, reproducible and valid.

3

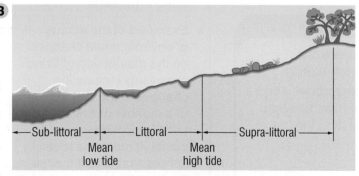

Figure 1

  a Figure 1 is a transect of a rocky shore. What is a transect?

  b What factors might affect the distribution of organisms along this transect?

  c How might you measure the distribution of organisms along this shore?

  d How will the distribution of organisms on a shore differ from the distribution of organisms in a field?

4

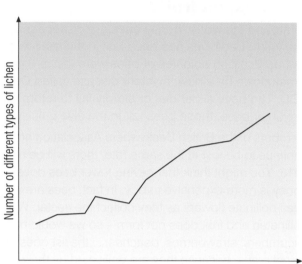

Figure 2

  a What does Figure 2 tell you about the distribution of lichens in the wood over the period of the recordings?

  b How can you explain the trend in the results?

  c What would you expect to happen if the level of sulfur dioxide emissions from the factories increases?

  d Why are lichens often used as bioindicators of environmental change?

5 **a** Describe how living organisms can be used as indicators of environmental change in an aquatic environment.

  b How repeatable, reproducible and valid do you think the data on change in an environment provided by living indicators might be?

  c Suggest three ways in which non-living indicators can also be used to measure environmental change.

6 Changes in the environment can have a very major effect on the distribution of living organisms. Describe in detail one example of a change in the distribution of an organism in response to measured environmental change.

AQA Examination-style questions

1 Both living and non-living indicators can be used to measure environmental change.

a i List A gives some indicators. List B gives some environmental factors.

Match each indicator in List A to the environmental factor in List B that it measures.

List A	List B
Lichens	Air or water temperature
Rain gauge	Dissolved oxygen in water
Freshwater invertebrates	Concentration of sulfur dioxide in the air
Oxygen meter	Rainfall
Thermometer	

(5)

ii Choose the living indicators from list A (1)

b Scientists have suggested that the decrease in numbers of sparrows in the countryside is due to farmers replacing the hedges around their fields with fences.

Suggest how destroying the hedges might affect the number of sparrows. (3)

2 A gardener investigated the best density of sowing carrot seed to get the heaviest crop.

The gardener:
- measured out four identical 1 m² areas of his garden
- sowed carrot seed at four different densities
- gave then equal amounts of water for two months
- dug up the carrots, washed and counted them and found the total mass for each area.

The table gives his results.

Area	1	2	3	4
Density of seed per cm²	1	3	10	20
Number of carrots in area	20	42	61	68
Total mass of carrots in kg	3.60	7.64	9.15	7.14
Mean mass of 1 carrot in g	180	182		

a i Complete the table by calculating the mean mass of 1 carrot for area 3 and area 4. (2)

ii What is the median of the mean mass of 1 carrot for the four areas? (1)

b Which density of seed gave the gardener his heaviest crop? (1)

c Describe what happened to the number and size of the carrots as the density of seed increased. (2)

d Name **two** environmental factors that could have caused the changes you described in part **c**.

Explain how each one could have affected the carrot growth. (4)

3 Students investigated the distribution of plantain plants in their local park. They made the hypothesis: **The further from an oak tree trunk, the more plantains will grow.**

Figure 1 shows how they set up their investigation.

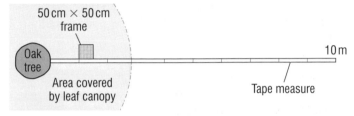

Figure 1

The students:
- laid out a 10 m tape from the base of the tree
- put down a 50 cm × 50 cm wooden frame against the 1 metre mark
- counted how many plantains were inside the frame and recorded it
- repeated the previous two steps for every metre mark.

The table shows the results:

Metre mark	1	2	3	4	5	6	7	8	9	10
Number of plantains	0	0	2	5	9	12	9	14	11	12

a Give the correct scientific name of the 10-m tape and of the 50 cm × 50 cm frame used in an environmental investigation. (2)

b Describe the trend in the number of plantains as you move further from the tree. (2)

c The students suggested that this trend was due to lack of sunlight under the oak tree.

How could the lack of sunlight affect the growth of plantain plants? (3)

d Suggest **one** other possible physical or biological factor that might have caused this trend. Explain your answer. (2)

e Suggest how **one** physical factor could be measured to give extra information to the students. (2)

f Suggest how the students could improve both the repeatability and reproducibility of this investigation. (2)

The effects of the human population explosion

Learning objectives

After this topic, you should know:

- the effect of the growth in human population on the Earth and its resources and the increased waste produced as a result.

Figure 1 The Earth – as the human population grows and standards of living increase, our impact on the planet gets bigger every day

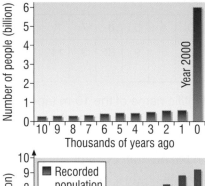

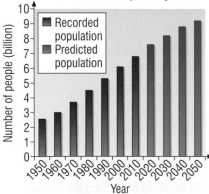

Figure 2 This record of human population growth shows the massive increase during the past 60 years – and predicts more to come

Humans have been on Earth for less than a million years. Yet our activity has changed the balance of nature on the planet enormously. Several of the changes we have made seem to be driving many other species to extinction. Some people worry that we may even be threatening our own survival.

Human population growth

For many thousands of years, people lived on the Earth in quite small numbers. There were only a few hundred million of us. We were scattered all over the world, and the effects of our activity were usually small and local. Any changes could easily be absorbed by the environment where we lived.

However, in the past 200 years or so, the human population has grown very quickly. In 2011, the human population passed 7 billion people, and it is still growing.

If the population of any other species of animal or plant suddenly increased like this, nature would tend to restore the balance. Predators, lack of food, build-up of waste products or diseases would reduce the population again. Yet we have discovered how to grow more food than we could ever gather from the wild. We can cure or prevent many killer diseases. We have no natural predators. This helps to explain why the human population has grown so fast.

In many parts of the world, our standard of living has also improved enormously. In the UK, we use vast amounts of electricity and fuel to provide energy for our homes and places of work. We use fossil fuels such as oil to generate this electricity. We also use oil and oil-based fuels to move about in cars, planes, trains and boats at high speed, and to make materials such as plastics. We have more than enough to eat, and if we are ill we can often be made better.

The effect on land and resources

The increase in the numbers of people has had an enormous effect on our environment. All these billions of people need land to live on. More and more land is used for the building of houses, shops, industrial sites and roads. Some of these building projects destroy the habitats of other living organisms.

We use billions of acres of land around the world for farming. Wherever people farm, the natural animal and plant populations are destroyed.

In quarrying, we dig up great areas of land for the resources it holds, such as rocks and metal ores. This also reduces the land available for other organisms.

In this way, the huge human population drains the resources of the Earth. Raw materials are rapidly being used up. This includes **non-renewable** energy resources such as crude oil and natural gas. Also, once metal ores are processed, they cannot be replaced.

 Did you know ...?

Current UN predictions suggest that the world population will soar to 244 billion by 2150 and 134 trillion by 2300!

Managing waste

Rapid growth in the human population along with an increase in the standards of living in many places around the world means that increasingly large amounts of waste are being produced. This includes human bodily waste and the rubbish from packaging, uneaten food and disposable goods. The dumping of this waste is another way in which we reduce the amount of land available for any other life apart from scavengers.

There has also been an increase in manufacturing and industry to produce the goods we want. This in turn has led to **industrial waste**.

The waste we produce presents us with some very difficult problems. If it is not handled properly, it can cause serious pollution. Our water may be polluted by **sewage**, by **fertilisers** from farms and by toxic chemicals from industry. The air we breathe may be polluted with smoke and poisonous gases such as sulfur dioxide.

The land itself can be polluted with toxic chemicals from farming such as pesticides and herbicides. It can also be contaminated with industrial waste, such as heavy metals. These chemicals in turn can be washed from the land into waterways.

If our ever-growing population continues to affect the **ecology** of the Earth, everyone will pay the price.

Figure 3 In the UK alone, hundreds of thousands of new houses and miles of new road systems are continuously being built. Every time we clear land like this, the homes of countless animals and plants are destroyed.

Summary questions

1 a Suggest reasons why the human population has increased so rapidly over the last couple of hundred years.
  b How do people reduce the amount of land available for other animals and plants?

2 What substances commonly pollute:
  a water?   b air?   c land?

3 a List examples of how the standard of living has increased over the past 100 years.
  b Give **three** examples of resources that humans are using up.

4 Explain clearly how the ever-increasing human population causes pollution in a number of different ways.

Key points

- The human population is growing rapidly and the standard of living is rising.

- More waste is being produced. If it is not handled properly, it can pollute the water, the air and the land.

- Humans reduce the amount of land available for other animals and plants by building, quarrying, farming and dumping waste.

B14.2 Land and water pollution

As the human population grows, more waste is produced. If it is not handled carefully, it may pollute the land, the water or the air.

Polluting the land

People pollute the land in many different ways. The more people there are, the more bodily waste and waste water from our homes (sewage) is produced. If the human waste is not treated properly, the soil becomes polluted with unpleasant chemicals and gut parasites. In the developed world, people produce huge amounts of household waste and hazardous (dangerous) industrial waste. The household waste goes into landfill sites, which take up a lot of room and destroy natural habitats. Toxic chemicals can also spread from the waste into the soil.

Toxic chemicals are also a problem in industrial waste. They can poison the soil for miles around. For example, after the Chernobyl nuclear accident in 1986, the soil was contaminated thousands of miles away from the original accident. Almost 30 years on, sheep from some farms in North Wales still cannot be sold for food because the radioactivity levels are too high.

Land can also be polluted as a side effect of farming. Weeds compete with crop plants for light, water and mineral ions. Animal and fungal pests attack crops and eat them. Farmers increasingly use chemicals to protect their crops. Weedkillers (or herbicides) kill weeds but leave the crop unharmed. Pesticides kill the insects that might otherwise attack and destroy the crop.

The problem is that these chemicals are poisons. When they are sprayed onto crops, they also get into the soil. From there, they can be washed out into streams and rivers (see next page). They can also become part of food chains when the toxins get into organisms that feed on the plants or live in the soil. The level of toxin in the animals that first take in the affected plant material is small, but sometimes it cannot be broken down in the body. So, at each stage along the food chain, more and more toxin builds up in the organism. This is known as bioaccumulation, and eventually it can lead to dangerous levels of poisons building up in the top predators (see Figure 2).

Total Caesium 137 deposition per 10 May 1986 in kBq/m²

- More than 1480
- 40 – 1480
- 10 – 40
- 2 – 10
- Less than 2
- No data

Note: the map shows total deposition resulting from both the Chernobyl accident and nuclear weapon tests. However, at the level above 10 kBq/m², in most cases the effects of the Chernobyl accident are predominant.

Figure 1 The accident at Chernobyl nuclear power plant polluted the land a long way away – including areas of the UK

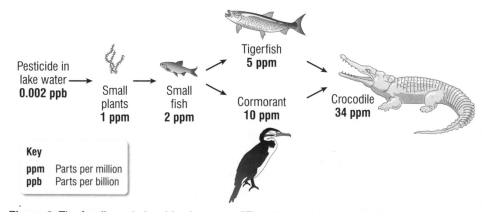

Key

ppm Parts per million
ppb Parts per billion

Figure 2 The feeding relationships between different organisms can lead to dangerous levels of toxins building up in the top predators

Polluting the water

A growing human population means a growing need for food. Farmers add fertilisers to the soil to make sure it stays **fertile** year after year. The minerals in these fertilisers, particularly the nitrates, are easily washed from the soil into local streams, ponds and rivers. Untreated sewage that is washed into waterways or pumped out into the sea also causes high levels of nitrates in the water. The nitrates and other mineral ions stimulate the growth of algae and water plants, which grow rapidly. Some plants die naturally. Others die because there is so much competition for light that they are unable to photosynthesise. There is a big increase in microorganisms feeding on the dead plants. These microorganisms use up a lot of oxygen during respiration.

This increase in decomposers leads to a fall in oxygen levels dissolved in the water. This means there isn't enough oxygen to support some of the fish and other aerobic organisms living in it. They die – and are decomposed by yet more microorganisms. This uses up even more oxygen.

Eventually, the oxygen levels in the water fall so low that all aerobic aquatic animals die, and the pond or stream becomes 'dead'. This is what we call **eutrophication**.

Toxic chemicals such as pesticides and herbicides or poisonous chemicals from landfill sites can also be washed into waterways. These chemicals can have the same bioaccumulation effect on aquatic food webs as they do on life on land. The largest carnivorous fish die or fail to breed because of the build-up of toxic chemicals in their bodies.

In many countries, including the UK, there are now strict controls on the use of chemicals on farms. The same restrictions apply to the treatment of sewage and to landfill sites, to help avoid these problems arising.

Pollution levels in water can be measured in many different ways. Oxygen and pH levels are measured using instruments. The water can be analysed to show the levels of polluting chemicals such as pesticides or industrial waste. Bioindicators – species such as salmon and bloodworms that can only be found in very clean or very polluted water – are also used to monitor pollution levels in our waterways.

links

To remind yourself of the use of bioindicators, look back to 13.4 'Measuring environmental change'.

Examiner's tip

Learn to describe the sequence of events for eutrophication.

Figure 3 This stream may look green and healthy, but all the animal life it once supported is dead as a result of eutrophication

Key points

- Human activities pollute the land and water in several ways.
- Toxic chemicals such as pesticides and herbicides can pollute the land.
- If sewage is not properly handled and treated, it can pollute the water.
- Fertilisers and toxic chemicals can be washed from the land into the water and pollute it.
- Sewage and fertilisers can cause eutrophication in waterways.

Summary questions

1 a What is sewage?
   b Which mineral ions does sewage contain in high levels?
   c Why is it so important to dispose of sewage carefully?

2 Explain how industrial waste can have a negative effect on the environment.

3 a Farming can cause pollution of both the land and the water. Explain how this pollution comes about, and how they are linked.
   b In the UK, a chemical called DDT was used to kill insects. Some large birds of prey and herons began to die and their bodies were found to have very high levels of the pesticide DDT in them. Explain how this would have happened.

B14.3

B14.3 Air pollution

Learning objectives

After this topic, you should know:

- how acid rain is formed
- how acid rain affects living organisms
- how air pollution causes global dimming and smog.

When the air you breathe is polluted, no one escapes the effects. A major source of air pollution is burning fossil fuels. As the human population grows and living standards increase, we are using more oil, coal and natural gas. We also burn huge amounts of petrol, diesel and aviation fuel derived from crude oil. Fossil fuels are a non-renewable resource – so eventually they will all be used up.

The formation of acid rain

When fossil fuels are burned, carbon dioxide is released into the atmosphere as a waste product. In addition, fossil fuels often contain sulfur impurities. These react with oxygen when they burn to form **sulfur dioxide** gas. At high temperatures, for example in car engines, nitrogen oxides are also released into the atmosphere.

Sulfur dioxide and nitrogen oxides can cause serious breathing problems for people if the concentrations get too high.

The sulfur dioxide and nitrogen oxides also dissolve in rainwater and react with oxygen in the air to form dilute sulfuric acid and nitric acid. This produces **acid rain**, which has been measured with a pH of 2.0 – more acidic than vinegar!

The effects of acid rain

Acid rain directly damages the environment. If it falls onto trees, it may kill the leaves, buds, flowers and fruit, and as it soaks into the soil, it can destroy the roots as well. Whole ecosystems can be destroyed.

Acid rain also has an indirect effect on our environment. As acid rain falls into lakes, rivers and streams, the water in them becomes slightly acidic. If the concentration of acid gets too high, plants and animals can no longer survive. Many lakes and streams have become 'dead' – no longer able to support life – as a result of this.

Figure 1 In some parts of Europe and America, huge areas of woodland are dying as a result of acid rain

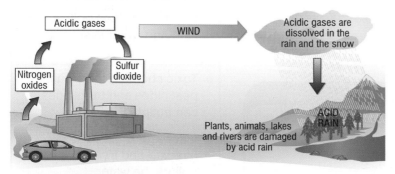

Figure 2 Air pollution in one place can cause acid rain – and serious pollution problems – somewhere else entirely, even in another country

Acid rain is difficult to control. It is formed by pollution from factories. It also comes from the cars and other vehicles we use every day. The worst effects of acid rain are often not felt by the country that produced the pollution (see Figure 2). The sulfur dioxide and nitrogen oxides are carried high in the air by the winds. As a result, it is often relatively 'clean' countries that get the acid rain from their dirtier neighbours. Their own clean air goes on to benefit someone else.

The UK and other countries have worked hard to stop their vehicles, factories and power stations producing the polluting gases. They have introduced measures to reduce the levels of sulfur dioxide and nitrogen oxides in the air. Low-sulfur petrol and diesel are now used in vehicles. More and more cars are fitted with catalytic converters. Once hot, these remove the acidic nitrogen oxides before they are released into the air. There are strict rules about the levels of sulfur dioxide and nitrogen oxides in the exhaust fumes of new cars.

In the UK, we have also introduced cleaner, low-sulfur fuels such as gas, rather than coal, in power stations and started generating more electricity from nuclear power. We have also put systems in power station chimneys to clean the flue gases before they are released into the atmosphere. These desulfurisation processes also produce sulfuric acid as a useful by-product, which can be used in a number of industrial processes. There is also an increasing interest in the use of **biofuels**, which only produce carbon dioxide and water as they burn.

As a result, the levels of sulfur dioxide in the air, and of acid rain, have fallen steadily over the past 40 years. Many European countries have done the same (see Figure 3). Unfortunately, there are still many countries around the world that do not have such controls in place.

Global dimming

One form of air pollution involves an increase in the number of tiny solid particles in the air. The sulfur products from the burning of fossil fuels are part of this problem. So is smoke from any type of burning. These particles reflect sunlight so less light hits the surface of the Earth. This causes a dimming effect. Global dimming could lead to a cooling of the temperatures at the surface of the Earth.

In Europe, where sulfur emissions and smoke are being controlled, dimming is being reversed. In many developing countries, dimming continues to get worse as air pollution grows.

Smog

Both smoke and chemicals such as sulfur dioxide and nitrogen oxides also add to another form of air pollution – **smog**. Smog forms a haze of small particles and acidic gases which can be seen in the air over major cities around the world. When China hosted the Olympics in 2008, in order to lower pollution so that the air was clean enough for the athletes to compete, the government introduced measures to halve the number of cars on the city roads and close down factories.

Did you know ... ?

In some countries such as Finland the acid rain falls as 'acid snow'. This can be even more damaging as all the acid is released in the first melt water of spring. This causes an 'acid flush' that magnifies the effect of the acid rain, producing water with a very low pH.

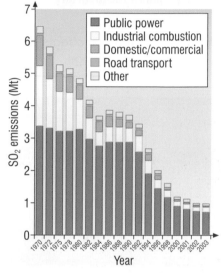

Figure 3 Bar chart to show the sources of sulfur dioxide emissions in the UK and the way in which they have been reduced over time

---

Summary questions

1 Produce a flowchart to show the production of acid rain and explain why some countries that have strict controls on sulfur emissions still suffer acid rain damage to their buildings and ecosystems.

2 a Explain how pollution from cars and factories burning fossil fuels pollutes:
   i the air
   ii the water
   iii the land.
   b In order to get rid of acid rain, it is important that all countries in an area control their production of sulfur dioxide and nitrogen oxides. Explain why this is.

3 a What is global dimming?
   b Look at Figure 3. What was the percentage reduction in sulfur dioxide emissions in the UK between 1980 and 2002?
   c What is the main source of sulfur emissions in the UK?
   d Global dimming has been reversed in the UK and Europe between 1980 and the present day. Suggest an explanation for this.

Key points

- When people burn fossil fuels, carbon dioxide is released into the atmosphere.

- Sulfur dioxide and nitrogen oxides can be released when fossil fuels are burned. These gases dissolve in rainwater and make it more acidic.

- Acid rain may damage trees directly. It can make lakes and rivers too acidic for plants and animals to live in them.

- Air pollution can cause global dimming and smog as tiny solid particles in the air reflect away the sunlight.

B14.4 Deforestation and peat destruction

Learning objectives

Learning objectives

After this topic, you should know:

- what is meant by deforestation
- why loss of biodiversity matters
- the environmental effects of destroying peat bogs.

Figure 1 Tropical rainforests are being destroyed by slash-and-burn clearance to provide cheap food for countries like ours

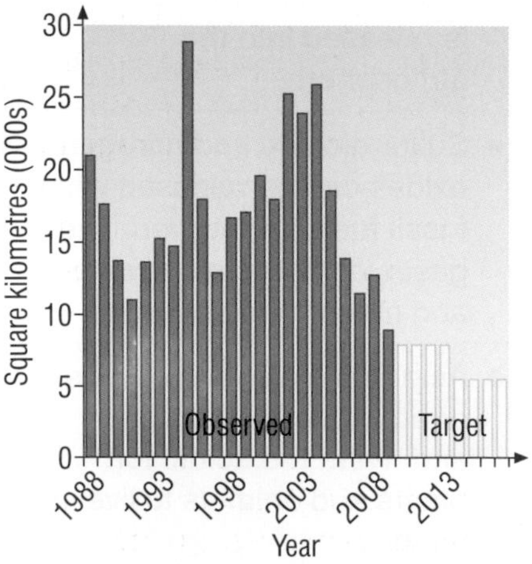

As the world population grows we need more land, more food and more fuel. One solution to this has been to cut down huge areas of forests. The loss of our forests may have many long-term effects on the environment and ecology of the Earth.

The effects of deforestation

All around the world, large-scale **deforestation** is taking place for timber and to clear the land for farming. When the land is to be used for farming, the trees are often felled and burned in what is known as 'slash-and-burn' clearance. The wood isn't used, it is just burned. The land produced is only fertile for a short time, after which more forest is destroyed. No trees are planted to replace those cut down.

There are three main reasons for the deforestation:

1. the land is used to grow staple foods such as rice, or ingredients for making cheap food in the developed world such as palm oil from oil palms
2. the land may be used to rear more cattle for the beefburger market
3. the land may be used to grow crops that can be used to make biofuels, such as sugarcane and maize for biofuels based on ethanol.

Large-scale deforestation in tropical areas has a number of negative effects.

- It increases the amount of carbon dioxide released into the atmosphere. Burning the trees leads to an increase in carbon dioxide levels from combustion.
- It increases the amount of carbon dioxide released into the atmosphere through the action of microorganisms. The dead vegetation left behind decays – it is attacked by decomposing microorganisms, which use up oxygen and release more carbon dioxide.
- It reduces the rate at which carbon dioxide is removed from the atmosphere. Normally, trees and other plants use carbon dioxide in photosynthesis. They take it from the air and it gets locked up for years (sometimes for hundreds of years) in plant material such as wood. This means that when we destroy trees, we lose a vital carbon dioxide 'sink'. Dead trees don't take carbon dioxide out of the atmosphere. In fact, they add to the carbon dioxide levels as they are burned or decay.

Loss of biodiversity

Tropical rainforests contain more diversity of living organisms than any other land environment. When we lose these forests, we also lose **biodiversity** as many species of animals and plants become extinct. Many of these species have not yet been identified or studied. We could be destroying sources of new medicines or food for the future.

For an animal such as the orang-utan, which eats around 300 different plant species, losing the forest habitat is driving the species to extinction. This is just one of hundreds if not thousands of species of living organisms of all different types that are endangered by the loss of their rainforest habitat.

Figure 2 The rate of deforestation is devastating. Even in the high profile Brazilian Amazon, where deforestation rates are dropping, around 8–10 000 km² of tropical rainforest is being lost each year

Square kilometres (000s)

Observed   Target

1988 1993 1998 2003 2008 2013

Year

Deforestation is taking place at a tremendous rate. In Brazil alone, an area about a quarter the size of England is lost each year. When the forests are cleared, they are often replaced by a monoculture (single species) such as oil palms. This process also greatly reduces biodiversity.

Cows, rice and methane

It isn't just carbon dioxide levels that are increasing in the atmosphere as a result of deforestation. Much of the deforested land is used to produce food for the ever-increasing world population. One of these foods is rice. As rice grows in swampy conditions, known as paddy fields, **methane** gas is released.

Figure 3 The loss of biodiversity, from large mammals such as the orang-utan to the smallest mosses or fungi, will potentially have far-reaching effects in the local ecosystems and for human beings

 Did you know … ?

Methane is another greenhouse gas that affects global warming. It has a more powerful greenhouse effect per molecule than carbon dioxide.

Another food – and another source of methane gas – is from cattle. Cows produce methane during their digestive processes and release it at regular intervals. In recent years, the number of cattle raised to produce cheap meat for fast food, such as burgers, has grown enormously. So the levels of methane are rising. Many of these cattle are raised on farms created by deforestation.

Peat bog destruction

Peat bogs are another resource that is being widely destroyed. Peat bogs form over thousands of years, usually in marshy areas. They are made of plant material that cannot decay completely because the conditions are very acidic and lack oxygen. Peat acts as a massive carbon store.

Peat can be burned as a fuel and is also widely used by gardeners because it helps to improve the properties of the soil. When peat is burned or used in gardens, carbon dioxide is released into the atmosphere and the carbon store is lost. Peat is formed very slowly so it is being destroyed faster than it is made.

Summary questions

1 a What is biodiversity?
  b What is deforestation?
  c How does deforestation affect biodiversity – and why does it matter?

2 Give **three** reasons why deforestation increases the amount of carbon dioxide in the atmosphere.

3 a Why are the numbers of:
    i   rice fields and cattle in the world increasing?
    ii peat bogs in the world decreasing?
  b Explain why this is cause for concern.

?? Did you know … ?

In the UK, the government is trying to persuade gardeners to use alternative 'peat-free' composts to reduce carbon dioxide emissions. Compost can be made from bark, from garden waste, from coconut husks and other sources – the problem is persuading gardeners to use them.

Examiner's tip

Remember that trees, plants in peat bogs and algae in the sea all use carbon dioxide for photosynthesis. Carbon compounds are then 'locked up' in these plants.

Key points

● Deforestation is the destruction or removal of areas of forest or woodland. Deforestation leads to loss of biodiversity.

● Large-scale deforestation has led to an increase in the amount of carbon dioxide released into the atmosphere (from burning and the actions of microorganisms). It has also reduced the rate at which carbon dioxide is removed from the air by plants.

● More rice fields and cattle have led to increased levels of methane in the atmosphere.

● The destruction of peat bogs releases carbon dioxide into the atmosphere.

B14.5 Global warming

Learning objectives

After this topic, you should know:

- what is meant by global warming

- how global warming could affect life on Earth.

Many scientists are very worried that the climate of the Earth is getting warmer. This is commonly called **global warming**.

Changing conditions

For millions of years, there has been a natural balance in the levels of carbon dioxide in the atmosphere. The carbon dioxide released by living things into the atmosphere from respiration has been matched by the amount removed. Around the world, carbon dioxide is removed from the atmosphere by plants all the time for photosynthesis. What is more, huge amounts of carbon dioxide are dissolved in the oceans and lakes. We say that the carbon dioxide is **sequestered** in plants and water, or that plants and water act as carbon dioxide sinks.

As a result, carbon dioxide levels in the air have stayed about the same for a long period. However, as a result of human activities, the levels of carbon dioxide are currently increasing. Unfortunately, the numbers of plants available to absorb the carbon dioxide are decreasing. The speed of these changes means that the natural sinks cannot cope. So the levels of carbon dioxide in the atmosphere are building up. At the same time, the levels of methane gas are increasing too.

links

For information on how plants use carbon dioxide to make food, look back to 9.1 'Photosynthesis'.

The greenhouse effect

Energy from the Sun reaches the Earth, warming it up, and much of it is radiated back out into space. However, gases such as carbon dioxide and methane absorb some of the energy released as the Earth cools down so it can't escape. As a result, the Earth and its surrounding atmosphere are kept warm and ideal for life. Because carbon dioxide and methane act like a greenhouse around the Earth, they are known as **greenhouse gases**. The way they keep the surface of the Earth warm is known as the **greenhouse effect**, and it is vital for life on Earth.

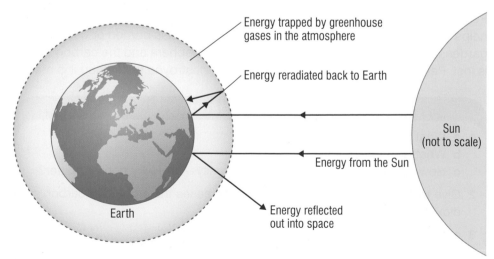

Figure 1 The greenhouse effect – vital for life on Earth

Examiner's tip

Remember which gas is which! Carbon dioxide increase causes global warming. Sulfur dioxide and nitrogen oxides cause acid rain.

Global warming

The greenhouse effect is necessary to keep the Earth's surface at a suitable temperature for life. However, as the levels of carbon dioxide and methane go up, the greenhouse effect is increasing. There are more greenhouse gases in the atmosphere to trap the energy of the Sun and the average temperature at the Earth's surface is going up. The change is very small – only about 0.55 °C from the 1970s to the present day. This is not much – but an increase of only a few degrees Celsius may cause the following changes:

- **Climate change:** As the Earth's climate changes due to global warming, many scientists think that we will see an increase in severe and unpredictable weather conditions. Some people think the very high winds and extensive flooding seen around the world in the 21st century are early examples of the effects of global warming.

- **Rising sea levels:** If the Earth warms up, the ice caps at the North and South Poles and many glaciers will melt. This will cause sea levels to rise. There is evidence that this is already happening. It will mean more flooding for low-lying shores and eventually parts of countries, or even whole countries, may disappear beneath the seas.

- **Changes in migration patterns:** As climates become colder or hotter, and the seasons change, the migration patterns of birds, insects and mammals may change.

- **Changes in distribution:** Some animals may extend their range as climate change makes conditions more favourable. Others may find their range shrinks. Some will disappear completely from an area or a country.

- **Reduced biodiversity:** As the climate changes, many organisms will be unable to survive and will become extinct, for example the potential loss of polar bears as Arctic ice melts.

??? Did you know … ?

The change in the distribution pattern of organisms as a result of global warming can affect the spread of tropical diseases. For example, as the range of the *Anopheles* mosquito increases, so does the area of the world affected by malaria.

What's more, gases get less soluble in water as the temperature increases. Therefore, as sea temperatures rise, less carbon dioxide can be sequestered in the water, which makes the situation worse. Global warming is a big problem for us all.

Summary questions

1 a Use the data in Figure 1 on page 198 to produce a bar chart showing the maximum recorded level of carbon dioxide in the atmosphere every tenth year from 1970 to the year 2010.
  b Explain the trend you can see on your chart.
  c Describe and explain the greenhouse effect. How does it affect the conditions on Earth?

2 What is meant by global warming? Explain how it is related to the greenhouse effect and why it is perceived as a problem.

3 Research **one** possible result of global warming and write a report, giving examples of organisms that have been or might be affected.

⬭ links

To find out more about changes in distribution of organisms, look at 13.4 'Measuring environmental change'.

Figure 2 Puffin populations in northern Scotland are failing to rear their chicks because a rise in sea temperatures reduces the numbers of small fish that puffins feed on. They may need to move to new breeding sites if they are to survive.

Key points

- Increasing levels of carbon dioxide and methane in the atmosphere give rise to an increased greenhouse effect, leading to global warming – an increase in the temperature of the surface of the Earth.

- Global warming may cause a number of changes including climate change, a rise in sea level, changes in migration patterns and distribution of species, and loss of biodiversity.

- Global warming will mean that less carbon dioxide is sequestered in oceans and lakes.

B14.6

Analysing the evidence

There is a lot of debate about environmental issues such as global warming and changing distributions of species. The great majority of scientists now think the evidence shows that global warming is at least partly linked to human activities such as the burning of fossil fuels and deforestation, but not everyone agrees. It is very important to analyse and interpret data concerning environmental issues very carefully, and be thorough in your evaluation of the methods used to collect the data. Remember, any data used should be repeatable, reproducible and valid.

Looking at evidence

There is hard scientific evidence for the build-up of greenhouse gases such as carbon dioxide in the atmosphere. For example, the monthly readings from the mountain top Mauna Loa observatory in Hawaii provide us with a clear pattern of the changes in carbon dioxide levels over recent years. Scientists do not argue with this data. It is recorded in a simple, repeatable, reproducible and valid way.

However, there are many other questions to which we do not have such clear-cut answers. These include:

- Has a similar rise in carbon dioxide and methane levels ever been seen before?
- Can the observed rise in greenhouse gases be clearly linked to human activities?
- Has the observed rise in greenhouse gases had any effect on temperature, climate or weather?

It is much more difficult to get valid data to answer these questions.

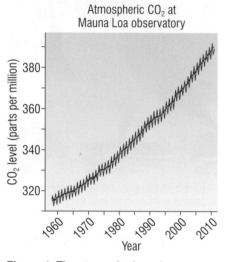

Atmospheric CO$_2$ at Mauna Loa observatory

Figure 1 The atmospheric carbon dioxide readings for this graph are taken monthly on a mountain top in Hawaii. There is a clear upward trend, which shows no sign of slowing down.

Some extreme weather patterns have certainly been recorded in recent years. Yet throughout history there is evidence of other, equally violent, weather patterns. These occurred long before fossil fuels were used so heavily and deforestation.

Also, weather is not the same as climate. Weather can change from day to day, but climate is the weather in an area over a long period of time. It is evidence of climate change rather than freak weather that scientists are looking for – but the freak weather may be evidence of climate change!

How can we be sure?

How valid, reproducible and repeatable are the data on which ideas about environmental change are based? Scientists measure the daily temperatures in many different places. They also look at how the temperature of the Earth has changed over time, and how levels of carbon dioxide in the atmosphere have changed over centuries. They collect many different types of evidence. For example, they use cores of ice that are thousands of years old (see Figure 2), the rings in the trunks of trees and the type of pollen found in peat bogs.

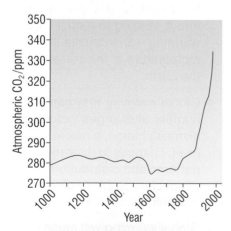

Figure 2 This graph shows how carbon dioxide levels in the atmosphere have changed over centuries, based on cores of pure, undisturbed ice from the Antarctic

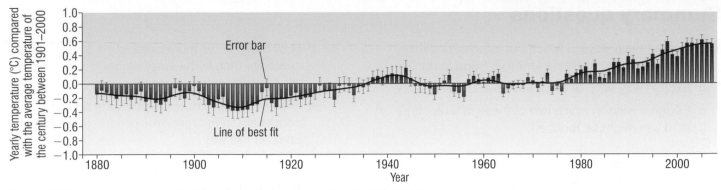

Figure 3 This graph shows how global surface temperatures have varied from the 1901–2000 mean over 130 years. These data are widely regarded as very repeatable and reproducible.

Putting evidence together

In 2002, 500 billion tonnes of ice broke away from Antarctica and melted. Scientists have looked back at data from a number of sources to show that:

- the global surface temperature has been rising steadily
- the snow and ice cover in the northern hemisphere has been reducing
- sea levels have been rising (as a result of all the melting ice).

Many of these changes can be related to changes in atmospheric carbon dioxide levels and increased human activities, but it is impossible so far to establish a complete link between the two.

Much of the evidence for climate change is published in well-respected journals, but there are some controversies. In 2009, it emerged that some scientists in the UK had hidden data that showed that global temperatures were falling slightly rather than rising. The scientists support the idea that human activities are causing global warming and did not want to publish data that might challenge this idea.

The evidence continues to be collected. At the moment, most people and governments are convinced that we need to change the way we live, use less fossil fuels and preserve our rainforests if we are to reduce the potential damage from global warming.

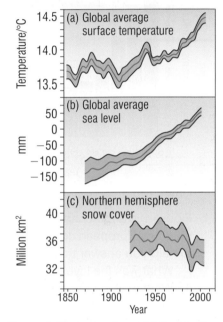

Figure 4 These graphs, published by the IPCC (Intergovernmental Panel on Climate Change), show what appears to be a clear correlation between rising temperatures, melting snow and rising sea levels

Summary questions

1 Why do you think it is so important that data looking at the links between human behaviour and environmental changes should be repeatable, reproducible and valid?

2 a Give a clear explanation of the difference between weather and climate.
   b What is the difference between an apparent correlation between factors such as carbon dioxide levels, human activities, global warming and climate change and one factor definitely causing an observed change?

3 Summarise the evidence shown on the graphs in Figures 2, 3 and 4. Explain what they appear to show and how these data might be used as evidence for a human influence on global warming.
   What other data might you need to help support that conclusion?

Examiner's tip

Look for examples in the media of how humans pollute the Earth and for ways of controlling pollution.

Key points

- There are a lot of data on environmental change.

- The validity, reproducibility and repeatability of all data must be evaluated before conclusions can be drawn.

Summary questions

1 a List the main ways in which humans reduce the amount of land available for other living things.

b Explain why each of these land uses is necessary.

c Suggest ways in which two of these different types of land use might be reduced.

2 a Draw a flowchart showing acid rain formation.

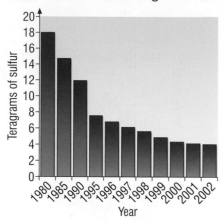

Figure 1

b Figure 1 is a bar chart showing the sulfur emissions made by European countries over time. Use this graph to help you answer the following questions:

i What was the level of sulfur emissions in 1980?

ii What was the approximate level of sulfur in the air in the year that you were born? (Make sure you give your birth year.)

iii What was the level of sulfur emissions in 2002?

c What do these data tell you about trends in the levels of sulfur emissions since 1980? Suggest explanations for the trends you have observed.

3

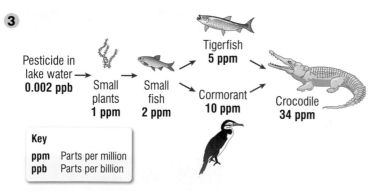

Key

ppm Parts per million
ppb Parts per billion

Figure 2

This diagram shows a food chain with increasing levels of pesticide in the bodies of the organisms involved.

a What is a food chain?

b How many times more pesticide is found in the body of a small fish than in the lake water?

c How many times more pesticide is found in the crocodile than in the small plants at the beginning of the food chain?

d Explain carefully how the pesticide becomes more concentrated in organisms progressing through a food chain in this way.

4 a Describe the environmental impacts of deforestation and peat bog destruction. Highlight the similarities and differences between the two.

b

Type of animal	Dairy cows	All other cattle	Sheep
Methane emissions (kg/year)	120	43	10

i Plot a bar chart of the data in this table, which show the amount of methane produced by different types of animal in a year.

ii Explain the advantages and disadvantages of farming different types of animals in terms of environmental effect and human benefits.

5 In Figure 1 in 14.6 'Analysing the evidence', you can see clearly annual variations in the levels of carbon dioxide recorded each year. These fluctuations are thought to be due to seasonal changes in the way plants are growing and photosynthesising through the year.

a Explain how changes in plant growth and rate of photosynthesis might affect carbon dioxide levels.

b How could you use the evidence of this data to argue against deforestation?

c How is the ever-increasing human population affecting the build-up of greenhouse gases?

d What type of evidence is used to investigate the effect of this build-up of greenhouse gases on the Earth's climate? Which types of evidence are most valid, repeatable and reproducible?

AQA Examination-style questions

1 The rapidly rising human population is increasing the amount of waste polluting the Earth.

Complete the following sentences about pollution.

a **Two** gases that pollute the air are .... which causes acid rain, and .... which contributes to global warming.

b **Two** toxic chemicals that can be washed into streams and lakes from farms are .... and ....

c If sewage or fertilisers pollute water it leads to .... , which reduces the .... concentration of the water. (6)

2 **a** List **three** ways that human activities are reducing the amount of land available for other animals and plants. (3)

b These activities are reducing biodiversity.
   i What is biodiversity? (1)
   ii Choose **one** of the human activities you named in part **a** and explain how it is reducing biodiversity. (3)

3 Tropical rainforests in Brazil are being cleared to provide land to grow vast areas of sugar cane and to graze cattle.

a Why does Brazil grow huge quantities of sugar? (2)

b Name the gas continuously produced by the digestive processes in cows. (1)

c This deforestation is contributing to global warming by increasing carbon dioxide levels in the atmosphere.
   i How is carbon dioxide naturally removed from the atmosphere? (2)
   ii Explain **two** ways that deforestation causes a rise in carbon dioxide levels in the air. (4)

d Give **three** likely effects of global warming on the Earth. (3)

4 Students investigated a stream where they thought a pipe may be discharging sewage into the water.

They chose four points – two upstream and two downstream from the pipe. They measured the percentage oxygen saturation of the water with an oxygen meter. At each point they also identified and counted the invertebrates found in a 3-minute kick sample.

The table shows the students' results.

Sample point	50 m upstream	25 m upstream	Pipe	25 m downstream	50 m downstream
% oxygen saturation	88	90		5	22
Mayfly larvae	6	5		0	0
Diving beetles	14	17		1	3
Freshwater hoglice	2	1		66	58
Bloodworms	3	2		8	9

a Suggest which two species of invertebrates are good indicators of dissolved oxygen levels in water. Explain your choices. (4)

b Evaluate the evidence that the students were correct in thinking that the pipe was discharging sewage. (3)

c *In this question you will be assessed on using good English, organising information clearly and using specialist terms where appropriate.*

   Describe how the sewage would lead to the process of eutrophication. (QWC) (6)

B15.1 Theories of evolution

We are surrounded by an amazing variety of life on planet Earth. Questions such as 'Where has it all come from?' and 'When did life on Earth begin?' have puzzled people for many generations.

Darwin's theory of **evolution** by **natural selection** tells us that all the species of living things alive today have evolved from the first simple life forms. Scientists think these early forms of life developed on Earth more than 3 billion years ago. Most of us take these ideas for granted – but they are really quite new.

Up to the 18th century, most people in Europe believed that the world had been created by God. They thought it was made, as described in the Christian Bible, a few thousand years ago. However, by the beginning of the 19th century, scientists were beginning to come up with new ideas.

Lamarck's theory of evolution

Jean-Baptiste Lamarck was a French biologist. He thought that all organisms were linked by what he called a 'fountain of life'. He made the great step forward of suggesting that individual animals adapted and evolved to suit their environment. His idea was that every type of animal evolved from primitive worms. The change from worms to other organisms was caused by the **inheritance of acquired characteristics**.

Lamarck's theory proposed that the way organisms behaved affected the features of their body – a case of 'use it or lose it'. If animals used something a lot over a lifetime, Lamarck thought this feature would grow and develop. Any useful changes that took place in an organism during its lifetime would be passed from a parent to its offspring. The neck of the giraffe is a good example (see Figure 1). If a feature wasn't used, Lamarck thought it would shrink and be lost.

Lamarck's theory influenced the way **Charles Darwin** thought. However, there were several problems with Lamarck's ideas. There was no evidence for his 'fountain of life' and people didn't like the idea of being descended from worms. People could also see quite clearly that changes in their bodies – such as big muscles, for example – were not passed on to their children.

We now know that in the great majority of cases, Lamarck's idea of inheritance cannot happen. However, his ideas paved the way for the scientists such as Darwin who followed him.

Charles Darwin and the origin of species

Our modern ideas about evolution began with the work of one of the most famous scientists of all time – Charles Darwin. Darwin set out in 1831 as the captain's companion and ship's naturalist on HMS *Beagle*. He was only 22 years old at the start of the voyage to South America and the South Sea Islands.

Darwin planned to study geology on the trip. Yet as the voyage went on, he became as excited by his collection of animals and plants as by his rock samples.

In South America, Darwin discovered a new form of the common rhea, an ostrich-like bird – although he had almost finished eating it before he noticed the differences! When he observed two different types of the same bird living in slightly different areas, this set Darwin thinking.

Figure 1 In Lamarck's model of evolution, giraffes have long necks because each generation stretched up to reach the highest leaves. So each new generation had a slightly longer neck.

On the Galapagos Islands, Darwin was amazed by the variety of species. He noticed that they varied from island to island. Darwin found strong similarities between types of finches, iguanas and tortoises on the different islands. Yet each was different and adapted to make the most of local conditions.

Darwin collected huge numbers of specimens of animals and plants during the voyage. He also made detailed drawings and kept written observations. The long journey home gave him plenty of time to think about what he had seen. Charles Darwin returned home after five years with some new ideas forming in his mind.

After returning to England, Darwin spent the next 20 years working on his ideas. Darwin's theory is that all living organisms have evolved from simpler life forms. This evolution has come about by a process of natural selection.

Reproduction always gives more offspring than the environment can support. Only those that have inherited features most suited to their environment – the 'fittest' – will survive. When they breed, they pass on the genes for those useful inherited characteristics to their offspring. This is natural selection.

When Darwin suggested how evolution took place, no one knew about genes. He simply observed that useful inherited characteristics were passed on. Today, we know it is useful genes/alleles that are passed from parents to their offspring in natural selection.

Figure 2 Darwin was impressed by the marine iguanas he found on the Galapagos Islands and he studied them very carefully, comparing them in detail to land-dwelling iguanas

Examiner's tip

Remember the key steps in natural selection:

Mutation of gene → advantage to survival → breed → pass on genes.

Figure 3 Darwin worked here in his study for around 20 years, carrying out experiments and organising his ideas on evolution by natural selection

Summary questions

1 Explain what is meant by the following terms:
   a evolution
   b natural selection.

2 How did Jean-Baptiste Lamarck affect the development of ideas about evolution?

3 Explain the importance of the following in the development of Darwin's ideas.
   a South American rheas
   b Galapagos tortoises, iguanas and finches
   c The long voyage of HMS *Beagle*
   d The 20 years from Darwin's return to the publication of his book, *The Origin of Species*.

Key points

- The theory of evolution states that all the species that are alive today – and many more which are now extinct – evolved from simple life forms that first developed more than 3 billion years ago.

- Darwin's theory is that evolution takes place through natural selection.

- The evidence for Darwin's theory came from his observations while on a scientific expedition to the Galapagos Islands in the 1830s.

- Darwin discovered that variations between species of finches, iguanas and tortoises reflected how each species had adapted and evolved to suit life on a different island.

B15.2 Accepting Darwin's ideas

Learning objectives

After this topic, you should know:

- why Darwin's theory of evolution was only gradually accepted.

Charles Darwin came back from his trip on HMS *Beagle* with new ideas about the variety of life on Earth. He read numerous books and thought about the ideas of many other people, such as Lamarck, Lovell and Malthus. He gradually built up his theory of evolution by natural selection.

Darwin knew his ideas would be controversial. He expected a lot of opposition, both from fellow scientists and from religious leaders.

Building up the evidence

Darwin realised that he would need lots of evidence to support his theories. This is one of the reasons why it took him so long to publish his ideas. He spent years trying to put his evidence together in order to convince other scientists.

He used the amazing animals and plants he had seen on his journeys as part of that evidence. They showed that organisms on different islands had adapted to their environments by natural selection. This meant they had evolved to be different from each other.

Darwin carried out breeding experiments with pigeons at his home. He wanted to show how features could be artificially selected. Darwin also studied different types of barnacles (small invertebrates found on seashore rocks) and where they lived. This gave him more evidence of organisms adapting and forming different species.

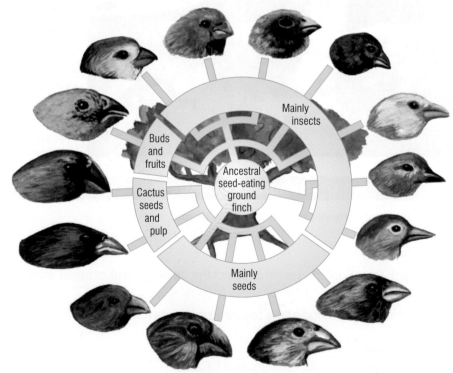

Figure 1 The finches found on the different Galapagos Islands look very different, but all evolved from the same original type of finch by natural selection

Darwin built up a network of friends, fellow scientists and pigeon breeders. He didn't travel far from home (he was often unwell), but he spent a lot of time discussing his ideas with this group of friends. They helped him get together the evidence he needed, and he trusted them as he talked about his ideas.

Eventually he was pushed to publish when he realised that someone else – Alfred Wallace – was developing similar ideas.

Why did people object?

In 1859, Darwin published his famous book *On the Origin of Species by Means of Natural Selection* (often known as *The Origin of Species*). The book caused a sensation. Many people were very excited by his ideas and defended them enthusiastically. Others were deeply offended, or simply did not accept them.

There were many different reasons why it took some scientists a long time to accept Darwin's theory of natural selection. They include:

- The theory of evolution by natural selection challenged the belief that God made all of the animals and plants that live on Earth. This religious view was the generally accepted belief among most people in early Victorian England.
- In spite of all Darwin's efforts and experiments, many scientists felt there was not enough evidence to convince them of his theory.
- There was no way to explain how variety and inheritance happened. The mechanism of how inheritance happens – by genes and genetics – was not known until 50 years *after* Darwin published his ideas. Because there was no mechanism to explain how characteristics could be inherited, Darwin's theory was much harder for people to accept and understand.

The arguments raged and it took some time before the majority of scientists accepted Darwin's ideas. However, by the time of his death in 1882, Darwin was widely regarded as one of the world's great scientists. He is buried in Westminster Abbey along with other great people such as Sir Isaac Newton.

Did you know ... ?

Darwin let his children use the back of his original manuscript of *The Origin of Species* as drawing paper. Not much of the original manuscript exists. Most of the pages that we do have, Darwin himself kept – but because of his children's drawings rather than his own writing!

Summary questions

1 Explain Darwin's theory of evolution.

2 Darwin set out in HMS *Beagle* in 1831.
   a What was his role on the ship?
   b Where did the expedition travel to?
   c How many years later did Darwin publish *The Origin of Species*?

3 What type of evidence did Darwin put together to convince other scientists his ideas were right?

4 Explain why it took some time before most people accepted Darwin's ideas.

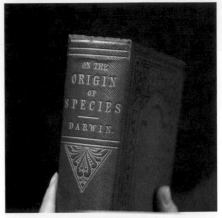
Figure 2 Darwin's famous book – it sold out on the first day of publication!

Figure 3 It wasn't just scientists who were interested in Darwin's ideas. Cartoonists loved the idea of evolution too.

Key points

- Darwin's theory of evolution by natural selection was only gradually accepted for a number of reasons. These include:
  - a conflict with the widely held belief that God made all the animals and plants on the Earth
  - insufficient evidence
  - no mechanism for explaining variety and inheritance (genetics were not understood for another 50 years).

B15.3 | Natural selection

Figure 1 The tiny number of thistles that will survive and grow into adults from this mass of floating seeds have a combination of genes that gives them an edge over all the others

⚭ links

For more information on the competition between plants and animals in the natural world, look back at 12.4 'Competition in animals' and 12.5 'Competition in plants'.

Figure 2 The natural world is often brutal. Foxes aren't the only animals to hunt rabbits! Only the best adapted predators capture prey and survive to breed – and only the best adapted prey animals escape to breed as well.

Scientists explain the variety of life today as the result of a process called natural selection. The idea was first suggested about 150 years ago by Charles Darwin.

Animals and plants are always in competition with each other. Sometimes an animal or plant gains an advantage in the competition. This might be against other species or against other members of its own species. That individual is more likely to survive and breed. This is known as natural selection.

Survival of the fittest

Charles Darwin was the first person to describe natural selection as the 'survival of the fittest'. Reproduction is a very wasteful process. Animals and plants always produce more offspring than the environment can support.

Genetic variation

The individual organisms in any species may show a wide range of variation. This is because of differences in the genes they inherit. Differences in the genes can arise as a result of mutation (see below). The offspring with the alleles that produce the characteristics best suited to the environment are more likely to survive to breed successfully. The alleles that have enabled these individuals to survive are then passed on to the next generation. Less well adapted alleles will be lost. This is natural selection at work.

Think about rabbits. The rabbits with the best all-round eyesight, the sharpest hearing and the longest legs will be the ones that are most likely to escape being eaten by a fox. They will be the ones most likely to live long enough to breed. What's more, they will pass those useful genes on to their babies. The slower, less alert rabbits will get eaten and their genes are less likely to be passed on.

The part played by mutation

New forms of genes (alleles) result from changes in existing genes. These changes are known as mutations. They are tiny changes in the long strands of DNA. Mutations occur quite naturally through mistakes made in copying DNA when the cells divide. Mutations introduce more variety into the genes of a species. In terms of survival, this is very important.

Many mutations have no effect on the characteristics of an organism, and some mutations are harmful. However, just occasionally a mutation has a good effect. It produces an adaptation that makes an organism better suited to its environment. This makes it more likely to survive and breed. The mutant allele will gradually become more common in the population and will cause the species to evolve.

??? Did you know … ?

Fruit flies can produce 200 offspring every two weeks. The yellow star thistle, an American weed, produces around 150 000 seeds per plant per year. If all those offspring survived, we'd be overrun with fruit flies and yellow star thistles!

Natural selection in action

When new forms of a gene arise from mutation, there may be a relatively rapid change in a species. This is particularly true if the environment changes. If the mutation gives the organism an advantage in the changed environment, it will soon become common.

Malpeque Bay in Canada has some very large oyster beds. In 1915, the oyster fishermen noticed a few small, flabby oysters with pus-filled blisters among their healthy catch. By 1922, the oyster beds were almost empty. The oysters had been wiped out by a destructive new disease (soon known as Malpeque disease).

Fortunately, a few of the oysters had a mutation that made them resistant to the disease. These were the only ones to survive and breed. The oyster beds filled up again, and by 1940 they were producing more oysters than ever.

A new population of oysters had evolved. As a result of natural selection, almost every oyster in Malpeque Bay now carries an allele that makes them resistant to Malpeque disease. So the disease is no longer a problem.

Figure 3 People will pay a lot of money for healthy oysters like these, so the evolution of a disease-resistant strain in Malpeque Bay allowed a new oyster business to emerge from the ruins of the old one

Timescales of evolution

Natural selection can bring about change very quickly. In bacteria, it can take a matter of days for the genetic make-up of a population to change. In the Malpeque Bay oysters, the population changed over about 20 years. However, to produce an entire new species rather than just a different population usually takes much longer. It has taken millions of years for the organisms present on Earth in the 21st century to evolve. There have been many different species that no longer exist, which lived on Earth many millions of years ago. The descendants of some of those species are the animals and plants we see around us.

⚭ **links**

For more information on genes, look back at 10.1 'Inheritance'.

⚭ **links**

You can find out about the evolution of antibiotic-resistant bacteria by natural selection in 8.5 'Changing pathogens'.

⚭ **links**

To find out more about evolutionary timescales, look ahead to 15.7 'More about extinction'.

Key points

- Natural selection works by selecting the organisms best adapted to a particular environment.

- Different organisms in a species may show a wide range of variation because of differences in their genes.

- The individuals with the characteristics most suited to their environment are most likely to survive and breed successfully.

- The genes that have produced these successful characteristics are then passed on to the next generation.

- The timescales of evolution vary depending on the complexity and life cycle of organisms; for example, simple organisms such as bacteria evolve much faster than complex multicellular organisms such as mammals.

Summary questions

1 Many features that help animals and plants survive are the result of natural selection. Give **three** examples, for example all-round eyesight in antelope, and use them to explain what is meant by natural selection.

2 **a** What is mutation?
  b Why is mutation important in natural selection?

3 Explain how the following characteristics of animals and plants have come about in terms of natural selection.
  a Male red deer have large sets of antlers.
  b Cacti have spines instead of leaves.
  c Camels can tolerate their body temperature rising far higher than most other mammals.

B15.4 Classification and evolution

Learning objectives

After this topic, you should know:
- how classification helps us to understand evolution.

Did you know ...?

The most widely accepted kingdoms of microorganisms are Monera, Protoctista and Fungi. However, there is still a lot of argument between scientists as to exactly which organisms fit into each kingdom.

Vanessa Atalanta (Red Admiral)

Pyronia Tithonus (Gatekeeper)

Inachis Io (Peacock)

Figure 1 Animals, plants and microorganisms are identified by the differences between them rather than the similarities. These three animals are all butterflies, but they each belong to a different species.

Examiner's tip

Remember, a species is a group of organisms that can successfully breed together to produce fertile offspring.

How are organisms classified?

Classification is the organisation of living things into groups according to their similarities.

There are millions of different types of living organisms. Biologists classify living things to make it easier to study them. Classification allows us to make sense of the living world. It also helps us to understand how life began and how the different groups of living things are related to each other.

Living things are classified by studying their similarities and differences. By looking at similarities and differences between organisms, we can decide which should be grouped together.

The natural classification system

The system we use for classifying living things is known as the **natural classification system**. In this system:

- The biggest groups are the **kingdoms**, and the best known are the animal kingdom and the plant kingdom. The microorganisms are then split between three different kingdoms.
  Kingdoms contain lots of organisms with many differences but a few important similarities. For example, all animals move their whole bodies about during at least part of their life cycle, and their cells do not have cellulose cell walls. On the other hand, plants do not move their whole bodies about and their cells have cellulose cell walls. Also, some plant cells contain chloroplasts full of chlorophyll for photosynthesis.

- The smallest group is a **species**. Members of the same species are very similar. Any differences are small variations of the same feature. A species is a group of organisms that can breed together and produce fertile offspring. Orang-utans, dandelions and brown trout are all examples of separate species of living organisms.

Classification and evolutionary relationships

In the past, we relied on careful observation of organisms to decide which species they belonged to. Out in the field, this is still the main way we identify an organism. However, scientists have developed different models to suggest relationships between living organisms.

Since Darwin's time, scientists have used classification to show the evolutionary links between different organisms. These models are called **evolutionary trees**. They are built up by looking at the similarities and differences between different groups of organisms.

One of the most famous evolutionary trees was produced by Darwin himself. It was found in one of the notebooks that he used to plan his book *The Origin of Species*. It starts off with the words 'I think'. Then it shows how Darwin was beginning to see relationships between different groups of living organisms (see Figure 2).

However, observation may not tell you the whole story. Some organisms look very different but are closely related. Others look very similar but come from very different groups. Now scientists are increasingly using DNA evidence to decide what species an organism belongs to. They look for differences as well as similarities in the DNA. This allows them to work out the **evolutionary relationships** between organisms.

It also means they can see how long ago different organisms had a common ancestor. The study of the evolutionary development of a species is sometimes called phylogeny, and the way the phylogeny of different species is linked makes up the study of evolutionary relationships.

Evolutionary and ecological relationships

Classifying organisms helps us to understand how they evolved. It can also help us to understand how species have evolved together in an environment. We call this their ecological relationships, and it is another way of modelling relationships between organisms.

For example, pandas have a thumb which they use to grip bamboo. However, it is not like a human thumb – It has evolved from specialised wrist bones. The only other animals to have a similar 'wrist thumb' are red pandas. Both red pandas and giant pandas eat bamboo. Based on their modern ecological feeding relationships, it looks as though they are closely related in evolution. However, based on their anatomy and DNA, giant pandas are closely related to other species of bears, and red pandas are much more closely related to raccoons.

Recently, scientists found a fossil ancestor of red pandas that also had a 'wrist thumb'. There is also evidence from the ecological relationships of this fossil animal. This suggests the thumb evolved as an adaptation for a quick escape into trees carrying prey stolen from sabre-toothed tigers. This is rather different from the giant panda evolving to feed on bamboo.

Now the ecological models and the evolutionary models match – the two species had a common ancestor a very long time ago, but the special 'wrist thumb' evolved separately as adaptations to solve two different ecological problems.

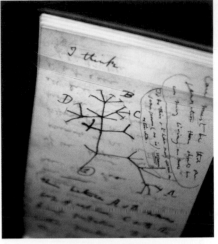

Figure 2 This evolutionary tree was found in one of the notebooks that Darwin used to plan his book *The Origin of Species*

Figure 4 Both the giant panda and the red panda use the 'wrist thumb' to eat bamboo, but they evolved this feature for different reasons

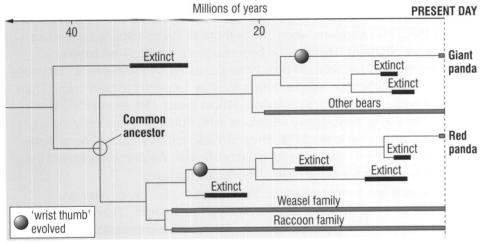

Figure 3 Evolutionary trees such as this show us the best model of the evolutionary relationships between organisms

Summary questions

1 **a** What is classification?
  b What are the main kingdoms of the living world?
  c What is a species? Give **five** examples of species of living organisms, including at least one plant species.

2 **a** What observations can be made to compare living organisms and how has modern technology affected the way we classify organisms?
  b How does classification help us to build up models of evolutionary relationships?

3 How are evolutionary trees useful to us?

Key points

- Studying the similarities and differences between organisms allows us to classify them into animals, plants and microorganisms.

- Classification also helps us to understand evolutionary and ecological relationships.

- Models such as evolutionary trees allow us to suggest relationships between organisms.

B15.5 The origins of life on Earth

There is no record of the origins of life on Earth. It is a puzzle that can never be completely solved. There is not much valid evidence for what happened – no one was there to see it! We don't even know exactly when life on Earth began. However, most scientists think it was somewhere between 3 to 4 billion years ago.

There are some interesting ideas and well-respected theories that explain most of what you can see around you. The best known of these is Darwin's theory of evolution by natural selection. The biggest problem that we have is finding the evidence to support the ideas.

What can we learn from fossils?

Some of the best evidence we have about the history of life on Earth comes from **fossils**. Fossils are the remains of organisms from many hundreds of thousands or millions of years ago that are found preserved in rocks, ice and other places. For example, fossils have revealed the world of the dinosaurs. These giant reptiles dominated the Earth at one stage and died out many millions of years before the evolution of the first human beings.

You have probably seen a fossil in a museum or on TV, or maybe even found one yourself. Fossils can be formed in a number of ways:

- They may be formed from the hard parts of an animal. These are the bits that do not decay easily, such as the bones, teeth, claws or shells.

- Another type of fossil is formed when an animal or plant does not decay after it has died. This happens when one or more of the conditions needed for decay are not there. This may be because there is little or no oxygen present. It could be because poisonous gases kill off the bacteria that cause decay. Sometimes the temperature is too low for decay to take place. Then the animals and plants are preserved almost intact – for example, in ice (see Figure 3) or peat. These fossils are rare, but they give a clear insight into what an animal looked like. They can also tell us what an animal had been eating or the colour of a long-extinct flower. We can even extract the DNA and compare it to the DNA of modern organisms.

- Many fossils are formed when harder parts of the animal or plant are replaced by other minerals and become part of the rock. This takes place over long periods. Mould fossils are formed when a impression of an organism is made in mud and then becomes fossilised, while cast fossils are made when a mould is filled in. Rock fossils are the most common form of fossils (see Figure 1).

- Some of the fossils we find are not of actual animals or plants, but of traces they have left behind. Fossil footprints, burrows, rootlet traces and droppings are all formed. These help us to build up a picture of life on Earth long ago.

An incomplete record

The fossil record is not complete for several reasons.

- Many of the very earliest forms of life were soft-bodied organisms. This means they have left little fossil trace. It is partly why there is so little valid evidence of how life began. There is no fossil record of the earliest life forms on Earth. This is why scientists cannot be absolutely certain about how life on Earth began.

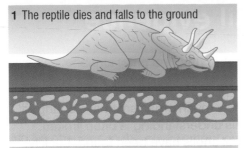

1 The reptile dies and falls to the ground

2 The flesh rots, leaving the skeleton to be covered in sand or soil and clay before it is damaged

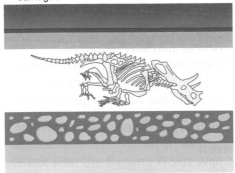

3 Protected, over millions of years, the skeleton becomes mineralised and turns to rock. The rocks shift in the earth with the fossil trapped inside.

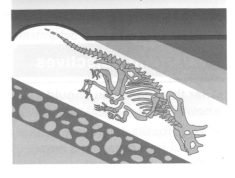

4 Eventually, the fossil emerges as the rocks move and erosion takes place

Figure 1 It takes a very long time for fossils to form, but they provide us with invaluable evidence of how life on Earth has developed

- Most organisms that died did not become fossilised – the right conditions for fossil formation were rare. Also, many of the fossils that were formed in the rocks have been destroyed by geological activity. Huge amounts of rock have been broken down, eroded (worn away), buried or melted over the years. As this happens, the fossil record is lost too.
- Finally, there are many fossils that are still to be found.

In spite of all these limitations, the fossils we have found can still give us a 'snapshot' of life millions of years ago.

Figure 2 Trilobites lived from between 525 and 250 million years ago, but some of the fossils are so good they still look almost alive

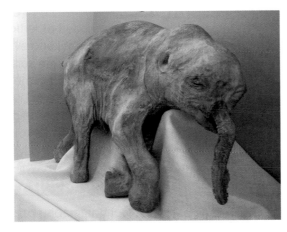

Figure 3 This baby mammoth was preserved in ice for at least 10 000 years. Examining this kind of evidence helps scientists to check the accuracy of ideas based on fossil skeletons alone.

Summary questions

1 There are several theories about how life on Earth began.
   a Why is it impossible to know for sure?
   b Why are fossils such important evidence for the way life has developed?

2 **a** Summarise the main ways in which fossils are formed.
   b What is the most common type of fossil?
   c How long ago were many of these fossils formed?

3 What is an ice fossil, what sort of age are most ice fossils, and how do ice fossils help scientists to check the evidence provided by the main fossil record?

Key points

- Fossils are the remains of organisms from millions of years ago that are found in rocks.

- Fossils may be formed in different ways.

- Fossils give us information about organisms that lived millions of years ago.

- It is very difficult for scientists to know exactly how life on Earth began because there is little evidence that is valid.

B16.1

Pyramids of biomass

Figure 1 Plants such as this sugarcane can produce a huge mass of biological material in just one growing season

Figure 2 The difference in the water content between fresh plants and dried plants makes a huge difference to the amount of biological material you appear to have

Radiation from the Sun (**solar** or **light energy**) is the source of energy for most communities of living organisms on Earth.

Light (solar) energy pours out continually on to the surface of the Earth. Green plants and algae absorb a small amount of this light energy using chlorophyll for photosynthesis. During photosynthesis, some of the light energy is transferred to chemical energy in the bonds of the glucose molecules that are made. This energy is then stored in the substances that make up the cells of the plants and algae. This new material adds to the **biomass**.

Measuring biomass

Biomass is the mass of material in living organisms. Ultimately, almost all of the biomass on Earth is built up using energy from the Sun.

Biomass is often measured as the dry mass of biological material in grams. The main problem with measuring dry biomass is that you have to kill the living organisms to dry them out.

Wet biomass in grams can be used instead. This does not involve killing the organisms but its value is less useful because the amount of water in living organisms can vary throughout the day and depending on conditions, so any results are less repeatable and reproducible.

The biomass made by plants is passed on through food chains or food webs. It goes into the animals that eat the plants. It then passes into the animals that eat other animals. No matter how long the food chain or complex the food web, the original source of all the biomass involved is the Sun.

In a food chain, there are usually more producers (plants) than primary consumers (herbivores). There are also usually more primary consumers than secondary consumers (carnivores). However, the number of organisms often does not accurately reflect what is happening to the biomass – the size of the organisms matters as well as the actual numbers. So, measuring the biomass produced is a useful way of looking at the feeding relationships between the different organisms.

Pyramids of biomass

The amount of biomass at each stage of a food chain is less than it was at the previous stage. We can draw the total amount of biomass in the living organisms at each stage of the food chain. When this biomass is drawn to scale, we can show it as a **pyramid of biomass**.

Interpreting pyramids of biomass

The amount of material and energy contained in the biomass of organisms at each stage of a food chain is less than it was at the previous stage. This is because:

- Not all organisms or parts of organisms at one stage are eaten by the stage above. For example, parts such as plant roots or animal bones may be left behind.
- Some of the materials and energy taken in are passed out and lost in the waste materials of the organism.
- Cellular respiration supplies all the energy needs for living processes in an organism, including movement. Much of the energy is eventually transferred to the surroundings as heat. For example, when a herbivore eats a plant, lots of the plant biomass is used in respiration by the animal cells to release energy. Only a relatively small proportion of the plant material is used to build new herbivore biomass by making new cells, building muscle tissue, etc. This means that very little of the plant biomass eaten by the herbivore in its lifetime is available to be passed on to any carnivore that eats it.

So, at each stage of a food chain, the amount of energy in the biomass that is passed on gets less. A large amount of plant biomass supports a smaller amount of herbivore biomass. This in turn supports an even smaller amount of carnivore biomass.

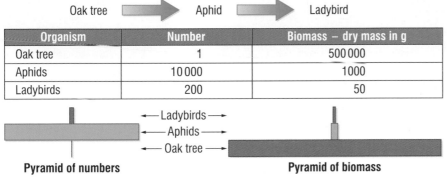

Organism	Number	Biomass – dry mass in g
Oak tree	1	500 000
Aphids	10 000	1000
Ladybirds	200	50

Figure 4 A pyramid of biomass is drawn to scale to represent the biomass of the organisms at each level of a food chain

Summary questions

1. **a** What is biomass?
   b Why is a pyramid of biomass always drawn to scale?

2.

Organism	Biomass, dry mass (g)
grass	100 000
sheep	5000
sheep ticks	30

   a Draw a pyramid of biomass for this grassland food chain.
   b Explain why the sheep ticks have so much less biomass than the grass cropped by the sheep.

3. Using the data in Figure 4, calculate the percentage biomass passed on from:
   a the producers to the primary consumers
   b the primary consumers to the secondary consumers.

Biomass of tertiary consumer (carnivore)

Biomass of secondary consumer (carnivore)

Biomass of primary consumer (herbivore)

Biomass of plants (producers)

Figure 3 Any food chain can be turned into a pyramid of biomass such as this. The blocks should always be drawn to scale.

Examiner's tip

Remember a pyramid of biomass gets smaller as you go up and that the plants go on the bottom step.

Key points

- Radiation from the Sun is the main source of energy for all living things. The Sun's light energy is captured by green plants and algae during photosynthesis, and transferred to chemical energy, which is stored in the substances that make up the cells. This is new biomass.

- Biomass is the mass of living material in an animal or plant. We can measure dry biomass or wet biomass.

- At each stage of a food chain, biomass is less than at the previous stage because some is lost in the waste materials of the organism and some is used for living processes such as movement.

- The biomass at each stage can be drawn to scale and shown as a pyramid of biomass.

Energy transfers

The amounts of biomass and energy contained in living things get less as you progress up a food chain. Only a small amount of the biomass taken in gets turned into new animal material. What happens to the rest?

Figure 1 The amount of biomass in a lion is a lot less than the amount of biomass in the grass that feeds the zebra it preys on. But where does all the biomass go?

Energy loss in waste

The biomass that an animal eats is a source of energy, but not all of the energy can be used.

Firstly, herbivores cannot digest all of the plant material they eat. The material they can't digest is passed out of the body in faeces.

The meat that carnivores eat is easier to digest than plants. This means that carnivores need to eat less often and produce less waste. However, as with herbivores, most carnivores cannot digest all of their prey, such as hooves, claws, bones and teeth. Therefore, some of the biomass that they eat is lost in their faeces.

When an animal eats more protein than it needs, the excess is broken down. It gets passed out as urea in the urine. This is another way in which biomass – and energy – are transferred from the body to the surroundings.

Energy loss due to movement

Part of the biomass eaten by an animal is used for respiration in its cells. This supplies all the energy needs for the living processes taking place within the body, including movement.

Movement uses a great deal of energy. The muscles use energy to contract and also get hot. So the more an animal moves about, the more energy (and biomass) it uses from its food.

Figure 2 Animals such as horses produce very large quantities of dung, which is made up of all the biomass they can't digest

Figure 3 Sea anemones are animals that don't move much, so they don't need much to eat

Keeping a constant body temperature

Much of the energy animals release from their food in cellular respiration is eventually transferred to their surroundings as heat. Some of this heat is produced by the muscles as the animals move.

Energy transfers to the surroundings are particularly large in mammals and birds. That is because they use energy all the time to keep their bodies at a constant temperature, i.e. to keep warm when it's cold or to cool down when it's hot. So mammals and birds need to eat far more food than animals such as fish and amphibians to achieve the same increase in biomass.

Practical

Investigating the energy released by respiration

Even plants transfer energy by heating their surroundings in cellular respiration. You can investigate this using germinating peas in a vacuum flask.

- What would be the best way to monitor the temperature continuously?
- Plan the investigation.

Figure 4 Only between 2% and 10% of the biomass eaten by an animal such as this horse will get turned into new horse. The rest of the stored energy will be used for movement or transferred, heating the surroundings, or lost in waste materials.

Examiner's tip

Make sure you can explain the different ways in which both mass and energy are lost between the stages of a food chain.

Key points

- The amounts of biomass and energy get less at each successive stage in a food chain.

- This is because some material and energy are always lost in waste materials, and some are used for respiration to supply energy for living processes, including movement. Much of the energy is eventually transferred to the surroundings as heat.

Summary questions

1 a Why is biomass lost in faeces?
  b Why do animals that move around a lot use up more of the biomass they eat than animals that don't move much?

2 Explain why so much of the energy from the Sun that lands on the surface of the Earth is not turned into biomass in animals.

B16.3 Making food production efficient

Learning objectives

After this topic, you should know:

- that short food chains make food production more efficient

- how we can manage food production to reduce energy losses.

⊙⊙ **links**

For information on pyramids of biomass, look back to 16.1 'Pyramids of biomass'.

Figure 1 Many people enjoy eating meat and it is a useful part of a balanced diet. Yet reducing the stages in the food chain – at the very least not feeding animal products to farm animals and eating less meat and more plant material – makes food production more efficient.

Pyramids of biomass show us that the organisms at each successive stage of a food chain contain less material and therefore less energy. This has major implications for the way we produce food.

Food chains in food production

In the developed world, much of our diet consists of meat or other animal products such as eggs, cheese and milk. The cows, goats, pigs and sheep that we use to produce our food eat plants. By the time it reaches us, much of the energy from the plant has been used up.

In some cases we even feed animals to animals. Ground up fish, for example, is often part of commercial pig and chicken feed. This means we have put another extra stage into the food chain. It goes from plant to fish, fish to pig, pig to people, making it even less efficient.

There is a limited amount of the Earth's surface that we can use to grow food. The most energy-efficient way to use this food is to grow plants and eat them directly. If we only ate plants, then in theory there would be plenty of food for everyone on the Earth. Biomass produced by plants would be used to feed people and produce human biomass.

However, every extra stage we introduce results in less energy getting to us at the end of the chain. An example is feeding plants to animals before we eat the food ourselves. In turn, this means less food to go around the human population.

Reducing the number of stages in food chains could dramatically increase the efficiency of our food production. Eating less meat would mean more food for everyone.

Artificially managed food production

As you saw in 16.2, animals don't turn all of the food they eat into new animals. Some of the food can't be digested and is lost as waste. Energy is also used in moving around and maintaining a constant body temperature.

Farmers apply these ideas to food production to make it more efficient. People want meat, eggs and milk – but they want them as cheaply as possible. So farmers want to get the maximum possible increase in biomass from animals without feeding them extra food. There are two ways of doing this:

- Limiting the movement of food animals so they don't use much energy in moving their muscles and so have more biomass available from their food for growth.

- Controlling the temperature of their surroundings so the animals will not have to use much energy keeping warm or cooling down. Again, this leaves more biomass spare for growth.

Controlling these factors means keeping the animals inside with restricted space to move, and a constant ideal temperature. This is what happens in the massive poultry rearing sheds where the majority of the chickens that we eat are produced.

⊙⊙ **links**

For information on energy losses through a food chain, look back to 16.2 'Energy transfers'.

Birds kept in these sheds can be ready to eat in a matter of weeks. They always have plenty of food, but there is not much room to move. There is also a risk of disease spreading quickly through the animals as they are so close together. The poultry need constant monitoring, which costs money, but they can be sold for meat very quickly.

Animals reared in this way can appear more like factory products than farm animals. That's why these intensive methods are sometimes referred to as factory farming.

Intensive farming methods are used because there has been a steady increase in demand for cheap meat and animal products. This is the only way farmers can meet these demands from consumers.

On the other hand, these animals live very unnatural and restricted lives. In comparison, birds reared outside grow more slowly but have a better quality of life. It takes more space, the weather can be a problem and it is a slower process, but there is no heating or lighting to pay for.

More people are now aware of how our cheap meat and eggs are produced. As a result, there has been a backlash against the conditions in which intensively reared animals live. However, it is easy to forget that animals living outside sometimes have to contend with cold, rain, wind and mud!

Increasingly, intensive systems are being developed with far greater awareness of animal welfare issues. Contented animals gain biomass more quickly than stressed ones, so everyone benefits. Many modern farming systems used in the UK are a careful compromise between maximum weight gain and animal well-being.

Food miles

Another aspect of efficiency in food production is how far the food travels. Food produced around the world can travel thousands of miles to reach your plate. This uses fuel, which increases the amount of carbon dioxide in the atmosphere. People are more aware of these 'food miles' now and many people try to buy meat, fruit and vegetables that have been grown relatively locally.

 Did you know … ?

The biggest herd of dairy cows in the world is in Saudi Arabia, where 37 000 cows are all kept inside water-cooled buildings.

Summary questions

1 Explain carefully why there would be more food for everyone if we all ate only plants.

2 a Why are animals prevented from moving much and kept indoors in intensive farming?
  b Why is it important to keep cattle and pigs cool in hot temperatures and warm when it is cold to get the maximum gain in biomass?

3 a What are the advantages and disadvantages for a farmer of rearing animals intensively?
  b What are the advantages and disadvantages of less intensive rearing methods?

4 What are food miles and why do many people aim to keep their food miles as low as possible?

Figure 2 Most people would like the animals that provide their meat to be reared in the best possible conditions, but what is best for the cattle is not always as easy to judge as you might think

Examiner's tip

Be clear about the ways in which the efficiency of food production can be improved to meet the needs of a growing human population. Make sure you have considered the advantages and disadvantages of each method before your examination.

Key points

- Biomass and energy are reduced at each stage of a food chain. The efficiency of food production is improved by reducing the number of stages in a food chain.

- The efficiency of food production can also be improved by restricting energy loss from animals by limiting their movement and by controlling the temperature of their surroundings.

B16.4 Sustainable food production

Figure 1 Atlantic cod have been fished almost to extinction, causing cod and chips to become almost a luxury dish

As the human population keeps increasing, we are becoming more aware of the need for **sustainable food production**. This means producing foods in ways that can continue for many years. It involves:

- maintaining the health of the soil so plant crops grow well year after year
- looking at ways to produce food that reduce the stages in the food chain and make it more efficient
- taking care of the fish stocks in our oceans so they do not run out.

Managing the oceans

People have fished for food throughout human history. However, in the past 60 years or so, commercial fishing fleets of large factory ships have built up. These are capable of taking huge quantities of fish on a regular basis. The result of this uncontrolled overfishing is that stocks of edible fish are falling. In some areas, such as the North Sea, fish stocks are becoming dangerously low because almost all of the breeding fish have been caught.

It is important to maintain fish stocks at a level where breeding continues successfully. Otherwise certain species, such as cod and bluefin tuna, may disappear completely in some areas. Many of these fish grow slowly for years before they are ready to breed. If the breeding stock is taken, then people fish for smaller, younger fish – but there are no more breeding animals to replace them.

People have been warning about the problems of overfishing for years. Populations of some fish are so low they could disappear altogether. At last, serious restrictions on fishing are being put in place.

Tackling the problem of overfishing

Ways in which we can conserve fish populations include controlling the size of the holes in the nets so only the biggest fish are caught. Younger, smaller fish can get through the nets and live to grow large enough to breed. There can also be bans on fishing in the breeding season and very strict quotas imposed on fishermen. This means they have a strictly enforced limit on the amount and type of fish they are allowed to catch. However, quotas can be of limited use. Once the fish are caught they are already dead – so if the fishermen are over quota they will simply throw the excess dead fish back into the sea, which does not help maintain the populations. However, quotas can substantially reduce the numbers of fishing trips made, though at some human cost. Fishermen need to fish to make a living and many traditional fishing families have lost their livelihood in the conservation of fish stocks.

Only with protection such as fishing quotas and net sizes will we be able to conserve the fish stocks. Then we will be able to fish them sustainably for years to come.

The need for a global solution

It is not just UK waters that have been dangerously overfished – the same phenomenon is seen all over the world. For example, many scientists think that only a complete fishing ban can now save the bluefin tuna, which has been overfished almost to extinction in spite of the introduction of measures designed to manage and control the stocks. Only by a massive reduction in catches – moving to line-caught fish only for sale – will the still relatively common skipjack tuna avoid the same fate. It will take international cooperation on a large scale to maintain fish stocks in the oceans of the world.

Novel foods

Another practical solution to the problems of food production and distribution has been for scientists to investigate new ways of growing foods and even novel foods. So in recent decades, fish farming has become increasingly common around the world, with species such as tilapia grown on many continents including India and Africa as well as the UK.

Almost 30 years ago in the UK, scientists developed a completely new food based on fungi. It is known as **mycoprotein**, which means 'protein from fungus'. It is produced using the fungus *Fusarium*, which grows and reproduces rapidly on a relatively cheap sugar syrup. In optimum conditions, it can double its mass every five hours! The fungal biomass is harvested and purified. Then it is dried and processed to make mycoprotein. This is a pale yellow solid with a faint taste of mushrooms. On its own, it has very little flavour.

However, mycoprotein is given a range of textures and flavours to make it similar to many familiar foods such as chicken and beef. It is a high-protein, low-fat meat substitute. The protein content of mycoprotein is similar to that of prime beef. So it is used by vegetarians and people who want to reduce the fat in their diet. Because the fungi use cheap food from plants and reproduce rapidly, this is a very sustainable food source.

In years to come, more novel foods may be developed that provide an efficient and ethically acceptable way of producing protein food quickly.

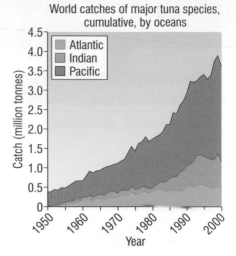

World catches of major tuna species, cumulative, by oceans

Figure 2 Tuna catches have increased enormously over time to the point where some species of tuna are almost extinct

---

Examiner's tip

Learn what can be done to conserve fish stocks so that we will have fish in the future.

Summary questions

1 a How has the fishing industry reached crisis point?
   b How can fish stocks be protected?
   c Why do you think these measures were not put in place a long time ago?

2 a Using the data in Figure 2, calculate the increase in the tuna catch from its lowest level to its highest in the three big oceans.
   b How can some species of tuna be conserved for future fishing?

3 Mycoprotein is an example of sustainable food production. Explain how it is similar to and how its production differs from intensive farming.

Key points

- Sustainable food production means producing food in a way which can continue for many years.

- It is important to control net size and impose fishing quotas to conserve fish stocks, so breeding continues and the decline in numbers is halted.

- New foods can be developed with reduced stages in the food chain for efficient production.

B16.5

Decay processes

Living organisms remove materials from the environment for growth and other processes. For example, plants take nutrients from the soil all the time. These nutrients are passed on into animals through food chains and food webs. If this was a one-way process, the resources of the Earth would have been exhausted long ago.

Fortunately, all these materials are returned to the environment and recycled. For example, many trees shed their leaves each year, and most animals produce droppings at least once a day. Animals and plants eventually die as well. A group of organisms known as the **decomposers** then break down the waste and the dead animals and plants. In this process, decomposers return the nutrients and other materials to the environment. The same material is recycled over and over again. This process often leads to very stable communities of organisms.

The decay process

Decomposers are a group of microorganisms that include bacteria and fungi. They feed on waste droppings and dead organisms.

Detritus feeders, or **detritivores**, such as maggots and some types of worms, often start the process of decay. They eat dead animals and produce waste material. The bacteria and fungi then digest everything – dead animals, plants and detritus feeders plus their waste. They use some of the nutrients to grow and reproduce. They also release waste products.

The waste products of decomposers are carbon dioxide, water, and nutrients that plants can use. When we say that things decay, they are actually being broken down and digested by microorganisms.

The decay process releases substances that plants need to grow. It makes sure that the soil contains the mineral ions that plants take up through their roots and use to make proteins and other chemicals in their cells. The decomposers also 'clean up' the environment, removing the bodies of all the dead organisms.

Figure 1 This orange is slowly being broken down by the action of decomposers. You can see the fungi clearly, but the bacteria are too small to be seen.

Conditions for decay

The speed at which things decay depends partly on the temperature. Chemical reactions in microorganisms, like those in most living things, work faster in **warm conditions**. They slow down and might even stop if conditions are too cold. Decay also stops if it gets too hot. The enzymes in the decomposers are denatured (change shape and stop working).

Most microorganisms also grow better in **moist conditions**. The moisture makes it easier for them to digest their food and also prevents them from drying out. So the decay of dead plants and animals – as well as leaves and dung – takes place far more rapidly in warm, moist conditions than it does in cold, dry ones.

Although some microorganisms are anaerobic (can survive without oxygen), most decomposers respire like any other organism. This means they need oxygen to release energy, grow and reproduce. This is why decay takes place more rapidly in aerobic conditions when there is **plenty of oxygen** available.

Did you know … ?

The 'Body Farm' is an American research site where scientists have buried human bodies in many different conditions. They are studying every stage of human decay, collecting data to help work out the time since death occurred. This will help police forces all over the world to solve murder cases.

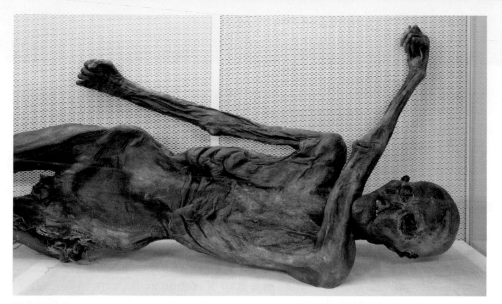

Figure 2 Decomposers cannot function at low temperatures, so if an organism – such as this 4000-year-old man – is frozen as it dies, it will be preserved with very little decay

The importance of decay in recycling

Decomposers are vital for recycling resources in the natural world. What's more, we can take advantage of the process of decay to help us recycle our waste.

In **sewage treatment plants**, we use microorganisms to break down the bodily waste we produce. This makes it safe to release into rivers or the sea. These sewage works have been designed to provide the bacteria and other microorganisms with the conditions they need. That includes a good supply of oxygen.

Another place where the decomposers are useful is in the garden. Many gardeners have a **compost heap**. Grass cuttings, vegetable peelings and weeds are put onto the compost heap. It is then left, to allow decomposing microorganisms to break all the plant material down. It forms a brown, crumbly substance known as compost, which can be used as a fertiliser.

Summary questions

1   a What type of organisms are involved in the processes of decay?
    b Why are the processes of decay so important in keeping the soil fertile?

2   a Garden and kitchen waste added to a compost bin rot down and become compost much more rapidly in summer than in winter. Why is this?
    b During a particularly hot dry summer, compost formation may slow down. Give a possible explanation for this.
    c Turning over the contents of a compost bin every so often can increase the rate at which decomposition takes place. Why is this?

B16.6

The carbon cycle

Figure 1 Within the natural cycle of life and death in the living world, mineral nutrients are cycled between living organisms and the physical environment

Imagine a stable community of plants and animals. The processes that remove materials from the environment are balanced by processes that return materials. Materials are constantly cycled through the environment. One of the most important of these is carbon.

All of the main **molecules** that make up our bodies (carbohydrates, proteins, fats and DNA) are based on carbon atoms combined with other **elements**.

The amount of carbon on the Earth is fixed. Some of the carbon is 'locked up' in **fossil fuels** such as coal, oil and gas. It is only released when we burn them. They are known as **carbon sinks**.

Huge amounts of carbon are combined with other elements in carbonate rocks such as limestone and chalk. There is a pool of carbon in the form of carbon dioxide in the air. Carbon dioxide is also found dissolved in the water of rivers, lakes and oceans. These things all act as carbon sinks. This stored carbon is described as 'sequestered'.

All the time, a relatively small amount of available carbon is cycled between living things and the environment. This constant cycling of carbon is called the **carbon cycle**.

Photosynthesis

Green plants and algae remove carbon dioxide from the atmosphere for photosynthesis. They use the carbon from carbon dioxide to make carbohydrates, proteins and fats. These make up the biomass of the plants and algae. The carbon is passed on to animals that eat the green plants and algae. The carbon goes on to become part of the carbohydrates, proteins and fats in these animal bodies. When these animals are eaten by other animals, some of the carbon becomes in turn the carbohydrates, fats and proteins that make up their bodies.

This is how carbon is taken out of the environment. But how is it returned?

Respiration

Living organisms respire all the time. They use oxygen to break down glucose, providing energy for their cells. Carbon dioxide is produced as a waste product. This is how carbon is returned to the atmosphere.

When plants, algae and animals die, their bodies are broken down by decomposers. These are animals and microorganisms such as blowflies, moulds and bacteria that feed on the dead bodies. The animals which feed on dead bodies and waste are called **detritus feeders**. They include animals such as worms, centipedes and many insects.

Carbon is released into the atmosphere as carbon dioxide when these organisms and microorganisms respire. All of the carbon (in the form of carbon dioxide) released by the various living organisms is then available again. It is ready to be taken up by plants and algae in photosynthesis.

Combustion

Wood from trees contains lots of carbon, locked into the molecules of the plant during photosynthesis over many years. Fossil fuels also contain lots of carbon, which was locked away by photosynthesising organisms millions of years ago.

When we burn wood or fossil fuels, carbon dioxide is produced, so we release some of that carbon back into the atmosphere. Huge quantities of fossil fuels are burned worldwide to power our vehicles and make electricity, while wood is burned to heat homes and (in many countries) to cook food.

Photosynthesis: carbon dioxide + water (+ **light energy**) → glucose + oxygen
Respiration: glucose + oxygen → carbon dioxide + water (+ **energy**)
Combustion: fossil fuel or wood + oxygen → carbon dioxide + water (+ **energy**)

The constant cycling of carbon in the carbon cycle is summarised in Figure 2.

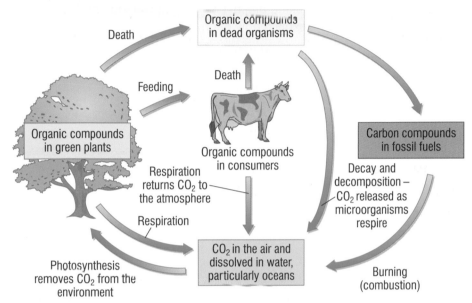

Figure 2 The carbon cycle in nature

Figure 3 Burning wood and fossil fuels to keep us warm, power our cars or make our electricity, all releases locked in carbon in the form of carbon dioxide

Energy transfers

When plants and algae photosynthesise, they transfer light energy into chemical energy that can be stored in the food they make. This chemical energy is transferred from one organism to another through the carbon cycle. Some of the energy can be used for movement or transferred by heating the organisms and their surroundings at each stage. The decomposers break down all the waste and dead organisms and cycle the materials as plant nutrients. By this time, all of the energy originally absorbed by green plants and algae during photosynthesis has been transferred elsewhere.

For millions of years, the carbon cycle has regulated itself. However, as we burn more fossil fuels we are pouring increasing amounts of carbon dioxide into the atmosphere. Scientists fear that the carbon cycle may not cope as the levels of carbon dioxide in our atmosphere increase, it may lead to climate change.

⚭ links

For more on the role of carbon dioxide in possible climate change, see 14.4 'Deforestation and peat destruction' and 14.5 'Global warming'.

Summary questions

1 a What is the carbon cycle?
  b What are the main processes involved in the carbon cycle?
  c Why is the carbon cycle so important for life on Earth?

2 a Where does the carbon come from that is used in photosynthesis?
  b Explain carefully how carbon is transferred through an ecosystem.

3 Explain the links between the processes of photosynthesis, respiration and combustion and describe the role of each process in the carbon cycle.

Summary questions

1

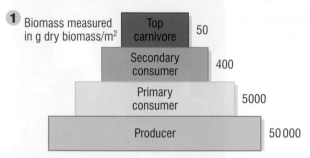

Biomass measured in g dry biomass/m²

Top carnivore	50
Secondary consumer	400
Primary consumer	5000
Producer	50 000

Figure 1

a Use the information in Figure 1 to calculate the percentage biomass passed on:
  i from producers to primary consumers
  ii from primary to secondary consumers
  iii from secondary consumers to top carnivores.

b In any food chain or food web, the biomass of the producers is much larger than that of any other level of the pyramid. Why is this?

c In any food chain or food web, there are only small numbers of top carnivores. Use your calculations to help you explain why.

d All of the animals in the pyramid of biomass shown here are cold blooded. What difference would it have made to the average percentage of biomass passed on between the levels if mammals and birds had been involved? Explain the difference.

2 The world population is increasing and there are food shortages in many parts of the world. Explain, using pyramids of biomass to help you, why there would be more efficient use of resources if people everywhere consumed much less meat and more plant material.

3 Chickens are often farmed intensively to provide meat as cheaply as possible. The birds arrive in the broiler house as 1-day-old chicks. They are slaughtered at 42 days of age when they weigh about 2 kg. The temperature, amount of food and water and light levels are carefully controlled. About 20 000 chickens are reared together in one house. The table below shows their weight gain.

Age (days)	1	7	14	21	28	35	42
Mass (g)	36	141	404	795	1180	1657	1998

a Plot a graph to show the growth rate of one of these chickens.

b Explain why the temperature is so carefully controlled in the broiler house.

c Explain why so many birds are reared together in a relatively small area.

d Why are birds for eating reared like this?

e Draw a second line to show how you would expect a chicken reared outside in a free-range system to gain in mass, and explain the difference.

4 Microorganisms decompose organic waste and dead bodies. We preserve food to stop this decomposition taking place. Use your knowledge of decomposition to explain how each method stops the food going bad:

a Food may be frozen.

b Food may be cooked – cooked food keeps longer than fresh food.

c Food may be stored in a vacuum pack – with all the air sucked out.

d Food may be tinned – it is heated and sealed in an airtight container.

5

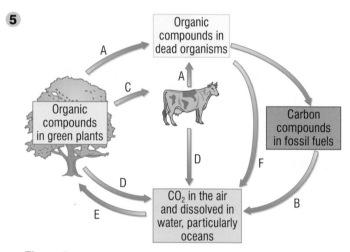

Figure 2

a How is carbon dioxide removed from the atmosphere in the carbon cycle?

b How does carbon dioxide get into the atmosphere?

c Where is most of the carbon stored?

d Why is the carbon cycle so important and what could happen if the balance of the reactions was disturbed?

e List each of the processes labelled A–F, in Figure 2 above.

6 a The temperature in the middle of a compost heap will be quite warm. Energy is produced as microbes respire. How does this help the compost to be broken down more quickly?

b In sewage works, oxygen is bubbled through the tanks containing sewage and microorganisms. How does this help to ensure that human waste is broken down completely?

AQA Examination-style questions

1 A woodland habitat contained the following:
- 40 trees
- 10 000 caterpillars, eating the leaves
- 350 birds, eating the caterpillars.

a Draw and label a pyramid of biomass for this woodland habitat. (3)

b Name the source of energy for the habitat. (1)

c Explain how this energy is captured, converted into chemical energy and transferred to chemical components in the bodies of the caterpillars. (6)

d Scientists estimated the amount of energy contained in each layer of the pyramid.

The results are shown in the table.

	Energy in MJ
Trees	5 000 000
Caterpillars	20 000
Birds	1000

i Calculate the percentage of energy present in caterpillars that is transferred to the birds. (2)

ii Suggest **two** reasons why not all the energy present in the caterpillars is transferred to the birds. (2)

e *In this question you will be assessed on using good English, organising information clearly and using specialist terms where appropriate.*

In autumn, the leaves fall from the trees.

Describe how the carbon in the dead leaves is recycled so that the trees can use it again. (QWC) (6)

2 The diagram shows what happens to the energy in the food a calf eats.

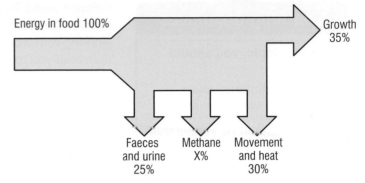

Energy in food 100%

Growth 35%

Faeces and urine 25%

Methane X%

Movement and heat 30%

In the calculations, show clearly how you work out your answer.

a Calculate the percentage of energy lost in methane (X). (2)

b The energy in the food the calf eats in one day is 10 megajoules.

Calculate the amount of this energy that would be lost in faeces and urine. (2)

c Name the process that transfers the energy from the food into movement. (1)

d The farmer decides to move his calf indoors so that it will grow quicker.

Suggest **two** reasons why. (2)

e The farmer's wife says she does not think that this is a good idea. Suggest a reason why. (1)

3 Many consumers will buy only fish that has been caught by 'sustainable fishing'.

a What is meant by 'sustainable fishing'? (2)

b Suggest what might happen if fish stocks in the ocean drop below a certain level. (2)

c Explain how the following methods help to keep fish stocks at a good level:
i Using only nets with a large size mesh (holes).
ii Giving fishing boats from different countries 'quotas' – a maximum limit of each type of fish they can catch and sell. (4)

d Suggest **two** reasons why the fish stocks are not significantly improving despite these rules. (2)

Investigations

Science works for us all day, every day. Working as a scientist you will have knowledge of the world around you and particularly about the subject you are working with. You will observe the world around you. An enquiring mind will then lead you to start asking questions about what you have observed.

Science usually moves forward by slow steady steps. Each small step is important in its own way. It builds on the body of knowledge that we already have.

Thinking scientifically

Deciding on what to measure

Variables can be one of two different types:

- A **categoric variable** is one that is best described by a label (usually a word). The colour of eyes is a categoric variable, e.g. blue or brown eyes.
- A **continuous variable** is one that we measure, so its value could be any number. Temperature (as measured by a thermometer or temperature sensor) is a continuous variable, e.g. 37.6°C, 45.2°C. Continuous variables can have values (called a quantity) that can be given by any measurements made (e.g. light intensity, flow rate, etc.).

When designing your investigation you should always try to measure continuous **data** whenever you can. If this is not always possible, you should then try to use ordered data. If there is no other way to measure your variable then you have to use a label (categoric variable).

Making your investigation repeatable, reproducible and valid

When you are designing an investigation you must make sure that others can repeat any results you get – this makes it **reproducible**. You should also plan to make each result **repeatable**. You can do this by getting consistent sets of repeat measurements.

You must also make sure you are measuring the actual thing you want to measure. If you don't, your data can't be used to answer your original question. This seems very obvious but it is not always quite so easy. You need to make sure that you have controlled as many other variables as you can, so that no-one can say that your investigation is not **valid**.

How might an independent variable be linked to a dependent variable?

The **independent variable** is the one you choose to vary in your investigation.

The **dependent variable** is used to judge the effect of varying the independent variable.

These variables may be linked together. If there is a pattern to be seen (for example as one thing gets bigger the other also gets bigger), it may be that:

- changing one has caused the other to change
- the two are related, but one is not necessarily the cause of the other.

Starting an investigation

Observation

As scientists we use observations to ask questions. We can only ask useful questions if we know something about the observed event. We will not have all of the answers, but we know enough to start asking the correct questions.

When you are designing an investigation you have to observe carefully which variables are likely to have an effect.

What is a hypothesis?

A **hypothesis** is an idea based on observation that has some really good science to try to explain it.

When making hypotheses you can be very imaginative with your ideas. However, you should have some scientific reasoning behind those ideas so that they are not totally bizarre.

Remember, your explanation might not be correct, but you think it is. The only way you can check out your hypothesis is to make it into a prediction and then test it by carrying out an investigation.

observation + knowledge → hypothesis → prediction → investigation

Starting to design an investigation

An investigation starts with a question, followed by a **prediction**. You, as the scientist, predict that there is a relationship between two variables.

You should think about a preliminary investigation to find the most suitable range and interval for the independent variable.

Making your investigation safe

Remember that when you design your investigation, you must:
- look for any potential **hazards**
- decide how you will reduce any **risk**.

You will need to write these down in your plan:
- write down your plan
- make a risk assessment
- make a prediction
- draw a blank table ready for the results.

Examiner's tip

Observations, backed up by creative thinking and good scientific knowledge can lead into a hypothesis.

Key points

- Continuous data can give you more information than other types of data.
- You must design investigations that produce repeatable, reproducible and valid results if you are to be believed.
- Be aware that just because two variables are related, does not mean that there is a causal link.
- Hypotheses can lead to predictions and investigations.
- You must make a risk assessment, make a prediction and write a plan.

Setting up investigations

Fair testing

A **fair test** is one in which only the independent variable affects the dependent variable. All other variables are controlled.

This is easy to set up in the laboratory, but almost impossible in fieldwork. Plants and animals do not live in environments that are simple and easy to control. They live complex lives with variables changing constantly.

So how can we set up the fieldwork investigations? The best you can do is to make sure that all of the many variables change in much the same way, except for the one you are investigating. Then at least the plants get the same weather, even if it is constantly changing.

If you are investigating two variables in a large population then you will need to do a survey. Again, it is impossible to control all of the variables. Imagine scientists were investigating the effect of diet on diabetes. They would have to choose people of the same age and same family history to test. The larger the sample size tested, the more valid the results will be.

Control groups are used in these investigations to try to make sure that you are measuring the variable that you intend to measure. When investigating the effects of a new drug, the control group will be given a **placebo**. The control group think they are taking a drug but the placebo does not contain the drug. This way you can control the variable of 'thinking that the drug is working' and separate out the effect of the actual drug.

Designing an investigation

Accuracy

Your investigation must provide **accurate** data. Accurate data is essential if your results are going to have any meaning.

How do you know if you have accurate data?

It is very difficult to be certain. Accurate results are very close to the true value. It is not always possible to know what that true value is.

- Sometimes you can calculate a theoretical value and check it against the experimental evidence. Close agreement between these two values could indicate accurate data.
- You can draw a graph of your results and see how close each result is to the line of best fit.
- Try repeating your measurements with a different instrument and see if you get the same readings.

How do you get accurate data?

- Using instruments that measure accurately will help.
- The more carefully you use the measuring instruments, the more accuracy you will get.

Precision

Your investigation must provide data with sufficient precision. If it doesn't then you will not be able to make a valid conclusion.

How do you get precise and repeatable data?

- You have to repeat your tests as often as necessary to improve repeatability.
- You have to repeat your tests in exactly the same way each time.
- Use measuring instruments that have the appropriate scale divisions needed for a particular investigation. Smaller scale divisions have better resolution.

Making measurements

Using instruments

You cannot expect perfect results. When you choose an instrument you need to know that it will give you the accuracy that you want, i.e. it will give you a true reading.

When you choose an instrument you need to decide how precise you need to be. Some instruments have smaller scale divisions than others. Instruments that measure the same thing can have different sensitivities. The resolution of an instrument refers to the smallest change in a value that can be detected. Choosing the wrong scale can cause you to miss important data or make silly conclusions.

You also need to be able to use an instrument properly.

Errors

Even when an instrument is used correctly, the results can still show differences. Results may differ because of a **random error**. This is most likely to be due to a poor measurement being made. It could be due to not carrying out the method consistently.

The error may be a **systematic error**. This means that the method was carried out consistently but an error was being repeated.

Anomalies

Anomalies are results that are clearly out of line. They are not those that are due to the natural variation that you get from any measurement. These should be looked at carefully. There might be a very interesting reason why they are so different. If they are simply due to a random error then they should be ignored.

If anomalies can be identified while you are doing an investigation, then it is best to repeat that part of the investigation. If you find anomalies after you have finished collecting the data for an investigation, then they must be discarded.

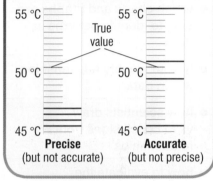

Using data

Learning objectives

After this topic, you should know:

- what is meant by the 'range' and the 'mean' of a set of data
- how data should be displayed
- which charts and graphs are best to identify patterns in data
- how to identify relationships within data
- how scientists draw valid conclusions from relationships
- how to evaluate the reproducibility of an investigation.

Presenting data

Tables

Tables are really good for getting your results down quickly and clearly. You should design your table before you start your investigation.

The range of the data

Pick out the maximum and the minimum values and you have the range. You should always quote these two numbers when asked for a range. For example, the range is between … (the lowest value) and … (the highest value) and don't forget to include the units!

The mean of the data

Add up all of the measurements and divide by how many there are.

Bar charts

If you have a categoric independent variable and a continuous dependent variable then you should use a **bar chart**.

Line graphs

If you have a continuous independent and a continuous dependent variable then use a **line graph**.

Scatter graphs

These are used in much the same way as a line graph, but you might not expect to be able to draw such a clear line of best fit. For example, if you want to see if lung capacity is related to how long people can hold their breath, you might draw a scatter graph of your results.

Using data to draw conclusions

Identifying patterns and relationships

Now you have a bar chart or a graph of your results you can begin looking for patterns in your results. You must have an open mind at this point.

Firstly, there could still be some anomalous results. You might not have picked these out earlier. How do you spot an anomaly? It must be a significant distance away from the pattern, not just within normal variation.

A line of best fit will help to identify any anomalies at this stage. Ask yourself – do the anomalies represent something important or were they just a mistake?

Secondly, remember a line of best fit can be a straight line or it can be a curve – you have to decide from your results.

The line of best fit will also lead you into thinking what the relationship is between your two variables. You need to consider whether your graph shows a **linear relationship**. This simply means can you be confident about drawing a straight line of best fit on your graph? If the answer is yes, then is this line positive or negative?

A **directly proportional** relationship is shown by a positive straight line that goes through the origin (0, 0).

Your results might also show a curved line of best fit. These can be predictable, complex or very complex!

Drawing conclusions

Your graphs are designed to show the relationship between your two chosen variables. You need to consider what that relationship means for your conclusion. You must also take into account the repeatability and the validity of the data you are considering.

You will continue to have an open mind about your conclusion.

You will have made a prediction. This could be supported by your results, it might not be supported, or it could be partly supported. It might suggest some other hypothesis to you.

You must be willing to think carefully about your results. Remember it is quite rare for a set of results to completely support a prediction and be completely repeatable.

Look for possible links between variables. It may be that:
- changing one has caused the other to change.
- the two are related, but one is not necessarily the cause of the other.

You must decide which is the most likely. Remember a positive relationship does not always mean a causal link between the two variables.

Your conclusion must go no further than the **evidence** that you have. Any patterns you spot are only strictly valid in the range of values you tested. Further tests are needed to check whether the pattern continues beyond this range.

The purpose of the prediction was to test a hypothesis. The hypothesis can:
- be supported,
- be refuted, or
- lead to another hypothesis.

You have to decide which it is on the evidence available.

Evaluation

If you are still uncertain about a conclusion, it might be down to the repeatability, reproducability and the validity of the results. You could check reproducability by:
- looking for other similar work on the Internet or from others in your class,
- getting somebody else to redo your investigation,
- trying an alternative method to see if you get the same results.

Key points

- The range states the maximum and the minimum value.
- The mean is the sum of the values divided by how many values there are.
- Tables are best used during an investigation to record results.
- Bar charts are used when you have a categoric independent variable and a continuous dependent variable.
- Line graphs are used to display data that are continuous.
- Drawing lines of best fit help us to study the relationship between variables. The possible relationships are linear, positive and negative; directly proportional; predictable and complex curves.
- Conclusions must go no further than the data available.
- The reproducibility of data can be checked by looking at other similar work done by others, perhaps on the Internet. It can also be checked by using a different method or by others checking your method.

In fish and chip shops, potatoes are cut into chips several hours before they are cooked.

The mass of water in the chips must be kept constant during this time.

To keep the water in the chips constant, the chips are kept in sodium chloride solution.

1 (a) The drawing shows some apparatus and materials.

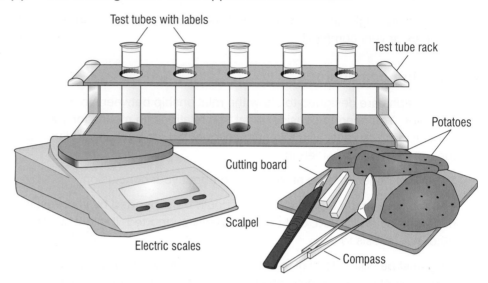

In this question you will be assessed on using good English, organising information clearly and using scientific terms where appropriate.

Describe how you would use the apparatus and materials shown in the drawing to find the concentration of sodium chloride in which to keep the chips so that the mass of water in the chips remains constant.

You should include:
– the measurements you would make
– how you would make the investigation a fair test.

First, I would cut up the potato using the scalpel so that I had chips exactly the same cross-section (say 5 mm × 5 mm) and length (say 5 cm). I would then dilute some 1.0 mol/dm³ sodium chloride solution with distilled water to give 0.1, 0.2, 0.3, 0.4, 0.5, 0.6, 0.7, 0.8 mol/dm³ solutions in separate test tubes and label them. I would use pure water as well. I would use forceps to blot each chip dry, find its mass on the balance and record the mass in a table. I would put one chip in each test tube, making sure I had the correct mass opposite each solution in my table.

I would leave them all for 24 hours. Next day, I would remove each one with forceps, blot it dry as before and find its mass. I would record the new mass in the next column of my table.

The concentration of sodium chloride where there was least change in mass would be the best one to use.

(6)

This answer would score 6 marks. The candidate has included all the necessary science points, they have used appropriate scientific terms for the apparatus and materials, and they have described a logical and detailed method.

1 (b) In a similar investigation, a student investigated the effect of the concentration of sodium chloride solution on standard-sized cylinders cut from a potato.

The table shows the student's results.

	Concentration of sodium chloride solution in mol/dm³					
	0	0.2	0.4	0.6	0.8	1.0
Change in length of cylinders in mm	+4.1	+1.5	−1.4	−3.6	−4.6	−5.2

1 (b) **(i)** On the graph paper below, draw a graph to display the student's results.
– Add a suitable scale and label to the *y*-axis.
– Plot the student's results.
– Draw a line of best fit.

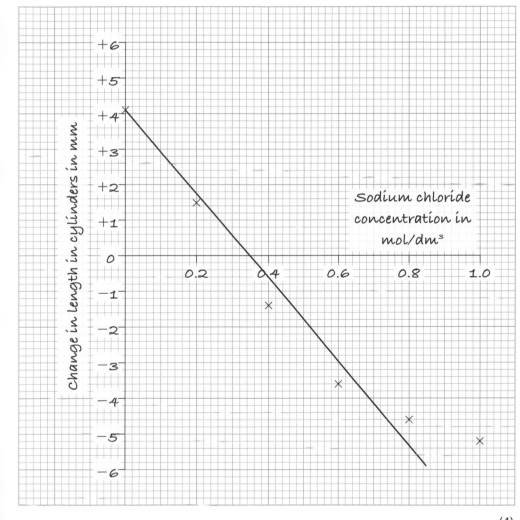

The candidate would score 3 marks, 1 for correct scale and label on the *y*-axis, and 2 marks for correct plots. However, the line of best fit is not close enough, as it should show a smooth curve.

(4)

1 (b) **(ii)** In which concentration of sodium chloride would the chips **not** change mass?

This answer gains 1 mark as it is correct for their line.

Concentration 0.35 mol/dm³

(1)

1 (b) **(iii)** Explain the changes in length of potato cylinders that were placed in the 1 mol/dm³ sodium chloride solution.

The cylinders shrank by 5.2 mm. This is because the liquid outside the cells had a higher concentration of salt than the liquid inside the cells and so water moved out of the cells by osmosis. This made the cells and the cylinders shrink in length.

(3)

The candidate would gain 2 marks for correctly identifying the concentration gradient and for knowing that therefore water moves out of the cells into the liquid outside. However, they did not gain the final point by saying that this is able to happen because the cell membranes are partially permeable

Glossary

A

Abdomen The lower region of the body. In humans it contains the digestive organs, kidneys, etc.

Accurate A measurement is considered accurate if it is judged to be close to the true value.

Acid rain Rain that is acidic due to dissolved gases, such as sulfur dioxide, produced by the burning of fossil fuels.

Active site The site on an enzyme where the reactants bind.

Active transport The movement of substances against a concentration gradient and/or across a cell membrane, using energy.

Adaptation Special feature that makes an organism particularly well suited to the environment where it lives.

ADH Anti-diuretic hormone secreted by the pituitary gland in the brain that affects the amount of water lost through the kidneys in the urine.

Adult cell cloning Process in which the nucleus of an adult cell of one animal is fused with an empty egg from another animal. The embryo which results is placed inside the uterus of a third animal to develop.

Adult stem cells Stem cells (cell with the potential to differentiate and form a variety of other cell types) that are found in small quantities in adult tissues.

Aerobic respiration Breaking down food using oxygen to release energy for the cells.

Agar The nutrient jelly on which many microorganisms are cultured.

Agglutinate Stick together.

Agriculture Growing plants or other organisms on farms to supply human needs e.g. for food, clothing etc.

Algae Single-celled or simple multicellular organisms that can photosynthesise but are not plants.

Algal cells The cells of algae, single-celled or simple multicellular organisms, which can photosynthesise but are not plants.

Allele A version of a particular gene.

Alveoli The tiny air sacs in the lungs which increase the surface area for gaseous exchange.

Amino acids The building blocks of protein.

Amylase The enzyme made in the salivary glands and the pancreas which speeds up the breakdown of starch into simple sugars.

Anaerobic respiration Breaking down food without oxygen to release energy for the cells.

Anomalous result Result that does not match the pattern seen in the other data collected or is well outside the range of other repeat readings. It should be retested and if necessary discarded.

Anther Makes pollen containing the male gametes of the plant.

Antibiotic Drug that destroys bacteria inside the body without damaging human cells.

Antibodies Proteins made by the white blood cells which bind to specific antigens.

Antigen The unique protein on the surface of a cell. It is recognised by the immune system as 'self' or 'non-self'.

Aorta The main artery leaving the left ventricle carrying oxygenated blood to the body.

Artery Blood vessel which carries blood away from the heart. It usually carries oxygenated blood and it has a pulse.

Artificial pacemaker An electrical device that can be implanted to act as pacemaker for the heart when the natural pacemaker region fails.

Asexual budding A form of asexual reproduction where a complete new individual forms as a bud on the parent organism e.g. yeast, hydra.

Asexual reproduction Reproduction that involves only one individual with no fusing of gametes to produce the offspring. The offspring are identical to the parent.

Atrium The small upper chambers of the heart. The right atrium receives blood from the body and the left atrium receives blood from the lungs.

Auxin A plant hormone that controls the responses of plants to light (phototropism) and to gravity (gravitropism).

B

Bacteria Single-celled microorganisms that can reproduce very rapidly. Many bacteria are useful, e.g. gut bacteria and decomposing bacteria, but some cause disease.

Bacterial colony A population of billions of bacteria grown in culture.

Bar chart A chart with rectangular bars with lengths proportional to the values that they represent. The bars should be of equal width and are usually plotted horizontally or vertically. Also called a bar graph.

Bases Nitrogenous compounds that make up part of the structure of DNA and RNA.

Benign tumours Tumours that grow in one location and do not invade other tissues.

Biconcave disc The shape of the red blood cells – a disc which is dimpled inwards on both sides.

Bile Yellowy-green liquid made in the liver and stored in the gall bladder. It is released into the small intestine and emulsifies fats.

Biodiversity The number and variety of different organisms found in a specified area.

Biofuel Fuel produced from biological material which is renewable and sustainable.

Biological detergent Washing detergent that contains enzymes.

Biomass Biological material from living or recently living organisms.

Biotic index of water cleanliness A measure of how clean water is by studying the type and numbers of living organisms found in it.

Bladder The organ where urine is stored until it is released from the body.

Blood circulation system The system by which blood is pumped around the body.

Blood vessel A tube which carries blood around the body, i.e. arteries, veins and capillaries.

Blood The liquid which is pumped around the body by the heart. It contains blood cells, dissolved food, oxygen, waste products, mineral ions, hormones and other substances needed in the body or needing to be removed from the body.

Breathing The physical movement of air into and out of the lungs. In humans this is brought about by the action of the intercostal muscles on the ribs and the diaphragm.

C

Callus A mass of unspecialised plant tissue.

Cancer The common name for a malignant tumour.

Capillaries The smallest blood vessels which run between individual cells. They have a wall which is only one cell thick.

Carbohydates Molecules which provide us with energy. They contain the chemical elements carbon, hydrogen and oxygen and are made up of single sugar units.

Carbohydrase Enzyme which speeds up the breakdown of carbohydrates.

Carbon cycle The cycling of carbon through the living and non-living world.

Carbon sinks Something that takes up more carbon dioxide than it produces e.g. plants, the oceans.

Carcinogens Chemicals that can cause mutations in cells and so trigger the formation of malignant tumours.

Carnivore Animal that eats other animals.

Carpel The female parts of a flower made up of the stigma, style and ovary.

Carrier Individual who is heterozygous for a faulty allele that causes a genetic disease in the homozygous form.

Catalyst A substance which speeds up a chemical reaction. At the end of the reaction the catalyst remains chemically unchanged.

Categoric variable See Variable – categoric.

Cell cycle The sequence of events by which cells grow and divide.

Cell membrane The membrane around the contents of a cell which controls what moves in and out of the cell.

Cell wall A rigid structure which surrounds the cells of living organisms apart from animals.

Cellulose A big carbohydrate molecule which makes up plant and algal cell walls.

Central nervous system (CNS) The central nervous system is made up of the brain and spinal cord where information is processed.

Cerebral cortex Region of the brain concerned with consciousness, memory and language.

Cerrebellum Region of the brain concerned with coordinating muscular activity and balance.

Charles Darwin The Victorian scientist who developed the theory of evolution by a process of natural selection.

Chemotherapy Treatment in which chemicals are used to either stop cancer cells dividing or to make them self-destruct.

Chlorophyll The green pigment contained in the chloroplasts.

Chloroplasts The organelles in which photosynthesis takes place.

Chromosome Thread-like structure carrying the genetic information found in the nucleus of a cell.

Classification The organisation of living things into groups according to their similarities.

Clone Offspring produced by asexual reproduction which is identical to its parent organism.

Cloning The production of offspring which are genetically identical to the parent organism.

Combustion The process of burning.

Competition The process by which living organisms compete with each other for limited resources such as food, light or reproductive partners.

Complex carbohydrates Carbohydrates made up of long chains of single sugar units e.g. starch, cellulose.

Compost heap A site where garden rubbish and kitchen waste are decomposed by microorganisms.

Concentration gradient The gradient between an area where a substance is at a high concentration and an area where it is at a low concentration.

Continuous variable See Variable – continuous.

Control group If an experiment is to determine the effect of changing a single variable, a control is often set up in which the independent variable is not changed, thus enabling a comparison to be made. If the investigation is of the survey type (q.v.) a control group is usually established to serve the same purpose.

Control variable See Variable – control.

Core body temperature The internal temperature of the body.

Coronary artery An artery which carries oxygenated blood to the muscle of the heart.

Coronary heart disease Heart disease caused by problems with the coronary arteries that supply the heart muscle with oxygenated blood.

Culture medium A substance containing the nutrients needed for microorganisms to grow.

Cuticle The waxy covering of a leaf (or an insect) which reduces water loss from the surface.

Cystic fibrosis A genetic disease that affects the lungs, digestive and reproductive systems. It is inherited through a recessive allele.

Cytoplasm The water-based gel in which the organelles of all living cells are suspended.

D

Data Information, either qualitative or quantitative, that have been collected.

Decomposer Microorganism that breaks down waste products and dead bodies.

Deforestation Removal of forests by felling, burning, etc.

Denatured Change the shape of an enzyme so that it can no longer speed up a reaction.

Deoxygenated Lacking in oxygen.

Dependent variable See Variable – dependent.

Detritivores Organisms that feed on organic waste from animals and the dead bodies of animals and plants.

Detritus feeder See decomposer.

Dialysis machine The machine used to remove urea and excess mineral ions from the blood when the kidneys fail.

Dialysis The process of cleansing the blood through a dialysis machine when the kidneys have failed.

Diaphragm A strong sheet of muscle that separates the thorax from the digestive organs, used to change the volume of the chest during ventilation of the lungs.

Differentiated Specialised for a particular function.

Diffusion The net movement of particles of a gas or a solute from an area of high concentration to an area of low concentration (along a concentration gradient).

Digested Broken down into small molecules by the digestive enzymes.

Digestive juices The mixture of enzymes and other chemicals produced by the digestive system.

Digestive system The organ system running from the mouth to the anus where food is digested.

Direct contact A way of spreading infectious diseases by skin contact between two people.

Directly proportional A relationship that, when drawn on a line graph, shows a positive linear relationship that crosses through the origin.

DNA fingerprints Patterns produced by analysing the DNA which can be used to identify an individual.

DNA Deoxyribonucleic acid, the material of inheritance.

Dominant The characteristic that will show up in the offspring even if only one of the alleles is inherited.

Donor The person who gives material from their body to another person who needs healthy tissues or organs, e.g. blood, kidneys. Donors may be alive or dead.

Double circulation The separate circulation of the blood from the heart to the lungs and then back to the heart and on to the body.

Droplet infection A way of spreading infectious diseases through the tiny droplets full of pathogens, which are expelled from your body when you cough, sneeze or talk.

Drug A chemical which causes changes in the body. Medical drugs cure disease or relieve symptoms. Recreational drugs alter the state of your mind and/or body.

E

Ecology The scientific study of the relationships between living organisms and their environment.

Effector organs Muscles and glands which respond to impulses from the nervous system.

Egg nucleus The nucleus of the female gamete that will form the embryo when it is fertilised.

Electron microscope An instrument used to magnify specimens using a beam of electrons.

Element A substance made up of only one type of atom. An element cannot be broken down chemically into any simpler substance.

Embryonic stem cell Stem cell with the potential to form a number of different specialised cell types, which is taken from an early embryo.

Emulsifies Breaks down into tiny droplets which will form an emulsion.

Endemic When a species evolves in isolation and is found in only one place in the world; it is said to be endemic (particular) to that area.

Endosperm nucleus The nucleus of the female gamete that will form the endosperm (food store) when it is fertilised.

Environmental causes External, not inherited conditions that affect the way in which characteristics of organisms develop.

Environmental isolation This is when the climate changes in one

area where an organism lives but not in others.

Enzyme Protein molecule which acts as a biological catalyst. It changes the rate of chemical reactions without being affected itself at the end of the reaction.

Epidermal tissue The tissue of the epidermis – the outer layer of an organism.

Epithelial tissue Tissue made up of relatively unspecialised cells which line the tubes and organs of the body.

Error – human Often present in the collection of data, and may be random or systematic. For example, the effect of human reaction time when recording short time intervals with a stopwatch.

Error – random Cause readings to be spread about the true value, due to results varying in an unpredictable way from one measurement to the next. Random errors are present when any measurement is made, and cannot be corrected. The effect of random errors can be reduced by making more measurements and calculating a new mean.

Error – systematic Cause readings to be spread about some value other than the true value, due to results differing from the true value by a consistent amount each time a measurement is made. Sources of systematic error can include the environment, methods of observation or instruments used. Systematic errors cannot be dealt with by simple repeats. If a systematic error is suspected, the data collection should be repeated using a different technique or a different set of equipment, and the results compared.

Eutrophication The process by which excessive nutrients in water lead to very fast plant growth. When the plants die they are decomposed and this uses up a lot of oxygen so the water can no longer sustain animal life.

Evaporation The change of a liquid to a vapour at a temperature below its boiling point.

Evidence Data which has been shown to be valid.

Evolution The process of slow change in living organisms over long periods of time as those best adapted to survive breed successfully.

Evolutionary relationship Model of the relationships between organisms, often based on DNA evidence, which suggests how long ago they evolved away from each other and how closely related they are in evolutionary terms.

Evolutionary tree Model of the evolutionary relationships between different organisms based on their appearance, and increasingly, on DNA evidence.

Exchange surface A surface where materials are exchanged.

Extinction Extinction is the permanent loss of all the members of a species.

Extremophile Organism which lives in environments that are very extreme, e.g. very high or very low temperatures, high salt levels or high pressures.

F

Fair test A fair test is one in which only the independent variable has been allowed to affect the dependent variable.

False negative A test that shows that a specific problem is not present when in fact it is.

False positive A test that shows that a specific problem is present when it is not.

Fatty acids Building blocks of lipids.

Fermentation The reaction in which the enzymes in yeast turn glucose into ethanol and carbon dioxide.

Fertile A fertile soil contains enough minerals e.g. nitrates, to supply the crop plants with the all nutrients needed for healthy growth.

Fertiliser A substance provided for plants that supplies them with essential nutrients for healthy growth.

Filament Attaches the anther to the flower.

Fossil fuel Fuel obtained from long-dead biological material.

Fossils The remains of organisms from many thousands or millions of years ago that have been preserved in rock, ice, amber, peat etc.

Fructose syrup A sugar syrup.

G

Gamete Sex cell which has half the chromosome number of an ordinary cell.

Gametocytes The stage in the lifecycle of the malaria parasite Plasmodium that reproduces sexually and infects female mosquitos.

Gaseous exchange The exchange of gases, e.g. the exchange of oxygen and carbon dioxide which occurs between the air in the lungs and the blood.

Gene probe A probe that will bind to a particular damaged gene or chromosome.

Gene A short section of DNA carrying genetic information.

Genetic causes The alleles inherited by an organism that determine its characteristics directly.

Genetic disorder Disease which is inherited.

Genetic engineering A technique for changing the genetic information of a cell.

Genetic material The DNA which carries the instructions for making a new cell or a new individual.

Genetically modified An organism that has had its genetic material modified, usually by the addition of at least one new gene.

Genetically modified crops (GM crops) Crops that have had their genes modified by genetic engineering techniques.

Genotype The genetic makeup of an individual regarding a particular characteristic.

Geographical isolation This is when two populations become physically isolated by a geographical feature.

Geological time The timescale covering billions of years used by Earth scientists to show the ages of the rocks and the major events in the history of the Earth.

Glandular tissue The tissue which makes up the glands and secretes chemicals, e.g. enzymes, hormones.

Global warming Warming of the Earth due to greenhouse gases in the atmosphere trapping infrared radiation from the surface.

Glucagon A hormone involved in the control of blood sugar levels.

Glucose A simple sugar.

Glycerol Building block of lipids.

Glycogen Carbohydrate store in animals, including the muscles, liver and brain of the human body.

Gravitropism Response of a plant to the force of gravity controlled by auxin.

Greenhouse effect The trapping of infrared radiation from the Sun as a result of greenhouse gases, such as carbon dioxide and methane, in the Earth's atmosphere. The greenhouse effect maintains the surface of the Earth at a temperature suitable for life.

Greenhouse gas Gases, such as carbon dioxide and methane, which absorb infrared radiated from the Earth, and result in warming up the atmosphere.

Guard cells The cells which surround stomata in the leaves of plants and control their opening and closing.

H

Haemoglobin The red pigment which carries oxygen around the body.

Hazard A hazard is something (e.g. an object, a property of a substance or an activity) that can cause harm.

Heart The muscular organ which pumps blood around the body.

Herbicide Chemical that kills plants.

Herbivore Animal that feeds on plants.

Herd immunity The target of vaccination programmes because when a large percentage of the population are immune to a disease, the spread of the pathogen is greatly reduced and it may disappear completely from a population.

Heterozygous An individual with different alleles for a characteristic.

Homeostasis The maintenance of constant internal body conditions.

Homozygous An individual with two identical alleles for a characteristic.

Hormones Chemicals produced in glands that carry chemical messages around the body.

Horticulture Growing plants for food and pleasure in gardens.

Hydrotropism The response of a plant to water.

Hypertonic A solution with a higher concentration of solute molecules than another solution.

Hypothermia The state when the core body temperature falls below the normal range.

Hypothesis A proposal intended to explain certain facts or observations.

Hypotonic A solution with a lower concentration of solute molecules than another solution.

I

Immune response The response of the immune system to cells carrying foreign antigens. It results in the production of antibodies against the foreign cells and the destruction of those cells.

Immune system The body system which recognises and destroys foreign cells or proteins such as invading pathogens.

Immunisation Giving a vaccine that allows immunity to develop without exposure to the disease itself.

Immunosuppressant drugs Drugs which suppress the immune system of the recipient of a transplanted organ to prevent rejection.

Impulse Electrical signal carried along the neurons.

Independent variables See Variables – independent.

Industrial waste Waste produced by industrial processes.

Infectious disease Disease which can be passed from one individual to another.

Infectious Capable of causing infection.

Inheritance of acquired characteristics Jean-Baptiste Lamarck's theory of how evolution took place.

Inherited disorder Passed on from parents to their offspring through genes.

Inoculate To make someone immune to a disease by injecting them with a vaccine which stimulates the immune system to make antibodies against the disease.

Insoluble molecule Molecule which will not dissolve in a particular solvent such as water.

Insulin A hormone involved in the control of blood sugar levels.

Intercostal muscles The muscles between the ribs which raise and lower them during breathing movements.

Internal environment The conditions inside the body.

Inter-specific competition Competition for resources between members of different species.

Intra-specific competition Competition for resources between members of the same species.

Ion A charged particle produced by the loss or gain of electrons.

Ionising radiation Radiation made of particles which produce ions in the materials that they pass through, which in turn can make them biologically active and may result in mutation and cancer.

Isomerase An enzyme which converts one form of a molecule into another.

Isotonic Having the same concentration of solutes as another solution.

J

Jean-Baptiste Lamarck French biologist who developed a theory of evolution based on the inheritance of acquired characteristics.

K

Kidney Organ which filters the blood and removes urea, excess salts and water.

Kidney transplant Replacing failed kidneys with a healthy kidney from a donor

Kidney tubule A structure in the kidney where substances are reabsorbed back into the blood.

Kingdom The highest group in the classification system e.g. animals, plants.

L

Lactic acid One product of anaerobic respiration. It builds up in muscles with exercise. Important in yoghurt and cheese making processes.

Light microscope An instrument used to magnify specimens using lenses and light.

Limiting factor Factor which limits the rate of a reaction, e.g. temperature, pH, light levels (photosynthesis).

Line graph Used when both variables are continuous. The line should normally be a line of best fit, and may be straight or a smooth curve. (Exceptionally, in some (mainly biological) investigations, the line may be a 'point-to-point' line.)

Linear relationship The relationship between two continuous variables that can be represented by a straight line on a graph.

Lipase Enzyme which breaks down fats and oils into fatty acids and glycerol.

Lipids Oils or fats.

Liver A large organ in the abdomen which carries out a wide range of functions in the body.

M

Male nuclei The nuclei found in pollen grains.

Malignant tumours Tumours that can spread around the body, invading health tissues as well as splitting and forming secondary tumours.

Mean The arithmetical average of a series of numbers.

Median The middle value in a list of data.

Medulla Region of the brain concerned with unconscious activities such as controlling the heart beat and breathing.

Meiosis The two-stage process of cell division which reduces the chromosome number of the daughter cells. It is involved in making the gametes for sexual reproduction.

Merozoites The stage in the lifecycle of the malaria parasite Plasmodium that is released from the liver to infect the red blood cells of the human host.

Metastase The way that malignant tumours spread around the body.

Methane A hydrocarbon gas with the chemical formula CH_4. It makes up the main flammable component of biogas.

Microorganism Bacteria, viruses and other organisms that can only be seen using a microscope.

Mineral ion Chemical needed in small amounts as part of a balanced diet to keep the body healthy.

Mitochondria The site of aerobic cellular respiration in a cell.

Mitosis Asexual cell division where two identical cells are formed.

Mode The number which occurs most often in a set of data.

Molecule A particle made up of two or more atoms bonded together.

Monitor Observations made over a period of time.

Monohybrid crosses Genetic crosses involving the inheritance of a single gene.

Motor neurones Neuron that carries impulses from the central nervous system to the effector organs.

MRSA Methicillin-resistant Staphylococcus aureus. An antibiotic-resistant bacterium.

Multicellular organism An organism which is made up of many different cells which work together. Some of the cells are specialised for different functions in the organism.

Multifactorial Involving many different factors.

Muscular tissue The tissue which makes up the muscles. It can contract and relax.

Mutation A change in the genetic material of an organism.

Mycoprotein A food based on the fungus Fusarium that grows and reproduces rapidly. It means 'protein from fungus'.

N

Natural classification system Classification system based on the similarities between different living organisms.

Natural selection The process by which evolution takes place. Organisms produce more offspring than the environment can support so only those which are most suited to their environment – the 'fittest' – will survive to breed and pass on their useful characteristics.

Negative feedback system A system of control based on an increase in one substance triggering the release of another substance which brings about a reduction in levels of the initial stimulus.

Negative pressure A system when the external pressure is lower than the internal pressure.

Nerve Bundles of hundreds or even thousands of neurons.

Nervous system See Central nervous system.

Net movement The overall movement of …

Neurones Basic cell of the nervous system which carries minute electrical impulses around the body.

Nitrate ion Ion which is needed by plants to make proteins.

Non-renewable Something which cannot be replaced once it is used up.

Nucleus (of a cell) An organelle found in many living cells containing the genetic information.

O

Obese Very overweight, with a BMI of over 30.

Optic nerve The nerve carrying impulses from the retina of the eye to the brain.

Organ A group of different tissues working together to carry out a particular function.

Organ system A group of organs working together to carry out a particular function.

Osmosis The net movement of water from an area of high concentration (of water) to an area of low concentration (of water) along a concentration gradient.

Ova Female sex cells (gametes) in animals.

Ovary Female sex organ which contains the eggs and produces sex hormones during the menstrual cycle.

Overweight A person is overweight if their body carries excess fat and their BMI is between 25 and 30.

Ovules The female gametes in a plant.

Oxygen debt The extra oxygen that must be taken into the body after exercise has stopped to complete the aerobic respiration of lactic acid.

Oxygenated Containing oxygen.

Oxyhaemoglobin The molecule formed when haemoglobin binds to oxygen molecules.

P

Pacemaker Something biological or artificial that sets the basic rhythm of the heart.

Palisade mesophyll Upper layer of mesophyll tissue in plant leaves that contains many chloroplasts for photosynthesis.

Pancreas An organ that produces the hormone insulin and many digestive enzymes.

Parasite Organism which lives in or on other living organisms and gets some or all of its nourishment from this host organism.

Partially permeable membrane Allowing only certain substances to pass through.

Pathogen Microorganism which causes disease.

Permanent vacuole A space in the cytoplasm filled with cell sap which is there all the time.

Pesticide Chemical that kills animals.

Petal Feature of a plant adapted to contain the sex organs. May be brightly coloured or patterned to attract insects and other pollinators.

Phenotype The physical appearance/biochemistry of an individual regarding a particular characteristic.

Phloem tissue The living transport tissue in plants which carries sugars around the plant.

Photosynthesis The process by which plants make food using carbon dioxide, water and light energy.

Phototropism The response of a plant to light, controlled by auxin.

Pigment A coloured molecule.

Pituitary gland Small gland in the brain which produces a range of hormones controlling body functions.

Placebo A substance used in clinical trials which does not contain any drug at all.

Plasma The clear, yellow liquid part of the blood which carries dissolved substances and blood cells around the body.

Plasmid Extra circle of DNA found in bacterial cytoplasm.

Plasmolysis The state of a plant cell when large amounts of water have moved out by osmosis and the protoplasm shrinks and pulls away from the cell wall leaving visible gaps.

Platelet Fragment of cell in the blood which is vital for the clotting mechanism to work.

Pollen tube The tube that grows out of the pollen grain down the style and through which the male nuclei travel to the ovules.

Polydactyly A genetic condition inherited through a dominant allele which results in extra fingers and toes.

Polytunnel Large greenhouse made of plastic.

Positive pressure A system where the external pressure is higher than the internal pressure.

Precise A precise measurement is one in which there is very little spread about the mean value. Precision depends only on the extent of random errors – it gives no indication of how close results are to the true value.

Predator An animal which preys on other animals for food.

Prediction A forecast or statement about the way something will happen in the future. In science it is not just a simple guess, because it is based on some prior knowledge or on a hypothesis.

Protease An enzyme which breaks down proteins.

Protein synthesis The process by which proteins are made on the ribosomes based on information from the genes in the nucleus.

Puberty The stage of development when the sexual organs and the body become adult.

Pulmonary artery The large blood vessel taking deoxygenated blood from the right ventricle of the heart to the lungs.

Pulmonary vein The large blood vessel bringing blood into the left atrium of the heart from the lungs.

Pyramid of biomass A model of the mass of biological material in the organisms at each level of a food chain.

Q

Quadrat A piece of apparatus for sampling organisms in the field.

Quantitative sampling Sampling which records the numbers of organisms rather than just the type.

R

Radiotherapy Cancer treatment when the cells are destroyed by targeted doses of radiation.

Range The maximum and minimum values of the independent or dependent variables; important in ensuring that any pattern is detected.

Receptor Special sensory cell that detects changes in the environment.

Recessive The characteristic that will show up in the offspring only if both of the alleles are inherited.

Recipient The person who receives a donor organ.

Red blood cell Blood cell which contains the red pigment haemoglobin. It is biconcave discs in shape and gives the blood its red colour.

Reflex arc The sense organ, sensory neuron, relay neuron, motor neuron and effector organ which bring about a reflex action.

Reflex Rapid automatic response of the nervous system that does not involve conscious thought.

Repeatable A measurement is repeatable if the original experimenter repeats the investigation using same method and equipment and obtains the same results.

Reproducible A measurement is reproducible if the investigation is repeated by another person, or by using different equipment or techniques, and the same results are obtained.

Respiration The process by which food molecules are broken down to release energy for the cells.

Respiratory (breathing) system The system of the body including the airways and lungs that is specially adapted for the exchange of gases between the air and the blood.

Ribosome The site of protein synthesis in a cell.

Risk The likelihood that a hazard will actually cause harm. We can reduce risk by identifying the hazard and doing something to protect against that hazard.

Root hair cell Cell on the root of a plant with microscopic hairs which increases the surface area for the absorption of water from the soil.

S

Salivary gland Gland in the mouth which produces saliva containing the enzyme amylase.

Sample size The size of a sample in an investigation.

Schizonts The stage in the lifecycle of the malaria parasite Plasmodium that bursts out of the red blood cells, destroying them and causing symptoms of disease.

Secreting Releasing chemicals such as hormones or enzymes.

Selective reabsorption The varying amount of water and dissolved mineral ions that are taken back into the blood in the kidney, depending on what is needed by the body.

Sense organ Collection of special cells known as receptors which responds to changes in the surroundings (e.g. eye, ear).

Sensory neurones Neuron which carries impulses from the sensory organs to the central nervous system.

Sepal Small green leaf-like structures that protect a flower when it is in bud.

Sequestered The storage of carbon dioxide directly or indirectly in plant material and water.

Sewage treatment plant A site where human waste is broken down using microorganisms.

Sewage A combination of bodily waste, waste water from homes and rainfall overflow from street drains.

Sex chromosome A chromosome which carries the information about the sex of an individual.

Sexual reproduction Reproduction which involves the joining (fusion) of male and female gametes producing genetic variety in the offspring.

Sickle-cell anaemia A genetic disorder affecting the structure of the haemoglobin which in turn affects the shape of the red blood cells, making them sickle shaped so they don't carry oxygen efficiently.

Simple sugars Small carbohydrate molecules made up of single sugar units or two sugar units joined together.

Sionatrial node The region of the special tissue that acts as the natural pacemaker region of the heart.

Small intestine The region of the digestive system where most of the digestion of the food takes place.

Smog A haze of small particles and acidic gases that form in the air over major cities as a result of the burning of fossil fuels in vehicles and pollution from industrial processes.

Solar (light) energy Energy from the Sun or other light source.

Solute The solid which dissolves in a solvent to form a solution.

Specialised Adapted for a particular function.

Speciation The formation of a new species.

Species A group of organisms with many features in common which can breed successfully producing fertile offspring.

Sperm Male sex cell (gamete) in animals.

Spongy mesophyll Lower layer of mesophyll tissue in plant leaves that contains some chloroplasts and also has big air spaces to give a large surface area for the diffusion of gases.

Sporozoites The stage in the lifecycle of the malaria parasite Plasmodium that is passed on to humans when the female mosquito takes a blood meal. This goes on to infect the liver.

Stamen The male part of a flower made up of the anthers and filament.

Stem cell Undifferentiated cell with the potential to form a wide variety of different cell types.

Stent A metal mesh placed in the artery which is used to open up the blood vessel by the inflation of a tiny balloon.

Stigma The part of the flower where pollen lands during pollination.

Stimuli A change in the environment that is detected by sensory receptors.

Stomata Openings in the leaves of plants (particularly the underside) which allow gases to enter and leave the leaf. They are opened and closed by the guard cells.

Style The part that transports the male sex cells to the ovary.

Sulfur dioxide A polluting gas formed when fossil fuels containing sulfur impurities are burned.

Sustainable food production Methods of producing food which can be sustained over time without destroying the fertility of the land or ocean.

Synapse A gap between neurons where the transmission of information is chemical rather than electrical.

T

Territory An area where an animal lives and feeds, which it may mark out or defend against other animals.

Therapeutic cloning Cloning by transferring the nucleus of an adult cell to an empty egg to produce tissues or organs which could be used in medicine.

Thermoregulatory centre The area of the brain which is sensitive to the temperature of the blood.

Thorax The upper (chest) region of the body. In humans it includes the ribcage, heart and lungs.

Tissue culture Using small groups of cells from a plant to make new plants.

Tissue A group of specialised cells all carrying out the same function.

Trachea The main tube lined with cartilage rings which carries air from the nose and mouth down towards the lungs.

Transect A measured line or area along which ecological measurements (e.g. quadrats) are made.

Translocation The movement of sugars from the leaves to the rest of a plant.

Transpiration stream The movement of water through a plant from the roots to the leaves as a result of the loss of water by evaporation from the surface of the leaves.

Transpiration The loss of water vapour from the leaves of plants through the stomata when they are opened to allow gas exchange for photosynthesis.

Transport system A system for transporting substances around a multicellular living organism.

Tropism The response of a plant to a

stimulus by growth e.g. phototropism.

Tuber Modified part of a plant which is used to store food in the form of starch.

Tumour A mass of abnormally growing cells that form when the cells do not respond to the normal mechanisms which control the cell cycle.

Turgor The state of a plant cell when the pressure of the cell wall on the cytoplasm cancels out the tendency for water to move in by osmosis, so the cell is rigid.

Type 1 diabetes Diabetes which is caused when the pancreas cannot make insulin. It usually occurs in children and young adults and can be treated by regular insulin injections.

Type 2 diabetes The form of diabetes that is linked to obesity, diet and exercise levels as well as genetics. The pancreas still makes insulin although the levels may reduce but the body cells stop responding to insulin.

U

Urea The waste product formed by the breakdown of excess amino acids in the liver.

Urine The liquid produced by the kidneys containing the metabolic waste product urea along with excess water and salts from the body.

Urobilin Yellow pigment that come from the breakdown of haemoglobin in the liver.

V

Vaccination Introducing small quantities of dead or inactive pathogens into the body to stimulate the white blood cells to produce antibodies that destroy the pathogens. This makes the person immune to future infection.

Vaccine The dead or inactive pathogen material used in vaccination.

Vacuum An area with little or no gas pressure.

Valid Suitability of the investigative procedure to answer the question being asked.

Valve Structure which prevents the backflow of liquid, e.g. the valves of the heart or the veins.

Variable Physical, chemical or biological quantity or characteristic.

Vein Blood vessel which carries blood away from the heart. It usually carries deoxygenated blood and has valves to prevent the backflow of blood.

Vena cava The large vein going into the right atrium of the heart

carrying deoxygenated blood from the body.

Ventilated Movement of air into and out of the lungs.

Ventricles The large chambers at the bottom of the heart. The right ventricle pumps blood to the lungs, the left ventricle pumps blood around the body.

Villi The finger-like projections from the lining of the small intestine which increase the surface area for the absorption of digested food into the blood.

Virus Microorganism which takes over body cells and reproduces rapidly, causing disease.

W

White blood cell Blood cell which is involved in the immune system of the body, engulfing bacteria,

making antibodies and making antitoxins.

Wilting The process by which plants droop when they are short of water or too hot. This reduces further water loss and prevents cell damage.

X

Xylem tissue The non-living transport tissue in plants, which transports water around the plant.

Y

Yeast Single-celled fungi which produce ethanol when they respire carbohydrates anaerobically.

Z

Zygote Cell formed when the male and female gametes fuse at fertilisation.

Answers

1 Cell activity

1.1

1 a Nucleus, cytoplasm, cell membrane, mitochondria, ribosomes.

b Cell wall, chloroplasts, permanent vacuole.

c Cell wall provides support and strengthening for the cell and the plant; chloroplasts for photosynthesis; permanent vacuole keeps the cells rigid to support the plant.

2 The nucleus controls all the activities of the cell and contains the instructions for making new cells or new organisms. Mitochondria are the site of aerobic respiration, so they produce energy for the cell.

3 Root cells in a plant do not have chloroplasts because they don't carry out photosynthesis – they are underground so have no light.

1.2

1 a It isn't contained in a nucleus and there are extra genes known as plasmids separate from the main genetic material.

b Yeast cells.

c Flagella are long protein strands found in some bacteria which are used for moving the bacteria about.

2

	Useful	Damaging
Bacteria	Food production, e.g. yoghurt and cheese Sewage treatment Making medicines Decomposers in natural cycles, e.g. carbon and nitrogen cycle Healthy gut	Diseases Decay
Fungi	Food production – bread Alcoholic drinks Antibiotics Decomposers in food chains and webs	Diseases Decay of food stuffs

3

Feature	Animal cell	Plant or algal cell	Bacterial cell	Yeast cell
Cell membrane	Yes	Yes	Yes	Yes
Nucleus	Yes	Yes	No	Yes
Plasmids	No	No	Yes	No
Chloroplasts	No	Yes	No	No
Cell wall	No	Yes	Yes	Yes
Cytoplasm	Yes	Yes	Yes	Yes

1.3

1 Fat cells: not much cytoplasm so room for fat storage; ability to expand to store fat; few mitochondria as they do not need much energy, so do not waste space. Cone cells from human eye: outer segment containing visual pigment; middle segment packed full of mitochondria; specialised nerve ending. Root hair cells: no chloroplasts so no photosynthesis; root hair increases surface area for water uptake; vacuole to facilitate water movement; close to xylem tissue. Sperm cells: tail for movement to egg; mitochondria to provide energy for movement; acrosome full of digestive enzymes to break down the outside layers of the egg cell; large nucleus full of genetic material.

2 a It takes lots of energy for muscle cells to contract and move things around and this is supplied by the mitochondria, which are the cell organelles where energy is released.

b Chloroplasts make food for the plant by photosynthesis. They need light energy for this. So having the cells near the top of the leaf packed with chloroplasts means they can make the best possible use of the light available.

3 Mitochondria – the number of mitochondria give an idea of how much energy the cell uses.
Flagella or cilia – used to move the cell around or to move substances past the cell.
Nucleus – tells you if the cell is capable of reproduction. Storage materials such as fat or starch.
Cellulose cell walls – suggest plant cell.
Chloroplasts – show photosynthesis takes place.
Any other valid point.

1.4

1 Particles in a liquid or a gas move randomly. As the particles move they bump into each other and this makes them move apart. Diffusion is the spreading of the particles of a gas or of a substance in solution along a concentration gradient and this happens as a result of the random collisions. When the particles are concentrated, there are more collisions. Many particles will move randomly towards the area of low concentration. Only a few will move randomly in the other direction.

2 a Heating the gas or solution will speed up diffusion as the particles are moving faster.

b Folded membranes provide an increased surface area so diffusion can take place more quickly.

3 a Concentration gradient between the gut (high concentration of digested food) and blood stream (low concentration of digested food) so digested food molecules move from the gut into the blood stream by diffusion. The large surface area of the lining of the small intestine gives a big area for diffusion to take place over and increases the rate at which it occurs.

b There is a concentration gradient between the carbon dioxide concentration in the blood (high) and the air in the lungs (relatively low) so carbon dioxide moves from the blood into the air in the alveoli of the lungs along a concentration gradient by diffusion. Again, a large surface area and rich blood supply speed up the process.

c The female moth produces chemicals which spread out into the air around her by diffusion. The further the distance from the female moth, the fewer molecules of the attractive chemical there will be. The male moth is sensitive to the chemical and flies up the concentration gradient, following the chemical as it gets stronger until it brings him to the female moth.

1.5

1 a In diffusion all the particles move freely along concentration gradients. In osmosis only water molecules move across a partially permeable membrane from an area of high concentration of water to an area of low concentration of water.

b If the cell makes water during chemical reactions and the cytoplasm becomes too dilute, water moves out of the cell by osmosis. If the cell uses up water in chemical reactions and the cytoplasm becomes too concentrated, water moves in by osmosis to restore the balance.

2 a Isotonic solution – a solution with the same concentration of solutes as the inside of a cell. Hypotonic solution – a solution which has a lower concentration of solutes than the cytoplasm of a cell. Hypertonic solution – a solution which has a higher concentration of solutes than the inside of a cell.

b If the solute concentration of the fluid surrounding the cells of the body is lower than the cell contents, water will move into the cells by osmosis, they will swell and may burst. If the solute concentration is higher than the cells then water will leave the cells by osmosis. The cells will shrink and stop working properly. So it is important for solute concentration of the fluid surrounding the body cells to be as constant as possible to minimise the changes in the size and shape of the cells of the body and to keep them working normally.

3 Plants rely on osmosis to support their stems and leaves. Water moves into plant cells by osmosis from the xylem. This causes the vacuole to swell and press the cytoplasm against the plant cell walls. The pressure builds up until turgor is reached when the pressure is so great that no more water can physically enter the cell. Turgor pressure makes the cells hard and rigid, which in turn keeps the leaves and stems of the plant rigid and firm.

4 The cytoplasm of *Amoeba* contains a lower concentration of water particles than the water in which the organism lives. The cell membrane is partially permeable, so water constantly moves into *Amoeba* from its surroundings by osmosis. If this continued without stopping, the organism would burst. Water can be moved into the vacuole by active transport, and then the vacuole moved to the outside of the cell using energy as well.

1.6

1 Transport protein or system in the membrane is usually used. The substrate molecule binds to the transport protein in the membrane. This moves across the membrane carrying the substance to the other side. The substrate is released and the carrier molecule returns to its original position. This all uses energy.

2 a In active transport substances are moved along a concentration gradient or across a partially permeable membrane which they cannot cross by diffusion. The process uses energy. Osmosis and diffusion both involve the movement of substances down a concentration gradient or across a partially permeable membrane and they do not use energy produced by the cell.

b Cellular respiration releases the energy needed for active transport. Cellular respiration takes place in the mitochondria so cells which carry out lots of active transport often have lots of mitochondria to provide the energy they need.

3 a They need to get rid of the excess salt from the salt water in the sea and they use active transport to secrete the salt against a concentration gradient into special salt glands that remove it from the body.

b Plants need to move mineral ions from the soil into their roots. Mineral ions are much more concentrated in the cytoplasm of plant cells than in soil water, so they have to be moved against a concentration gradient. This involves active transport and the use of energy from cellular respiration.

1.7

1 As living organisms get bigger and more complex, their surface area to volume ratio gets smaller (diagrams to show this are useful here). As a result it is increasingly difficult to exchange materials quickly enough with the outside world. Gases and food molecules can no longer reach every cell inside the organism by simple diffusion and metabolic waste cannot be removed fast enough to avoid poisoning the cells. So in many larger organisms, there are special surfaces with very large surface areas where the exchange of materials takes place.

2 a It is covered in tiny buds with a very good blood supply.

b The tiny buds give it a large surface area so the turtle can use them for breathing – they absorb oxygen from the water which diffuses into the blood. It is so effective that the turtles can stay underwater for months at a time.

3 a Having a large surface area that provides a big area over which exchange can take place; being thin, which provides a short diffusion path having an efficient blood supply (in animals); this moves the diffusing substances away and maintains a concentration (diffusion) gradient; being ventilated (in animals) to make gaseous exchange more efficient by maintaining steep concentration gradients.

b Any three suitable exchange surfaces, e.g. alveoli of lungs, villi of small intestine, gills of fish, roots and leaves of plants with correct adaptations, e.g. examples of large surface area, thin, etc.

1.8

1 A 3, B 4, C 1, D 2

2 A folded gut wall has a much larger surface area over which nutrients can be absorbed.

3 a Because they have flattened villi, so much smaller surface area is available for absorption of digested food; so much less food is absorbed; they don't get enough glucose and other nutrients and so lose weight and tend to be thin.

b Someone with coeliac disease is affected by gluten. The villi are flattened and surface area for absorption of digested food products is lost. Without gluten in the diet, the gut can recover and the villi will reappear. Then the body can absorb nutrients properly from the gut and so gain weight, etc.

Answers to end of chapter summary questions

1 a A genetic material, B cytoplasm, C cell membrane, D slime capsule, E cell wall, F plasmids, G flagella.

b H vacuole, I food storage granule, J cytoplasm, K cell wall, L cell membrane, M nucleus.

c Similarities: Both have cell walls, cell membrane and cytoplasm. Both have genetic material but that of the plant involves chromosomes contained in a nucleus and that of a bacterial cell is a long circular strand of DNA found free in the cytoplasm with additional small loops of DNA known as plasmids.
Differences: Bacterial cells are much smaller than plant cells. Plant cells contain chloroplasts which can carry out photosynthesis, bacteria do not. Plant cells have permanent vacuoles, bacterial cells do not, bacterial cells may have slime capsules, plant cells do not. Bacterial cells may have flagella to move them about, plant cells do not.

d Similarities: Both have cell membrane, cytoplasm and nucleus.
Differences: Yeast cells are much smaller than animal cells. Yeast cells have food storage granules which most animal cells do not. Yeast cells have cell walls, animal cells don't, yeast cells have permanent vacuoles, animal cells do not.

2 a

Diffusion	Osmosis	Active transport
The net movement of particles from an area of high concentration to an area of lower concentration.	The net movement of water from a high concentration of water molecules to a lower concentration (dilute to more concentrated solution) across a partially permeable membrane.	The movement of a substance from a low concentration to a higher concentration, or across a partially permeable membrane.
Takes place because of the random movements of the particles of a gas or of a substance in solution in water	Although all the particles are moving randomly, only the water molecules can pass through the partially permeable membrane.	Involves transport or carrier proteins which carry specific substances across a membrane.
Takes place along a concentration gradient.	Takes place along a concentration gradient of water molecules.	Takes place against a concentration gradient.
No energy from the cell is involved.	No energy from the cell is involved.	Uses energy from cellular respiration.

b Expect water to move into both A and B by osmosis as the inside of the bag is hypertonic to the outside. Expect water to move into bag B faster than bag A because at a higher temperature. Increase in temperature gives increased rate of random movements of the particles and so would increase the rate at which water particles would pass through the partially permeable membrane, so the rate of osmosis would increase.

3 a An amoeba is a simple organism with a large surface area to volume ratio. It is able to get sufficient oxygen through diffusion across the cell membrane. The stickleback is a more complex organism with a lower surface area to volume ratio. Diffusion cannot provide sufficient oxygen for each cell and so a more effective exchange system of gills is required.

b The feathery structure of the gills greatly increases the surface area available for exchanging gases, whilst pushing water across the gills increases the rate of absorption. The circulating blood delivers the oxygen to the cells and removes the metabolic waste. The circulating blood also maintains a steep concentration gradient at the exchange surfaces in the gills, helping to increase diffusion further.

4 A large surface area – increases the area over which exchange can take place, e.g. villi of the small intestine, alveoli of lungs, roots of plants any other sensible example.
Being thin – this gives a short diffusion path which makes the process quicker and more efficient, e.g. leaf, distance from alveolar air to blood in the lungs, distance from inside of gut to blood vessels in villi in small intestine.
Having an efficient blood supply (in animals) – this moves the diffusing substances away from the diffusion surfaces to maintain a steep concentration gradient which increases the rate and efficiency of the exchange process.
Being ventilated – moving fresh gases in for exchange – makes the exchange more efficient by maintaining steep diffusion gradients, e.g. breathing, moving water over gills of a fish.

Answers to end of chapter examination-style questions

1 a A – nucleus; B = mitochondria; C = ribosomes; D = plasmid (4)

b Controls all the activities of the cell (1); contains the genetic material (1)

c Plasmids (1); and loop of genetic material (1)

d i 0.1 mm;
ii 0.04 mm;
iii 0.002 mm (3)

e Two from: enzymes or named enzyme; to make cell parts or named cell parts; antibodies; antigens; hormones (2)

f Bacterial cells are too small to contain them (1)

2 a Root hair cells absorb water from the soil (1) by osmosis (1), for photosynthesis. The mesophyll leaf cell absorbs light energy from the sun (1) which it uses in photosynthesis (1) to make glucose for the plant. (1)

b Compare: both have cell wall for support; cell membrane for exchange of materials; mitochondria to provide energy by cell respiration and ribosomes to make proteins. *(Maximum of 3 marks)* Contrast: leaf cell has chloroplasts with chlorophyll to capture (absorb) light energy but root hair cells have none as they are underground in dark; root hair cell has long, thin projection to give maximum surface area for water absorption/active transport of minerals; root hair cell has larger permanent vacuole to store more water and pass it on to adjacent cells. *(Maximum of 3 marks)*

3 a Pot A = turgid cell (1) – cell membrane in contact with cell wall and large amount of cell sap (1); Pot B = plasmolysed cell (1) – cell membrane coming away from cell wall and small amount of cell sap (1)

b Water from roots passed up via xylem to stem and leaf cells (1) which keeps them turgid (1) so the contents press out against cell membrane and cell wall giving strength (1). (Answer could be reverse for wilting plant.)

4 a Isotonic (1)

b 0.28 mol/dm^3 (1)

c There is a higher concentration (of salts/sugars) inside the cell/ higher concentration of water outside the cell (1), so the solution is hypotonic. (1) This causes water to diffuse into the cell (1) by osmosis (1), across the partially/semi-permeable cell membrane. (1) The cell fills up with water, swells and eventually bursts, (1) as it does not have a rigid cell wall like a plant cell to contain it. (1) *(Maximum of 6 marks)*

2 Cell division, differentiation and organisation

2.1

1 Chromosomes are structures made of DNA found in pairs in the nucleus of the cells which contain the inherited material.
A gene is a small packet of information that controls a characteristic, or part of a characteristic, of your body. It is a section of DNA.
An allele is a particular form of a gene which codes for a particular characteristic.

2 a Cells need to be replaced with identical cells to do the same job.

b In mitosis a cell divides to form two identical daughter cells. Copies are made of the chromosomes in the nucleus. Then the cell divides in two which each get a copy of the full set of chromosomes. Mitosis is important for forming the identical cells needed for growth or the replacement of tissues.

3 a Differentiation is the process by which cells become specialised and adapted to carry out a particular function in the body of a living organism. It is important because all of the cells of an early embryo are the same but organisms need different cells to carry out different roles in the body, e.g. muscle cells, sperm cells and gut lining cells.

b In animals, it occurs during embryo development and is permanent. In plants, it occurs throughout life and can be reversed or changed.

c Plants can be cloned relatively easily. Differentiation can be reversed, mitosis is induced, conditions can be changed and more mitosis induced. The cells redifferentiate into new plant tissues. In animals, differentiation cannot be reversed, so clones cannot be made easily. In order to make clones, embryos have to be made.

2.2

1 a 23 (pairs)

b 23

c 46

2 Sexual reproduction involves the fusing of two special sex cells or gametes so it brings genetic information from two individuals together, which introduces variety. The gametes are made during the process of meiosis. During meiosis each gamete receives a random mixture of the original chromosome pairs so the gametes are all different from the original cells as well, which also introduces variety.

3 a Meiosis. After the chromosomes are copied, the cell divides twice quickly resulting in sex cells each with half the number of chromosomes.

b In the reproductive organs/in the ovary or the testes.

c Meiosis is important because it halves the chromosome number in the gametes, Then when two gametes fuse during sexual reproduction, the new individual has the correct normal number of chromosomes in pairs in the cells, e.g. in humans, 23 chromosomes in the gametes, 46 chromosomes in 23 pairs in a normal somatic cell.
Meiosis is also important because it introduces variety as each gamete receives a random mixture of the original chromosomes.

2.3

1 a A stem cell is undifferentiated cell which has the potential to differentiate and form different specialised cells in the body. A normal body cell is specialised for a specific function and if divided by mitosis can only form cells with the same specialisation.

b Embryonic stem cells, adult stem cells.

2 a They can be used to make any type of adult cell to repair or replace damaged tissues, with no rejection issues.

b Treating paralysis, treating degenerative diseases of the brain, growing new organs for transplant surgery, treating blindness, any other sensible suggestion.

c Changing all the time – so far stem cells used successfully to treat cancers of the bone marrow, beginning to be used for restoring eyesight, some success in healing hearts after heart attack, any valid ideas as this will change from year to year.

3 a There are ethical objections and concerns over possible side effects.

b By using stem cells from umbilical blood, adult stem cells and therapeutic cloning.

2.4

1 a The set sequence in which cells grow and divide. It involves a period of active mitotic cell division followed by a long period of when the cell does not divide but gets bigger, increases mass and replicates DNA ready for the next division.

b i Expect the cell cycle to lengthen – at its most rapid in the early embryo and fetus when new cells are forming every few hours in the process of growth, differentiation and development, still fast in child which is growing but slower than before birth.

ii Expect cell cycle to be much longer in the older person. 13 year old in puberty and so cells growing and dividing rapidly with growth spurt and development of secondary sexual characteristics. In 70 year old no more growth and less replacement so cell cycle slows right down.

2 a A mass of abnormally growing cells formed when the normal control of the cell cycle is lost and the cells divide rapidly without growing and maturing.

b A benign tumour grows in one place and does not invade other tissues. A malignant tumour can spread around the body invading different healthy tissues.

c A benign tumour can grow very large and cause pressure on and damage to an organ which can be life-threatening. The original tumour may split into pieces which are carried around the body in the blood or lymph where they continue their uncontrolled division to form secondary tumours. These tumours disrupt normal tissue and will usually cause death if untreated.

3 a They either stop the cancer cells dividing or make them self-destruct.

b The drugs used to treat cancer are designed to target the rapidly dividing cancer cells. They also tend to affect other rapidly dividing cells. The cells of the hair follicles, the skin, the blood-forming bone marrow and the stomach lining are always dividing rapidly so they are more likely than other body cells to be affected by chemotherapy.

2.5

1 a A group of cells with similar structure and function working together to carry out a particular function in the body or in an organ.

b Several different tissues working together to carry out a particular function in the body.

2 a Sperm – specialised cell – found individually.

b Kidney – organ – several tissues working together.

c Stomach – organ – several tissues working together.

3 a The palisade mesophyll near the top surface of the leaf where the light falls contains lots of chloroplasts for photosynthesis. The spongy mesophyll is deeper in the leaf. It also contains chloroplasts but there are big air spaces between the cells and the cells have a large surface area, which makes gas exchange between the air and the cells much easier (exchange of carbon dioxide from the air into the leaf cells and oxygen from the leaf cells into the air). The stomata allow the diffusion of gases into and out of the leaf. The xylem vessels carry water to the cells from the soil. The phloem vessels remove the products of photosynthesis and carry them around the plant to the cells where they are needed.

b The stomach has a layer of muscular tissue that contracts to churn up the food, mixing it with the digestive juices and helping physical and chemical digestion; it has glandular tissue that produces enzymes to break down the food and tough epithelial tissue, which covers the inside and outside of the organ.

2.6

1 A 3, B 4, C 1, D 2.

2 An organ is a collection of several different tissues that work together to carry out a particular function in the body, e.g. heart pumps blood around the body, the stomach collects the food you eat and continues the digestive process (any two examples).
An organ system is a number of organs that work together to carry out a major function in the body, e.g. the digestive system gradually breaks down insoluble food molecules into soluble molecules which can be taken into the blood stream, and then gets rid of the waste material (any two examples).

3 Each part of the digestive system relies on the parts before it, e.g. the stomach relies on the mouth, teeth and salivary glands to deliver chunks of chewed food; the small intestine depends on the stomach to continue the process of digestion and then on the enzymes made by the pancreas to help with the digestive process. The large intestine can only deal with the remains of the food which has already been digested in the small intestine and the soluble molecules absorbed into the blood. This leaves the waste material and lots of water, so the large intestine can absorb the water and remove faeces from the body.

Answers to end of chapter summary questions

1 a Mitosis is cell division that takes place in the normal body cells and produces genetically identical daughter cells.
   b [Marks awarded for correct sequence of diagrams with suitable annotations.]
   c All the divisions from the fertilised egg to the baby are mitosis. After birth, all the divisions for growth are mitosis, together with all the divisions involved in repair and replacement of damaged tissues.

2 Meiosis is a special form of cell division to produce gametes in which the chromosome number is reduced by half. It takes place in the reproductive organs (the ovaries and testes).

3 a Meiosis is important because it halves the chromosome number of the cells, so that when two gametes fuse at fertilisation, the normal chromosome number is restored. It also allows variety to be introduced.
   b [Marks awarded for correct sequence of diagrams with appropriate annotations.]

4 a Stem cells are unspecialised cells which can differentiate (divide and change into many different types of cell) when they are needed.
   b They may be used to repair damaged body parts, e.g. grow new spinal nerves to cure paralysis; grow new organs for transplants; repair brains in demented patients. [Accept any other sensible suggestions.]
   c For: They offer tremendous hope of new treatments; they remove the need for donors in transplants; they could cure paralysis, heart disease, dementia etc; can grow tissues to order.
   Against: Many embryonic stem cells come from aborted embryos or from fertility treatment and so this raises ethical issues about the use of unborn humans in research. Some people are also concerned about whether using stem cells may trigger cancer. There are also issues surrounding the cost and amount of time stem cell research takes.

5 a An abnormally growing mass of cells where the normal control of the cell cycle has been lost.
   b Similarities: either type of tumour can get very large and cause pressure or damage to an organ, which can be life threatening in itself; both can be treated by surgery, radiotherapy or chemotherapy. Differences: malignant tumours can split into small pieces which spread to other areas of the body in the blood stream or lymph and grow into secondary tumours in other organs. They are much more difficult to treat than benign tumours because of this spread so the outlook for the patient if the cancer has spread is less positive.

6 a Epidermis, mesophyll, xylem, etc. – any three plant tissues.
   b Stem – supports other areas of the plant, transports materials around the plant; roots – anchors plant in soil, enables uptake of water and mineral ions from the soil; leaves – photosynthesis.
   c Xylem and phloem – because xylem brings water and minerals to all the cells from the roots, and phloem transports dissolved food (glucose, sugars) which all the cells need for energy from respiration.

7 a An organ system is a group of organs that all work together to carry out a particular function in the body.

b

Body part	Function
A – mouth	Takes food into the body/chews food/mixes with saliva
B – oesophagus	Muscular tube which squeezes food down to the stomach
C – stomach	Adds acid and enzymes to food, squeezes and mixes food
D – pancreas	Produces digestive enzymes for the duodenum
E – large intestine	Absorbs water from undigested food/stores faeces
F – anus	Muscular sphincter by which faeces leave the body
G – small intestine	Produces digestive enzymes/breaks down large insoluble molecules into small soluble molecules/absorbs digested soluble food molecules into the blood
H – duodenum	First part of the small intestine which breaks down large insoluble molecules into small soluble molecules
I – liver	Produces bile/many other functions

c Muscle tissue – contracts so it can squeeze food, mix food and digestive enzymes, etc. Glandular tissue specialised to contain cells which secrete substances such as mucus, acid, enzymes needed by the body. [Any other sensible suggestion.]

Answers to end of chapter examination-style questions

1 One mark for each correctly matched term and definition, as follows:
Chromosome – a structure carrying a large number of genes.
Allele – a different form of one gene.
Gene – a section of genetic material coding for one characteristic.
Nucleus – the part of a cell that contains the genetic material.
Gamete – a cell with a single set of chromosomes.

2 a B with chromosomes all doubled to make 12 in total (1); C with 2 cells each containing 3 pairs (1); D with all cells containing 3 different chromosomes (1).
   b Gametes, ova, eggs, sperm. (1)
   c Identical to cell at A. (1)

3 a One mark for each correct row *(Maximum of 5 marks)*.

Differentiated cells	v
Cells with a single set of chromosomes	i
Undifferentiated cells	ii or iii or iv
Cells dividing rapidly by mitosis	iii or iv
An embryo	ii

   b CELL → TISSUE → ORGAN → ORGAN SYSTEM → ORGANISM (2 marks all correct; 1 mark if 1 error)
   c Phloem = tissue (1); stem = organ (1); root hair = cell (1); water transport system = organ system (1); sunflower plant = organism (1)
   d Half of the genes/genetic material (1) for the seed came from the pollen (1), which may have had a gene/coded for a different colour.

4 a Stem cells are undifferentiated (1) so they can be differentiated to grow the tissue needed (1), whereas body cells are already differentiated and will not grow a different new tissue (1).
   b 1 mark for each issue identified, with at least 1 from each section, to a maximum of 6 marks:
   Medical – there might not be an unaffected embryo which is a match; IVF is very expensive; IVF is very stressful and unpleasant; they would need to decide if this is a good time to have another baby.
   Social – all the treatment will be stressful/disrupt their lives; they may find religion/friends/family disagree with them.
   Ethical – they may not believe in destroying embryos; they may believe the embryo can't give permission so it is wrong.

5 a Uncontrolled growth of abnormal cells. (1)
   b Malignant (1), because it has spread to other tissues (1) and formed secondary tumours (1).
   c Via the bloodstream. (1)
   d He may have been a cigarette smoker (1) and taken carcinogens from the smoke (1) into his lungs. (Allow any correct alternatives, e.g. he may have worked with asbestos (1) and breathed it in to his lungs (1).)

3 Carbohydrates, lipids, proteins and enzymes

3.1

1 a A molecule made up of long chains of amino acids.
  b As structural components, as hormones, as antibodies and as catalysts (enzymes).

2 Similarities: all vital components of a balanced diet; all contain carbon, hydrogen and oxygen; all large molecules made up of smaller molecules joined together; any other sensible point.
  Differences: Carbohydrates are made of sugar units. Complex carbohydrates are long chains of sugar units joined together by condensation reactions. They are broken down into glucose in the body, which is used to provide energy in cellular respiration. Carbohydrate-rich foods include bread, potatoes, rice and pasta. [Any other sensible point.] Proteins are made up of single units called amino acids joined together. They contain nitrogen as well as carbon, hydrogen and oxygen. They are joined by peptide links. Molecules have complex 3-D shapes. Protein-rich foods include meat, fish, pulses and cheese. [Any other sensible point.] Lipids may be solids (fats) or liquids (oils). They are made up of three fatty acid molecules joined to a molecule of glycerol. They are the most energy-rich food. They are insoluble in water. Lipid-rich foods include olive oil, butter, cream. [Any other sensible point.]

3 a Iodine test – iodine turns from yellowy-red to blue-black in the presence of starch.
  b Ethanol test – cloudy white layer forms at the boundary if lipid is present.

4 a It depends on the fatty acids which are joined to the glycerol.
  b Complex carbohydrates are made up of long chains of simple sugars joined together by condensation reactions when a molecule of water is released each time two simple sugars are joined.

3.2

1 a Catalyst: a substance that speeds up a chemical reaction but is not used up or involved in the reaction and can be used many times over.
  b Enzyme: large protein molecules which act as biological catalysts.
  c Active site: an area in the structure of the enzyme that is a specific shape and which enables the substrate of the catalysed reaction to fit into the enzyme protein. This allows the enzyme to catalyse the reaction.

2 a Protein
  b The substrate (reactant) of the reaction to be catalysed fits into the active site of the enzyme like a lock and key. Once it is in place, the enzyme and the substrate bind together. The reaction takes place rapidly and the products are released from the surface of the enzyme, which is then ready to catalyse another reaction. [A diagram can help with this explanation and students should be given credit for a well labelled diagram used as part or all of their explanation.]

3 a Building up large molecules from smaller ones; breaking down large insoluble molecules into smaller soluble ones; changing one molecule into another; any other sensible suggestion.
  b The reactions needed for life to continue could not take place fast enough without enzymes to speed them up. Enzymes also control the many reactions so that they can take place in the same small area without interfering with each other.

3.3

1 To begin with, enzyme controlled reactions go faster as the temperature increases – increase in the speed of random movements of particles mean collisions between enzyme and substrate are more likely. However, once the temperature reaches around 40 °C the structure of the protein making up the enzyme starts to be affected. The bonds holding the protein in its complex 3-D shape start to break down and the shape of the active site changes. The substrate can no longer bind to the active site and so the enzyme cannot catalyse the reaction. [Students should include a diagram to show the effect of temperature on enzyme action and could draw a diagram to show the change in the shape of the active site.]

2 a About pH 2.
  b About pH 8.
  c The activity levels fall fast.
  d The increase in pH affects the shape of the active site of the enzyme, so it no longer bonds to the substrate. It is denatured and no longer catalyses the reaction.

3.4

1 Proteases: predigested baby food. Carbohydrases: convert starch to glucose syrup. Isomerase: converts glucose syrup to fructose syrup.

2 a The protease and lipase enzymes digest proteins and fats on the clothes, so the clothes get cleaner than detergent alone. The enzymes work best at lower temperatures. Detergent alone needs higher temperatures to work at its best, so biological detergents are much more effective at low temperatures.

  b At temperatures above about 45 °C, the enzymes may be denatured and so have no effect on cleaning.

3 Microorganisms can provide industrial enzymes – they are easy and cheap to grow in very large quantities, the enzymes work at low temperatures and using genetic engineering bacteria and yeast can be made to produce a wide range of useful enzymes. Some of the enzymes pass out of the microorganism and can be used. Sometimes the enzymes are used within the microorganism itself e.g. in the production of human insulin. The disadvantages of using enzymes in industry is that temperature and pH conditions need to be carefully controlled to prevent the enzyme becoming denatured. Microorganisms have to be supplied with food and oxygen and their waste products have to be removed to prevent contamination.

Answers to end of chapter summary questions

1 a A simple sugar is a carbohydrate made up of a single sugar molecule. A complex carbohydrate is made up of long chains of simple sugar units joined together by condensation reactions with the loss of a molecule of water each time.
  b They provide us with energy – they are broken down to give glucose used in cellular respiration to provide energy.
  c Test for simple sugar: add blue Benedict's solution and heat in a water bath. If Benedict's turns brick red, a simple reducing sugar such as glucose is present. Test for complex carbohydrate, e.g. starch: yellow-red iodine solution turns blue-black in the presence of starch.

2 a A lipid contains carbon, hydrogen and oxygen and consists of three fatty acid molecules joined to a single molecule of glycerol. Complex carbohydrates are made up of carbon, hydrogen and oxygen and are made up of long chains of simple sugar units joined together by condensation reactions with the loss of a molecule of water each time. Proteins contain carbon, hydrogen, oxygen and nitrogen. They are made up of long chains of small amino acids joined using peptide links.
  b i Solid lipids – fats; liquid lipids – oils.
   ii Depends on the fatty acids which are joined to the molecule of glycerol – the different fatty acids affect the characteristics of the lipid.

3 a A protein molecule is made up of long chains of amino acids joined by peptide links. Different arrangements of the amino acids give you different proteins. The long amino acid chains are folded, coiled and twisted to make specific 3-D shapes and they are held in these shapes by weak bonds.
  b Diagram similar to Figure 1 to show enzyme action – explain shape of active site results from protein structure, substrate fits into active site like a lock and key, reaction takes place and products released from active site which can then work again.
  c The bonds which hold the 3-D structure of the protein together are sensitive to pH and temperature and are easily broken down. Once they are broken, the shape of the protein molecule changes and the active site is lost, so that the substrate can no longer bond to the enzyme.

4 a [Marks awarded for well-drawn graph correctly labelled.]
  b The reaction speeds up with the increase in temperature. Particles moving faster with more energy, so more likely to collide and react.
  c [Marks awarded for well-drawn graph correctly labelled.]
  d Catalase
  e That it increases the rate up to about 40 °C and after that, the rate of the reaction decreases and eventually stops.
  f Manganese(IV) oxide is a chemical and not adversely affected by temperature. Catalse is an enzyme made of protein – as temperature goes up, the enzyme is denatured, the shape of the active site is lost and it can no longer catalyse the reaction.
  g Carry out the test on temperatures around 40 °C to see which temperature took the shortest time.

5

Pros	Cons
Good at removing biological stains such as grass, blood and food. Effective at low temperatures, which uses less electricity so is: a good for the environment b cheaper for the consumer.	May be a problem with enzymes going into rivers, etc. Low temperatures used for washing with biological detergents less good at killing pathogens on clothes.

Answers to end of chapter examination-style questions

1 a i Sugars/glucose (1)
   ii Glycerol (1)
   iii Amino acids (1)
   iv Fatty acid (1)

b **i** A biological catalyst (1).
   ii The shape of the active site (1) binds the substrate/reactant (1) so that the reaction happens faster to make the products (1).
   iii Denatured (1).
   iv High temperature/temperature above 45°C (1) and incorrect pH (1).

c Structural proteins/named structural protein (1), to build body parts (1); antibodies (1), for defence against infection (1); hormones (1), to control body functions (1).

2 a Microorganisms (1)
   b **i** Proteases (1) **ii** Amino acids (both words) (1)
   c **i** 14 minutes (1)
      ii Enzyme Z (1) – it takes the least time (to pre-digest protein)/works fastest (1) (*Allow only 7 minutes/less time/faster; do not allow 'works best'.*)
      iii Temperature (1); pH (1)

3 a The darker blue colour produced absorbs more light (1).
   b **i** 6.7–7 (minutes) (Correct answer with or without working gains 2 marks; if final answer incorrect award 1 mark for evidence of selection of 40(% light intensity), either in working or in graph 2)
      ii All starch is broken down.
   c Because 40°C is the optimum temperature for the enzyme's action (1) and the enzyme is denatured/destroyed/damaged at higher temperatures (1).
   d Fructose is sweeter than glucose (1) therefore needed in smaller quantities/so fewer calories in the slimming food (1).

4 Human biology – breathing

4.1

1 Intercostal muscles contract to move your ribs up and out and diaphragm muscles contract to flatten the diaphragm, so the volume of your thorax increases, the pressure decreases and air moves in. Intercostal muscles relax and the ribs move down and in and the diaphragm relaxes and domes up so the volume of your thorax decreases. The pressure increases and air is forced out.

2 Gaseous exchange is the exchange of the gases oxygen and carbon dioxide in the lungs. This is vital because oxygen is needed by the cells for cellular respiration to provide energy, while carbon dioxide is a poisonous waste product which must not be allowed to build up.

3 a [Marks awarded for well-drawn bar chart correctly labelled.]
   b Bar chart shows that we breathe in air which is mainly nitrogen with oxygen and a tiny bit of carbon dioxide. The air we breathe out has less oxygen and more carbon dioxide. So we take oxygen out of the air into the blood and pass carbon dioxide out of the blood into the air and change the composition of the air. BUT we only breathe in oxygen and only breathe out carbon dioxide.
   c Good ventilation system – breathing – to maintain a good concentration gradient; large surface area; good blood supply; small diffusion distances – alveoli.

4.2

1 Because breathing depends on the intercostal muscles and diaphragm contracting and relaxing and this has to be stimulated by nerves. If someone is paralysed and the spinal cord no longer works, the nerve messages can no longer reach the breathing muscles and so spontaneous breathing is lost.

2 a The patient is sealed into a unit and the air is then pumped out which lowers the pressure. As a result the chest wall moves up and out which increases the volume and decreases the pressure inside the chest. So air from the outside is drawn into the lungs as a result of the pressure differences, just like ordinary breathing. The vacuum is then switched off and air moves back into the chamber which increases the pressure again. This in turn pushes down on the ribs, increasing the pressure in the chest and forcing air out of the lungs.
   b The principle is similar to normal breathing in that the chest is expanded and compressed, which causes the pressure to be lowered and then increased; this in turn forces air into the lungs and then out again. However, the changes are the result of artificial pressure changes in the machine rather than the movement of the ribs and diaphragm by muscles under the control of the nervous system.
   c The patient has to be enclosed in a machine or a shell which fits around the chest all the time to maintain their breathing.

3 a It forces a carefully measured unit or breath of air into the lungs under positive pressure, rather like blowing up a balloon. Once the lungs are inflated the positive pressure stops and the lungs deflate as the ribs move down under gravity, forcing the air back out of the lungs.
   b The method for getting air into the lungs is completely different from the natural process. The way air is removed from the lungs is similar to normal quiet exhalation.

c Advantages: it can be given with a simple face mask or tube into the trachea; it can be given very simply using a bag ventilator or using sophisticated machines that can keep breathing for people for many years. Can be delivered by simple mask over nose and mouth. Patients can remain mobile. Few disadvantages.

4.3

1 a Glucose + oxygen → carbon dioxide + water (+ energy)
   b $C_6H_{12}O_6 + 6O_2 \rightarrow 6CO_2 + 6H_2O$ (+ energy)
   c Muscle cells are very active and need a lot of energy so they need large numbers of mitochondria to supply the energy. Fat cells use very little energy so need very few mitochondria.

2 a The main uses of energy in the body are for movement, building new molecules and heat generation.
   b The symptoms of starvation are: people become very thin; stored energy is used up and growth stops; new proteins are not made and there is not enough energy or raw materials; people lack energy, as there is a lack of fuel for the mitochondria, people feel cold, as there is not enough fuel for the mitochondria; to produce heat energy.

3 [See Practical box 'Investigating respiration' on page 48 of the Student Book. Any sensible suggestions for practical investigations.]

4.4

1 a Glycogen is a complex carbohydrate stored in the muscles.
   b Glycogen can be converted rapidly to glucose to provide fuel for aerobic respiration, which provides the body cells with energy. Muscle tissue often needs sudden supplies of energy to rapid contraction in a way that most other tissues do not, so muscle needs a glycogen store. Other tissues don't need the energy in the same way so have not evolved to have glycogen stores.

2 Heart rate: increases before exercise starts as a result of anticipation. It rises rapidly, followed by a steady rise and then falls quite sharply as the exercise finishes. Increased heart rate supplies muscles with the extra blood they need to bring glucose/sugar and oxygen to the muscle fibres, and to remove the carbon dioxide that rapidly builds up.
Breathing rate: increases more slowly and evenly than the heart rate, but remains high for some time after exercise. To begin with, increased heart rate supplies enough oxygen, then the breathing rate needs to increase to meet demand. When exercise stops, breathing rate remains high until the oxygen debt is paid off.

3 [Award marks based on ideas presented when predicting results. Look for clear, sensible ideas, safe investigation, realistic expectations, appropriate methods of recording and analysing, awareness of weakness in investigation. Look also for clear understanding of independent, dependent and control variables.]

4.5

1 The muscles become fatigued. After a long period of exercise, your muscles become short of oxygen and switch from aerobic to anaerobic respiration, which is less efficient. The glucose molecules are not broken down completely, so less energy is released than during aerobic respiration. The end products of anaerobic respiration are lactic acid and a small amount of energy.

2 The waste lactic acid you produce during exercise as a result of anaerobic respiration has to be broken down to produce carbon dioxide and water. This needs oxygen, and the amount of oxygen needed to break down the lactic acid is known as the oxygen debt. Even though your leg muscles have stopped, your heart rate and breathing rate stay high to supply extra oxygen until you have broken down all the lactic acid and paid off the oxygen debt.

3 a Cellular respiration which takes place without oxygen.
   b Animals – anaerobic respiration takes place in the muscles when there is not enough oxygen and the waste product is lactic acid and a relatively small amount of energy. This allows animals to continue running, etc., even when they cannot breathe fast enough to supply the oxygen they need.
   Glucose → lactic acid (+ energy)
   $C_6H_{12}O_6 \rightarrow 2C_3H_6O_3$ (+ energy)
   Plants and yeast – when they respire anaerobically they form ethanol and carbon dioxide. This allows them to continue to respire in low oxygen atmospheres. Not common in plants as they form oxygen during photosynthesis. Quite common in yeasts. People make use of it and deprive yeasts of oxygen to make alcoholic drinks.
   Glucose → ethanol + carbon dioxide (+ energy)
   $C_6H_{12}O_6 \rightarrow 2C_2H_5OH + 2CO_2$ (+ energy)

Answers to end of chapter summary questions

1 a The alveoli provide a very large surface area with thin walls and a rich blood supply.

b Air is moved in and out of the lungs by movements of the ribcage and diaphragm. Breathing in: intercostal muscles contract, pulling ribs upwards and outwards. Diaphragm muscles contract flattening the diaphragm. These things increase the volume of the thorax, which lowers the air pressure so it is lower than the outside air. This is then pushed into the lungs by atmospheric pressure.
Breathing out: intercostal muscles relax so ribs drop down and in. Diaphragm muscle relaxes so diaphragm domes up. These things reduce the volume of the thorax and increase the pressure, so air is forced out of the lungs.
Constantly refreshing the air in the lungs maintains the best possible concentration gradients between the air and the blood for the movement of oxygen from the air into the blood and carbon dioxide out of the blood into the air in the lungs. This makes gaseous exchange more efficient.

2 a A system which forces a carefully measured unit or breath of air into the lungs under positive pressure, rather like blowing up a balloon. Once the lungs are inflated the positive pressure stops and the lungs deflate as the ribs move down, forcing the air back out of the lungs.

b In normal breathing, the increase in volume of the chest creates a negative pressure – so that air is drawn into the lungs by the force of the atmospheric air. In positive pressure ventilation, the pressure in the chest does not change and air is forced in under pressure from the outside.

c Doesn't involve the patient being encased in an artificial lung or shell, so much easier for them to be mobile.

3 a [Award marks for standard of graphs, axes, etc.]

b As the peas start to grow, they began to respire aerobically. As a result, a small amount of heat energy is produced so the temperature increased.

c Because the seeds were dry and not growing, so there was no respiration or heat produced.

d As a control level.

e i Any reasonable explanation, e.g. the important thing about flask C is that the peas are dead so the temperature for the first five days remains at 20 °C as they are not respiring.

ii Peas had gone mouldy and mould respiring so temperature goes up. Anomaly, e.g. sun on thermometer, poor reading, etc.

4 a [Credit will be given in the subsequent answers for extracting and using the information on the bar charts.]

b i Increased fitness means that the heart has a greater volume and pumps more blood at each beat. The heart therefore beats more slowly at rest.

ii Increased fitness affects the lungs by lowering the breathing rate.

5 a The breakdown of glucose in a cell using oxygen to release energy that can be used by the cell. Carbon dioxide and water are waste products of the reaction.
Glucose + oxygen → carbon dioxide + water (+ energy)
$C_6H_{12}O_6 + 6O_2 \rightarrow 6CO_2 + 6H_2O$ (+ energy)

b The breakdown of glucose in the cell in the absence of oxygen to release a small amount of energy to be used by the cell.

c In a human being the waste product is lactic acid.
Glucose → lactic acid (+ energy)
$C_6H_{12}O_6 \rightarrow 2C_3H_6O_3$ (+ energy)
In a yeast cell the waste products are ethanol and carbon dioxide.
Glucose → ethanol + carbon dioxide (+ energy)
$C_6H_{12}O_6 \rightarrow 2C_2H_5OH + 2CO_2$ (+ energy)

d This is the amount of oxygen needed to convert the lactic acid produced during a period of anaerobic exercise in the muscles to carbon dioxide and water with the release of energy.

e When exercise begins the heart and breathing increase to bring more oxygen into the body. The capacity of the heart and lungs will be bigger in a fit individual than in an unfit person, and so the breathing and heart rate will not increase as much as a fit person can bring more air into the body and pump more oxygenated blood around the body with each breath or heartbeat than an unfit individual. The muscles of a fit individual will be bigger with a better blood supply than the muscles of an unfit individual, so they will contract more efficiently and use aerobic respiration for longer. So a fit individual will build up a smaller oxygen debt than an unfit individual for the same amount of exercise, and will be able to convert the lactic acid to carbon dioxide and water faster as they bring more oxygen into their body.

6 a Aerobic respiration produces more energy to allow the muscles to contract more efficiently, so athletes want it to continue as long as possible before changing to less efficient anaerobic respiration.

b Red blood cells carry oxygen to the tissues, so if you have more red blood cells, you have more oxygen so aerobic respiration continues longer and muscles work more effectively.

c It increases the red blood cells in the body just before a performance and so allows more oxygen to be carried to the working muscles.

d They start anaerobic respiration where glucose is incompletely broken down to form lactic acid. Less energy is produced and the lactic acid can cause muscle fatigue.

Answers to end of chapter examination-style questions

1 a A = intercostal muscles (1); B = bronchi (1); C = diaphragm (1)

b Any five from the following (must be in correct order):
The intercostal muscles contract (1) and the ribcage is pulled up and out (1). The diaphragm contracts (1), which causes it to flatten (1). This increases the volume in the thorax (1), so the pressure decreases (1), pulling air in/air pushed in from the atmosphere where the pressure is now greater/there is greater atmospheric pressure (1).

2 a Rounded/bubble shape (1) gives maximum surface area (1). Because walls are only one-cell thick/there are thin cells lining alveolus and/or capillary (1) this gives shorter diffusion path/there is a short distance for gases to diffuse (1). Allow – layer of water lining alveolus (1) to dissolve oxygen molecules (1). (Maximum of 4 marks)

b Fresh air with more oxygen is continually brought into alveolus by ventilation/breathing in (1). Blood in capillary is continually moving away taking oxygen with it (1).

c i Glucose (1), water (1), $C_6H_{12}O_6$ (1), $6H_2O$ (1) (Ignore energy)

ii Mitochondria (1)

iii Muscle cells require a lot of energy to contract (1), and mitochondria are the cell parts where energy is released in aerobic respiration. (1)

3 a When exercising, muscle cells need to contact more (1) so more energy is supplied from aerobic respiration (1). This means the muscle cells need to be supplied with more oxygen and glucose via the bloodstream (1). The heart beats faster to pump blood to the cells more quickly (1). Breathing rate (and depth of breaths) increases so that more air goes into the lungs (1), so oxygen diffuses quicker into the bloodstream. (1) (Maximum of 5 marks)

b 115–90 = 25 beats per minute (1)

c Lactic acid (1), because her muscle cells have run out of oxygen and are respiring anaerobically (1).

d Student B was fitter. She had a lower resting heart rate which rose to a lower maximum (1). She had a much quicker recovery time for her heart rate to reach the resting level again (1).
Student B had a lower resting breathing rate which did not rise as high as student A (1). Her breathing rate returned to normal much quicker (1). Student B did not complain of pain, so her muscles were probably not respiring anaerobically (1), meaning her lung and heart capacity was greater and could supply enough oxygen (1). (Maximum of 5 marks)

4 Marks awarded for this answer will be determined by the Quality of Written Communication (QWC) as well as the standard of the scientific response.

• There is a clear description of most of the features of a normal lung which must be copied and at least two advantages of the artificial lung. The answer shows almost faultless spelling, punctuation and grammar. It is coherent and in an organised, logical sequence. It contains a range of appropriate or relevant specialist terms used accurately. (5–6 marks)

• There is a description of at least three features of a normal lung which must be copied and at least one advantage of the artificial lung. There are some errors in spelling, punctuation and grammar. The answer has some structure and organisation. The use of specialist terms has been attempted, but not always accurately. (3–4 marks)

• There is a description of at least two features of the lung which must be copied and at least one advantage of the artificial lung. The spelling, punctuation and grammar are very weak. The answer is poorly organised with almost no specialist terms and/or use demonstrating a general lack of understanding of their meaning. (1–2 marks)

• No relevant content. (0 marks)

Examples of biology points made in the response:
• large surface area
• method of removing carbon dioxide
• thin membrane
• method of filtering the air going in/ventilation described
• no need for tissue matching
• no operation needed
• few lungs become available
• no need for (immunosuppressant) drugs
• reference to ethics involved with transplants.

5 a Glucose (1) → carbon dioxide (1) + ethanol (1) (*Ignore energy*)
b Carbon dioxide (1) as it is a gas and will form bubbles (1).
c i 40 °C (1)
ii Anaerobic respiration in yeasts is controlled by enzyme(s) (1). At 0 °C enzymes are inactive (1) so no carbon dioxide is produced and the volume does not increase (1). 40 °C is the optimum temperature so there is most activity and volume increase (1). By 60 °C/80 °C/ higher temperatures, the enzyme(s) have been denatured (1), so there is no volume increase (1). (*Maximum of 5 marks*)

5 Human biology – circulation and digestion

5.1

1 Most of the cells of the body are too far away from the air or even from the lungs to be able to get oxygen and get rid of their waste carbon dioxide by diffusion. They are also too far from the digestive system to be able to get the food they need by diffusion, and from the excretory organs to get rid of waste products. This is why people need a circulatory system. The blood carries everything that is needed by the cells and is carried close to every cell in the body in the capillary network, so food and oxygen can pass into the cells by diffusion along a concentration gradient. Waste products diffuse from the cells into the blood along a concentration gradient. The circulation of the blood by the pumping of the heart means substances are constantly renewed or removed which maintains the steep concentration gradients into and out of the cells. Any other sensible points.

2 Blood carried from heart to lungs is deoxygenated blood from the body, so it is dark (purply) red until it picks up oxygen again in the lungs. It is called an artery because it carries blood leaving the heart.

3 Vena cava, right atrium, atrium contracts, blood through valve, right ventricle, ventricle contracts, blood out through valves into pulmonary artery, to lungs where blood is oxygenated, back to heart through pulmonary vein, through valve into left atrium, left atrium contracts, blood through valve into left ventricle, left ventricle contracts, blood through valve into aorta, round body.

4 a Blood enters the atria of the heart (the top chambers). Deoxygenated blood comes into the right atrium from the body through the vena cava. Oxygenated blood from the lungs comes into the left atrium through the pulmonary vein. The atria contract together and force blood down into the larger lower chambers, the ventricles. Valves close to stop the blood flowing backwards as the ventricles contract. The right ventricle sends deoxygenated blood to the lungs in the pulmonary artery. The left ventricle pumps oxygenated blood around the body in the aorta. As the blood leaves the heart, more valves close to prevent it flowing backwards.
b i The heart valves prevent the blood flowing backwards into the chambers they have just left, which makes the heart more efficient.
ii The coronary arteries supply the heart muscle with oxygenated blood so that they can respire aerobically and contract efficiently.
iii The thickened muscle of the left ventricle wall allows the heart to pump the blood all around the body very efficiently as it can pump harder than the right side, which only has to send blood to the lungs.

5.2

1 It is controlled by a group of cells called the sinoatrial node found in the right atrium of the heart, which act as a natural pacemaker. It produces a regular electrical signal that spreads through the heart and makes it contract.

2 An artificial pacemaker is a device which can be implanted into the chest and which sends regular electrical signals to the heart to stimulate it to contract and beat. If the heart is beating normally the artificial pacemaker doesn't do anything, but if the heart rhythm changes then the pacemaker kicks in and sends regular signals to the heart again. Some pacemakers can even measure additional demands during exercise and increase the heart rate to compensate.

3 Artificial hearts can be used to keep a patient alive until a suitable heart for transplant becomes available. In some cases they can be used to rest the heart of a patient and give it chance to recover. Eventually they may be used to replace the natural heart over the long term.

4 [Award marks for well-argued points backed by evidence where possible.]

5.3

1 a Artery – blood vessel that carries blood away from the heart; has pulse from blood forced through them from the heart beat; have a small lumen and thick walls of muscle and elastic fibres.
b Vein – blood vessel that carries blood towards the heart; no pulse; valves to keep blood flowing in the right direction; large lumen; relatively thin walls.
c Capillary – very tiny vessel with narrow lumen and walls one-cell thick, so ideal for diffusion of substances in and out.

2 a [Make sure students' diagrams show the capillary network between arteries and veins and link the arteries and veins to the heart.]
b [These should be labelled: heart, lungs, artery to lungs, capillaries in lungs, vein to heart, artery to body, capillaries in organs of the body, vein to heart.]

3 a A stent is a metal mesh which is placed in an artery and opened up by the inflation of a tiny balloon. The stent holds a narrowed blood vessel open so the blood can flow freely.
b Stent advantages: no anaesthetic, relatively cheap, effective. Stent disadvantages: can't open the most blocked or narrowed arteries. Bypass advantages: very effective against severe blockages. Bypass disadvantages: needs general anaesthetic, more expensive.

4 a Valves prevent the backflow of blood in the heart. If a valve does not close properly blood can flow backwards, which means that the full amount of blood does not leave the heart and the blood coming into a heart chamber mixes with blood that hasn't left, so the heart cannot pump as effectively as it should.
b Doctors can operate on the heart and replace a leaky valve with either a mechanical valve made of titanium and plastic or a biological valve, which are based on valves taken from the hearts of pigs or cattle.

	Advantages	Disadvantages
Mechanical valve	Lasts a very long time, works well	Need to take medication to prevent clotting for the rest of life, open-heart surgery
Biological valve	Works extremely well, no medication needed	Has to be replaced after about 15 years

5.4

1 Any three from: transporting oxygen from the lungs to the cells of the body; transporting carbon dioxide from the cells of the body to the lungs; transporting digested food molecules from the gut to the cells; transporting urea from the liver to the kidneys; transporting the white blood cells of the immune system around the body; any other sensible point.

2 a Blood plasma is a yellow liquid with cells suspended in it.
b Red blood cells.
c Any three from: transports waste products, digested food, carbon dioxide, blood cells, hormones.

3 White blood cells form antibodies and actively digest microorganisms. Platelets help with clotting, which keeps the microorganisms out.

5.5

1 An antigen is a protein on the surface of the cell which is unique to that individual. An antibody is a protein made in the white blood cells in response to a foreign antigen.

2 a The cells have no antigens so they do no stimulate an immune response from other individuals regardless of their blood group. So blood group O can be given to anyone.
b People with blood group O have both antibody a and b in their blood so they can only be given blood group O otherwise agglutination will take place.

3 It is necessary to match the antigens on the surface of the cells of the donor organ as closely as possible to the antigens on the surface of the cells of the person receiving the transplant to minimise the risk of rejection of the transplanted organ due to an immune response by the white cells.

4

Artificial organ	Transplant
In theory machines available to everyone, but in most cases tied to hospital while attached to artificial heart	Need donor, often not available
No problem with tissue matching	Need tissue match
Usually only a short-term solution until transplant available or heart recovers	Further surgery usually needed eventually as donor heart doesn't last forever
Expensive over the long term	After surgery, relatively low cost of medicine
Only with modern 'portable' hearts can lead anything like normal life and still very limited	Can lead relatively normal life

5.6

1

Enzyme	Where it is made	Reaction catalysed	Where it works
Amylase	Salivary glands, pancreas, small intestine	Starch → sugars/glucose	Mouth, small intestine
Protease	Stomach, pancreas, small intestine	Proteins → amino acids	Stomach, small intestine
Lipase	Pancreas, small intestine	Lipids → fatty acids and glycerol	Small intestine

2 Large insoluble molecules in food cannot be absorbed into the blood so have to be digested to form small insoluble molecules that can be absorbed.

5.7

1 a Acidic conditions
  b Hydrochloric acid is made in glands in the stomach.
  c Alkaline/alkali
  d The liver produces bile that is stored in the gall bladder and released when food comes into the small intestine.

2 [Marks for a good diagram showing a large fat droplet coated in bile splitting into many small fat droplets.] This produces a larger surface area so enzymes can get to many more fat molecules and break them down more quickly.

3 Bread is mainly carbohydrate, butter is a lipid and egg has large amounts of protein.
All food taken into the mouth and chewed (physically broken up) and coated in saliva to make it easier to swallow and to start the digestion of starch using amylase from the salivary glands.
Food swallowed down the oesophagus.
Stomach muscles churn the food and mix it with digestive juices – protease enzymes (pepsin) to break down proteins to amino acids and hydrochloric acid to give the acid pH needed for pepsin to work at its best.
Food squirted out of the stomach into the first part of the small intestine (duodenum). Bile added from gall bladder to emulsify fats and give a bigger surface area for digestive enzymes to work on. It also neutralises the acid from the stomach and gives an alkaline pH, which is needed for the enzymes from the pancreas to work at their best.
In the duodenum (first part of the small intestine), digestive enzymes are added from the pancreas – amylase breaks down starch (carbohydrates) to glucose, proteases break down protein to amino acids and lipases break down lipids to give fatty acids and glycerol.
Semi-digested food squeezed on by peristalsis to the rest of the small intestine. Amylase, proteases and lipases are made in the wall of the small intestine. The lining is covered with villi giving a large surface area so the products of digestion can be absorbed into the blood stream as efficiently as possible.
The remains of the sandwich, which cannot be digested, pass into the large intestine. Here water is removed. What is left is the faeces and these are passed out of the body through the anus.
Any other sensible points.

Answers to end of chapter summary questions

1 a Not enough blood is pumped out of the heart into the circulation so the patient will suffer from a lack of oxygen. Because the heart never empties properly it will not pump as efficiently.
  b The gap in the centre of the heart allows the oxygenated blood on the left of the heart to become mixed with the deoxygenated blood on the right side of the heart. This means that the blood pumped around the body is not fully oxygenated so the baby will suffer the symptoms of lack of oxygen – lack of energy, blue colour, etc.
  c The coronary arteries supply the oxygen needed by the heart muscle to beat and pump blood around the body. If they are narrowed or blocked then not enough oxygen reaches the heart muscle so it cannot contract properly or may die. This is particularly noticeable when a person exercises and their heart needs more oxygen as it needs to beat harder and faster. If the heart cannot pump properly, not enough oxygen gets to the body either.

2 a They will have fewer red blood cells than normal so cannot carry so much oxygen in their blood so their muscles will get less oxygen. This is likely to mean they will perform poorly and develop a much bigger oxygen debt than usual.
  b They will not be able to produce haemoglobin, the red pigment that is found in the red blood cells which carries oxygen around in the body. As a result, the person may become anaemic – lacking in red blood cells and tired and weak because their blood cannot carry the oxygen they need.

3 a A stent is a metal mesh which is placed in an artery and opened up by the inflation of a tiny balloon. The stent holds a narrowed blood vessel open so the blood can flow freely.
  b Stents, because the percentage of patients dying or having a heart attack or stroke was substantially lower after stents were fitted than after bypass surgery.
  c Whether the type of patients who were given stents were at exactly the same stage of illness/had the same number of risk factors for future illness as the patients given bypass surgery; whether the patients were all treated at the same hospital or at different hospitals, by the same doctors or different doctors, etc.; any sensible suggestion.

4 a Whether one blood group can receive a blood donation of another blood group without undergoing agglutination.
  b i If the wrong blood group is given, the blood of the patient will clot and agglutinate. This can block the blood vessels and cause death.
  ii The same as in blood transfusions plus the need for the tissue match of donor and recipient to be as close as possible and blood group is an important aspect of that.
In an organ transplant, patients are given immunosuppressant drugs which stop the immune response and so the wrong blood group type would not result in a damaging reaction. In a normal blood transfusion this doesn't happen, so if the groups are wrong the blood will agglutinate.

5 a [Award marks for clearly labelled axes, correct axes, accurate plotting of points on graph etc.]
  b Alkaline
  c Probably found in the duodenum (first part of the small intestine) where alkaline bile is added to the contents to neutralise the stomach acid and give an alkaline pH for the action of the pancreatic enzymes.

Answers to end of chapter examination-style questions

1 a i Right atrium (1)
  ii pulmonary artery (1)
  iii pulmonary vein (1)
  iv aorta (1)
  b To prevent the blood flowing back (into the left atrium) (1)
  c Advantages: smaller; does not get in the way; less likely to be damaged *(Maximum of 2 marks)*
Disadvantages: needs operation to insert/remove; harder to check/change battery *(Maximum of 2 marks)*

2 a Helps defend the body against pathogens/engulfs pathogens/produces antibodies against pathogens (1).
  b Starts the clotting mechanism at a wound site (1).
  c Absorbed by diffusion in lungs (1); binds to haemoglobin in red cells to form oxyhaemoglobin (1); splits from haemoglobin in tissues and diffuses into cells (1).
  d Any two from: urea (1); waste product from liver to kidneys for removal (1); carbon dioxide (1); waste product from cells to lungs for removal (1); soluble food molecules/glucose/amino acids/fatty acids/glycerol(1); from gut to cells/liver (1).

3 a A unique/specific protein on the surface of a cell (1).
  b Tissue typing (1); immunosuppressant drugs (1).
  c A, because her cells have the A antigen (1) and so her body recognises the new cells as 'self' (1); O, because the new cells have no antigen (1), so her body will react against them (1).

4 a i A = Large intestine (1), B = pancreas (1), C = gall bladder (1), D = stomach (1)
  ii D (1); C (1); B (1) and D (1); A (1).
  b Marks awarded for this answer will be determined by the Quality of Written Communication (QWC) as well as the standard of the scientific response.
Scientific points:
  • salivary amylase and/or pancreatic amylase and/or small intestine amylase break down insoluble starch into soluble sugars/glucose
  • stomach/pancreatic/small intestine protease breaks down insoluble proteins into soluble amino acids
  • pancreatic/small intestine lipase breaks down insoluble fats/lipids into soluble fatty acids and glycerol
  • the small soluble molecules can be absorbed into the blood from the small intestine. *(6 marks maximum)*

5 a Any two from: temperature of test tubes; volume of solution; volume of A and B protease; concentration of A and B protease. (2)
  b Repeated the investigation/repeat each test three times and take a mean/repeat and discard any anomalous results. (1)
  c Optimum activity of enzyme A is pH 10 (1); optimum pH of B is 2 (1).
  d Enzyme B must be pepsin (1) because stomach is acid/has a pH of about 2 (1). Enzyme A must be trypsin (1) as pancreatic enzymes work best at alkaline pH/pH of 8–9 (1).

6 Marks awarded for this answer will be determined by the Quality of Written Communication (QWC) as well as the standard of the scientific response.
- There is a clear, balanced and detailed description of the roles of both the liver and pancreas. The answer shows almost faultless spelling, punctuation and grammar. It is coherent and in an organised, logical sequence. It contains a range of appropriate or relevant specialist terms used accurately. (5–6 marks)
- There is some description of the roles of both the liver and pancreas which lacks some details. There are some errors in spelling, punctuation and grammar. The answer has some structure and organisation. The use of specialist terms has been attempted, but not always accurately. (3–4 marks)
- There is a brief description reference to the role of either the liver or pancreas. The spelling, punctuation and grammar are very weak. The answer is poorly organised with almost no specialist terms and/or their use demonstrating a general lack of understanding of their meaning. (1–2 marks)
- No relevant content. (0 marks)

Examples of biology points made in the response:
- liver produces bile
- bile neutralises acid
- acid produced by stomach
- pancreas produces lipase
- lipase is an enzyme
- lipase works best in neutral/alkaline conditions
- lipase catalyses the breakdown of fat
- to fatty acids and glycerol
- allow reference to, or a description of emulsification.

6 Nervous coordination

6.1

1 a To take in information from the environment around you and coordinate the response of the body so you can react to your surroundings.
b A neurone is a single nerve cell, a nerve is a bundle of hundreds or thousands of neurones.
c A sensory neurone carries impulses from your sense organs to the central nervous system, a motor neurone carries information from the CNS to the effector organs – muscles and glands – of your body.
2 [Marks awarded for table showing receptors for light, sound, position, smell (could also have temperature, pain, pressure) with student example of a stimulus for each one.]
3 Light from the fruit is detected by the sensory receptors in the eyes, an impulse travels along the sensory neurone to the brain, information is processed in the brain and an impulse is sent along a motor neurone to the muscles of the arm and hand so you pick up the fruit and put it in your mouth. [Give credit if students add anything further, e.g. sensory impulses from mouth/nose to brain with information about taste, smell of fruit, touch sensors send impulses about presence of fruit, motor impulses to muscles for chewing, etc.]

6.2

1 a They enable you to avoid damage and danger because they happen very fast. They control many of the vital functions of the body, such as breathing, without the need for conscious thought.
b It would slow the process down so would not be so effective at preventing damage. It would be very difficult to consciously control breathing, heart rate, digestion, etc., and still be able to do anything else.
2 Reflex actions to operate automatically, even when you are asleep, so cannot rely on conscious thought processes, unlike speaking and eating, which we choose when to do.
3 Stimulus → receptor → sensory neurone → synapse → chemical message → relay neurone → synapse → chemical message → motor neurone → muscles in leg lift the foot.

6.3

1 a Millions of interconnected neurones arranged in different regions to carry out different functions.
b Because it takes in all the sensory information and coordinates the responses as well as allowing conscious thought, intelligence, emotions, etc.
2 a Cerebral cortex – consciousness, intelligence, memory and language.
Cerebellum – coordinating muscular activity and balance.
Medulla – controls unconscious activities such as gut movements and breathing.

b Cerebral cortex involved with intelligence, memory and language. Apes are more intelligent, have better memories and have a more complex social structure than rats and mice, and this is made possible by the larger cerebral cortex. Humans have higher intelligence and memory than apes, and are the only animals with full verbal language, which has developed with the evolution of bigger cerebral cortexes to deal with all the additional information.
3 Studying people with brain damage – can be very useful but no control over which areas damaged; don't know what else is involved if caused by disease; any sensible point.
Electrical stimulation of different parts of the brain – this has been done on animals and people during surgery and has allowed scientists to see which areas of the brain are associated with hunger, thirst, anger, etc. MRI scans allow images to be taken of the brain in living people to see which areas – if any – are damaged. More recently new scanning techniques allow us to see images of the brain as someone carries out a simple task and so identify which areas of the brain are being used to control it.

Answers to end of chapter summary questions

1 a F
b C
c D
d B
e A
f E
2 a It enables you to react to your surroundings and to coordinate your behaviour.
b i Eye
ii Ear
iii Skin
iv Skin
c Diagram of reflex arc. The explanation needs to include the following points: reference to three types of neurone: a sensory neurone; a motor neurone; a relay neurone. The relay neurone is found in the CNS, often in the spinal cord. An electrical impulse passes from the sensory receptor, along the sensory neurone to the CNS. It then passes to a relay neurone and straight back along a motor neurone to the effector organ (usually a muscle in a reflex). This is known as the 'reflex arc'. The junction between one neurone and the next is known as a 'synapse'. The time between the stimulus and the reflex action is as short as possible. This allows you to react to danger without thinking about it.
3 a X is a sensory neurone, Y is a motor neurone.
b A neurone is an individual nerve cell, a nerve is a bundle of many neurones – it may be all sensory neurones, all motor neurones or a mixture.
c

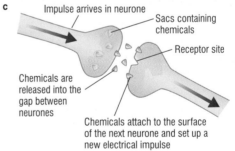

Impulse arrives in neurone
Sacs containing chemicals
Receptor site
Chemicals are released into the gap between neurones
Chemicals attach to the surface of the next neurone and set up a new electrical impulse

d Your neurones are not joined up directly to each other. There are junctions between them called synapses, which form physical gaps between the neurones. The electrical impulses travelling along your neurones have to cross these synapses. They cannot leap the gap. When the impulse reaches the synapse, sacs containing special chemicals release the chemicals into the gap between the two neurones. The chemical molecules are picked up on receptor sites on the membrane of the next neurone on the other side of the synapse. This sets up a new electrical impulse in the next neurone.
4 a Region C is the medulla which controls many basic functions such as breathing, heart rate and the movements of the gut. If this area is destroyed the person can not longer breathe, etc., and so they die.
b Area B is the cerebellum. This area of the brain controls balance and coordination so if it is damaged you would expect the person to fall over/have problems with balance and become very clumsy and uncoordinated.
c Area A is the cerebral cortex, which covers the brain and is involved in many different things including intelligence, emotions and memory. The effect on the patient will depend on exactly which area is damaged, but could include memory loss, loss of intelligence, change in emotional responses, etc.

5 Studying dead brains allowed scientists to map and identify different areas of the brain. Then they could correlate damage in certain areas (discovered after death) to behaviour in life. MRI scans allowed scientists to confirm their mapping. It also made it possible to identify damaged areas of the brain, such as those damaged by a stroke or traumatic injury, and relate them to the impact on the behaviour of the living patient. Modern MRI scans allow scientists to see which areas of the healthy brain appear to be active when someone carries out a particular task, so it lets them see how the brain works normally.

Answers to end of chapter examination-style questions

1 a X – Cerebral cortex (1); Y – Cerebellum (1); Z – Medulla (1)
  b i Electrical stimulation (1); MRI (scanning) (1)
  ii Loss of (some) muscular coordination (1)
2 a Receptor (1), relay neurone (1), motor neurone (1), response (1)
  b Stimulus = hot saucepan/heat/high temperature (1); Effector = (arm) muscle (1)
  c i When the (electrical) impulse reaches the synapse it causes a chemical substance to be released (1), which diffuses across the gap and causes an impulse to be initiated/triggered/started in the next neurone (1).
  ii Central nervous system (allow brain, spinal cord) (1).
  d 1.2/0.02 = 60 metres per second (*2 marks for correct answer, even if no working shown. If answer is incorrect allow 1 mark for 1.2/0.02*)
3 a Independent variable = number of frames it took the hammer to move to the knee/speed of hammer (1); dependent variable = distance moved by lower leg (1); control variable = distance hammer moved (1)
  b Can measure very short times/fast speeds (1); keeps a permanent record (1).
  c Repeating the trial and calculating means (1).
  d The faster the speed of the hammer the greater the movement (1), up to a maximum of 10 cm movement (1).

7 Homeostasis

7.1

1 a Chemical substances that coordinate many body processes. Made by endocrine glands and secreted directly into the blood stream. They are carried to their target organs in the blood.
  b Hormones: chemical, made by glands and carried in the blood stream, often relatively slow response, often act over a long period of time. Nerves: electrical, impulses travel in neurones, very fast response, act instantly.
2 a To stop too much water moving in or out of cells, damaging and destroying them.
  b Because the enzymes work best at 37 °C.
  c Because blood sugar that is too high or too low causes problems in the body.
3 a i Losing water through sweating.
  ii Losing salt through sweating.
  iii Temperature going up with exercising.
  b Sweating cools you down and helps to keep the body temperature constant – a costume makes you sweat more (as you get hotter), which means you lose more water – but also makes it harder for sweat to evaporate (so you don't cool so effectively). Also, a costume is heavy so it's harder work to run.

7.2

1 a Carbon dioxide: formed during aerobic respiration:
glucose + oxygen → energy + carbon dioxide + water
Urea: excess amino acids from protein/worn out tissues; amino group removed from amino acids and converted to urea in the liver.
  b Both are poisonous to the cells/damage the body.
  c Carbon dioxide removed in the lungs.
Urea removed by the kidneys.
2 a The waste product formed when excess amino acids are broken down in the liver.
  b Excess amino acids carried to the liver in the blood stream. The liver removes the amino group from the amino acids in a process called deamination. This initially forms ammonia, which is converted into urea. It is passed into the blood and carried to the kidneys to be excreted.
  c Involved in a number of processes which help to maintain a steady internal state in the body, e.g. deamination of excess amino acids to form urea; detoxifying poisonous substances such as ethanol and paracetamol so the levels do not build up in the blood; passing the breakdown products into the blood to be excreted; breaking down worn out red blood cells and storing the iron until it is needed again; any other sensible suggestion.

3 [Look for as many accurate points and connections as possible.]

7.3

1 a To filter out urea; to balance the water and salt level of blood.
  b They filter the blood – sugar, mineral ions, amino acids, urea and water are filtered out of the blood into the kidney tubule and then selectively reabsorbed as the liquid travels along the tubule. All of the sugar is taken back into the blood but the amounts of mineral ions and water vary with the needs of the body. Some urea returns to the blood along a concentration gradient.
2 Processed food often contains high levels of salt. Salt affects the concentration of the body fluids. The kidney is involved in balancing the levels of salt in the body and if salt levels go up the kidneys remove salt and excrete them in the urine.
3 a Your blood would become diluted. The kidneys would retain all but the excess salt and lose a lot of water, so you would produce a lot of very dilute urine.
  b Your kidneys would conserve both salt (because you are losing it in sweat) and water, so you would produce small quantities of very concentrated urine.

7.4

1 a Because kidneys remove toxins such as urea from the body and maintain the correct salt and water balance of the body fluids. If levels of urea build up or the water and salt balance of the body is not maintained, it can cause damage to the cells so they no longer function properly and this can lead to death.
  b Diffusion along a concentration gradient.
2 Blood out of artery → through pump → blood thinners added to prevent clotting → blood passes through dialysis membranes and excess salt and urea are removed → clean blood into bubble trap → blood returns to vein in an arm.
3 a People with kidney failure cannot remove excess salt or get rid of the urea produced by the breakdown of excess amino acids.
  b The excess salt and urea are removed during the process of dialysis.
4 a There is no urea, so a steep concentration gradient exists from the blood to the dialysis fluid.
Normal plasma levels of salt, glucose, etc., are present, so there is no net loss or gain due to diffusion.
  b To help maintain concentration gradients for diffusion.

7.5

1 a The transplanted kidney takes on the functions of the failed kidneys, balances the blood chemistry and gets rid of urea.
  b If one identical twin acts as a living donor for the other twin. They are genetically identical so have the same antigens on their cells so there is no risk of a rejection reaction as the recipient will recognise the donor tissue as its own.
2 a Live organs have no tissue damage; family donors are a close tissue match.
  b Taking organs from a living healthy person can threaten their health, so it is a big step to take.

3

Dialysis	Transplant
Machines available	Need donor, often not available
No problem with tissue matching	Need tissue match
Twice a week at least, for life	Surgery every ten years or more
Expensive long term	After surgery, relatively low cost of medicine
Always have to watch diet, spend time on dialysis machine, etc.	Can lead relatively normal life

[Preferable treatment personal choice, but must be justified by rational argument.]

7.6

1 a This is the temperature at which enzymes work best.
  b Above around 40 °C the enzymes which are made of protein start to denature. This means the shape of the active sites change and the enzymes can no longer catalyse the reactions of the cell so the cells die. This quickly results in death of the whole organism and is irreversible. Below 35 °C the reactions of the body slow down even with enzymes catalysing them and they cannot take place fast enough to maintain life.
2 a The thermoregulatory centre in the brain is sensitive to the temperature of the blood flowing through it. It also receives information about the skin temperature from receptors in the skin and coordinates the body responses to keep the core temperature at 37 °C.
  b Temperature sensors in the skin send impulses to the thermoregulatory centre in the brain giving information about the temperature of the skin and the things it touches. This is important for

maintaining the core temperature because if the external surroundings and the skin are cold, the body will tend to conserve heat to keep the core temperature up, and vice versa.

3 If core temperature increases, to lower body temperature: blood vessels supplying capillaries in skin dilate; more blood in capillaries so more heat is lost, more sweat produced by sweat glands, which cools the body as it evaporates. If core temperature decreases, to raise body temperature: blood vessels supplying blood to skin capillaries constrict; less blood transported to surface of skin so less heat is lost, shivering occurs by rapid muscle movement, which needs respiration – releasing heat energy.

7.7

1 Hormone: a chemical message carried in the blood which causes a change in the body.
Insulin: a hormone made in the pancreas which causes glucose to pass from the blood into the cells where it is needed for energy.
Diabetes: a condition when the pancreas cannot make enough insulin to control the blood sugar.
Glycogen: an insoluble carbohydrate stored in the liver.

2 a Blood glucose levels go up above the ideal range. This is detected by the pancreas, which then secretes insulin. Insulin causes the liver to convert glucose to glycogen. This causes glucose to move out of the blood into the cells of the body, thus lowering blood glucose levels. When the blood sugar level falls, glucose is released back into the blood.
If the blood glucose level drops below the ideal range, this is detected by the pancreas. The pancreas secretes glucagon, which causes the liver to convert glycogen into glucose, which increases the blood glucose level.

   b Glucose is needed for cellular respiration, which releases energy for everything. Too much or too little glucose in the blood causes problems.

3 Type 1 diabetes is a condition where the pancreas does not make enough or any insulin. It is treated by injections of insulin to help control blood glucose levels. Your diet needs to be carefully controlled with regular meals and the intake of carbohydrate carefully monitored.
Type 2 diabetes is a condition where either the pancreas does not make enough insulin or your body does not react properly to the insulin than is produced. Type 2 diabetes is linked to obesity, old age and a lack of exercise. It can be treated by improving the diet, the amount of exercise and losing weight as well as insulin injections.

7.8

1 a People with type 1 diabetes need insulin injections but they also need to monitor and control their food intake carefully.

   b Type 2 diabetes can often be treated and controlled or even cured by eating a carefully controlled balanced diet, losing weight and taking regular exercise. Because it can be caused by too little insulin being produced or by the cells becoming insensitive to insulin, it can also sometimes be treated by drugs that help the insulin the body makes have a bigger effect on the body cells, help the pancreas make more insulin or reduce the amount of glucose absorbed from the gut. If none of these treatments work, the patient will have to use insulin.

2 a Original – from pancreases of cattle and pigs used for meat; no control over quantities as used what was available from slaughterhouses; not exactly the same chemically.
Modern – produced by genetically modified bacteria; exact quantity and quality control; exactly the same as naturally occurring human insulin.
Genetically modified insulin is better as it is a match for the natural hormone and both quantity and quality of the product can be controlled to give better glucose control.

   b Insulin treatment widely available; patient deals with it themselves; relatively cheap, etc.
Pancreatic transplant is a good idea but complex surgery; high risk; expensive; patients have to be on immunosuppressant drugs for the rest of their lives; needs repeating eventually; not enough donors. These are the reasons why it is not more widely used.

Answers to end of chapter summary questions

1 a The maintenance of a constant internal environment, for example in terms of a constant core temperature, the water and ion content of the body and the blood glucose levels.

   b For cells to work properly they need to be at the right temperature (so enzymes work optimally); they need to be surrounded by the correct concentration of water and mineral ions in the blood so osmosis doesn't cause problems; they need glucose to provide energy and they need waste products to be removed as build up can change pH or poison systems. This is why the body systems must be controlled within fairly narrow limits.

2 a i
ii
iii
b

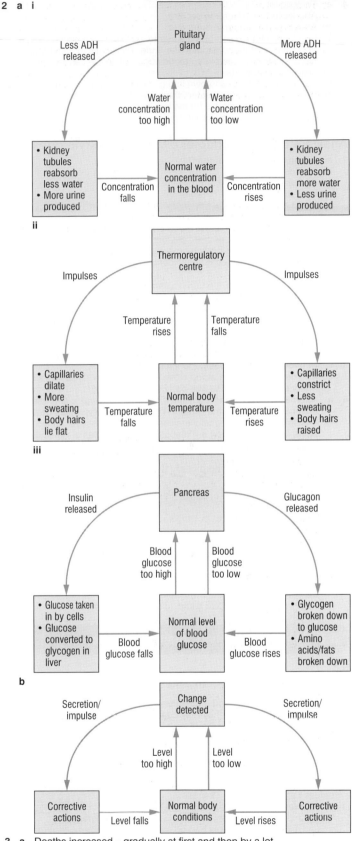

3 a Deaths increased – gradually at first and then by a lot.
   b Around 25 °C.
   c When very hot (often humid), sweat doesn't evaporate to cool people down; people lose a lot of water by sweating so become dehydrated and therefore can't sweat and cool down; exercise in heat generates heat in muscles; body can't get rid of it by sweating, etc.; any sensible points.

4 a They go up.
  b About 60–120 milligrams per litre.
  c About 50–310 milligrams per litre.
  d Insulin injections keep blood sugar levels within a reasonable range; prevent loss of blood sugar in the urine; allow cells to take up glucose etc. Limitations – can't keep blood sugar within the narrow range of natural insulin control.
  e Carbohydrates broken down into glucose (blood sugar), so the more carbohydrate-rich food eaten, the higher the blood sugar levels will climb and the harder it is for the insulin injections to maintain safe and healthy levels of blood sugar.

Answers to end of chapter examination-style questions

1 a Receptor(s) (1), effector(s) (1)
  b i Nose/tongue (1)
    ii Ear (1)
    iii Eye (1)
    iv Skin (1)
  c By a nerve impulse to a muscle to contract (1); by causing a gland to secrete a hormone into the blood (1).
2 a Homeostasis (1)
  b Any three from: core body temperature, water content of body, ion content of body, blood glucose concentration (3).
  c i Brain (1)
    ii Pancreas (1)
3 a i Thermoregulatory centre (allow thermoregulation centre/hypothalamus) (1).
    ii It has receptors (1) (ignore receptors in skin) that detect changes in the temperature of the blood/plasma (1).
  b Shivering causes the muscles to contract (1) resulting in increased respiration/more heat released/produced (1).
  c i Blood vessels/arteries/arterioles dilate/widen (1).
    ii There will be more blood close to/near surface (1) so more heat is lost/heat is lost faster/the body cools faster (1).
4 a All small molecules (accept list if it contains both waste and useful molecules) pass into the filtrate (1), but large ones such as proteins and lipids do not (1). Useful molecules (accept glucose, amino acids, some ions, some water) are reabsorbed (1), but waste molecules (accept urea, water, ions, poisons) are passed into urine. (1)
  b i Brain (1)
    ii ADH (anti-diuretic hormone) (1)
    iii Pituitary (1)
  c Marks awarded for this answer will be determined by the Quality of Written Communication (QWC) as well as the standard of the scientific response.
    Scientific points:
    As it was hot the worker sweated a lot so the water content of his blood fell. This was detected in the brain and the pituitary gland released ADH. The ADH caused the kidneys to reabsorb more water, so his urine was low volume and concentrated. After he drank the water the water content of his blood went up, so the brain caused the pituitary to stop making ADH, so less water was reabsorbed by the kidney and the urine was higher in volume and dilute. (6 marks maximum)

8 Defending ourselves against disease

8.1
1 a Microorganisms known as pathogens. Pathogens include bacteria and viruses.
  b Bacteria may make you ill as a result of the toxins they produce as they divide rapidly or they may cause direct damage to your cells. Viruses take over the cells of your body as they reproduce, damaging and destroying cells, which is how they cause disease.
  c Pathogens make you ill as a result of the way your body reacts to the toxins they make or the cell damage they cause.
2 Any sensible suggestions should be accepted, such as: wiping work surfaces, cleaning toilets, using tissues to blow nose, washing hands before handling food, for example:
3 Any sensible points e.g.
  • Pathogens are very small so until the development of microscopes people had no way of seeing bacteria or viruses.
  • Because we couldn't see microorganisms it was very difficult to work out or understand how diseases spread.
  • Evidence, such as doctors handwashing reducing the deaths of women after giving birth, was seen as against the Bible, which was very powerful.
  • Still difficult to convince people if their ideas are entrenched, e.g. Barry Marshall attempting to show people that most stomach ulcers are the result of bacterial infections.

8.2
1 a Droplet infection, direct contact, contaminated food and drink, break in the skin.
  b When we cough, sneeze or talk, droplets full of pathogens pass into the air to be breathed in by someone else.
    Pathogens on skin passed to someone else's skin on contact.
    Pathogens taken in on food or in drink.
    Pathogens can get through the barrier of the skin to the tissue underneath.
2 a Pathogens cannot be stopped from getting into cuts.
  b You have not got enough white blood cells to ingest pathogens or to produce antibodies/antitoxins, so pathogens are not destroyed.
3 a Prevents pathogens getting from your hands to the food.
  b Removes pathogens from where they might come into contact with other people or get on your hands.
  c Prevents pathogens from the gut being taken in with drinking water.
4 Explanation to include the ingestion of microorganisms, the production of antibodies and antitoxins.

8.3
1 a A unique protein found on the surface membrane of the cells of any organism.
  b A protein made by white blood cells in response to specific antigens. The antibodies attach themselves to the antigens and destroy the cell/pathogen.
  c Any sensible suggestions, for example: bacterial – TB, tetanus, diphtheria; viral – polio, measles, whooping cough.
2 a Every cell has unique proteins on its surface called 'antigens'. Your immune system recognises that the antigens on the microorganisms that get into your system are different from the ones on your own cells. Your white blood cells then make antibodies to destroy the antigens/pathogens. Once your white blood cells have learnt the right antibody needed to tackle a particular pathogen, they can make that antibody very quickly if the pathogen gets into your system again, and in this way you develop immunity to that disease.
  b A small quantity of dead or inactive pathogen is introduced into your body. This gives your white blood cells the chance to develop the right antibodies against the pathogen without you getting ill. Then, if you meet the live pathogens, your body can respond rapidly, making the right antibodies just as if you had already had the disease.
3 Vaccines can be made using inactive viruses or bacteria so can stimulate antibody production against either type of pathogen, thereby developing immunity.

8.4
1 Paracetamol relieves symptoms/makes you feel better, whereas antibiotics kill the bacteria and actually make you better.
2 a He noticed a clear area around mould growing on bacterial plates.
  b It was difficult to get much penicillin out of the mould and it does not keep easily.
  c Florey and Chain.
3 Viral pathogens reproduce inside your cells, so it is very difficult to develop a drug that destroys them without destroying your cells as well.

8.5
1 Students should show clear understanding of the different stages involved in the development of antibiotic resistance. Colony of bacteria treated with antibiotic 1 → 5% have mutation and survive → the surviving bacteria are treated with antibiotic 2 → 5% have a mutation and are resistant to antibiotic 1 and 2 → etc.
2 a Bacterium
  b MRSA has developed resistance to many antibiotics including methicillin as a result of them being used extensively in hospitals. Increasingly small colonies of antibiotic-resistant bacteria have survived and reproduced until now the majority of Staphylococcus aureus in hospitals are resistant to common antibiotics.
3 a Increased use of antibiotics leading to more resistant bacteria, lower hygiene standards in hospitals, people failing to wash their hands between patients, visitors, etc. Any other sensible point.
  b Possible reasons include: men are more likely to pick up infections than women; men are less likely to wash their hands thoroughly or use the alcohol gel in hospitals as patients or visitors than women; more men die than women; more men go into hospital than women; men are less likely to complete a course of medicine than women and so develop a resistant strain; any other sensible point.
  c A big effort has been made to reduce these infections including: reduction in prescription of antibiotics; treating conditions with very specific antibiotics for the pathogen rather than broad spectrum antibiotics; constant reminders to medical staff to wash hands/use alcohol gel between patients; constant reminders to patients and visitors to wash hands/use alcohol gels on entering and leaving hospitals, doctor's surgeries, wards, etc.; increasing hygiene standards in hospitals; nursing patients affected by antibiotic-resistant strains of bacteria in isolation; any other sensible point.

8.6

1 a To find out more about them. To find out which nutrients they need to grow and to investigate what will affect them and stop them growing.

b Agar jelly is a culture medium containing nutrients. It provides the carbohydrates and other nutrients needed by bacteria, which are grown on it.

2 Using up the available food and oxygen; build up of waste products such as carbon dioxide and other toxins.

3 a Because this reduces the chances of growing microorganisms which might be harmful to people.

b Because at higher temperatures the microorganisms grow much more rapidly.

Answers to end of chapter summary questions

1 a Breathed into the lungs; taken in through the mouth; through cuts and breaks in the skin; any other sensible suggestion.

b They reproduce rapidly and often produce toxins or may damage cells directly. The body's reaction to these situations causes the symptoms of disease.

c Viruses take over the cells of your body as they reproduce, damaging and destroying the cells. This, along with the reaction of the body to the damage, causes the symptoms of disease.

2 a Droplet infection, through contaminated food and drink, by direct contact with someone who has an infection and through cuts and breaks in the skin, which give pathogens on the skin direct access to the body.

b Any sensible suggestions, such as: handwashing after using the toilet, coughing/sneezing into hand/handkerchief, good food hygiene, cooking food properly.

c Alcohol hand gels available at entrance and exit; good hygiene measures – clean offices, toilets, etc.; encourage staff to stay away when ill so don't spread pathogens; good food hygiene in canteen; any other sensible suggestions.

3 a Each time a colony of bacteria are exposed to an antibiotic, some individual bacteria may survive due to genetic mutations unique to them. The population of this resistant strain will steadily increase as the non-resistant strain are killed by the antibiotic. Resistance to vancomycin can develop through this process of natural selection. The pathogen can then spread quickly as patients will not have immunity against the new strain.

b Use antibiotics carefully – only when they are needed – and make sure people always finish the course.

4 a Use sterile Petri dish and agar.
Sterilise the inoculating loop by heating it to red hot in the flame of a Bunsen and then let it cool. Do not put the loop down as it cools.
Innoculate agar with zigzag streaks of bacteria using sterile loop.
Replace the lid on the dish quickly to avoid contamination.
Secure the lid with adhesive tape but do not seal.
Label the culture and incubate at no warmer than 25 °C.

b Include points such as: Inoculate agar plates with bacteria – ideally from school floor.
Add circles of filter paper soaked with different strengths of the disinfectant and incubate at no higher than 25 °C.
Look for areas of clear agar around the disinfectant-soaked disk.
Recommend lowest concentration that destroys the bacteria.

5 The skin covers the body and prevents entry of pathogens; if your skin is cut you bleed, washing pathogens out, and then the blood clots forming a seal over the healing skin and preventing the entry of any pathogens. The breathing system produces sticky mucus, which traps pathogens from the air, and cilia, which move the mucus away from the lungs out of the body or into the stomach. The stomach produces acid, which kills most of the pathogens taken in through. The mouth the white blood cells of the immune system form antibodies against the antigens on any pathogens that get into the body.
Some of the white blood cells of the immune system engulf and digest pathogens.
Some of the white blood cells of the immune system produce antitoxins against the toxins produced by some bacteria so they no longer make you ill.

6 a A vaccine contains a dead or weakened form of a disease-causing pathogen. It works by triggering the body's natural immune responses. A small amount of the vaccine is injected into the body. The white blood cells develop the antibodies needed to destroy the pathogen without you becoming ill. Then, if you take the live pathogens into your body, the immune system can provide the right antibodies very quickly (as if you had had the disease) and destroy the pathogen before it can make you ill.

b Some diseases are so dangerous that you can be dead or permanently damaged before the body has time to develop the right antibodies. These are the diseases you are usually vaccinated against. It is not worth the expense of vaccinating against less serious diseases.

7 a 1998

b It has varied but the general trend has been for it to increase, particularly in the late 2000s.

c It went up dramatically.

d Because initially the majority of children were still vaccinated against measles and mumps. As years passed there was a bigger and bigger population of unvaccinated children who were vulnerable to the diseases.

e i So that the population has herd immunity – when most people are immune to a disease, it cannot spread; this protects the small number of people not vaccinated.

ii Expect it to continue to rise for a few more years perhaps and then gradually fall again as the proportion of the population who are vaccinated continues to rise.

Answers to end of chapter examination-style questions

1 a Pathogens (1)
b Viruses (1)
c Toxins (1)

2 a i Lives inside cells (1)
ii Inactive (1)
iii Antibodies (1)

b i 1950 (1)
ii 8 (years) (1)
iii Any one from: disease could be reintroduced (from abroad); disease would spread if it came back; protection on holiday abroad; high proportion of immune people needed to prevent epidemic (1). (1 mark maximum)

3 a Any **four** from: May already have had the disease (1) so will rapidly produce antibodies/antitoxins against it (1); the bacteria were caught by the sticky mucus (in respiratory tract/trachea/bronchi) (1) and would be wafted up to be swallowed (1) and killed by acid in the stomach (1); there were not enough bacteria (1) and the body destroyed them before they could cause the disease (1). (4 marks maximum)

b Ingesting the bacteria (1) which kills them (1). Producing antibodies (1) which bind to the antigen on the bacteria (1) and removes them. Producing antitoxin (1) which neutralises the toxin (1).

4 a i Defence (accept specific functions of white cells) (1).
ii Forming clot at site of wound (1).
iii 100 ÷ 0.008 (1); equals 12 500 (1) (Correct answer with or without working gains 2 marks; ignore any units)
iv The size of red blood cell is approximately same size as capillary or red blood cell is too big (1); therefore there is no room for more than one cell or only one can fit (1). (Allow use of numbers; do not accept capillaries are narrow)
v In lungs, oxygen diffuses from the alveoli into the blood (1); in the red blood cell, oxygen combines with haemoglobin, forming oxyhaemoglobin (1); in tissues, oxyhaemoglobin splits up, releasing oxygen, which diffuses into the cells (1). (For each mark, whole statement is required)

b i (Student Y) because she had the lower resting heart rate (1); the lower heart rate increase (1) and the quicker recovery time (1). (Accept converse for Student X)
ii When exercising the rate of aerobic respiration in the muscles is higher (1); (the increased heart rate) increases rate of delivery of oxygen to the (respiring) muscles (1); and increases rate of delivery of glucose to the (respiring) muscles (1); and results in faster removal of carbon dioxide and lactic acid (1).

9 Plants as organisms

9.1

1 a CO_2 comes from the air; water from the soil; light energy from the Sun/electric light.

b Carbon dioxide and water from the water it lives in; light from Sun or electric light.

2 From the air into the air spaces in the leaf; into plant cells; into chloroplasts; joined with water to make glucose; converted to starch for storage.

3 When a plant is in the light it carries out photosynthesis. During photosynthesis, the plant makes glucose from carbon dioxide and water using energy from light. This glucose is converted to starch to be stored and used for energy when the plant is in the dark and cannot photosynthesise. Iodine solution turns blue-black in the presence of starch. So carrying out an iodine test on a plant that has been in the light for 24 hours will give a positive blue-black colour for starch because the plant has been photosynthesising for a long time and much of the glucose will have been stored as starch. If the plant is then left in the dark for 24 hours, it cannot photosynthesise and so the cells will use the stored starch for energy. This means there is little or no starch left in the leaves so they do not affect iodine solution.

9.2

1 Carbon dioxide, light and temperature.
2 a i Light levels are low until sunrise, temperature falls overnight.
   ii Carbon dioxide will limit photosynthesis.
   iii Low light levels in winter, days are shorter, temperature colder.
   iv Trees will limit the light, temperature will be warm so carbon dioxide will be limiting.
  b Each case is within the natural environment and light, temperature and carbon dioxide levels can interact meaning that at any time, any one of them may be the limiting factor for photosynthesis.
3 a As light intensity increases, so does the rate of photosynthesis. This tells us that light intensity is a limiting factor.
  b An increase in light intensity has no effect on the rate of photosynthesis, so it is no longer a limiting factor; something else probably is.
  c Temperature acts as a normal limiting factor to begin with; increase in temperature increases the rate of photosynthesis. But above a certain temperature, the enzymes in the cells are destroyed so no photosynthesis can take place.

9.3

1 Respiration; energy for cell functions; growth; reproduction; building up smaller molecules into bigger molecules; converted into starch for storage; making cellulose; making amino acids; building up fats and oils for a food store in seeds.
2 a Glucose is soluble and would affect the movement of water into and out of the plant cells. Starch is insoluble and so does not disturb the water balance of the plant.
  b Leaves, stems, roots and storage organs.
  c [Any sensible suggestions involving a slice of potato and dilute iodine solution.]
3 Bogs are wet and peaty and the soil contains very few minerals, especially nitrates. Plants need nitrates form the soil to make amino acids and build them into proteins. So many plants cannot grow well on bogs. Carnivorous plants trap insects and digest their bodies, which provides a good supply of nitrates and other minerals. So they can grow and thrive on bogs as they do not rely on them for their minerals.

9.4

1 a Stomata are small openings all over the leaf surface.
  b The stomata open during daylight allowing air into the leaves so that carbon dioxide enters the cells for photosynthesis, but they close the rest of the time to control the loss of water.
  c The opening and closing of the stomata is controlled by the guard cells.
2 Plant roots are thin, divided structures with a large surface area (SA). The cells on the outside of the roots near the growing tips also have extensions, called root hairs, which increase the SA for the uptake of substances from the soil. These tiny projections from the cells push out between the soil particles. The membranes of the root hair cells also have microvilli that increase the SA for diffusion and osmosis even more. The water then has only a short distance to move across the root to the xylem, where it is moved up and around the plant. Plant roots are also adapted to take in mineral ions using active transport. They have plenty of mitochondria to supply the energy they need, as well as all the advantages of the large SA and short pathways needed for the movement of water as well.
3 The adaptations are very similar: large SA, and small distances to travel. Plants are not always as effective as animals at maintaining concentration gradients through active circulation, but they have plenty of active transport systems to help them.

9.5

1 a Transpiration is the loss of water vapour from the surface of plant leaves through the stomata.
  b Water evaporates from the surface of the leaves. As this water evaporates, water is pulled up through the xylem to take its place. This constant movement of water molecules through the xylem from the roots to the leaves is known as the 'transpiration stream'.
2 a The waxy cuticle and the guard cells reduce the loss of water vapour.
  b Reduces water loss a little, as it would not cover all the stomata. Not a big effect as most stomata are on the underside of the leaves.
  c Greatly reduce the loss of water from the leaf, as most of the stomata would be covered and therefore little evaporation would take place. In turn, the rate of water uptake would be very much reduced.
  d The rate of transpiration would increase because the rapid air movement across the leaf would increase the rate of evaporation of water and so increase the uptake of water as well.
  e The uptake of water from the cut end of the plant stem.
3 a Transpire rapidly as stomata exposed directly to light and heat from the Sun.

b Not a problem as they live in water, so never a shortage to bring up from the roots.

9.6

1 a To move food made in the leaves to the rest of the plant and to transport water and mineral ions taken from the soil to the rest of the plant.
  b All the cells need dissolved sugar for cellular respiration and also as the basis for making new plant material. Water is needed for photosynthesis to make sugar, and also to keep the cells rigid to support the plant.

2

Xylem	Phloem
Mature cells are dead	Living cells
Transports water and minerals from the soils around the plant	Transports dissolved sugars from photosynthesis around the plant
Found on the inside of vascular bundles in the stem	Found on the outside of vascular bundles in the stem

3 The transport tissue of young trees is on the outside of the trunk under the bark. In young trees the bark is relatively soft and animals such as deer and even rabbits will eat it. If the bark is nibbled off all around the tree, water cannot move up from the roots and sugars cannot move down to the roots and the young tree will die. Plastic covers protect the young bark so it cannot be eaten. They can be removed once the trees are more mature. If this isn't done, most of the young trees are likely to be destroyed and the woodland will eventually die as the old, mature trees are not replaced.

9.7

1 Plants need to be able to respond to their surroundings so that the roots grow down into the soil when a seed germinates and the shoots grow up towards the light for photosynthesis to take place. They need to be able to grow into light if something shades them. The roots need to be able to grow towards water if there is a damp area of soil. Trophic responses enable plants to respond to light, gravity and water. Shoots have a positive phototropism – they grow towards the light, and roots grow away from the light. In gravitropisms, shoots grow away from the force of gravity and roots grow towards the force of gravity. Roots grow towards water in a hydrotropism.

2

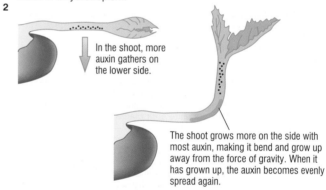

In the shoot, more auxin gathers on the lower side.

The shoot grows more on the side with most auxin, making it bend and grow up away from the force of gravity. When it has grown up, the auxin becomes evenly spread again.

3 a When the light is shining directly from above, both sets of shoots grow upwards in the same way. However, in one-sided light, the exposed shoots will grow and bend towards the light. In response to the one-sided stimulus, auxin moves across to the darker side of the shoots. This increased concentration of auxin stimulates the cells on that side to grow faster, which causes the shoots to bend towards the light until they are effectively illuminated evenly again. This sensitivity to one-sided light is in the tip of the shoots, so the shoots covered in foil caps do not respond and continue to grow straight up as there is no change in the auxin concentrations.
  b The seedlings would start to grow towards the light because the shoot tips are now exposed and the auxin movement will occur. However, they won't bend as much as the shoots exposed all the time as they will have had less time to grow.

9.8

1 a A chemical that brings about a growth response in a plant.
  b Hormone rooting powder contains auxin, a plant hormone which does lots of things including stimulating the growth of roots in a cut stem. By using rooting hormones, gardeners greatly increase the likelihood that a cutting will develop roots and grow well, making it much easier to propagate plants by taking lots of cuttings.
2 They can be used to cause excessive growth that kills plants. They are absorbed more by broad-leaved plants that are often weeds rather than by cereals. Hormones can also be used to cause leaf fall, which kills plants as well.

3 Auxin stimulates growth in plants. If excess auxin is absorbed through the leaf, the plant will go into uncontrolled rapid growth and eventually die. Farmers use hormone weedkillers – broad-leaved weeds absorb lots of hormone and die, while the narrow-leaved cereal plants are untouched. This means the crop plants grow without competition, giving a much better yield, which helps provide food for people. Auxin is also used when taking cuttings, to help propagate good strains of crop plants, and when cloning plants. Any other sensible suggestions.

9.9

1 a Male sex organs: anther and filament make up the stamen. Anther produces pollen grains, which contain the male gametes; filament is the stalk that attaches it to the flower. Female sex organs: stigma, style and ovary. Stigma is where the pollen lands during pollination; the style is the stalk down which the male nuclei travel to the ovule; the ovary produces the female gametes, the ovules, and forms a fruit to protect them once they have been fertilised.

b Male gametes are much smaller than the female gametes; there are many more male gametes than female gametes; male gametes have to travel to the female gametes; any other sensible point.

2 The petals are often brightly coloured and marked to attract insect pollinators and direct them in to the nectar so they brush against the anthers and collect pollen on the way. The sepals protect the petals in the bud.

3 a The transfer of pollen from the anther to the stigma, often from one flower to another.

b Insects and wind.

c If insect pollinated expect: big flower with big petals, coloured and/or patterned to attract insects and guide them in; scent to attract insects; nectar in the flower to attract insects; anthers inside the petals so insects brush past pollen on way to nectar; stigma inside petals so insects brush past it and offload pollen on way to nectar. Relatively few large sticky pollen grains to stick to insects.

If wind pollinated expect: small flower with small brown or green petals and no scent or nectar as these are no use in attracting the wind. Anthers outside the flowers so pollen blows off into wind. Huge numbers of very small light pollen grains so travel easily in the wind; stigma large, feathery and sticky to capture pollen from the air.

9.10

1 Pollination is the arrival of a pollen grain on the stigma; fertilisation is the fusing of the male nucleus from the pollen grain with the egg nucleus from the ovule to form a zygote.

2 Pollination → growth of the pollen tube from the pollen grain into the style → the pollen tube grows into the ovary and into an ovule → the male nuclei from the pollen grain migrate into the pollen tube → the male nuclei move down into the ovule → one male nucleus fuses with egg nucleus to form the zygote, which will form the embryo plant → other male nucleus fuses with two more female nuclei to form endosperm nucleus, which will make foodstore of the seed.

3 a The fertilised ovule forms a seed containing an embryo plant and a food store contained within a tough outer coat called the testa.

b The ovary wall develops into the fruit and is often adapted to help with the dispersal of the seeds away from the parent plant, for example as a fleshy fruit or a winged seed. It is important for the seeds to spread as far from the parent plant as possible because this avoids competition with the adult plant and between the growing seedlings.

4 Any three sensible choices, e.g. a fleshy fruit, a winged fruit, a floating fruit, an explosive fruit, a hooked fruit, along with a valid explanation of how they work.

Answers to end of chapter summary questions

1 a

$$\text{carbon dioxide} + \text{water} \xrightarrow{\text{light energy}} \text{glucose} + \text{oxygen}$$

$$6CO_2 + 6H_2O \xrightarrow{\text{light energy}} C_6H_{12}O_6 + 6O_2$$

b Starch

c i Credit accurately drawn graphs, correctly labelled axes, etc.

ii Plants in higher light intensity photosynthesise faster and therefore produce more food and grow well. Light will not limit them – CO_2 or temperature might. For plants in lower light, the light is a limiting factor on their growth.

2 a Because conditions are good for photosynthesis – plenty of light, water and warm temperatures allow rapid photosynthesis, which gives rapid growth.

b Made from glucose made in photosynthesis.

c Energy store for the developing embryo as the seed germinates and grows but before it can photosynthesise.

d Energy for the plant cells for growth; to make complex carbohydrates such as cellulose for plant cell walls and starch for storage; combined with nitrates from the soil to make amino acids and proteins; any other sensible point.

3 Adaptations of leaves: thin and flat to give short diffusion distances; specialised cells with big air spaces and big surface area for gases to diffuse in and out of cells; xylem tissue bringing water into the leaf; stomata to allow carbon dioxide, oxygen and water vapour to diffuse in and out of leaves. All depends on passive processes of diffusion along concentration gradients.

Adaptations of roots: long and thin to give big surface area for the absorption of water and mineral ions; specialised root hair cells to increase the surface area for movement of water into the roots and active transport of mineral ions; movement of water passive along concentration gradients, movement of mineral ions active.

4 A One-sided light, seedling grows towards it in a phototropism.

B Tip removed – seedling grows straight – suggests the sensitivity comes from the tip.

C Opaque cap – again no response – confirms sensitivity to one-sided light in the tip of the shoot.

D Shoot bends towards light – shows that when light can reach tip it will respond.

E Base covered – shoot bends to light – base not involved in sensitivity to one-sided light.

F Shoot bends to one-sided light – suggests that the message from the tip to the growing cells may be chemical and water soluble – can pass through gelatine block from severed tip to growing cells.

G Shoot doesn't respond – plastic stops the message getting through, which again suggests it is chemical.

5 a

	Insect pollinated	Wind pollinated
Petals	Large, brightly coloured; many are patterned to guide insects in	Small, usually brown or green
Scent	Often scented to attract insects	Not scented
Nectar	Often make sugary liquid called nectar to attract insects	No nectar
Stigma	Found inside the petals so insects brush against them on way to nectar; may be sticky	Large, feathery; hangs outside the petals to collect pollen from the air; may be sticky
Anthers	Inside the petals so insects brush past on way to nectar	Hang outside petals so pollen blown away by wind
Pollen grains	Relatively few, large and sticky to attach onto the insects that visit the flower	Many, small and light to float easily in the wind

b The pollen grain attaches to the top of the stigma in pollination. A special pollen tube grows out of the pollen grain and down the style. The pollen tube grows into the ovary and into an ovule. The male nuclei from the pollen grain migrate into the pollen tube and move down into the ovule. Here, one of the male nuclei from the pollen grain fertilises the egg nucleus in the ovule to form a zygote, which grows and divides to form the embryo plant in the seed. The other male nucleus fuses with two more female nuclei to form the endosperm nucleus. The fertilised endosperm nucleus and egg cell nucleus of the ovule give rise to a seed. The endosperm forms a food store, while the tissue that results from the female egg nucleus forms the embryo plant. If there are several ovules, most or all of them will be fertilised. As the seeds form, the ovary grows into a fruit, which surrounds and protects the seeds.

6 a Transpiration is the loss of water vapour from the surface of plant leaves through the stomata.

b Potometer measures uptake of water by the shoot. Transpiration is the evaporation of water from the leaves. Some of the water taken up by the shoot is used by the plant for photosynthesis, support, etc., so not all the water taken up is transpired, although it gives a good approximation.

c i The rate of transpiration would increase because the rapid air movement across the leaf would increase the rate of evaporation of water and so increase the uptake of water as well.

ii It would greatly reduce the loss of water from the leaf, as most of the stomata would be covered and therefore little evaporation would take place. In turn, the rate of water uptake would be very much reduced.

Answers to end of chapter examination-style questions

1 a Carbon dioxide (1), oxygen (1).

b The sun (1). The light energy is absorbed by chlorophyll/chloroplasts (1) in the leaf (mesophyll) cells (1).

c Temperature (1) may be limiting as the enzymes work slowly in cold temperatures(1), or light (1) may be limiting as December is a very dark month and it is early morning (1).

d Any **three** from: for storage as starch (1); for storage as fats/oils (1); to make proteins/enzymes/ named protein or enzyme (1); to make cellulose for cell walls. (*3 marks maximum*)

2 a Weedkillers (1); rooting (powders) (1).

b Gravity (accept gravitropism/geotropism) (1) caused redistribution of auxin/hormone to lower side of stem (1); these hormones stimulate growth of cells on the lower side of stem only (1); so the stem grows upwards (1).

3 a Translocation – The movement of sugars from the leaves to other tissues (1); Xylem – The cells which transport water around the plant (1); Stomata – Openings in the lower surface of the leaf for gas exchange (1); Phloem – The cells which transport sugars around the plant (1); Transpiration stream – The transport of water from roots to leaves (1).

b To provide turgor for cells to support leaves and stems (1); to dissolve gases/ions/small food molecules for transport (1).

c Any four from the following possible answers, but they must be in the correct order:
The transpiration stream is driven by the evaporation of water from the leaves (1). In hot weather, photosynthesis is faster and uses more water (1). Stomata will be open to take in more carbon dioxide (or at a faster rate), meaning that more water vapour can escape (1). Evaporation happens faster if it is hot, dry and windy, so more water is lost from leaves (1) and more water is drawn in by the roots to replace what is being used up and lost (1). (*4 marks maximum*)

d Active transport (1), in which energy is required (1) (and a protein in the membrane transports the ion across against the concentration gradient).

e To make (amino acids for) proteins/for DNA synthesis (1).

4 a Marks awarded for this answer will be determined by the Quality of Written Communication (QWC) as well as the standard of the scientific response.
- There is a clear, balanced and detailed description referring to the data in the graph about light, temperature and carbon dioxide and how to set up a controlled experiment. The answer shows almost faultless spelling, punctuation and grammar. It is coherent and in an organised, logical sequence. It contains a range of appropriate or relevant specialist terms used accurately. (*5–6 marks*)
- There is some description of setting up a controlled experiment, including at least two variables. There are some errors in spelling, punctuation and grammar. The answer has some structure and organisation. The use of specialist terms has been attempted, but not always accurately. (*3–4 marks*)
- There is a brief description with reference to setting up several tunnels and mention of at least one variable, but little clarity and detail. The spelling, punctuation and grammar are very weak. The answer is poorly organised with almost no specialist terms and/or their use demonstrating a general lack of understanding of their meaning. (*1–2 marks*)
- No relevant content. (*0 marks*)

Examples of biology points made in the response:
- use of term limiting factors
- the more photosynthesis, the more growth
- carbon dioxide optimum around 4%
- plants need water
- control of light intensity
- types of light
- temperature control/25 °C
- idea that light changes with type of plastic/colour of plastic/thickness of plastic
- idea that might need heating/ventilation to control/monitor temperature
- idea that need to contain the carbon dioxide/have a source of carbon dioxide gas
- reference to having different sets of conditions in each model tunnel to be able to determine optimum/idea that might try slightly lower/higher temperature/carbon dioxide level to check cost effectiveness.

b Any one from the following: possible to mimic large scale events/idea of/on a small scale; can be used to predict changes/changes in variables; use of a description, e.g. to predict the spread of disease/can predict the effect of a chemical on all bacteria using a safe organism/can use fast breeding organisms to mimic processes which occur slowly in others/can predict the effect of global warming on organisms in a locality. (*1 mark maximum*)

10 Variation and inheritance

10.1

1 a The gene.

b Offspring inherit information from both parents and so end up with a combination of characteristics, some from the father and some from the mother.

2 a You inherit one set from each parent.

b Genes are carried on the chromosomes, so because chromosomes come in pairs, so do the genes – one from each parent.

c 20 000–25 000.

3 a This is because there are genetic differences between all the members of a species unless they are identical twins or produced by asexual reproduction.

b There are two sources of variety in individuals. One is the genetic information they inherit. The other is the variety in the environment in which they grow and develop. If both of these are identical – both the genetics and the environment – then the organisms should be identical too.

c It is almost impossible for two organisms to experience identical environmental conditions, so there will always be environmentally caused differences between them.

10.2

1 a No fusion of gametes, only one parent, no variety.

b Two parents, fusion of gametes, variety.

c Sex cell.

d The differences between individuals as a result of their genetic material.

2 Advantages of sexual reproduction: mixes genes, leads to variation, allows process of evolution, increases chances of a species surviving if environment changes.
Disadvantages of sexual reproduction: need to find a partner, risk of gametes not finding each other, generally slower.
Advantages of asexual reproduction: only involves one parent, simple and efficient, genes and characteristics conserved.
Disadvantages of sexual reproduction: no genetic variety – only produces clones, no evolution through natural selection.

3 a i By bulbs.
ii By flowers.

b They have the safety and reliability of asexual reproduction but the genetic variety which is introduced by sexual reproduction to help them survive changes in conditions.

c Asexually produced offspring will all be genetically identical to the single parent. Sexually produced offspring will be genetically different from both parents and from each other as each will be the result of the fusing of a different egg and sperm and each one will have a different genetic mixture.

10.3

1 Often we do not know the exact genetic makeup of individuals unless they are clones or identical twins. Also environmental differences can be very subtle, e.g. all children in same family in same home with same parents but will all have a slightly different environment depending on position in the family, etc. Not easy to get genetically identical groups of many animals for experimentation and certainly not of people to investigate effects of environment. Easier to use plants than animals because it is relatively easy to produce large numbers of genetically identical plants by either taking cuttings or tissue culture cloning; easier to control and manipulate the environment of plants as they do not move around and no ethical issues to giving plants a poor environment to observe the effect.

2 a Height seems to be most closely controlled by genetics as there is least difference between the identical twins regardless of whether they are brought up together or apart. Mass seems to be most affected by the environment as identical twins brought up apart are no more identical than ordinary siblings.

b For comparison with the normal population: studying identical twins reared together and twins reared apart allows you to compare the impact of different environments on genetically identical humans. Even twins brought up in the same household will not have identical environments – and there are small differences between them for all features. But when twins are reared apart, if they remain very similar, then that is largely controlled by genetics; while if there are big differences then the environment is having a big effect. Non-twin siblings show the level of similarity you would expect from two siblings (not genetically identical) reared in the same environment.

3 Credit for any sensible suggestions along with recognition of the need to control variables, how to get the most reliable and valid data from the investigation, etc.

10.4

1 **a** Dominant allele – an allele which controls the development of a characteristic even when it is present on only one of the chromosomes.

b Recessive allele – an allele which only controls the development of a characteristic if it is present on both chromosomes.

c Marks for each case where students identify correctly the single gene characteristic and the dominant and recessive alleles.

2 Marks awarded for drawing a Punnett square correctly with the appropriate gametes. DD, Dd, dD have dimples; dd has no dimples.

3 **a** He found that characteristics were inherited in clear and predictable patterns. He realised some characteristics were dominant over others and that they never mixed together.

b No one could see the units of inheritance, so there was no proof of their existence. People were not used to studying careful records of results.

c Once people could see chromosomes, a mechanism for Mendel's ideas of inheritance became possible.

10.5

1 A gene is made up of groups of three base pairs. Each group of three base pairs codes for a single amino acid.
The order of the base pairs in the gene determines the sequence of the amino acids, which are joined together to make a protein – so each gene codes for a unique protein.

2 **a** R r

b Genotypes of offspring 1RR:2Rr:1rr
Phenotypes of offspring: 3 round pea plants: 1 wrinkled pea plant.

	R	r
R	RR	Rr
r	rR	rr

c Genotypes of offspring 2Rr:2rr
Phenotypes of offspring: 2 round pea plants: 2 wrinkled pea plants

	R	r
r	rR	rr
r	rR	rr

3 From the top: D = dimples, d = no dimples. D is the dominant allele. Man Dd, woman dd. Their offspring: female dd (her male partner dd), male dd, male Dd (his female partner Dd). The offspring of the couple without dimples – both dd. The offspring of the couple with dimples, one boy dd, one boy either DD or Dd.

10.6

1 **a** A genetic disorder which causes extra fingers or toes.

b The faulty allele is dominant, so only one parent needs to have the allele and pass it on for the offspring to be affected.

c **A** Pp only – as produced a child that was unaffected.
B Pp – because mother must pass on a recessive allele to produce two unaffected children.
C–E – could be PP or Pp as each parent has the genotype Pp.

2 **a** Carriers have a normal dominant allele, so their body works normally.

b CF (cystic fibrosis) is recessive – must inherit one from each parent to get the disease. But if parents had the disease themselves, they would almost certainly be infertile, so parents must be carriers.

3 [Marks awarded for genetic diagram based on Figure 3 in Student Book, showing how cc (cystic fibrosis) arises.]

10.7

1 **a** This is a disorder caused by a faulty recessive allele which can be passed on from one generation to another. Because it is recessive parents can carry the allele without realising it. Any affected offspring have to inherit a faulty allele from both parents.

b The main symptoms are breathlessness, lack of energy and tiredness along with pain and tissue death and sometimes death of the individual. In sickle cell anaemia the red blood cells are sickle shaped instead of the normal biconcave discs. As a result they do not carry oxygen efficiently so the person does not get enough oxygen – they feel breathless and tired. The sickle cells can block small blood vessels and this can cause pain and tissue death. This leaves the person open to severe infections and even death.

2 **a** RR × Rr

	R	R
R	RR	RR
r	Rr	Rr

None of the offspring have sickle cell anaemia. 50:50% (1 in 2) chance of a child being a carrier.

b Rr × Rr

	R	r
R	RR	Rr
r	Rr	rr

1 in 4 of the offspring have sickle cell anaemia. 50:50% (1 in 2) chance of a child being a carrier.

c RR × rr

	R	R
r	Rr	Rr
r	Rr	Rr

None of the offspring have sickle cell anaemia. All of the offspring are carriers.

3 **a** A whole chromosome disorder when an extra copy of chromosome 21 is inherited. It means the person affected has 47 chromosomes instead of 46.

b Down's syndrome involves the whole chromosome not a single faulty allele.

10.8

1 Amniocentesis is done at around 15–16 weeks of pregnancy. It involves taking some of the fluid from around the developing fetus. This fluid contains fetal cells, which can then be used for genetic screening. Chorionic villus sampling of embryonic cells is done at an earlier stage of pregnancy – between 10 and 12 weeks – by taking a small sample of tissue from the developing placenta. This again provides fetal cells for genetic screening.

2 **a** Ultrasound used to show the position of the fetus and the needle → needle inserted through the body wall into the amniotic fluid → sample of the amniotic fluid which contains fetal cells drawn up into syringe → DNA is isolated from the fetal cells → gene probes for particular genetic disorders are added → UV light is used to screen the DNA – if the gene probe has bound to a faulty allele it will fluoresce, showing that the fetus is affected by the condition.

b A single cell is removed from the early embryo → DNA is isolated from the embryonic cell (and copied many times) → gene probes for particular genetic disorders are added → UV light is used to screen the DNA – if the gene probe has bound to a faulty allele it will fluoresce, showing that the fetus is affected by the condition.

3 Any two arguments for and two against universal embryo screening.

Answers to end of chapter summary questions

1 **a** From a runner – a special stem from the parent plant with small new identical plant on the end.

b Asexual

c By sexual reproduction (flowers, pollination, etc.).

d The new plants from the packet will be similar to, but not identical to their parents – each one will be genetically different. The plants produced by asexual reproduction will be identical to their parents.

2 **a** A sex cell, e.g. ovum and sperm in humans, pollen and ovule in plants.

b There are half the number of chromosomes in a gamete than in a normal body cell.

3 **a** DNA

b A section of DNA made up of hundreds and thousands of bases which code for a particular protein.

c A DNA strand is made up of combinations of bases. They are grouped into threes, and three bases codes for a particular amino acid. The arrangement of the bases determines the string of amino acids which is joined together to make a protein. Proteins are important in the structure of cells and also form the enzymes that catalyse all the other reactions of a cell. So by determining the proteins which are made, the DNA strand determines how the organism is put together and what it looks like – its phenotype.

4 Mendel carried out large numbers of genetic crosses on plants, particularly peas, growing in the monastery garden where he lived and worked. He carried out specific breeding experiments and counted the different offspring carefully, kept careful records and analysed his results. This was very unusual for the time, when statistical analysis of data was very rare. Mendel realised that there were clear patterns emerging from his data and made the hypothesis that there were individual units of inheritance, that some characteristics were dominant over others and that the units did not mix. Chromosomes and genes had not been discovered, so people found it very hard to accept Mendel's ideas. Also, there was no model of how it worked. It was the development of the microscope that enabled people to see chromosomes and how they were passed on when cells divided; this meant people eventually recognised Mendel's work.

5 **a** Sami's alleles are ss. We know this because she has curved thumbs and the recessive allele is curved thumbs. She must have inherited two recessive alleles to have inherited the characteristic.

b If the baby has curved thumbs, then Josh is Ss. The baby has inherited a recessive allele from each parent, so Josh must have a recessive allele. We know he also has a dominant allele as he has straight thumbs.

	Sami	
	s	s
Josh S	Ss	Ss
s	ss	ss

c If the baby has straight thumbs, then Josh could be either Ss or SS. We know that the baby has inherited one recessive allele from the mother, and we know that Josh has one dominant allele, but we do not know if he has two dominant alleles.

	Sami	
	s	s
Josh S	Ss	Ss
S	Ss	Ss

6 a As an anomaly, the white-flowered plant should be investigated, e.g. to see if the colour was a result of a mutation or because of the particular conditions in which it was grown. He could breed from it, plant it in a different soil, etc.

b i To have white flowers, both of the parent plants must have contained a recessive white allele, so:

	P	P
P	PP	Pp
p	Pp	pp

ii Expect a 3 : 1 ratio; actual results 295 : 102 – very close.

c Suggest cross purple flowers with white flowers (pp). If purple flowers homozygous PP, all the offspring will be purple (Pp):

	P	P
p	Pp	Pp
p	Pp	Pp

If purple flowers heterozygous, half of the flowers will be purple (Pp) and half will be white (pp).

	P	p
p	Pp	pp
p	Pp	pp

7 a The inheritance of a single pair of genes which influence a particular phenotype characteristic.

b Dominant allele – controls the development of a phenotype characteristic even if only present on one of the chromosome pair. Recessive alleles – only control the development of a phenotype characteristic if they are present on both chromosomes of a pair.

c Any two correct answers; for example: dimples, dangly earlobes, straight or curved thumbs.

d There is a faulty recessive allele that causes the condition cystic fibrosis, but only if it is present on both chromosomes in a pair. An individual can be a carrier – have one recessive allele – but not be aware of it because they also have a healthy dominant allele and so have no symptoms of disease. For example, F dominant normal, f recessive cystic fibrosis, normal parents Ff – heterozygotes gives a 3:1 chance of having a child with cystic fibrosis.

	F	f
F	FF	Ff
f	Ff	ff

e H dominant Huntington's, h recessive normal. Affected Hh (50% or 1 in 2 chance of having affected children) or HH (all children will be affected as only affected alleles can be passed on by the homozygous parent, normal parent hh).

	H	h
h	Hh	hh
h	Hh	hh

Answers to end of chapter examination-style questions

1 a Genes (1); DNA (1).
b Chromosomes (1); gamete (1).
c Alleles (1).
d Heterozygous (1); homozygous (1).
2 a Asexual reproduction (1).
b Red (1) because the cutting plants have exactly the same genes/genetic material as the parent plant (1).
c Any **two** from: (different amounts of) water (1), light (1), fertiliser with mineral ions (1). (*2 marks maximum*)
d Having clones/all plants with same genes (1), will be a control variable (1).
3 DNA (1); protein (1); amino acids (1); DNA (1); double helix (1); three (1); amino acid (1).
4 Marks awarded for this answer will be determined by the Quality of Written Communication (QWC) as well as the standard of the scientific response.
- All, or nearly all, scientific points are included in a clear and logical order. There is almost faultless spelling, punctuation and grammar. (*5–6 marks*)
- Many scientific points are correctly made, expressed clearly. There are very few mistakes in spelling, punctuation and grammar. (*3–4 marks*)
- A few scientific points are made although they may not be clearly expressed and the order may be confused. There are many mistakes in spelling, punctuation and grammar. (*1–2 marks*)

Examples of scientific points are: identical twins have same genes/genetic material (1); girls have nearly the same height, so likely to be mainly genetic variation (1); girls have very different weights (1) and this must be due to the environment (1); probably different diets/amount of exercise (1); hair is very different now but would have been same when born (1); hair differences must be due to environment as girls have treated it differently (1); eyes are same colour as eye colour is controlled by genes and cannot change (1).

5 a Parental genotypes HbAHbs, HbAHbs (accept explanations in terms of the symbols A and s) (1); gamete genotypes HbAHbs, HbAHbs correctly derived (1); children's genotypes HbAHbA, HbAHbs, HbAHbs, HbsHbs correctly derived (1); HbsHbs clearly defined as having sickle-cell anaemia (1).
b i HbAHbA individuals are more likely to die of malaria (1); HbsHbs individuals are likely to die of the condition before maturity (1); but crosses between heterozygotes keeps frequency of Hbs allele high (1).
ii There is partial coincidence between distribution of malaria and sickle-cell allele (1), but there could be another factor that influences both distributions (1).

11 Genetic manipulation

11.1

1 a Cuttings: taking a small piece of a stem or leaf and growing it in the right conditions to produce a new plant.
b Tissue cloning: getting a few cells from a desirable plant to make a big mass of identical cells, each of which can produce a tiny identical plant.
c Asexual reproduction: reproduction which involves only one parent; there is no joining of gametes and the offspring are genetically identical to the parent.
d Embryo cloning: splitting cells apart from a developing embryo before they become specialised, to produce several identical embryos.
2 a It allows the production of far more calves from the best cows; can carry good breeding stock to poor areas of the world as frozen embryos; can replicate genetically engineered animals quickly.
b Either: cow given hormones to produce large numbers of eggs → then cow inseminated with sperm → embryos collected and taken to the lab → embryos split to make more identical embryos → cells grown on again to make more identical embryos → embryos transferred to host mothers.
Or: cow given hormones to produce large numbers of eggs → eggs collected and taken to lab → eggs and sperm mixed → embryos grown → embryos split up to make more identical embryos → cells grown on to make bigger embryos → embryos transferred to host mothers.
c Marks awarded for understanding of issues involved in embryo cloning. For example, economic issues – only wealthy farmers/wealthy countries can afford the technology, is it acceptable to produce large numbers of identical cattle, etc.

3

Tissue cloning in plants	Embryo cloning in cattle
Based on normal body cells	Based on cells from an embryo
Involves using hormones to make a mass of unspecialised tissue and then using different hormones to stimulate the production of many plantlets	Involves splitting an individual embryo into a number of cells and allowing them to grow into small balls of cells before implanting them in surrogate mothers prepared using hormones
Produces thousands of genetically identical offspring	Produces up to thirty genetically identical offspring a year

11.2

1 The nucleus is removed from an unfertilised egg cell → the nucleus is taken from an adult body cell → the nucleus from the adult cell is inserted (placed) in the empty egg cell → new cell is given a tiny electric shock → new cell fuses together → begins to divide to form embryo cells → ball of cells inserted into womb to continue its development.

2 Natural mammalian clones occur when an early embryo completely splits in two to form two identical embryos, which continue to develop into genetically identical twin individuals.
Embryo clones are made artificially when the cells of a very early embryo are split so the individual cells can all continue to grow and divide and form a number of genetically identical individuals.
Adult cell cloning involves taking the nucleus of an unfertilised egg cell and replacing it with the nucleus of a cell from an adult cell of another animal of the same species. A small electric shock is needed to start the new cell dividing and developing to form an embryo, which can be implanted into a surrogate mother and eventually forms a new individual that is a clone of the original source of the adult cell nucleus. Very few of these adult cell clones survive – it is still a very difficult and experimental technique.

3 Advantages: enables us to clone adult animals so we can clone genetically engineered organisms, making it possible to clone new tissues and organs for people with diseases or needing transplants; could help infertile couples; could help conserve very endangered species. Any other valid points.
Disadvantages: people are concerned about human cloning; reduces variety in a population; objections to the formation of embryos that are then used to harvest tissues; people object to the cloning of endangered or extinct animals. Any other valid points. Students should also give an opinion as to the validity of the main concerns expressed. Award marks for reasoned consideration of the relevant scientific points.

11.3

1 Modifying the genome of different organisms enables us to use them to make useful substances, for example: bacteria making human insulin; modifying animals and plants to make human proteins in milk; modifying organisms to be resistant to disease, resistant to toxins or pesticides, to glow or change when attacked, to have an increased yield, shorter stems so less easily damaged, etc.; any other sensible points.

2 Cut a gene for a short stem from a plant closely related to the one you want to engineer using enzymes → take a plasmid out of a bacterium and cut it open using enzymes → insert the short stem gene into the bacterial plasmid, which acts as a vector → insert the vector into the cells of the plant you want to engineer → then clone those plant cells using tissue culture to make thousands of identical genetically engineered plants.

3 Any three sensible choices, e.g. golden rice, drought-resistant strains, plants that can withstand being under water, short-stemmed crops, pesticide resistance, etc. For whichever choices are made, award marks for sensible suggestions as to how the change has increased the crop yield and why it is important.

11.4

1 Advantages: improved growth rates of plants, bigger yields, plants that will grow in a range of conditions, plants that make their own pesticides or are resistant to herbicides. Disadvantages unknown but concerns about: insects may become pesticide-resistant if they eat pesticide-resistant plants repeatedly, GM organisms may affect human health, genes from GM plants may spread into wildlife and cross-breed with wild plants.

2 Credit for relevant comments backed by science. Examples of relevant points:
No: cloning has many potential benefits such as reproducing genetically engineered organisms, saving organisms from extinction, producing cheap plants. Some forms of cloning have been going on for centuries (cuttings) and these have been/may be used to produce medical treatments, etc.
Yes: most animals produced by adult cell cloning have problems, wasteful process, risk of human cloning for the wrong reasons, etc.

3 Relatively few successes so far; genetic engineering tried in cystic fibrosis so far with little success; some success in SCID; any other recent developments.

Answers to end of chapter summary questions

1 a Traditional cuttings used parts of whole stems and roots, but tissue culture uses minute collections of cells as the starting point. Cuttings result in up to hundreds of identical plants; tissue culture can give thousands.
  b Embryo cloning – flushing out early embryos and dividing them before replacing in surrogate mother cows.
  c Both allow large numbers of genetically identical individuals to be produced from good parent stock much faster and more reliably than would be possible using traditional techniques.
  d Cloning plants uses bits of the adult plant as the raw material for the cloning. Animal embryo cloning, as it is used at the moment, involves using embryos as the raw material for the cloning, although this may change in the future.
  e There are more and more people in the world needing to be fed, so techniques for reproducing high yielding plants and animals are always helpful and are financially beneficial for farmers. Also, in developed countries people demand high quality but cheap food, so techniques that reproduce valuable animals and plants are valued.

2 a Clear description of adult cell cloning, e.g. the nucleus is removed from an unfertilised egg cell. At the same time the nucleus is taken from an adult body cell, e.g. a skin cell of another animal of the same species. The nucleus from the adult cell is inserted (placed) in the empty egg cell. The new cell is given a tiny electric shock, which fuses the new cells together and causes it to begin to divide to form embryo cells. These contain the same genetic information as the original adult cell and the original adult animal. When the embryo has developed into a ball of cells, it is inserted into the womb of an adult female to continue its development.
  b Plant cloning has been accepted for a long time and doesn't threaten people – only advantages seen in general. Cloning animals is seen as worrying in itself but also raises concerns of human cloning. Cloning pets, etc., is seen as frivolous.

3 a

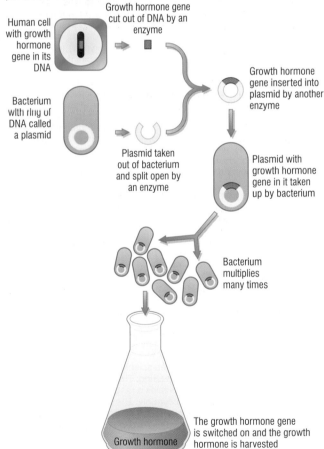

Human cell with growth hormone gene in its DNA

Growth hormone gene cut out of DNA by an enzyme

Bacterium with ring of DNA called a plasmid

Plasmid taken out of bacterium and split open by an enzyme

Growth hormone gene inserted into plasmid by another enzyme

Plasmid with growth hormone gene in it taken up by bacterium

Bacterium multiplies many times

The growth hormone gene is switched on and the growth hormone is harvested

Growth hormone

  b It is pure – free from any contamination. It is the human version of a hormone. It can be produced in large amounts relatively easily and cheaply as and when it is needed.

4 a They have been raised and trained on different establishments so it is environmental factors which are influencing their racing ability.
  b As a control – to see how the animal turns out if not trained up as a racing mule.
  c Data on effect of diet, handling, intensity of training, etc., on the temperament, running speed, stamina, etc., of the mules.

5 a Crops that have been genetically modified by adding genetic material from another organism.

b People are concerned about effects on human health, possible spread to other wild organisms through cross-breeding, insects becoming pesticide resistant, etc.

c Increasing the yield by: getting bigger seed heads; shorter stems so less damage by wind; drought, temperature or flood resistant so get crops in difficult conditions; making pesticides so prevent crops from being destroyed by insects, etc.; any other sensible points.

d Any sensible suggestions – look for awareness of good experimental design.

Answers to end of chapter examination-style questions

1 a A clone is a group of organisms created by asexual reproduction from a single parent and has exactly the same genetic material as the parent. (1) (Credit answer in terms of mitosis, provided that identical genetic material is explained.)

b Tissue culture (1).

c An embryo is split (1) at a very early stage/when it is still a ball of cells (1) and the divided embryos are implanted into different mothers (1). In adult cell cloning, a nucleus from a cell of the animal to be cloned is removed (1) and put into an egg cell that has had the nucleus removed (1). An electric shock makes the egg cell start to divide (1) and when it is a ball of cells/embryo it is implanted in the uterus of a (surrogate) mother (1).

d Any four from: embryo splitting would be better (1); as you could take embryos created by eggs and sperm from known champion cows and bulls (1); split them and put them into many other cows to produce calves (1). It is a method that has been done before (1); and it is likely to be cheaper (1) than adult cell cloning, which is still very new. (4 marks maximum)

2 a Any four from: nucleus/DNA/chromosomes/genetic material removed (1) from (unfertilised) egg/ovum (1). (Allow empty egg cell for the first two marks: do not allow fertilised egg.) Nucleus from the body cell of champion (cow) (1); inserted into egg/ovum (1); electric shock (1); to make cell divide or develop into embryo (1);(embryo) inserted into womb/host/another cow (1) (allow this point if wrong method, e.g. embryo splitting). (4 marks maximum)

b Any four from: Pros – economic benefit, e.g. increased yield/ more profit (1); clone calf not genetically engineered (1); genetic material not altered (1); milk safe to drink/same as ordinary milk (1). (2 marks maximum) Cons – consumer resistance (1); caused by misunderstanding process (1); not proved that milk is safe (1) (ignore 'God would not like it' or 'it's not natural'); ethical/religious argument (1); reduce gene pool (1). (2 marks maximum) Conclusion: sensible conclusion for or against, substantiated by information from the passage and/or own knowledge conclusion at end (1). (5 marks maximum)

3 a i Any one from: kills insects (which eat crop) (1); increases yield (1). (1 mark maximum)

ii Any two from: kills insects which may not be pests (1); poisonous to humans (1); expensive (1); pollutes the environment (1); other relevant suggestions, e.g. is not organic (1) (2 marks maximum)

iii Any one from: increases crop yield (1); reduces cost of pesticide use (1). (1 mark maximum)

iv Any one from: may lead to increased use of pesticides in the long run/description of or reference to last paragraph (1); ethical considerations, e.g. alters genes of crop (1). (Do not allow 'not natural' or 'genes may get into wildlife idea' or 'against religion' or 'not organic'.) (1 mark maximum)

b Marks awarded for this answer will be determined by the Quality of Written Communication (QWC) as well as the standard of the scientific response.

• There is a clear and detailed scientific description of the sequence of events in genetic engineering. The answer is coherent and in a logical sequence. It contains a range of appropriate or relevant specialist terms used accurately. The answer shows very few errors in spelling, punctuation and grammar. (5–6 marks)

• There is some description of the sequence of events in genetic engineering, but there is a lack of clarity and detail. The answer has some structure and the use of specialist terms has been attempted, but not always accurately. There may be some errors in spelling, punctuation and grammar. (3–4 marks)

• There is a brief description of the genetic engineering, which has little clarity and detail. The answer is poorly constructed with an absence of specialist terms or their use demonstrates a lack of understanding of their meaning. The spelling, punctuation and grammar are weak. (1–2 marks)

• No relevant content. (0 marks)

Examples of biology points made in the response:

• gene from the bacterium
• is cut from the chromosome
• using enzymes
• gene transferred to the cotton
• (cotton) chromosome (allow cell)
• (the gene) controls characteristics
• causes the cotton (cells) to produce the poison.

12 Adaptation and interdependence

12.1

1 Animals – food and oxygen, water and a mate. Plants: water, carbon dioxide, light energy, minerals from soil. Plants can make their own food using photosynthesis and produce oxygen. Animals have to eat food and need oxygen to break it down to release energy.

2 a An organism that can live in extremely difficult conditions in which most other organisms cannot survive.

b Enzymes which function in very high temperatures; enzymes which function at very low temperatures; ability to get rid of excess salt; ability to respire without oxygen; any other valid point.

3 An adaptation is a feature which makes it possible for an organism to survive in its particular habitat. Award marks for any three good examples of adaptations in animals or plants.

12.2

1 a It is very cold, so there is a problem in keeping warm and finding enough food.

b It is very hot, so the main problems are keeping the body cool and finding enough water.

2 Small ears reduce surface area of thin-skinned tissue to reduce heat loss; thick fur acts as an insulating layer to help prevent heat loss; layer of fat/ blubber provides insulating layer; any other relevant adaptations, e.g. furry feet to insulate against contact with ice; large size reduces surface area: volume ratio so reduces heat loss, etc.

3 a Large, thin ears for heat loss; loose wrinkled skin to aid heat loss; little or no fur; any other sensible suggestions.

b Animals living in hot dry conditions keep cool without sweating by avoiding the heat of the day and by having large ears, baggy skin, little fur, thin and silky fur and a large surface area to volume ratio to increase heat loss.

c Insulation against cold of water, e.g. blubber/internal fat; thick fur externally; small surface area to volume ratio by being big; small extremities such as ears; ability to take deep breaths, heart rate slows when they dive; any other sensible points.

12.3

1 a For photosynthesis; to support the cells, to support the stems; to transport substances around the plant; any other sensible point.

b Through their roots from the soil.

2 a By evaporation through the stomata.

b Dry places are often hot, so photosynthesis and respiration occur at a faster rate. The stomata are open more, so there is more evaporation. If the air is dry, evaporation occurs at a faster rate.

3 a Small leaves; curled leaves – reduce surface area; thick cuticle – reduces rate of evaporation.

b Any three sensible suggestions, e.g. reduction of leaves to spines; thickened water-filled stems or leaves as a store of water; long, deep roots; rolled leaves to reduce evaporation; reduction of stomata, etc.

12.4

1 a If anything happens to their food supply, such as another animal eating it, fire or disease, then they will starve.

b Any suitable examples, such as lions, cheetahs and leopards.

c Any suitable examples, such as rabbits, limpets on a sea shore.

d Members of the same species are all competing for exactly the same things, whereas different species often have similar but slightly different needs. Members of the same species tend to live in the same area.

2 a Fighting: strength, antlers, teeth, etc. Displaying: spectacular appearance, colours, part of body to display (e.g. peacock's tail).

b The answer to this will depend on the method selected for the first part of the answer.
Fighting: advantages – possibility of winning lots of mates, becoming dominant, fathering lots of offspring, females don't usually have any choice, preventing others from mating; disadvantages – the animal could be hurt or killed, needs lots of body resources to grow antlers and to fight.
Display: advantages – don't risk getting hurt, possibility of attracting several mates; disadvantages – uses up lots of resources to grow feathers/carry out displays, females usually choose and may not get noticed, vulnerable to disease or lack of food so don't produce good display, need to be seen. Any other sensible points.

3 a Very good eyesight, good hearing, good sense of smell, binocular vision so they can pounce, any other sensible points.

b Special teeth to grind grass and break open cells, ability to run fast away from predators to avoid being caught, good all round eyesight to detect predators creeping up, good hearing to detect predators, etc.

c Good camouflage, good eyesight, hearing and sense of smell to detect predators, good all-round vision, any other sensible points.

d Teeth and gut adapted to eating plants – crushing the cells to release the cell contents/breaking down cellulose cell walls, ability to reach the top of trees (long neck or good at climbing) to get to the tender leaves, ability to grip on to branches to get to the tender leaves/hold them to pull off the tree, possibly use tail for balance to get to the top of the tree.

12.5

1 a Grow and flower very early before many bigger plants get their leaves; growing tall very fast; growing larger leaves; making more chlorophyll to make the most of any light that arrives; any other sensible points.

b They produce flowers before the oak tree's leaves have grown to full size, so they are not shaded.

2 a To avoid competition between the seedlings and the parent plants and to avoid competition between the seedlings, as far as possible.

b Any three suitable adaptations – look for different ones, for example, fluffy seeds, winged seeds, seeds in berries/fruits which are eaten, explosive seeds, sticky seeds, hooked seeds, seeds that float on water. Any other sensible suggestion.

3 For example, deep taproot (difficult to remove, can regenerate well if severed); low rosette of leaves (avoids blades of lawnmowers and grazing animals); long flowering period, so produces large numbers of seeds; very effective wind dispersal of seed over a large area.

12.6

1 They have sharp mouthparts to pierce the skin of their hosts and suck blood; chemical in saliva to prevent the blood from clotting; flattened body shape so not easily dislodged; very hard bodies so not damaged by the animal scratching; long and powerful back legs so they can jump from host to host and from floor to host; can survive for long spells of time in the environment.

2 Internal parasites have hooks and suckers to attach to the gut wall, made of very thin, flattened segments, which give a big surface area for absorbing food from the gut easily. Segments produce many eggs for reproduction without a male. A thick cuticle protects the tapeworm from the digestive enzymes.

3 Effective parasite because it spends part of its lifecycle in one organism and part in another. In humans it spends time actually inside human liver cells and blood cells, which makes it very difficult for the immune system to attack it and also difficult to develop vaccines which depend on an immune response, because the parasite is hidden in the human cells. Difficult to develop medicines against it which don't also destroy the human cells and cause problems. Any other sensible point.

Answers to end of chapter summary questions

1 a D
b C
c A
d B

2 a The temperatures are too cold for reactions in the body to work and so for the organisms to survive.

b Problems: overheating in day, too cold at night and early morning to move much, water loss. How they cope with problems: bask in the Sun in the morning to warm up, hide in burrows or shade of rocks to avoid heat of day and cold of night, reduce water loss by behaviour and don't sweat.

c Large surface area: volume ratio allows them to lose heat effectively.

3 a Lots of water loss through the leaves, not much water taken up by roots.

b Most water is lost through the leaves, so less leaf surface area means less water loss.

c Spines, rolled leaves.

d Water storage in stems, roots or leaves; thick waxy cuticle; ability to withstand dehydration.

e They have several different adaptations to enable them to withstand water loss/little water available (spines, water storage in stem, etc.).

4 Pandas feed almost exclusively on bamboo, so if it dies out they have no food and will die out as well. Other animals – bamboo only part of the diet so they simply eat other plants.

5 a Because they are competing for exactly the same things.

b Makes sure there is plenty of food for the animals and their young; advertise their territory to reduce conflict with predators.

c Big advantage is that there is no risk of being hurt or killed if you have a courtship ritual/colouration, whereas fighting can lead to both and/or infection and death after injury. Disadvantages is that it uses up a lot of resources to develop the colouration/carry out the display and also the female gets to choose and you might not be chosen.

6 Students use the bar charts in the practical activity on page 84 to answer these questions.

a First month: crowded seedlings taller than spread out seedlings. Crowded seedlings shade each other so each seedling grows taller to avoid the shade. Spread seedlings don't have that pressure. But over six months, the crowded seedlings do not get light as they shade each other. They photosynthesise less so they cannot grow as tall as the spread out seedlings, which can make as much food as possible.

b i They relied mainly on the food stored in the seed – the crowded ones were taller but the spread ones had thicker stems and bigger leaves.

ii The spread out seedlings get the full effect of the light and grow as well as possible, making lots of new plants (and so wet mass). The crowded plants each get less light therefore less photosynthesis and less wet mass.

c To eliminate as far as possible the effects of genetic variety in the seedlings – the bigger the sample, the more reproducible the results.

d i Any of: light level, amount of water and nutrients available, temperature.

ii So that any differences would be the result of the crowding of the seedlings.

7 Malaria is caused by the single-celled parasite *Plasmodium falciparum*, which has a very complicated life cycle. It spends part of its life cycle in a mosquito and part in the human body. The parasites are passed on to people when the female Anopheles mosquitoes take two blood meals from people before laying their eggs. Once inside the human body, the parasites damage the liver and blood and cause serious disease symptoms including fevers, chills and exhausting sweats.

There are several forms of the malarial parasite, and each form is adapted to survive in different places in different hosts. Gametocytes infect mosquitoes, and this form reproduces sexually. The female mosquito takes them in when she feeds on the blood of someone infected with malaria. The gametocytes make their way to the salivary glands of the mosquito and change into a new form called sporozoites. Sporozoites are passed on to humans next time the mosquito takes a blood meal. The female injects saliva into the blood vessels of her host to prevent the blood from clotting as she feeds. Sporozoites enter the blood stream with the saliva and are carried in the blood to the liver where they enter the liver cells. In the liver cells, some of the sporozoites divide asexually to form thousands of merozoites, another form of the malaria parasite.

The merozoites are released from the liver into the blood where they enter the red blood cells. Here, hidden from the immune system of the body, some of the merozoites become schizonts. After a time, the schizonts burst out of the red blood cells, destroying them and releasing more merozoites. It is the reaction of the body to this release of schizonts and the destruction of red blood cells that causes the terrible fever attacks that are seen when someone suffers from malaria. Some of the merozoites in the blood go into a stage of sexual reproduction and produce female gametocytes, which can then be transferred to the female mosquito when she bites, and so the whole cycle starts again.

Answers to end of chapter examination-style questions

1 Marks awarded for this answer will be determined by the Quality of Written Communication (QWC) as well as the standard of the scientific response.

- There is a clear and detailed scientific explanation of adaptations. The answer is coherent and in a logical sequence. It contains a range of appropriate or relevant specialist terms used accurately. The answer shows very few errors in spelling, punctuation and grammar. (*5–6 marks*)
- There is some explanation of adaptations, but there is a lack of clarity and detail. The answer has some structure and the use of specialist terms has been attempted, but not always accurately. There may be some errors in spelling, punctuation and grammar. (*3–4 marks*)
- There is a brief explanation of adaptations, which has little clarity and detail. The answer is poorly constructed with an absence of specialist terms or their use demonstrates a lack of understanding of their meaning. The spelling, punctuation and grammar are weak. (*1–2 marks*)
- No relevant content. (*0 marks*)

Examples of biology points made in the response:

- large ears give large surface area to volume ratio, which allows more heat to be lost in hot conditions
- thin ears means blood flows near the surface so there is a shorter distance for heat energy to travel to surroundings
- no fat layer reduces insulation, which would keep heat in body
- bristles do not trap air layer, which would be an insulating layer
- by feeding in early morning, elephants do not create so much heat in the hot middle of the day and their food will have maximum water content collected overnight.

2 a No wings makes it easier to move in fur (1)
b Piercing mouth parts enable flea to suck blood from host as food (1)
c Flattened bodies make it easier to move in fur (1)
d Hard exterior means it is hard to kill/crush (1)
e Long back legs enable flea to jump from host to host (1)
f Bristles and combs secure it in the fur (1)

3 a Herbicides are chemicals that (selectively) kill some plants/weeds. (1)
b The herbicide will kill the weeds but not the vegetable plants (1) and so the vegetable plants will not have to compete (1) so hard for water (1), mineral ions (1), light (1) or space (1) to grow (*allow maximum of 2 marks for factors listed*). This means the vegetables will photosynthesise more (1) and so grow bigger. (*5 marks maximum*)

4 a i From 21.00 to 06.00 (1)
ii Any one from: same area of study (1); same mass of grass analysed (1); same herd of gemsboks (1). (*1 mark maximum*)
b The water content of grass rises during the night (some time after 18.00 hours to a maximum of 25% at 09.00 hours and then falls (more rapidly at first) to a minimum of 5% at 18.00 hours. (1) (Some accurate reference to actual figures in the table is necessary to obtain the mark.)
c Between 24.00 hours and 06.00 hours. (1) (The important words here are 'more than'. Candidates who ignore these words will include the figure of 30% and therefore give a response of 21.00 hours to 09.00 hours.)
d The water content of the grasses that it eats are high over this period (1). It is night and the gemsboks are therefore less easily seen by predators (1). It is cooler and therefore they are less likely to have to sweat and so this helps them conserve precious water (1).

13 Environmental change and the distribution of organisms

13.1
1 A community of organisms is where several different organisms exist close to each other and can often be dependent on, or have relationships with each other.
2 Temperature, amount of light, level of nutrients, availability of water, oxygen and carbon dioxide.
3 Carnivorous plants capture and digest animals and use the nitrate ions produced as the animal proteins are broken down. Other plants rely on taking nitrate ions from the soil so cannot survive in areas with very low levels of nitrate ions.
4 Temperature affects animals directly because some animals are adapted to life in cold climates and others to hot climates.
Animals are only found in appropriate temperatures and if the temperature of an area changes, it can have a significant impact on the distribution of animals, e.g. bird distribution.
Carbon dioxide levels affect animals directly because some animals are attracted to the carbon dioxide produced by other animals, e.g. mosquitoes.
Light affects the distribution of animals because it often affects the breeding cycles of animals, and also how well they can see to hunt.
All three influence indirectly because of their effect on plant growth as limiting factors – and the distribution of plants has a major impact on the distribution of animals as a major food source.
5 A new predator/carnivore will eat some of the same prey animals as other predators already in the community. It will compete with them. It will reduce the numbers of prey animals available to the existing predators. If it is a very successful competitor, it will reduce the number of prey animals a lot and may cause a big fall in numbers or even the local extinction of other predators. If it is not such a successful predator, it will just reduce the prey animals and other predators slightly.

13.2
1 A quadrat is a square frame made of wood or metal that you lay on the ground to outline your sample area.
Use the same size quadrat every time, and sample as many areas as you can to make results as valid as possible. Take as many samples as possible as sample size is very important in making the results valid. You must choose your sample areas at random so the results reflect the true distribution of the organisms and any findings you make will be valid. There are several ways of taking random samples: two common ones are the person dropping the quadrat, closing your eyes, spinning round, opening your eyes and walking 10 paces before dropping the quadrat. More scientifically, a random number generator is used to determine the drop point. Count the number of organisms you are investigating in the quadrat. It doesn't matter if you count organisms that are partly in the quadrat as in or out, as long as you do the same each time. Once you have collected all your readings, work out the mean number of organisms per m².

The limitations of this technique include: works well for plants and slow moving animals such as sea anemones, but not useful for other animals; difficult to be sure that the samples are completely random; need to take a very large sample size to get valid results over a large area, which is very time consuming and difficult to do; animals, presence can depend on conditions; any other sensible points.

2 a Spin round with eyes closed, keep eyes closed, walk a given number of paces and drop the quadrat, or any other sensible method.
b To give a representative and unbiased sample.
c Mean 6 (6.3), median 6.5, mode 6, 7 and 8.

3 Information similar – often use quadrats along the transect so using the same technique in different ways. Quadrats used for random measurements to get an overall picture of population or distribution of an organism or variety of organisms. Transect is a very specific study of a particular section of a habitat and measures zonal changes.

13.3
1 Repeatable – you must be able to repeat your own experiment and get similar results. Reproducible – other people should be able to repeat your investigation and get similar results. Valid – the investigation must answer the question you are asking.
2 a 1987 and 1989
b 2000 – heavy rain 2 years running which killed a lot of chicks.
c Evidence shows increase in numbers of years with heavy rainfall – often linked to climate change. And also change in sea temperatures with change in numbers of fish species often linked to climate change and changes in the ocean currents.
3 Data is reproducible because it has been carried out over many years on the same transect, on the same nests by different people every time. When a wider variety of nests are examined, the same pattern of results emerges. In a year of heavy rain there is a much lower level of chick survival. Different groups of students were involved in different years and the results still follow the same pattern. So, in these ways, the results can be seen to be reproducible. Results are valid because they answer the question, 'what is happening to the penguin population at Punta Tomobo', 'is the penguin population at Punta Tombo falling?' (or any of a number of other pertinent questions).

13.4
1 Living: presence of predators, food plants, disease-causing pathogens, any other sensible suggestions. Non-living: temperature, pH of an aquatic environment or the air, rainfall, light levels, local climate, oxygen levels (in water), any other sensible point.
2 This type of survey used bioindicators. These are species of animals or plants which are known to survive in particularly clean (e.g. trout, salmon) or particularly polluted (e.g. blood worms) conditions, or to be susceptible to particular pollutants. The presence or absence of these species gives information about the pollution levels. Also the biodiversity of the species of invertebrates and vertebrates in water such as the Thames is a good indicator of pollution levels. A rise in biodiversity suggests the water is less polluted, while a fall in biodiversity can be a clear indicator that pollution levels are rising again.
3 Methods along with evaluation of usefulness – should include at least one physical factor and one example of a bioindicator. Methods could include: measuring a non-living factor, e.g. rainfall, temperature, oxygen levels, levels of pollutants. For each method student must choose a suitable method of measuring changes in the factor they choose, e.g. rain gauge for rainfall, oxygen meter and datalogging for oxygen levels. They need to show that they realise that these measurements need to be taken over time, and using the same equipment to build up a record of data over time.
Measuring the changing distribution of living organisms is another way. This can be done using quadrats, field surveys – again data collected over time in the same place in the same way; examples could be lichens on trees, invertebrates in water. In that case students need to mention capture techniques, identification keys – again over time; measuring number of different species found and the types of different species is also indicative of the cleanliness of the water. Any other valid suggestions.

13.5
1 Temperature changes.
2 Multifactorial means that more than one factor is involved in bringing about a change in distribution of an organism. Bluebell numbers are affected by climate change – as springs get warmer, ground plants are growing earlier than in the past. They grow vigorously and get tall very quickly so they can outcompete the bluebells for light, water and other resources when they are around at the same time. This reduces the numbers of bluebells and the germination of bluebell seedlings. Woodland habitat is also being lost to building; conifer woodlands have lower light levels than deciduous woodlands so bluebells find it harder to get enough light; people go into woodlands to pick bluebells or may trample them; there is also cross-breeding with imported Spanish bluebells, so many factors affect the long-term distribution of the native bluebell.

3 a Bees act as pollinators to many different plants, including many food crops, especially fruit. Also loss of honey and beeswax.

b Colony collapse disorder (could be viral disease, could be spread by parasitic mites); change in flowering patterns due to global warming affecting the foodplants for the bees; farmers spraying chemicals which poison the bees; mobile phones could affect the bee's navigation systems; any other sensible suggestion.

c Because the way the problem is tackled will be very different – if it is a disease caused or carried by parasitic mites, then it becomes important to eradicate or control the mites or treat the disease. If it is a physical factor then we need to look at the environment and what, if anything, can be done to improve the situation for the bees.

Answers to end of chapter summary questions

1 a Nesting sites needed for birds to reproduce successfully, e.g. sand martins need sandy cliffs or river banks. Some plants need shady sheltered areas to thrive, e.g. violets. Any suitable examples.

b This is particularly a problem for plants that take minerals from the soil – so if levels of nitrates are low, very few plants can grow. Therefore in bogs there are very few plants except carnivorous plants such as sundew, Venus fly trap. Any other suitable examples.

c Temperature acts as a limiting factor on photosynthesis, so in cold areas this limits the size and types of plants that can grow. In turn this limits the animal life that can be found in an area, e.g. Arctic plants are small and this limits the range and numbers of reindeer and other Arctic herbivores. Any other sensible suggestions.

d Light affects the numbers and types of plants that can grow by affecting the rate of photosynthesis, e.g. rainforest plants grow very large as there is a plentiful supply of light (and other limiting factors are reduced too). Many animal breeding cycles are affected by light levels as well, e.g. sheep become fertile in autumn as days shorten so they lamb in the spring as the grass starts growing well. Any other suitable examples.

2 a To avoid bias in the results – students might choose areas with lots of casts as they look more interesting, for example.

b Either: the person dropping the quadrat closes their eyes, spins round, opens their eyes and walks 10 paces before dropping the quadrat OR (more scientifically) a random number generator is used to determine the drop point.

c The mean is the sum of the values divided by how many values there are (the average); the median is the middle value in the data set; the mode is the most common value in the data set.

d Trampled area – mean 3.4 (1 dp), median 4, mode 4. Flowerbed – mean 7.1 (1 dp) median 7, mode 6, 9.

e There are more worms in a flowerbed than in an area of trampled grass.

f Ensure quadrats spread randomly, increase the number of quadrat readings taken, get another group to repeat the investigation another day under different conditions, any other sensible suggestions.

3 a A transect is a line across a habitat made by stretching a tape between two points.

b Wave action, height of tides, amount of sunlight, amount of time exposed and not under water, any other sensible points.

c Placing a quadrat at regular intervals along the transect and counting the organisms that fall within it allows you to investigate how the distribution of organisms changes along the line of the transect.

d On a shore: there will be organisms that need to live under water all the time, organisms that can deal with the waves breaking on them, organisms that can survive time in the sea and time exposed, organisms that can live in a very salty environment, relatively few plants. etc. In a field, conditions are much more constant so there will be many more plants, greater variety of invertebrate life in plants and soil, insects, birds, mammals, etc. Any other sensible points to make the comparison between the organisms in the two different environments.

4 a The number of species of lichens has increased.

b As the time since the reduction in sulfur dioxide emissions increases, the levels of air pollution in the area have fallen. This has enabled more and more lichen species to recolonise the area.

c The number of lichen species would fall again.

d Lichens are very sensitive to the levels of sulfur dioxide in the air. In clean air, many lichen species will grow on tree bark, roofs, etc., but sulfur dioxide pollution kills many of the species. So they act as a good bioindicator for air pollution, and in particular for sulfur dioxide pollution, because if lichen species start to disappear it suggests pollution levels are rising, but if more lichen species appear then the air is getting cleaner.

5 a If levels of pollutants increase in water – particularly nitrate levels – this can result in a drop in the oxygen levels in the water. As a result of the increased nitrate, more plants grow and then die, and oxygen is used up by the decomposers in breaking down the excess plant material. This means less oxygen is available for the animal life in the water.

Levels of biodiversity drop and only organisms such as blood worms, which can live in water with very low oxygen levels, will survive. So both the specific species that can be found in the water and the overall levels of biodiversity can be used as bioindicators of pollution levels in aquatic environments.

b This depends on how and where the data was collected, the size of the samples, the frequency with which the samples were repeated, etc. It should be very reliable BUT being living organisms, lots of things can affect how easily they are collected for analysis. Any other sensible points.

c Oxygen levels in water (oxygen meter), temperature (thermometer), pH of water or rainfall (pH meter) – any sensible suggestions for measuring non-living indicators.

6 Any suitable example chosen. Look for detail and accuracy in the account.

Answers to end of chapter examination-style questions

1 a i Lichens – Concentration of sulfur dioxide in the air (1); Rain gauge – Rainfall (1); Freshwater invertebrates – Dissolved oxygen in water (1); Oxygen meter – Dissolved oxygen in water (1); Thermometer – Air or water temperature (1)

ii Lichens and freshwater invertebrates (1)

b Any **three** from: lack of grass seeds and berries as food (1); lack of places to shelter/hide from predators (1); lack of places to build nests/find mates (1); so birds do not survive to produce new offspring and numbers fall. (3 marks maximum)

2 a i Area 3 = 150 g (1); Area 4 = 105 g (1)

ii Median mass = 150 g and 180 g (even number) (1)

b 10 per cm² (1)

c The number of carrots increased rapidly up to 10 seeds per cm² then increased slowly up to 20 seeds per cm² (1). The size increased up to 3 seeds per cm² but decreased after that (1).

d Any two pairs from:
- availability of water (1); as the number of carrots increased the amount of water for each decreased and so they were able to photosynthesise and grow less rapidly (1);
- availability of mineral ions (1); the more carrots the fewer ions available for each one so growth is restricted (1)
- availability of space (1); as there are more carrots, there is less space for their roots and so they cannot grow as much (1). (4 marks maximum)

3 a Transect (1); quadrat (1)

b As you move away from the tree the number of plantains increases (1), but after 5–6 metres it levels off/stays about the same (1).

c Energy from the sun's radiation is required for photosynthesis (1). Photosynthesis produces the sugars/glucose (1) that is then used to make all the other chemicals needed for growth (1).

d Any one from:
- lack of water under tree (1) because leaves shelter ground from rain/because tree roots use it all up (1)
- lack of mineral ions (1) because they have all been used up by the tree (1). (2 marks maximum)

e Any one from:
- light by light meter (1) to see how much sunlight energy is blocked under tree (1)
- water by moisture sensor or rain gauge (1) to see if it is drier under tree (1). (Do not accept measuring oxygen or temperature.) (2 marks maximum)

f Repeatability by doing more transects around tree (1); reproducibility by other groups doing same investigation on different oak trees in park (1).

14 Human population and pollution

14.1

1 a Ability to farm large amounts of food; ability to cure and prevent infectious diseases; no natural predators that we can't shoot; ability to take fish from oceans in huge quantities; ability to control our environment with heating, lighting, etc., so fewer deaths from cold; any other sensible suggestions.

b By building houses and roads, by farming, by quarrying and by dumping waste.

2 a Sewage, fertilisers, pesticides, industrial chemicals; any other sensible suggestion.

b Sulfur dioxide, nitrogen oxides, smoke from burning fossil fuels, and other substances, methane, CFCs; any other sensible suggestions.

c Household waste, sewage, industrial waste, nuclear accidents, fertilisers, pesticides; any other sensible suggestions.

3 a Any sensible suggestions, e.g. use of electricity for lighting, heating, TV, etc.; use of fossil fuels for transport (cars, planes, etc.); plastics.

b Any three suitable suggestions, such as fossil fuels, wood, land, metals, etc.

4 Look for clarity of explanation without copying the Student Book. Points covered should include:
- Growing human population increases the amount of waste, including bodily waste and the rubbish from packaging, uneaten food and disposable goods.
- The dumping of waste produced by the ever-expanding human population makes large areas of land unavailable for other life.
- Driving cars, etc., leads to gases from exhausts.
- Farming leads to the use of pesticides and fertiliser sprays that cause pollution.

14.2

1 a Human bodily waste mixed with waste water.

b Nitrate ions, (phosphates).

c Because high levels of nitrate ions lead to eutrophication, when there is excess plant growth due to the high nitrate levels followed by death and decay. Decomposers use high levels of oxygen, which depletes the oxygen supply in the water and causes the death of fish and other animals.

2 Any sensible points including: toxic waste can poison soils; acidic gases from burning fossil fuels in factories can lead to acid rain; global warming as a result of carbon dioxide produced by burning in industry as well as vehicles; global dimming as a result of smoke from industrial processes leading to cooling temperatures; radiation damage, e.g. Chenobyl; toxic chemicals can poison land or waterways.

3 a Pollution of the land – pesticides and herbicides, sprayed to reduce pest damage and overcrowding of crops, soak into the soil and pollute it; they can become part of food webs and damage predators. Pollution of the water – pesticides and herbicides sprayed as above, and fertilisers added to the soil to improve crop yields can be washed out of the soil into waterways by rain. Toxic chemicals can kill water organisms through food webs. Nitrates from fertilisers cause eutrophication – excess plant growth, needing many microorganisms to decompose the plants, using up oxygen in water so fish and other animals die from lack of oxygen. This adds to the problem – more death, more decay, etc.

b Levels of pesticide in water needed to kill insects very low. DDT not broken down in the body. So the small fish that feed on the insects killed by DDT, or on plants which have absorbed DDT from the water, accumulate a higher level of DDT in their body. Larger fish eat them and the same thing happens so levels of DDT build up. Bigger fish eat lots of the medium-sized fish and the levels of DDT in their bodies get even higher. Birds of prey and herons eat the bigger fish then get a high enough level of DDT building up in their bodies to cause health problems and to kill them.

14.3

1

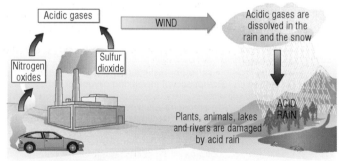

Sulfur dioxide and nitrogen oxides are often carried high in the air by the winds. This means they can be blown from a country that does not control its sulfur emissions to a country that has strict emission controls and fall as acid rain. This can cause as much damage to buildings and ecosystems as if the country did not control its emissions – and the clean air can be blown on to benefit other neighbours.

2 a i Sulfur dioxide, carbon dioxide and nitrogen oxides are produced from impurities when fossil fuels are burned. These cause air pollution.

ii Sulfur dioxide and nitrogen oxides in the air dissolve in the rain and fall to the ground. The water runs into streams, rivers, etc., and lowers the pH, making them more acidic.

iii Acid rain falls on the ground, soaks in and causes it to be acidic.

b The sulfur dioxide and nitrogen oxides produced by burning fossil fuels are carried high in the air by the prevailing winds. They can be blown hundreds of miles before they dissolve in rain and are carried to the ground. So every country needs to control emissions from the burning of fossil fuels to prevent any country being affected by acid rain.

3 a Global dimming is the reduction in light reaching the surface of the Earth because light is reflected away by the build up of pollution particles in the air (from sulfur compounds and smoke particles).

b Sulfur dioxide emissions in 1980 = 4.8; sulfur dioxide emissions in 2002 = 1.0; so, reduction in sulfur dioxide emissions between 1980 and 2002 = $(4.8 - 1.0)/4.8 \times 100 = 79\%$.

c Car engines, power stations and industry, but all are under strict controls and levels of sulfur emissions have fallen steadily for many years.

d Europe has controlled air pollution as seen by reduction in sulfur emissions; smoke will be controlled at the same time; this reduces the number of particles in the air reflecting the light and so reverses dimming effect of air pollution.

14.4

1 a The number and variety of different organisms found in a specified area.

b The removal of large areas of forests by felling, often linked to burning as well.

c Tropical rainforests contain more biodiversity than any other land environment so the loss of the forests means the biodiversity of animal and plant life is also lost. It matters because many species are being destroyed before they have even been identified, yet they could be extremely useful for crop breeding, medicines or food for the future. Any other sensible points.

2 Carbon dioxide produced by burning of trees; carbon dioxide produced by decomposition; less carbon dioxide removed from atmosphere by growing plants.

3 a i Rice fields are increasing because there is a population explosion; rice is the staple diet for many people, so more rice is needed. Cattle are increasing because there is a demand for cheap beef to supply burgers. Increased standards of living also means a greater demand for animal products generally.

ii Peat bogs decreasing as peat is used as a fuel and for compost for gardeners.

b Rice and cows lead to increased levels of methane in the atmosphere. Methane is a greenhouse gas. Loss of peat bog leads to an increase in carbon dioxide levels as peat is burnt or used as compost.

14.5

1 a Look for an accurately drawn bar chart from the figures given, correctly labelled axes, neat columns, etc.

b Levels of carbon dioxide have risen steadily since 1970 as a result of deforestation, burning fossil fuels, etc.

c The Sun's energy heats the Earth. Much of this heat is reflected back into space but some is absorbed by greenhouse gases, which re-radiate it back. Therefore the Earth's surface is kept warm enough for life. Increased levels of greenhouse gases leads to excess warming. This could result in climate change such as more extreme weather events. Melting of polar ice caps may also increase sea levels and flood low-lying land.

2 Global warming is a very small observed increase in the mean temperature at the surface of the Earth. The greenhouse effect is the way that the surface of the Earth is kept warm enough for life to exist as a result of the impact of greenhouse gases, such as carbon dioxide and methane, on the loss of heat energy from the surface. Energy from the Sun reaches the Earth, warming it up, and much of it is radiated back out into space. However, gases such as carbon dioxide and methane absorb some of the energy released as the Earth cools down, so it can't escape, keeping the Earth and its surrounding atmosphere warm and ideal for life. However, if the levels of carbon dioxide and methane in the atmosphere of the Earth increase, the amount of heat retained will also increase and this will cause global warming.

3 Look for accurate information and good examples.

14.6

1 Because if human behaviour and environmental changes are linked there needs to be some very big changes in human behaviour that people are not going to like and governments are not going to want to impose. If they are not linked then we need to know so that we do not make unnecessary changes. So all the evidence needs to be as repeatable, reproducible and valid as possible, so that if people challenge the findings they can check for themselves and get the same results. Any other sensible points.

2 a Weather is local and changes from day to day. Climate is the weather in an area over an extended period. Weather can be very variable but climates tend to be stable and predictable.

b Correlation is not the same as causation. If, in an investigation, it can be clearly, reproducibly and repeatably seen that one factor always causes an observed change, then that is relatively quickly and easily accepted, e.g. heating water makes it boil. However, it is very difficult to make such clearcut observations about human activities, carbon dioxide levels, etc., and certainly very difficult to know what has happened in the past. In some instances there is a very clear correlation between things that have no causative effect at all. So scientists have to be very careful and very thorough and build up their evidence over time.

3 Figure 2 shows a general pattern that before the late 1930s, the mean global temperature each year was below the average for the century. And that from the late 1970s the mean global temperature has been above the average for the century. This data certainly suggests that global warming is taking place. Figure 3 shows that there have been spikes in carbon dioxide, dust and temperature levels through the millennia. It shows that raised carbon dioxide levels are usually associated with raised mean temperature levels, and that raised dust levels are usually associated with lower mean temperatures. This confirms our models of global warming and global dimming. We currently have raised carbon dioxide and raised temperature, which ties in with data from Figure 2. Any other sensible suggestions.

Answers to end of chapter summary questions

1 a Building houses, shops, industrial sites and roads; for farming; for waste disposal; any other sensible suggestion.
 b People need places to live; to buy food; to produce things they need; transport systems to move people and goods; to grow food; to get rid of waste and rubbish; any sensible suggestions.
 c Any two sensible suggestions, e.g.: recycle rubbish; build fewer houses; more flats which use up less land; use public transport so fewer roads needed; etc.
2 a Cars and factories produce sulfur dioxide and nitrogen oxides → up into the atmosphere → carried along by winds → dissolve in rain → fall as acid rain on land and in water.
 b i 18 Tg per year.
 ii As appropriate.
 iii 4 Tg per year.
 c Sulfur dioxide emissions have fallen steadily and levelled out at a greatly reduced level. There are strict rules about the levels of sulfur dioxide and nitrogen oxides in the exhaust fumes of new cars, and catalytic converters remove sulfur dioxide. Cleaner, low-sulfur fuels are used in cars and power stations. More electricity is generated from gas and nuclear power. Systems are in place in power station chimneys that clean the flue gases.
3 a A model which shows the feeding relationships between plants and animals in an environment.
 b ×1 000 000
 c ×34
 d Levels of pesticide in water very low. DDT not broken down in living organisms. Plants absorb DDT and accumulate it through photosynthesis and diffusion. The small fish that feed on the plants absorb DDT from the water, eat lots of plants and accumulate a higher level of DDT in their body. Larger fish eat them and the same thing happens so levels of DDT build up. Cormorants eat lots of the medium-sized fish and the levels of DDT in their bodies get even higher. Crocodiles eat the bigger fish and cormorants and then get a high enough level of DDT building up in their bodies to cause health problems and even to kill them.
4 a Tropical rainforests contain more biodiversity than any other land environment so the loss of the forests means the biodiversity of animal and plant life is also lost. It matters because many species are being destroyed before they have even been identified, yet they could be extremely useful for crop breeding, medicines or food for the future. Tropical rainforests also have huge amounts of sequestered carbon dioxide in the bodies of the trees, which is locked up for the lifetime of the tree and then released slowly as it decays, but which is released all in one go if the trees are burned. Also. loss of trees means carbon dioxide is not being taken out of the atmosphere by photosynthesis in all the plants that make up the forest, including the trees. Any other sensible points.

Peat bogs are thousands of years old and contain huge amounts of stored carbon dioxide in the incompletely decomposed plant material. When peat is removed from the bogs and burnt as a fuel or used in the garden, the stored carbon dioxide is released back into the atmosphere. Peat forms very slowly so it is being destroyed faster than it can form.

Similarities: Both take a long time to form, both store huge amounts of carbon dioxide, both cause the release of carbon dioxide into the atmosphere when they are destroyed, both are very difficult to replace. Any other sensible points.

Differences: Rainforests lose huge amounts of biodiversity when destroyed. Peat bogs have small numbers of very rare, specially adapted organisms associated with them, which are lost, but less overall biodiversity goes. Any other sensible points.

---

 b i Look for clearly labelled and appropriate axes, well drawn graph.
 ii Advantages: Dairy cows produce huge amounts of milk, which is the basis of a very large range of human foods and drinks, and leather; beef cattle produce meat to eat and leather; sheep produce meat, milk in much smaller volumes than cows and wool. Any other sensible points.
 Disadvantages: All produce greenhouse gas methane (and carbon dioxide from respiration). Dairy cattle produce the most methane. Rainforests cut down to farm cattle to get cheap beef for burgers. Any other sensible points.
5 a In summer months, plants photosynthesising a lot and growing fast so take a lot of carbon dioxide out of the atmosphere. In winter, in all temperate regions, plants die back and trees lose their leaves so much less photosynthesis takes place, so carbon dioxide levels rise.
 b We can see the difference it makes when plants are actively photosynthesising in the summer, so we need plants there. If plants were not there to photosynthesise, imagine how carbon dioxide levels would build up, so it is vital to prevent deforestation.
 c More people; more cars and factories means more CO_2; more deforestation means less uptake of CO_2; more paddy fields to grow rice to feed people means more methane; more cows to produce cheap beef also produces methane. These greenhouse gases could change the Earth's climate, producing more extreme weather events and altering rainfall and temperatures in different ways in different parts of the world. Any other sensible point.
 d All sensible suggestions e.g. ice core data, measuring temperature at the surface of the Earth, monitoring weather patterns, tree rings, peat bog cores, etc. Most valid, repeatable and reproducible – data that can be checked and confirmed against other measures; data presented by groups without a bias; any sensible suggestions recognising that some data are is more valid, repeatable and reproducible than others.

Answers to end of chapter examination-style questions

1 a Sulfur dioxide/nitrogen dioxide (1); carbon dioxide/methane (1).
 b Pesticides (1) and herbicides (1).
 c Eutrophication (1); oxygen (1).
2 a Any three from: building, quarrying, mining, farming, dumping waste. (3 marks maximum)
 b i Biodiversity is the number of different species of living organisms/ plants and animals found in a particular habitat/place. (1)
 ii Any three from: taking away the land means clearing the plants (1) which are the producers (1) in the food chains, so other species cannot get enough food. The plants/trees are also needed for shelter/homes (1) so animals are easily caught by predators/have nowhere to breed (1). (3 marks maximum)
3 a Brazil grows sugar for fermentation/ produces ethanol (1) to use as a biofuel (1).
 b Methane (1)
 c i Any two from: by plants for photosynthesis (1); by dissolving in the rain (1); by dissolving in the lakes/oceans (1); by being used by sea organisms for shells/skeletons (1). (2 marks maximum)
 ii Any two pairs from:
 – Removing trees/plants (1) means they no longer take in carbon dioxide for photosynthesis (1).
 – Burning the wood/debris (1) releases more carbon dioxide that was locked in the wood (1).
 – Micro-organisms decay all the debris left behind (1) and release carbon dioxide as they respire (1). (4 marks maximum)
 d Any three from: ice caps melting; sea levels rising/flooding low-lying lands; more desserts; more storms/flooding; climates change; upsetting ocean current patterns; upsetting birds' migration patterns. (Do not accept animals die because it gets too hot.) (3 marks maximum)
4 a Any two pairs from:
 – Mayfly larvae (1) are present in high oxygen concentrations but none in low oxygen concentrations (1);
 – Diving beetles (1) as there are many at high oxygen levels but few in low oxygen levels (1);
 – Freshwater hoglice (1) live in low oxygen concentrations (1). (4 marks maximum)
 b Likely to be correct because less oxygen downstream (1) suggests eutrophication has occurred (1) but either there is not enough evidence/needs more results/repeats/samples OR there might be something else/a chemical causing the low oxygen levels (1).
 c Marks awarded for this answer will be determined by the Quality of Written Communication (QWC) as well as the standard of the scientific response.
 • There is a clear and detailed scientific description of the sequence of events. The answer is coherent and in a logical sequence.

It contains a range of appropriate or relevant specialist terms used accurately. The answer shows very few errors in spelling, punctuation and grammar. (*5–6 marks*)
- There is some description of the sequence of events, but there is a lack of clarity and detail. The answer has some structure and the use of specialist terms has been attempted, but not always accurately. There may be some errors in spelling, punctuation and grammar. (*3–4 marks*)
- There is a brief description, which has little clarity and detail. The answer is poorly constructed with an absence of specialist terms or their use demonstrates a lack of understanding of their meaning. The spelling, punctuation and grammar are weak. (*1–2 marks*)
- No relevant content. (*0 marks*)

Examples of biology points made in the response (in correct order):
- sewage contains organic matter/mineral ions/nutrients
- so algae/water plants grow (on surface of) in water
- algae/plants underneath top layer do not get enough light
- for photosynthesis
- so they die
- and microorganisms/decomposers decay them
- using up all the oxygen in the water
- so invertebrates/fish/aerobic creatures die too.

15 Evolution

15.1

1 a All the species of living organisms that are alive today (and many more which are now extinct) have evolved from simple life forms, which first developed more than 3 billion years ago.
  b Only the animals and plants most suited to their environment – the 'fittest' – will survive to breed and so pass on their characteristics.
2 Any thoughtful point, e.g. Lamarck helped to pave the way for Darwin's ideas; Lamarck's ideas stimulated Darwin's thinking; people had already come to terms with a theory other than the Bible so were more ready to accept Darwin's ideas, debate on the origins of life was opened up; Darwin's theory made more sense than Lamarck's and had an evidence base that Lamarck's did not, which made it easier for it to be accepted.
3 a South American rheas – Darwin found a new species. Two types of the bird living in slightly different areas made Darwin start to think about how they came about.
  b Galapagos tortoises, iguanas and finches – these were some of the animals in the Galapagos Islands that varied from island to island, and made Darwin wonder what had brought about the differences.
  c The long voyage of HMS *Beagle* – this gave Darwin lots of opportunities to collect specimens and time to think about his theories and ideas.
  d The twenty years from his return to the publication of the book *The Origin of Species* gave Darwin time to work out his ideas very carefully and to collect a lot of evidence to support them.

15.2

1 Darwin's theory is that all living organisms have evolved from simpler life forms by a process of natural selection. Reproduction always produces more offspring than the environment can support. Only those that have inherited features most suited to their environment – the 'fittest' – will survive. When they breed, they pass on the genes for those useful inherited characteristics to their offspring. This is natural selection.
2 a Captain's companion and ship's naturalist.
  b South America and the South Sea Islands.
  c *On the Origin of Species* published in 1859, so 28 years.
3 He used evidence from the voyage of HMS *Beagle* to show different organisms on different islands that were very similar but had adapted to fill different niches, etc., breeding experiments with pigeons, and evidence of different species of barnacles, discussion with and use of observations from fellow scientists.
4 There was a clash between the establishment, which was based on the Church and the idea that everything had its place and was created by God. A lot of inertia and strong belief to overcome. Also, it was just the status quo. Although Darwin had put together a lot of evidence, it wasn't enough for some scientists, particularly the links higher up the evolutionary tree thinking about human evolution. He was missing the fossil records that would fill in some of the gaps. No obvious mechanism until genes and genetics were discovered, so it was a process without an obvious model of how it came about.

15.3

1 [Any suitable examples from the spread.]
2 a New forms of genes (alleles) result from changes in existing genes known as mutations. Mutations are tiny changes in the long strands of DNA. Mutations occur quite naturally through mistakes made in copying DNA when the cells divide, but the rate of mutation can be increased by radiation or certain chemicals.

  b Mutations introduce more variety into the genes of a species and can increase the chances of survival. Many mutations have no effect on the characteristics of an organism, and some mutations are harmful but sometimes a mutation has a good effect by producing an adaptation that makes an organism better suited to its environment. This makes it more likely to survive and breed. The mutant allele will gradually become more common in the population and will cause the species to evolve. If a new form of a gene arises from mutation and this coincides with a change in the environment, there may be a relatively rapid change in a species. If the mutation gives the organism an advantage in the changed environment, it will soon become common. This is why mutations are important in natural selection.
3 a Mutation gave some deer antlers to make them more successful in battles with other stags and more attractive to females. This means that they are more likely to mate and pass on their genes. This process continues until antlers become normal in the population. The stags with the biggest or most effective antlers are the ones which mate most successfully.
  b Mutation produced spines instead of leaves. Cactus loses very little water and so survives well and reproduces, passing on advantageous genes until normal in population.
  c Mutation gives increased temperature tolerance. These camels have an advantage, so more likely to survive and breed, passing on the mutation until it is normal in the population.

15.4

1 a The organisation of living organisms into groups according to their similarities.
  b Animals, plants, monera, protoctista and fungi.
  c The smallest main group in classification. Often defined as a group of organisms that can breed together and produce fertile offspring. Any five examples of species including at least one plant species.
2 a Look for similarities and differences – traditionally these were physical appearance, including internal structures such as the skeleton, but biochemistry and how the cells work is now part of the picture. Modern technology has made big changes – the use of microscopes but most particularly the use of DNA analysis, which allows us to identify relationships between organisms very precisely.
  b Classifying organisms and seeing how closely they are related to other organisms allows us to build up evolutionary trees. The use of DNA technology makes it easier to recognise when organisms look similar but are not closely related or when they look very different but have evolved into separate species very recently.
3 Evolutionary trees look at the relationships between different groups of animals and how long ago they divided away from a common ancestor. They are very useful for helping to understand evolutionary pathways and relationships between species. DNA evidence has become very important in the development of evolutionary trees and changed some of the ideas based on observation alone.

15.5

1 a No one was there to see it and there is no direct evidence for what happened.
  b They show us how plants and animals have changed over time, how many animals have appeared and that some no longer exist.
2 a They may be formed from the hard parts of an animal, such as the bones, teeth, claws or shells.
     They may be formed when an animal or plant does not decay after it has died, e.g. in ice or peat.
     They may be formed when harder parts of the animal or plant are replaced by other minerals and become part of the rock. Mould fossils are formed when a impression of an organism is made in mud and then becomes fossilised, while cast fossils are made when a mould is filled in.
     They may be fossils not of actual animals or plants, but of traces they have left behind, e.g. fossil footprints, burrows, rootlet traces and droppings.
  b Rock fossils.
  c Millions of years ago.
3 An ice fossil is formed when an animal or plant does not decay after death because the temperature is too low for decay to take place. The animals and plants are preserved almost intact.These fossils are rare, but they give a clear insight into what an animal looked like. Ice fossils are often thousands of years old. They can tell us details such as what an animal had been eating or the colour of a long-extinct flower. We can even extract the DNA and compare it to the DNA of modern organisms. They mean that when we compare a more traditional fossil against an ice fossil, we can see how accurate our picture really is, because the ice fossils give us such a clear picture of the organism in life.

15.6

1 Helps us see how organisms have changed over millions of years to evolve into the animals we see today. Often what we can learn from

fossils is limited because the fossil record is often incomplete, but when we get a compete record, such as the horse, we can build up a clear picture of how a species evolves over time in response to changing environmental conditions; this is also revealed through the fossil record of plants, etc. Also shows organisms that have changed very little over millions of years, e.g. sharks.

2 It shows us how tall they were, what their feet were like, what their jaws and teeth were like and the basic body shape. This in turn tells us how they might have lived, how fast they moved, what they ate; it also allows us to compare them to modern horses.

3 a The cat has kittens, the kittens breed and soon there are lots of cats. Cats catch black-tailed mice easily, the mice numbers fall until there are not enough to breed and mice become extinct. Knock-on effect on owls and hawks as part of their diet has gone – which in turn will affect other prey animals.

   b European primroses will make more food and have bigger leaves – however, seeds will germinate sooner so will be too much competition for the English primrose and eventually it could become extinct.

15.7

1 a Any four sensible suggestions, e.g. new predators, new diseases, new, more successful competitors, environmental changes such as global warming, more rainfall, etc.

   b Any sensible suggestions, e.g. massive volcanic eruptions, collision of giant asteroids with the Earth.

2 Because without extinction, unsuccessful species would not die out. There would be too much competition for resources. New species would find it difficult to evolve. Any thoughtful point.

3 a Evidence for giant asteroid strike – crater, layer of rock debris, mineral formed when massive force hits rocks. The age of the rocks suggest this happened immediately before the mass extinction of dinosaurs.

   b An asteroid impact would have blasted huge amounts of dust and debris into the atmosphere. It would have triggered huge fires, earthquakes and landslides that would generate smoke and dust. This would have greatly reduced the levels of light reaching the Earth. In turn, this would have stopped plants growing and caused very low temperatures. This global winter would have caused the extinction of up to 70% of all the species on the Earth, including the dinosaurs because of the lack of food and an inability to keep warm, etc.

15.8

1 a Geographically by the formation of mountains, rivers, continents breaking apart, etc.
      Environmentally – climate change in one area and not another or different types of change in different areas.

   b Natural selection means organisms best suited to a particular environment will be most likely to survive and breed. So in two different environments, different features will be selected for and the organisms will become more and more different until they cannot interbreed and new species have evolved.

2 a An organism which is found in only one place in the world, where it has evolved.

   b Endemic organisms evolve as a result of geographical isolation. When an area of land becomes an island, the plants and animals on it are isolated from the organisms on the mainland and so, as they evolve, they often form new species. These are different from the original species and are unique and endemic to the island.

   c Our current model of speciation is that an organism has a wide range of alleles controlling its characteristics as a result of genetic variation from sexual reproduction and mutation. In each population, the alleles that are selected will control characteristics that help the organism to survive and breed successfully. This is natural selection. In the formation of endemic species, part of a population becomes isolated with new environmental conditions. Alleles for characteristics that enable organisms to survive and breed successfully in the new conditions will be selected. These are likely to be different from the alleles that gave success in the original environment. As a result of the selection of these different alleles, the characteristic features of the isolated organisms will change. Eventually, they can no longer interbreed with the original organisms and a new species forms. This is what has happened on islands such as Borneo, Australia and the Galapagos Islands, and it acts as evidence that our model of speciation reflects what happens in the natural world.

3 All populations have natural genetic variation due to sexual reproduction and mutation. This results in a wide variety of alleles in the population. If part of the population becomes isolated and conditions are different from the original population, different alleles are likely to give an advantage. These alleles will be selected for, as the organisms which have them will be most likely to survive and reproduce successfully in the new environment. As a result the characteristics of the organism will change until eventually they can no longer interbreed with the original population and a new species has evolved.

Answers to end of chapter summary questions

1 Lamarck thought that animals adapted and evolved to suit their environment and that they had all evolved from primitive worms by the inheritance of acquired characteristics. Lamarck's theory was that an organism's behaviour affected their structures, so if an animal used something a lot over several generations it would grow and develop, and this improved feature would be passed from parents to offspring. If a structure wasn't used, Lamarck thought it would shrink and be lost.

2 a He started with his work on barnacles, but it was the observations he made on the voyage on HMS *Beagle* that really made him recognise the great variety of life and start to consider how it had come about.

   b Darwin's theory is that all organisms produce more offspring than can survive. Some of these are better fitted to the environment than others, and these are the ones that are most likely to survive, breed and pass on those beneficial characteristics. This process of natural selection is most noticeable if there is a change in the environment.

3 a Similarities: They both suggest evolution of living things from simpler organisms, both suggest it took a long time; both suggest changes passed from parents to offspring. Differences: Lamarck suggests primitive worms as a starting point, suggests it is acquired characteristics which are passed on; Darwin suggests it is inherited features which are passed on, and the process of natural selection ('survival of the fittest') to decide which organisms survive and breed.

   b Any thoughtful point, e.g. it helped to pave the way for Darwin's ideas, people had already come to terms with a theory other than the Bible, debate was opened up, the idea of organisms evolving and changing was already there, Darwin's ideas of natural selection then made more sense – (people could see it happening with their own livestock) – than the idea of acquired characteristics, which people could see didn't happen in their own experience.

4 Credit careful explanations that include an understanding of the basic concepts. E.g. a pair of founder finches on one island with a high insect population has a mutation which results in birds with a slightly different shape beak. This makes it easier (for example) to poke its beak into cracks to find insects. These birds can get food that others can't reach which gives them an advantage. They get more food therefore more likely to survive, breed and pass on the genes for the thinner beak shape. Eventually a whole group of birds evolve with thinner beaks which feed on insects. As they are separate from the other birds, a new species has been formed. A similar process occurs on another island where there are a lot of fruit bushes – these birds evolve beaks suited to eating fruit and buds, etc. The birds evolve to take advantage of the available food on the islands.

5 a That species exist in different forms and the species which are not well adapted to conditions are most likely to die out.

   b They are both relatively isolated islands with lots of organisms that are found only there and are well adapted to the conditions. These different organisms would have helped Wallace as the differences were clear and obviously related to the conditions in Borneo, just as Darwin observed the very specialised organisms on the Galapagos islands.

   c Darwin was still working on his ideas and building up evidence – he was not expecting someone else to come up with basically the same idea on the strength of a short period of work.

   d Darwin had many different species that were closely related but showing adaptations from the Galapagos islands. He had years of breeding experiments with pigeons; huge collections of drawings and classification of barnacles with adaptations to different environments, etc.

6 a The organisation of living organisms into groups based on the similarities and differences between them.

   b Simple observation of external physical characteristics, habitat, etc. Analysis of the DNA to show the genetic links between the organisms.

   c Both show the ways in which organisms are related and may have evolved from a common ancestor.
      An evolutionary relationship shows how closely linked different organisms are genetically and so shows when the different species evolved away from each other. An ecological relationship shows how different organisms have developed together within their environment, and how this has affected their evolution.

7 a The remains of organisms from many years ago, often found in rocks. They can be formed in a number of different ways.

   b Rock fossil formation: The animal dies and falls to the ground and the flesh rots away, leaving the skeleton. This is covered with sand, soil or clay before it is damaged. Protected under layers of soil and rocks for millions of years, the skeleton becomes mineralised and turns to rock. Eventually it comes to the surface as a result of earth movements and erosion.
      Ice fossil formation: The animal died in conditions where decay could not take place. In this case, it was frozen immediately after death and preserved.

c Evidence of species which are now extinct; can be used to show links to modern species and relationships between different fossil species. Bone fossils show anatomical structures of organisms, size, etc., while ice fossils show appearance of animals in life, colours, can show food, etc. and give DNA for comparison with modern specimens. Limitations – not many fossils found; fossil record often incomplete; rarely find complete skeleton; skeletal fossils do not show what organisms actually looked like; few soft-bodied fossils; few complete evolutionary sequences; most fossils do not yield DNA, etc. Any sensible points.

d Earliest organisms all soft bodied – do not form fossils so little or no fossil evidence of the earliest life forms.

8 a The loss of all members of a species in an area or on the Earth.

b Species extinction is the loss of an entire species. Mass extinction the loss of a large percentage of all the species alive on the Earth over a relatively short period of time.

c Evidence in the fossil record of huge number of species disappearing.

d Any two theories, e.g. asteroid strike, volcanic eruption, global temperature change due to carbon dioxide levels, etc., with examples of relevant evidence.

e Importance – they have led to the evolution of many new species adapted to the new conditions to fill the available niches, and so moved the development of life forward.

9 The student should focus on the role of isolation – geographical or otherwise – as a reason for speciation to take place. Students should describe how organisms are unable to interbreed, natural genetic variety and how particular mutations become advantageous in isolated situations, leading to the formation of new species through natural selection. Look for good explanations and varied examples.

Answers to end of chapter examination-style questions

1 a In Darwin's theory, all life forms developed from simpler organisms/characteristics suited to a particular environment are selected (1). Lamarck/others suggested that characteristics acquired by an organism in its lifetime could be passed on to offspring (1).

b Any **two** from: it was believed that God created all the plants and animals on the Earth just as they are (1); scientists did not know about genes or how inheritance worked (1); Darwin did not have enough evidence at the time to convince people (1). (2 marks maximum)

c Mutations caused some finches to have sharper, thinner beaks (1). These birds found it easier to catch the insects so they survived and bred (1). So more offspring inherited the sharper, thinner beak as the genes were passed on (1). After many (or idea of) generations, all the finches had sharp thin beaks.

2 a Amphibia, reptiles, birds, mammals (1).

b Cartilage fish (1).

c From fossils (1).

d Diseases (1); predators (1).

3 Any **five** from:
- The population of the common ancestor had variation in size/size of jaw.
- The smaller, faster swimmers caught more fish which were easy to swallow.
- The larger ones with bigger jaws were able to catch and eat the rodents.
- The populations gradually separated to live where their food was.
- Natural selection occurred/different genes were selected and made them more different.
- Eventually they were so different they could no longer interbreed. (5 marks maximum)

4 a All members of a species die out. (2)

b i 900 million (must have the units) (1);

ii 11 (1);

iii As the human population rises, the number of extinctions rises. (2)

c i 4 (2) (If answer incorrect then 68–64 = 1 mark)

ii At the beginning of the century, people using more land for housing, etc. so loss of habitat/industrialisation/rise in pollution (1). At the end of the century, there were more protected species/idea of conservation of habitats/reintroduction (1).

16 Energy and biomass in food chains and natural cycles

16.1

1 a The mass of material in an animal or plant.

b Because it shows the amount of biological material at each level more accurately.

2 a Check students' answers for accuracy of pyramids.

b This is because the amount of material and energy contained in the biomass of the organisms at each stage of a food chain is less than it was at the previous stage. Not all of the organism at one stage is eaten by the stage above (e.g. roots of plants not eaten by sheep, only the blood of the sheep eaten by ticks). Some of the materials and energy taken in are passed out and lost in the waste products of the organism. Much of the material taken in is used in cellular respiration to produce energy, and much of that energy is eventually lost to the surroundings as heat. A relatively small amount of the food eaten is converted into new biomass in the next organisms in the food chain. So a large percentage of the biomass in the grass cropped by the sheep is not available to be passed on to the sheep ticks – and a large percentage of the biomass of the sheep is also not available to the sheep ticks, which is why they have so much less biomass than the original grass.

3 a $5000/100\,000 \times 100 = 5\%$

b $30/5000 \times 100 = 0.6\%$

16.2

1 a Not all of the material eaten can be digested by the animal and the indigestible material – cellulose cell walls in plants, hooves, bones, hair, etc., in animals – are passed out of the body in the faeces.

b The biomass taken in is used in cellular respiration to provide energy for movement and to supply the energy needed and the raw materials for building new biomass. The more energy from the food that is used to provide energy for movement, the less is available.

2 Most of the Sun's energy is not captured by plants. Plant biomass eaten by animals cannot all be digested. Some is broken down and used in respiration to release energy.
Most energy is used for movement and control of body temperature. A small amount is used for growth to produce new biomass in animals.

16.3

1 Biomass and energy is lost at every stage of a food chain – not all food eaten is digested, biomass is used as fuel for cellular respiration, energy lost to surroundings as heat, etc. Therefore the fewer stages there are in a food chain, the more efficient it is – so if people all ate plants instead of feeding plants to animals and then eating the animals, it would reduce the stages in the food chain. This would greatly reduce the loss of biomass and energy which results in adding another stage in the food chain, and so there would in theory be enough food available to feed everyone.

2 a Movement uses energy, so the less the animals move, the more energy is available for conversion into biomass. Animals that are kept indoors can have their temperatures controlled, so they don't use energy generating extra heat if temperatures fall, or sweating to lose heat if temperatures get too hot. Again, this maximises the conversion of food to biomass.

b Livestock such as cattle and pigs use a lot of energy in regulating their body temperature, cooling themselves down if they get too hot and keeping warm if the temperature falls. If the temperature in their accommodation is kept ideal, then they don't use energy from the biomass of their food regulating their body temperature. This means there is more energy available for building new animal biomass. As a result the livestock grow as fast as possible.

3 a Advantages: Work indoors, animals grow faster so can be sold sooner and next lot started off.
Disadvantages: He has to heat animal houses, light animal houses, build animal houses and animals may be stressed, higher feed bills.

b Advantages: Animals reared more naturally (more contented?), animals healthier so lower vets bills, no heating/lighting bills, lower feed bills.
Disadvantages: Have to deal with the weather, animals grow more slowly, need land.

4 Food miles are a measure of how far food has travelled from the farm where it was grown to your plate. Food produced around the world can travel thousands of miles flying or sailing to get to the UK and then on roads to get to shops and homes, using fuel to do so. Burning fossil fuels increases the carbon dioxide in the atmosphere, which may contribute to global warming. As people become aware of the effect of food miles on the environment, they aim to reduce the miles travelled by their food to lower the carbon dioxide implications (carbon footprint) of the food they eat.

16.4

1 a Development of large commercial fleets and huge factory ships have overfished the seas.

b Methods include controlling the size of the holes in the nets so only the largest fish are caught, banning fishing during the breeding season and strict catch quotas.

c Because people earn a living from fishing and didn't want to lose their income; no-one believed fish stocks would fall so dramatically; sea is big and seemed as if supply of fish is endless; any other sensible points.

2 a Atlantic 1000× bigger, Indian 6500× bigger, Pacific 1000× bigger.

b By rigid fishing quotas, eating only line-caught tuna, strict protection of fishing seasons and size of fish that can be caught; any other sensible point.

3 Similar: the fermenter like the enclosed shed or barn; the temperature is regulated and food supply (glucose) maintained to give the organism (*Fusarium*) the optimum conditions for maximum growth as fast as possible; cost of maintaining conditions outweighed by increase in production. Differs: fungus not an animal so conditions cause no stress – in fact ideal conditions; pH not monitored and maintained in farming; no free-range alternative.

16.5

1 a Detritivores such as maggots and some types of worms; decomposers, which are microorganisms such as bacteria and fungi.

  b Plants remove minerals such as nitrates from the soil through their roots all the time. When animals eat the plants these minerals are passed on through food chains and webs. If plants took minerals out but they were never returned, the soil would soon be infertile as there would be no minerals left. Decay is the process by which the minerals that have become part of the bodies of living organisms are recycled and returned to the environment.

2 a The rate of the chemical reactions in the microorganisms that act as decomposers gets faster with an increase in temperature. Average temperatures are much warmer in the summer than in the winter and so the reactions of decomposition occur much faster – and garden and kitchen waste are turned into compost more rapidly.

  b The microorganisms involved in the process of decomposition grow better in moist conditions. If it is too dry they cannot digest their food so easily and they may dry out and stop growing completely. So if it is particularly dry, even if it is also hot, at least some of the microorganisms involved in the formation of compost from garden and kitchen waste may slow down or stop growing and so in turn compost formation slows down.

  c Many of the microorganisms which bring about the decomposition of material in a compost bin are aerobic – they need oxygen to respire and so need aerobic conditions. Turning over the contents of a compost bin increases the air in the mixture and ensures that the microorganisms have plenty of oxygen so they can work as efficiently as possible, increasing the rate at which compost is formed.

16.6

1 a The cycling of carbon between living organisms and the environment.

  b Photosynthesis, respiration and combustion.

  c Because it prevents all the carbon from getting used up; returns carbon dioxide to the atmosphere to be available for photosynthesis.

2 a Carbon dioxide in the air.

  b Students can produce a written description of the carbon cycle or a diagram (e.g. Figure 2, The carbon cycle in nature) to summarise the stages (must cover all points in the carbon cycle).

3 Photosynthesis is the process by which plants use carbon dioxide and water to make glucose and oxygen, using energy from light.
carbon dioxide + water (+ light energy) → glucose + oxygen
Photosynthesis takes carbon dioxide out of the environment.
The glucose made by the plants is used in the plants and by animals (both those that eat plants and those that eat animals which eat plants) in the process of respiration. In respiration, glucose is broken down using oxygen to produce carbon dioxide, water and energy, which can be used in the reactions within cells.
glucose + oxygen → carbon dioxide + water (+ energy)
Respiration returns carbon dioxide to the atmosphere.
Combustion is the burning in oxygen of organic material from living or once-living organisms, e.g. wood, fossil fuels such as oil. It produces carbon dioxide, water and energy – it is the same as respiration but occurs in a rapid, uncontrolled way.
fossil fuel or wood + oxygen → carbon dioxide + water

Answers to end of chapter summary questions

1 a i 10%
   ii 8%
   iii 12.5%

  b The mass of the producers has to support the whole pyramid, relatively little energy is transferred from producers to primary consumers (difficult to digest).

  c Relatively little energy is passed up the chain, so not enough to support many carnivores.

  d Less energy passed on as warm blooded animals use energy to generate warmth. This is transferred to the environment and so that energy is no longer available to pass on up the chain.

2 The amount of biomass transferred along food chain gets less. Biomass is needed for energy. So by eating plants, the maximum amount of biomass is passed on to people.
Eating meat – plant biomass transferred to animals, animal biomass to people – biomass lost at both stages. Students could draw pyramid of biomass to show plant/person and plant/cow or sheep/person, etc.

3 a Graph plotting, correct scale, labelled axes, axes correct way round, accurate points.

  b So that chickens use little energy maintaining their body temperature, so have more energy for growth.

  c To reduce movement and thereby reduce energy used in movement, so more energy for growth.

  d So they grow fast to a weight when they can be eaten and another set of chickens started up – economic reasons.

  e The line should be below the first line. Chickens outside use energy moving around and keeping warm or cool, so convert less biomass from their food for growth.

4 a Low temperatures prevent growth of decay – causing microorganisms.

  b Cooking destroys the microorganisms, denatures enzymes so no decay.

  c Most decomposers need oxygen to respire – no air, no oxygen, so microbes cannot grow.

  d Heat kills microorganisms, no oxygen so no decay.

5 a Photosynthesis.

  b Respiration, burning (decay and decomposition).

  c Oceans, air (carbonate rocks).

  d CO_2 is important for photosynthesis and keeping surface of Earth warm. Excess CO_2 means surface gets warmer; this affects sea levels, living organisms. Less CO_2 means surface cools, affects life.

  e A death B burning (combustion) C feeding D respiration E photosynthesis F decay and decomposition.

6 a Higher-temperature means faster reactions. Warm compost means microorganisms digest, grow and reproduce faster. More decomposers results in faster decomposition.

  b Makes sure all the decomposing microorganisms have enough oxygen to respire as fast as possible.

Answers to end of chapter examination-style questions

1 a Three layers (1), each one getting smaller as you go up (1), labelled: trees, caterpillars, birds going up (1).

  b Sunlight/radiation from the sun (1)

  c Any five from: chloroplasts/chlorophyll (1) in the leaves absorbs/captures the light energy to use in photosynthesis (1) which makes sugar/glucose (1). When the leaves are eaten by the caterpillar they are digested (1) so the glucose /sugar is absorbed (1) into the caterpillar. It is used to make proteins/fats/new cells/new tissues in the caterpillar (1). (*5 marks maximum*)

  d i 1000/20 000 x 100 (1) = 5% (1);
    ii Any two from: some used for movement/contraction of muscles; some lost as heat to the environment; some lost as waste/faeces; not all caterpillars are eaten; not all parts of caterpillars are digested. (*2 marks maximum*)

  e Marks awarded for this answer will be determined by the Quality of Written Communication (QWC) as well as the standard of the scientific response.

   • All scientific points are made using appropriate scientific terms. The account of decay and recycling of carbon dioxide is presented in a clear and logical order. The answer contains a range of appropriate or relevant specialist terms used accurately. The answer shows very few errors in spelling, punctuation and grammar. (*5–6 marks*)

   • There are many correct scientific points presented in a clear manner, although they may not all be in logical order or complete. The answer has some structure and the use of specialist terms has been attempted, though not always accurately. There may be some errors in spelling, punctuation and grammar. (*3–4 marks*)

   • There are few scientific points about decay, which may be presented in an unclear or confused way. The answer is poorly constructed with an absence of specialist terms, or their use demonstrates a lack of understanding of their meaning. The spelling, punctuation and grammar are weak. (*1–2 marks*)

   • No relevant content. (*0 marks*)

   Examples of scientific points are:

   • Microorganisms/bacteria/fungi decay/decompose the leaves.

   • They use the carbohydrates/sugar/glucose to respire.

   • Respiration releases carbon dioxide into the air ready to be used again for photosynthesis.

2 a 10(%) (2) (If incorrect answer, allow 100% – 25 – 35 – 30 for 1 mark)

  b 2.5 (megajoules) (2) (If incorrect answer, allow 1 mark for correct working)

  c Respiration (1)

  d It reduces the calf's movement because it won't walk about, therefore it will use that energy for growth (1). It also reduces the energy transferred by heating/the calf will need to use to keep warm, and that energy can be used for growth (1).

e It is not cost effective as you have to pay for heat OR the calf might catch a disease more easily if it is inside with other animals OR any other sensible suggestion. (1)

3 a Fishing in a way that conserves the fish stocks at a constant level (1) so that they continue to breed (1).

b If they fish all the adults in a population there will not be enough left to breed (1) and so some species may die out/become extinct (1).

c i Only the biggest fish are caught (1) because the younger ones fit through the mesh/holes, so the younger ones are left to mature and breed (1).

ii More popular fish (1) are not all caught and so the stocks don't drop below a sustainable level (1).

d Any two from: fishing boats don't always obey the rules; extra fish are caught but if they are the wrong type they are just dumped overboard dead; the quotas are not tight enough to let the fish stocks regenerate; people find it hard to eat new/unusual species of fish; there is not time for the younger fish to breed properly before they are big enough to be caught in nets; or any other sensible suggestion. (*2 marks maximum*)

Index

Photo acknowledgements

B1.1.1 Wim van Egmond/Visuals Unlimited/Corbis; B1.1.2 Steve Gschmeissner/Science Photo Library; B1.1.4 iStockphoto; B1.2.2T Eye of Science/Science Photo Library; B1.2.2B Scott Camazine/Alamy; B1.2.3 Science Photo Library/Alamy; B1.4.3 Dr R. Dourmashkin/Science Photo Library; B1.6.4 ImageBroker/Imagebroker/FLPA; B1.7.1 Juniors Bildarchiv/Alamy; B1.8.1T Manfred Kage/Science Photo Library; B1.8.1B Dr. Richard Kessel & Dr. Gene Shih/Getty Images; B2.1.2 Science Photo Library; B2.2.2 Eye of Science/Science Photo Library; B2.3.2 Lewis Whyld/PA Archive/Press Association Images; B2.4.3 Cancer Research UK; B2.5.1 Cancer Research UK; B2.5.4 Eric Grave/Science Photo Library; B2.6.3 Nigel Cattlin/Alamy; B2.SQ5 Simon Fraser/Royal Victoria Infirmary, Newcastle upon Tyne/Science Photo Library; B3.1.1 Image Source/Alamy; B3.1.2 Maximilian Stock Ltd/Science Photo Library; B3.1.3 Dorling Kindersley/Getty Images; B3.2.1 J.C. Revy, ISM/Science Photo Library; B3.2.P Martyn F. Chillmaid/Science Photo Library; B3.3.1 Ingo Arndt/Minden Pictures/FLPA; B3.4.1 Martyn F. Chillmaid; B3.4.2 Alex Yeung/fotolia.com; B3.4.3 Ray Tang/Rex Features; B4.2.1 Penny Tweedie/Science Photo Library; B4.2.2 BSIP Laurent/ Trunyo/Science Photo Library; B4.2.3 Claire Deprez/Reporters/Science Photo Library; B4.3.1 Gary Carlson/Science Photo Library; B4.3.2 iStockphoto; B4.4.1 Eye of Science/Science Photo Library; B4.5.1 Erik Dreyer/Getty Images; B4.5.3 Paul Bock/Alamy; B5.1.2 Science Photo Library; B5.2.3 2010 SynCardia Systems, Inc.; B5.2.4 Sean Dempsey/PA Archive/Press Association Images; B5.3.3L Medical-on-Line/Alamy; B5.3.3R Steve Allen/Science Photo Library; B5.4.2 St Bartholomew's Hospital/Science Photo Library; B5.4.4 National Cancer Institute/Science Photo Library; B5.5.1 withGod/Fotolia.com; B5.5.2 Getty/Louie Psihoyos; B5.6.1 Nancy Hamilton/Science Photo Library; B5.7.1 Martyn F. Chillmaid/Science Photo Library; B5.7.3 Dr P. Marazzi/Science Photo Library; B5.ESQ1a Corbis Flirt/Alamy; B5.ESQ1b Trout55/iStockphoto; B6.1.1 Philippe Lissac/Godong/Corbis; B6.1.2 Christian Larue/fotolia.com; B6.2.3 Mauro Fermariello/Science Photo Library; B6.3.2 HO/AP/Press Association Images; B6.3.3 Sovereign, ISM/Science Photo Library; B7.1.1 Gavin Rodgers/Rex Features; B7.1.3 Gorilla/fotolia.com; B7.2.1 Kamila Panasiuk/fotolia.com; B7.2.2 MedicalRF.com/Corbis; B7.4.1 Life in View/Science Photo Library; B7.5.2 Geoffrey Robinson/Rex Features; B7.6.1T Gavin Hellier/Getty Images; B7.6.1B iStockphoto; B7.7.3 Steve Gschmeissner/Science Photo Library; B7.8.1 Lea Paterson/Science Photo Library; B7.8.2 Scott Camazine/Science Photo Library; B7.8.3 Assembly/Getty Images; B7.ESQ1 Ann Fullick; B8.1.1 Eric Erbe/Science Photo Library; B8.1.2 Dr. Harold Fisher, Visuals Unlimited/Science Photo Library; B8.1.3 Karl Schoendorfer/Rex Features; B8.2.1 Scott Camazine/Alamy; B8.2.2 Eye of Science/Science Photo Library; B8.3.1 Jenifer Harrington/Getty Images; B8.4.1 Tek Image/Science Photo Library; B8.4.2 St Mary's Hospital Medical School/Science Photo Library; B8.4.3 CC Studio/Science Photo Library; B8.5.3 iStockphoto; B8.6.1 CDC/Science Photo Library; B8.6.3 Phototake Inc./Alamy; B8.ESQ4 Christian Darkin/Alamy; B9.1.1 SAPS; B9.2.3 Fuse/Getty Images; B9.3.1 iStockphoto; B9.3.2 Cordelia Molloy/Science Photo Library; B9.3.3 FLPA/Chris Mattison; B9.5.1 iStockphoto; B9.6.1 FLPA/Nigel Cattlin; B9.6.2 FLPA/Wayne Hutchinson; B9.6.3 Steve Gschmeissner/Getty Images; B9.7.1 Graham Jordan/Science Photo Library; B9.8.1 Photos Lamontagne/Getty Images; B9.8.2 JoeFox/Alamy; B9.8.3 FLPA/Wayne Hutchinson; B9.9.1 Anthony Short; B9.9.2L iStockphoto; B9.9.2R iStockphoto; B9.10.1 Garry Delong/Science Photo Library; B9.10.3 Volff/fotolia.com; B10.1.1 iStockphoto; B10.1.2 Steve Gschmeissner/Science Photo Library; B10.2.1 iStockphoto; B10.2.2 Mat Hayward/fotolia.com; B10.2.3TL iStockphoto; B10.2.3BL iStockphoto; B10.2.3TM iStockphoto; B10.2.3BM iStockphoto; B10.2.3TR iStockphoto; B10.2.3BR iStockphoto; B10.3.1 Newspix/Rex Features; B10.3.2 Radius Images/Alamy; B10.3.3 iStockphoto; B10.4.1 CNRI/Science Photo Library; B10.4.3 Bettmann/Corbis; B10.6.1 Zephyr/Science Photo Library; B10.7.1 Dr. Stanley Flegler, Visuals Unlimited/Science Photo Library; B10.7.3L Look at Sciences/Science Photo Library; B10.7.3R iStockphoto; B10.8.2 Health Protection Agency/Science Photo Library; B11.1.1 Steve Hamilton/Getty Images; B11.2.1 Roslin Roslin Institute/Press Association Images; B11.3.2 International Rice Research Institute (IRRI); B11.4.1 Courtesy Golden Rice Humanitarian Board. www.goldenrice.org; B11.4.2L A&M UNIVERSITY/Rex Features; B11.4.2R PAT SULLIVAN/AP/Press Association Images; B11.4.3 european pressphoto agency b.v.; B12.1.1 iStockphoto; B12.1.2 Norbert Wu/Minden Pictures/FLPA; B12.1.3 B. Murton/Southampton Oceanography Centre/Science Photo Library; B12.2.1 Louise Murray/Science Photo Library; B12.2.2 Anthony Short; B12.2.3 FLPA/Mike Lane/Holt; B12.3.1 FLPA/Bob Gibbons; B12.3.2L iStockphoto; B12.3.2R David Hughes/fotolia.com; B12.4.1 iStockphoto; B12.4.2 iStockphoto; B12.4.3 iStockphoto; B12.4.4 Nature Picture Library/Phil Savoie; B12.5.1 Roxana/fotolia.com; B12.5.2 Lynwood Chase/Science Photo Library; B12.5.3 iStockphoto; B12.6.1 Cosmin Manci/fotolia.com; B12.6.2 Steve Gschmeissner/Science Photo Library; B12.ESQ1 WLDavies/iStockphoto; B12.ESQ2 coopder/iStock; B13.1.1 FLPA/Jurgen & Christine Sohns; B13.1.2 FLPA/Bob Gibbons/Holt; B13.1.3 Roberto Danovaro; B13.2.1 Edward Fullick; B13.2.4 Edward Fullick; B13.3.1 FLPA/imagebroker/Wolfgang Lampe; B13.3.3 ImageBroker/Imagebroker/FLPA; B13.4.1 Copyright 2010 Photolibrary; B13.4.2 William Mullins/Science Photo Library; B13.5.1 Mike Lane/FLPA; B13.5.3 FLPA/Mike Lane; B13.5.4 iStockphoto; B14.1.1 NOAA/Science Photo Library; B14.1.3 Skyscan Photolibrary/Alamy; B14.2.3 Hans Schouten/FN/Minden/FLPA; B14.3.1 Rob & Ann Simpson/Getty Images; B14.4.1 Ton Koene/Visuals Unlimited/Corbis; B14.4.3 Suzi Eszterhas/Minden Pictures/FLPA; B14.5.2 fotolia.com; B15.1.2 sodapix/Getty Images; B15.1.3 English Heritage Photo Library; B15.2.2 Nils Jorgensen/Rex Features; B15.2.3 Mary Evans Picture Library/Alamy; B15.3.1 Phil Degginger/Alamy; B15.3.2 Zoonar GmbH/Alamy; B15.3.3 NickR/fotolia.com; B15.4.1T iStockphoto; B15.4.1M S.R. Miller/fotolia.com; B15.4.1B S.R. Miller/fotolia.com; B15.4.2 Getty Images; B15.4.4T iStockphoto; B15.4.4B Pat & Tom Leeson/Science Photo Library; B15.5.2 Sinclair Stammers/Science Photo Library; B15.5.3 AFP/Getty Images; B15.6.DYK John Wright/Rex Features; B15.7.1 artpartner-images.com/Alamy; B15.7.3 Martin Bond/Science Photo Library; B15.8.1 ZSSD/Minden Pictures/FLPA; B15.8.2 iStockphoto; B15.8.3 Ulla Lohman; B15.SQ4 Dr Jeremy Burgess/Science Photo Library; B16.1.1 David R. Frazier Photolibrary, Inc./Alamy; B16.1.2 Westend61 – WEP/Getty Images; B16.2.1 iStockphoto; B16.2.2 iStockphoto; B16.2.3 iStockphoto; B16.2.4 iStockphoto; B16.3.1 Neil Holmes Freelance Digital/Alamy; B16.3.2T FLPA/John Eveson; B16.3.2B FLPA/Gerard Lacz; B16.4.1T Jan Van Arkel/FN/Minden/FLPA; B16.4.1B Pixelbliss/fotolia.com; B16.4.2 Oliver Leedham/Alamy; B16.5.1 iStockphoto; B16.5.2 Copper Age/Getty Images; B16.6.1 iStockphoto; B16.6.3T iStockphoto; B16.6.3B Steve Morgan/Alamy